Puzzle Baron

Picture Puzzles

Stephen P. Ryder

ALPHA

Publisher Mike Sanders
Editor Christopher Stolle
Book Designer Lindsay Dobbs
Compositor Ayanna Lacey
Proofreader Monica Stone

First American Edition, 2018
Published in the United States by DK Publishing
6081 E. 82nd Street, Indianapolis, Indiana 46250

Copyright © 2018 Dorling Kindersley Limited
DK, a Division of Penguin Random House LLC
20 21 22   10 9 8 7 6 5 4 3 2
002–308597–April/2018

Published in the United States by Dorling Kindersley Limited

A catalog record for this book
is available from the Library of Congress.
ISBN 978-1-4654-7024-9

DK books are available at special discounts when purchased
in bulk for sales promotions, premiums, fund-raising, or educational use.
For details, contact: DK Publishing Special Markets, 1745 Broadway,
New York, New York 10019
SpecialSales@dk.com

Printed and bound in China

All images © Dorling Kindersley Limited
For further information see: www.dkimages.com

A WORLD OF IDEAS:
SEE ALL THERE IS TO KNOW

www.dk.com

How to play!

This book contains 100 puzzles separated into three categories:

EASY
pp. 4–61

MEDIUM
pp. 62–155

HARD
pp. 156–180

Within each category are three kinds of puzzles:

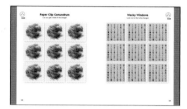

Spot the differences:
Compare the two images to find the differences. Each puzzle of this kind has a score section with a square for each difference. Mark each square for each change you find.

Unscramble the photo:
Put these images in the right order to create the completed photo. Use the blank squares at the bottom of these puzzles to mark where each numbered image should go.

Which one's different?:
Just one thing has changed between the photos shown: four images in the easy section; six images in the medium section; and nine images in the hard section.

ANSWERS

You'll find an answer key at the back of this book to help you check your answers:
• *Spot the differences:* Use the grid to find the changes.
• *Unscramble the photo:* Numbered boxes and the full photo show the answer.
• *Which one's different?:* A circle pinpoints where the single change occurred.

Now it's time to turn the page and have some fun!

Child's Play

Remember to have fun looking for what's different!

SCORE

Hearts and Crafts

Some felt and a bit of ribbon are sometimes all you need to cheer someone up.

Domo Arigato
Mister Roboto!

SCORE

Outfox the Toy Box

Can you spy with your little eye what's changed?

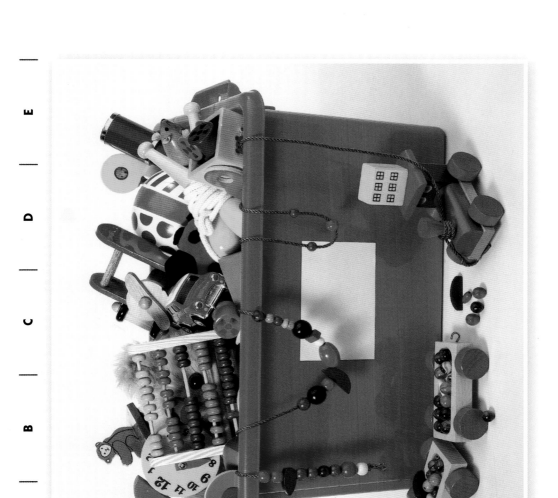

You've Gotta Be Kitten Me

Can you find the right places for these cute little kittens?

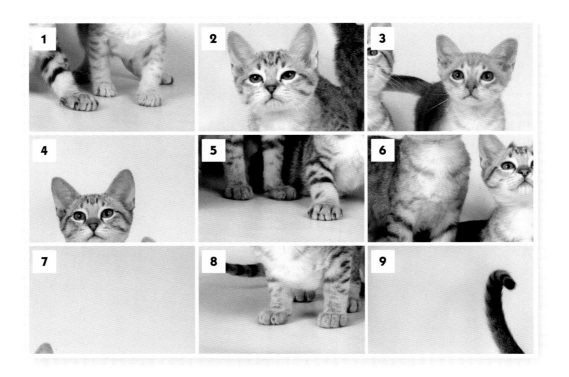

SCORE

Day at the Beach

Help Teddy enjoy the sunshine again!

EASY

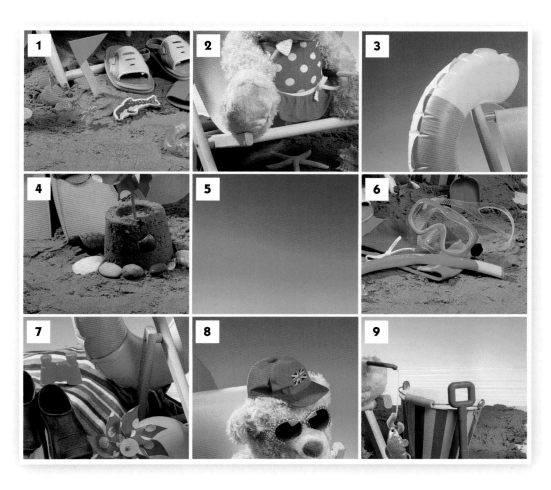

SCORE

Hail to the Chef

And to her collection of colorful cookware!

Fun in the Kitchen

Looks like Mom and Dad are getting breakfast in bed this morning!

A

B

C

D

E

1   2   3   4   5

Practical Pantry

Are your dry goods this well organized?

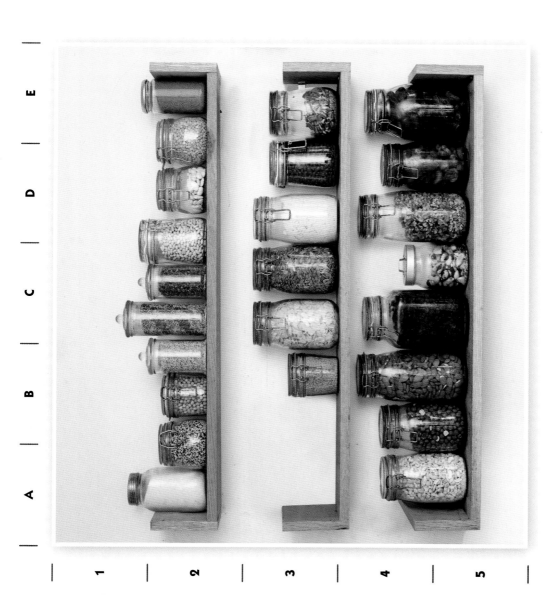

Creative Space

This is where the muse magic happens.

A

B

C

D

E

1   2   3   4   5

Building Blocks

Which one of these blocks changed?

Art Project

Which one of these isn't like the others?

Getting Organized

Never underestimate the value of a good travel organizer.

Wrap It Up

You don't want to be late for the party.

SCORE

Working From Home

It sure beats driving to the office each day.

A B C D E

1 2 3 4 5

The Dark Room

Looks like someone still hasn't upgraded to a digital camera.

EASY

SCORE

A B C D E

1 2 3 4 5

31

Flag Day

Wave your banner if you can find the change.

Put a Pin in It

Can you pinpoint what changed between these two images?

If You Can't Take the Heat ...

… don't leave the kitchen—just change the thermostat!

A

B

C

D

E

| 1 | 2 | 3 | 4 | 5 |

SCORE

Without a Shadow of a Doubt

These are some "shady" characters indeed!

A

B

C

D

E

1   2   3   4   5

The Moon Party Fizzled Out

There just wasn't any atmosphere.

A

B

C

D

E

1   2   3   4   5

Garden Games

Time for some outdoor gardening fun!

SCORE

A   B   C   D   E

1   2   3   4   5

Tile Style

Which tile has been replaced?

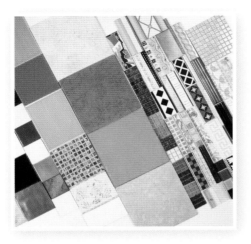

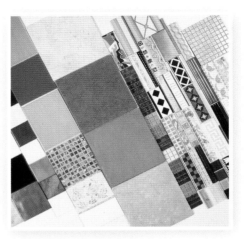

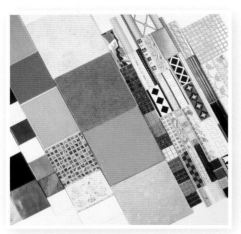

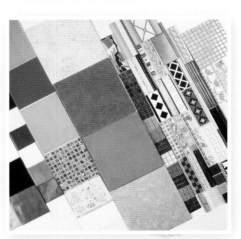

All Buttoned Up

Which button moved or changed?

EASY

Duly Noted

Can you jot down all the changes between the two photos?

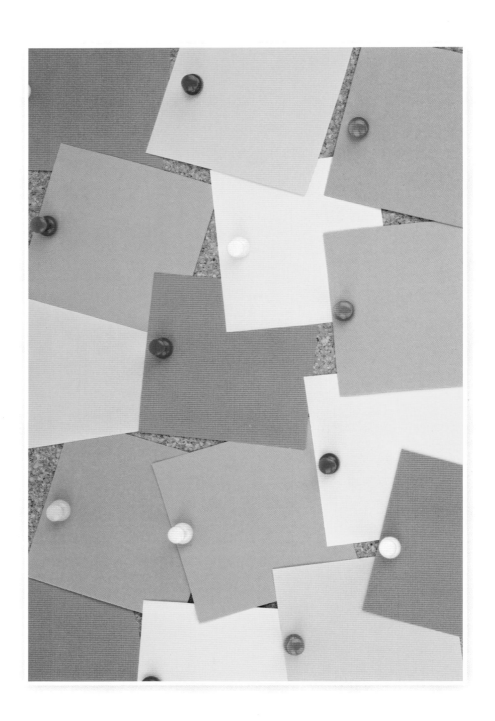

SCORE

A   B   C   D   E

1   2   3   4   5

Row, Row, Row Your Boat

You might need to wait for the tide to come in first though!

A

B

C

D

E

1   2   3   4   5

A Batch Made in Heaven

They're almost too cute to eat! Almost …

SCORE

A

B

C

D

E

1 2 3 4 5

They Say You Can't Take It With You

They've obviously never been to a souvenir shop.

EASY

A

B

C

D

E

1   2   3   4   5

SCORE

51

Little Drummer Boys

Can you put these cute guys and their percussion back together?

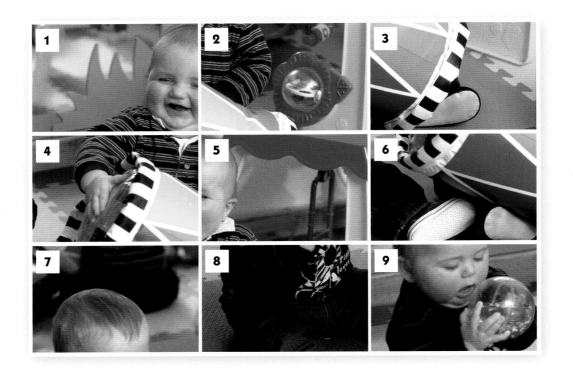

SCORE

All the World's a Stage

Can you put these theater images in their places before the show begins?

EASY

SCORE

We Had a Joke for This One

But we decided it was too cheesy.

A

B

C

D

E

1 2 3 4 5

Pencil Power

Think we've got enough colored pencils for this project?

A

B

C

D

E

| 1 | 2 | 3 | 4 | 5 |

Wool Pile

This must be a knitter's idea of heaven.

A

B

C

D

E

1   2   3   4   5

Newspaper Caper

Papier-mâché projects are lots of fun, but don't get any glue on the table!

A

B

C

D

E

1   2   3   4   5

SCORE

Quilt Quandary

Sail the sea of changes, but don't let the wind blow you in the wrong direction.

MEDIUM

A

B

C

D

E

| 1 | 2 | 3 | 4 | 5 |

Sew Much to Do ...

... and sew little time to do it!

A

B

SCORE

C

D

E

1   2   3   4   5

Music Boxes

What strange iPods—they're made of wood and only play one song!

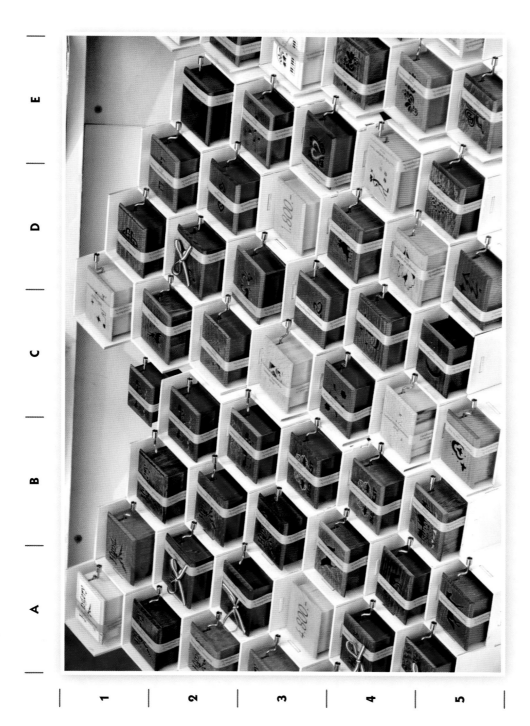

SCORE

Clean Up Your Toys!

Just because life is messy doesn't mean your room has to be.

A

B

C

D

E

1   2   3   4   5

Be Creative

Just don't spill any paint on the table!

A

B

SCORE

C

D

E

1   2   3   4   5

You Can Paint It Any Color …

… as long as it's white!

SCORE

Dollhouse Delight

What's changed with Isabella and Alexandria's playhouse?

A

B

C

D

E

1   2   3   4   5

SCORE

Hong Kong at Night

Can you return this street scene to its neon glory?

SCORE

Stuck in Traffic

Hope you've got a good audiobook to help you pass the time.

SCORE

X Marks the Spot

Follow the clues to figure out what's different.

Rumpus Room

If only mine were this clean and organized.

A

B

C

D

E

1   2   3   4   5

SCORE

81

Toys, Toys, Toys!

So many toys, but they're not all the same. Can you find the differences?

SCORE

Did You Hear the Story About the Bed?

It was all made up.

A

B

SCORE

C

D

E

1   2   3   4   5

Idyllic Iceland

The weather might be cold, but at least the people are warm and friendly!

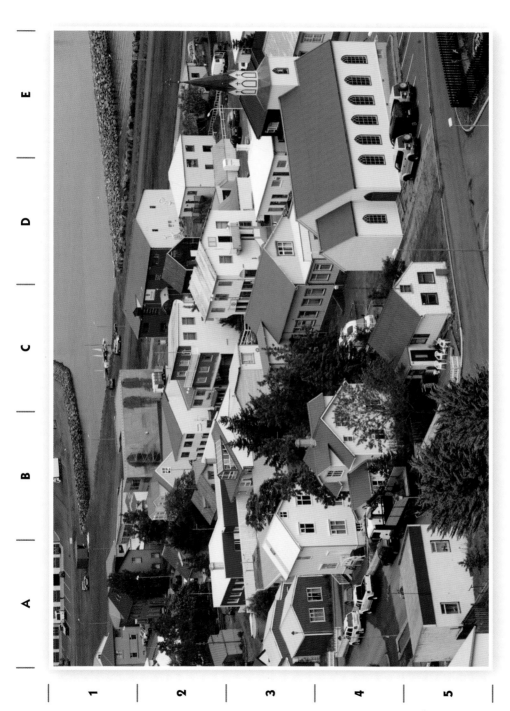

A | B | C | D | E

1 | 2 | 3 | 4 | 5

Moroccan Mementos

You'll never forget your trip to Marrakech if you pick up one of these items.

SCORE

A

B

C

D

E

| 1 | 2 | 3 | 4 | 5 |

Sunday in Slovenia

It seems the whole town's come out to enjoy the day.

Lamp Rays

Can you shed some light on where these puzzle pieces belong?

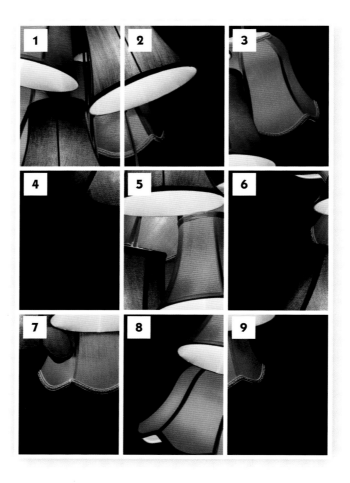

SCORE

Gift Decorations

Tag, you're it—except one isn't like the others. Which one?

Any Port in a Storm

As long as you can find an open spot!

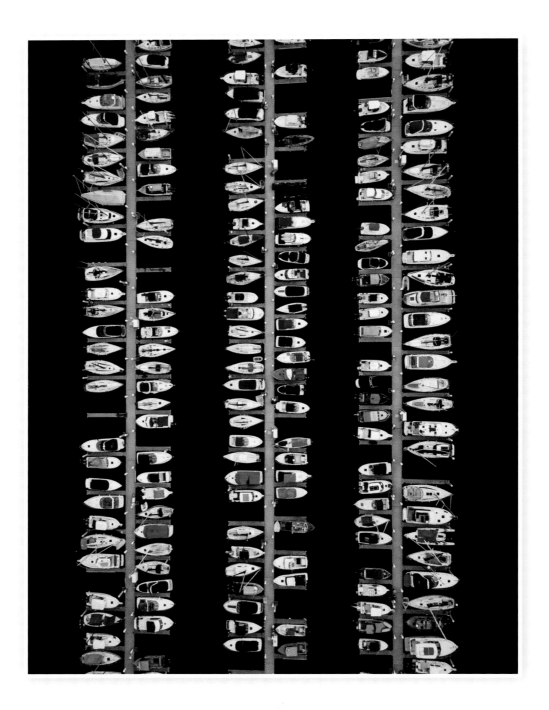

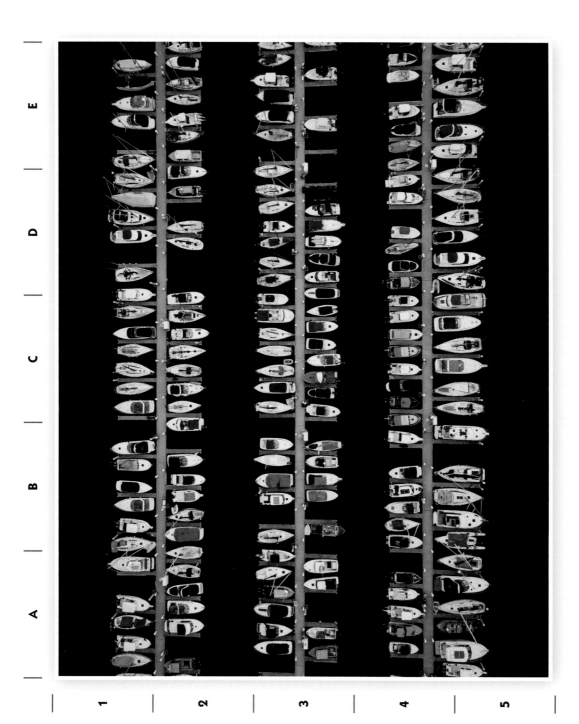

SCORE

A   B   C   D   E

1   2   3   4   5

It Looks Like Rain

Any idea where we could find an umbrella?

A

B

C

D

E

1   2   3   4   5

SCORE

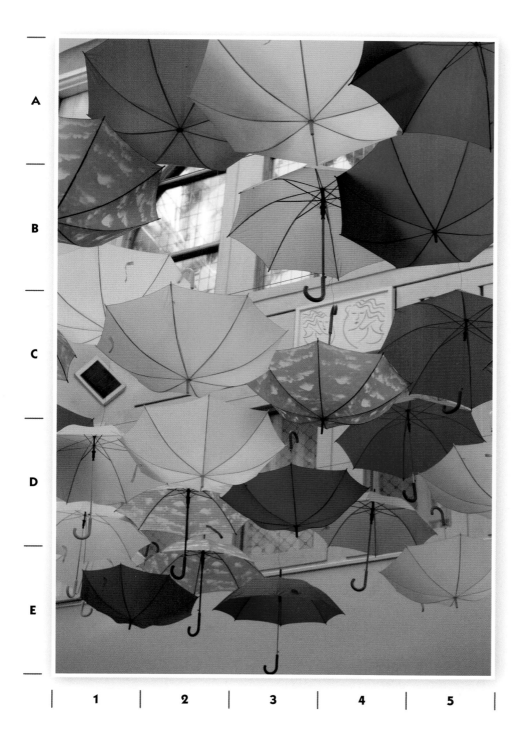

On-Street Parking

Hurry up before that last spot's taken!

MEDIUM

SCORE

E

D

C

B

A

1 2 3 4 5

Hitting the Shops

Who doesn't love a downtown shopping spree?

MEDIUM

SCORE

A   B   C   D   E

1   2   3   4   5

101

Holiday Gifts

Don't forget that fruitcake for Aunt Natalie.

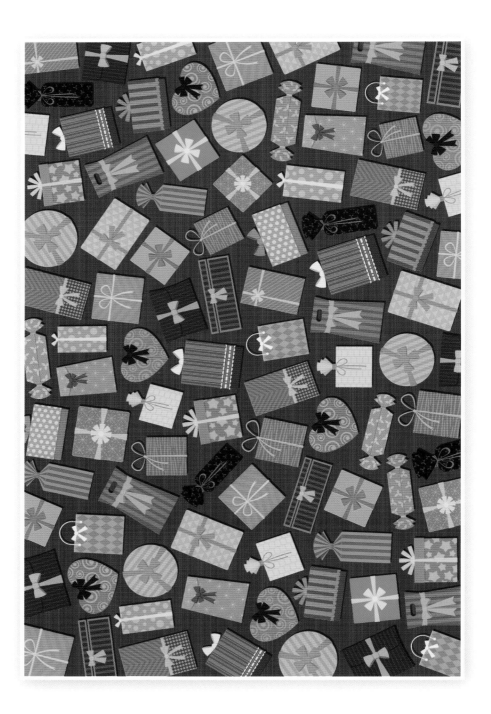

SCORE

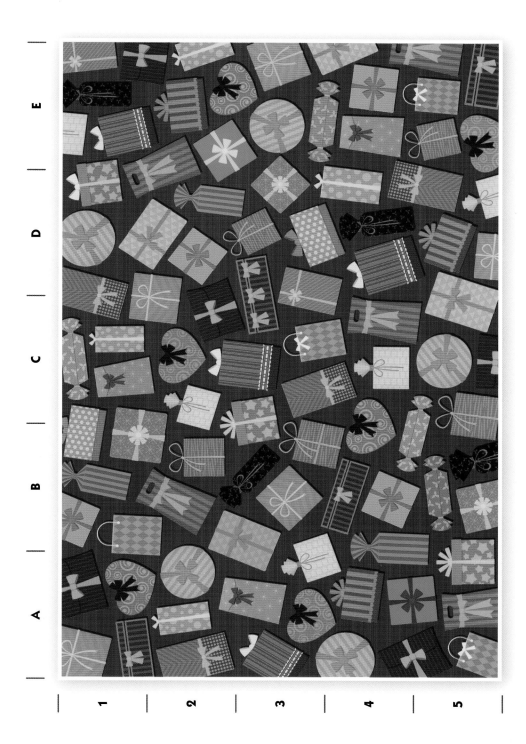

Too Many Towels

Stripes are the latest style, don't you know?

MEDIUM

SCORE

105

Market Madness

It might look crowded, but you can have a great time finding the differences.

A

B

SCORE

C

D

E

1   2   3   4   5

Out of the Office

Something's misplaced. Can you find it?

Matching Mosaics

One change can make all the difference in art. Can you find it?

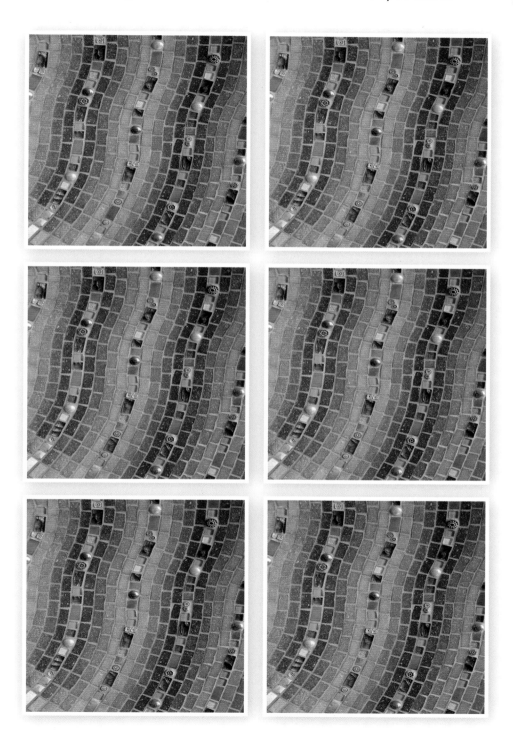

Raise the Roof

But before you do, see if you can find the changes we've made.

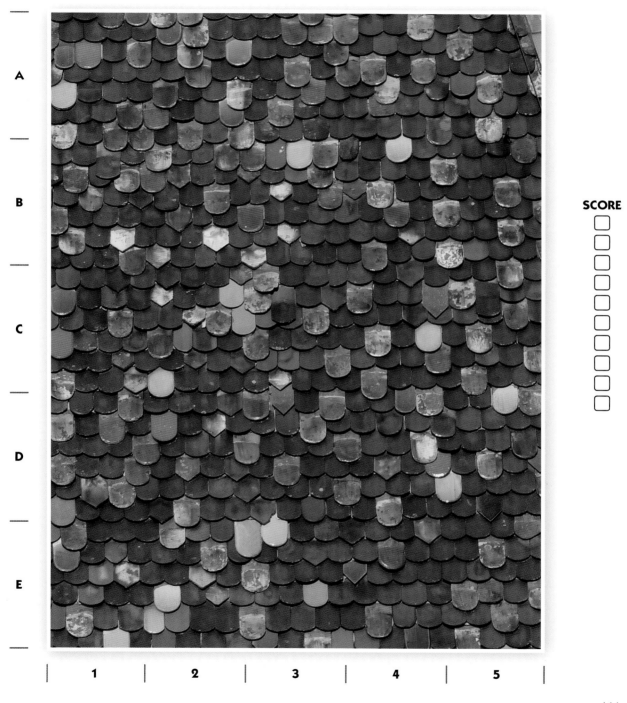

A

B

C

D

E

1   2   3   4   5

All Aboard!

The treat train is leaving the station.

MEDIUM

A

B

C

D

E

SCORE

1   2   3   4   5

Oh Sugar!

See if you can find all the changes without being tempted to eat the pages!

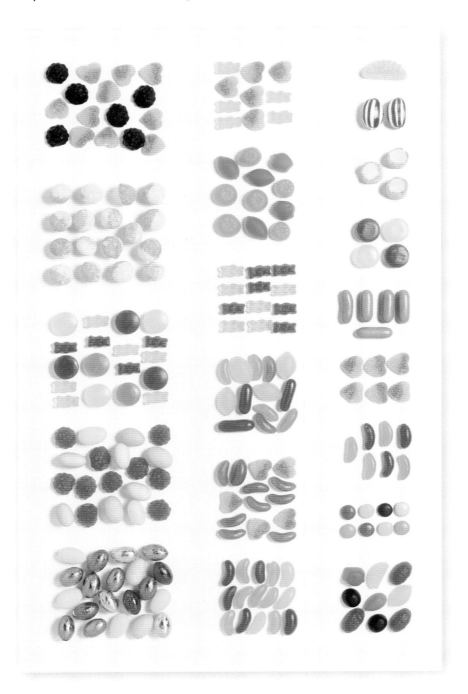

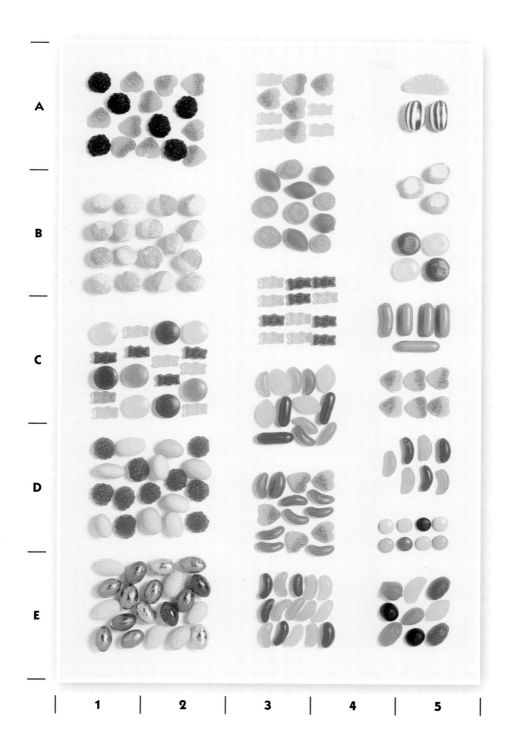

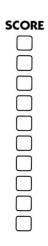

MEDIUM

SCORE

A

B

C

D

E

1   2   3   4   5

Shields Up!

Something tells me this town is big into heraldry.

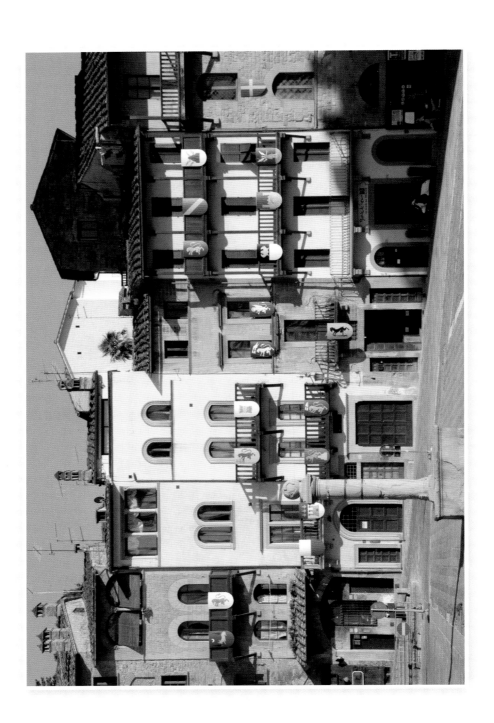

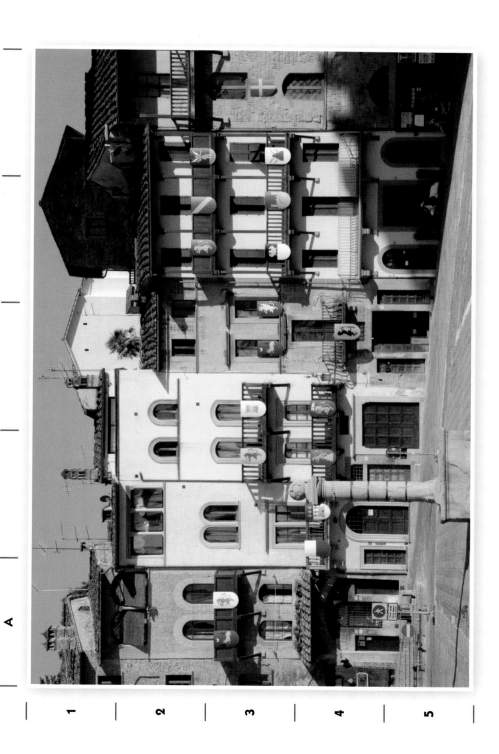

A B C D E

1 2 3 4 5

What a Crock!

Seriously, that's some good-looking crockery!

A

B

C

D

E

1   2   3   4   5

Unbearable

No lions or tigers—but plenty of bears!

A

B

C

D

E

1   2   3   4   5

Birds of a Feather ...

... flock together, especially when there's free food!

SCORE

A   B   C   D   E

1   2   3   4   5

Beguiling Bookshelf

How does the story change from one photo to the next?

School Spirit

Can you put this scene back together before recess ends?

MEDIUM

SCORE

Safe Harbor

This looks like a great place to park your boat.

A

B

SCORE

C

D

E

1   2   3   4   5

Target Practice
Closest to the bull's-eye wins!

SCORE

Anyone Seen My Boat?

I know I parked it around here somewhere!

MEDIUM

A
B
C
D
E

1   2   3   4   5

SCORE

Do You Like Magic?

Pick a card—any card.

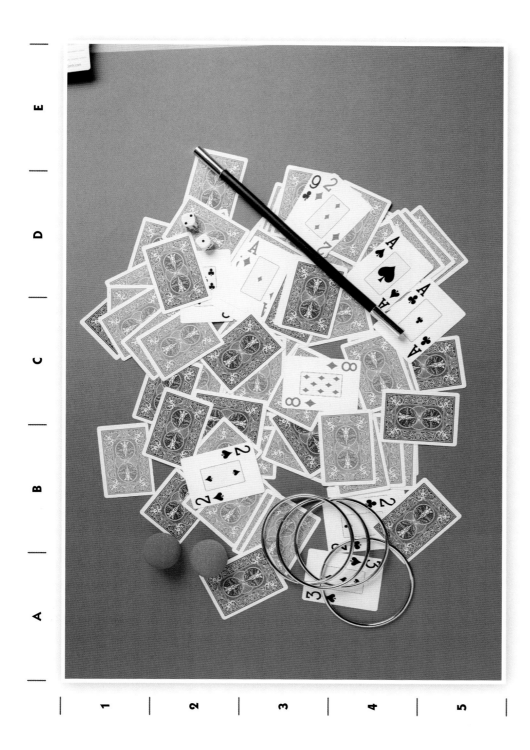

Knickknack Drawer

Don't you wish yours were this organized?

A

B

C

D

E

1   2   3   4   5

All These Plates ...

... and not a single one clean enough to eat from!

MEDIUM

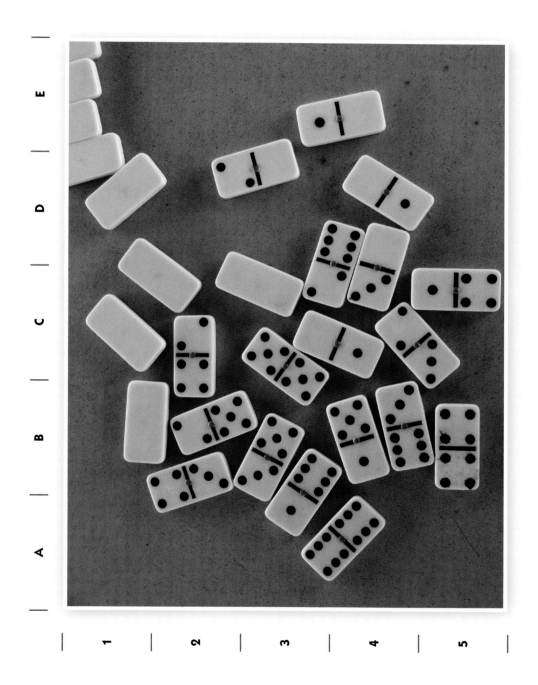

SCORE

E | D | C | B | A

1 | 2 | 3 | 4 | 5

Marching Band

Can you put this marching band back into its proper formation?

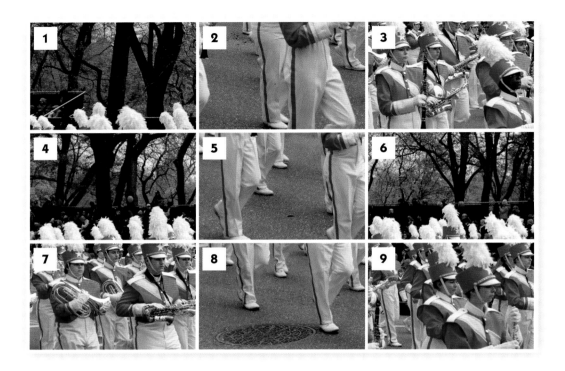

SCORE

Cycling Chaos

Can you put these cyclists in place before the race ends?

SCORE

Finding Fossils

Everything you need to discover a new dinosaur!

Jelly Bean Bonanza

What's your favorite flavor?

MEDIUM

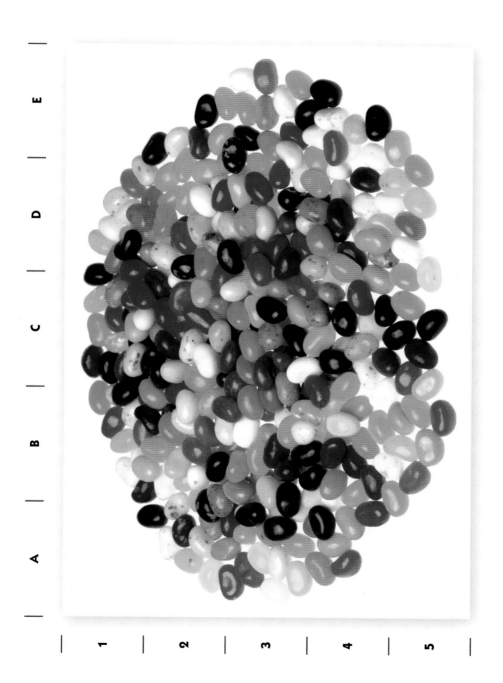

SCORE

A | B | C | D | E

1 | 2 | 3 | 4 | 5

Flower Power

Guess there must have been quite a few April showers!

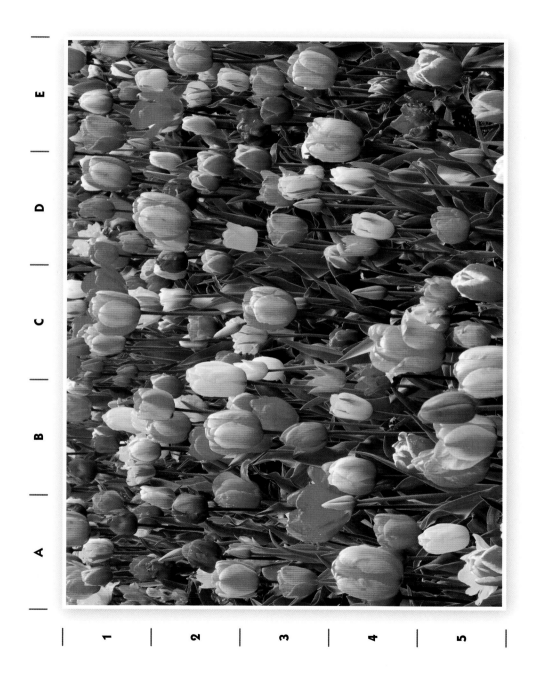

It's in the Mail

But whether it's in the right mailbox is anybody's guess!

P Is for ...

... plenty of permutations in this perplexing puzzle.

MEDIUM

SCORE

A Real Mind-Number

Tally up all the changes.

Tool Time

And yet I still can't find a Phillips-head screwdriver when I need one.

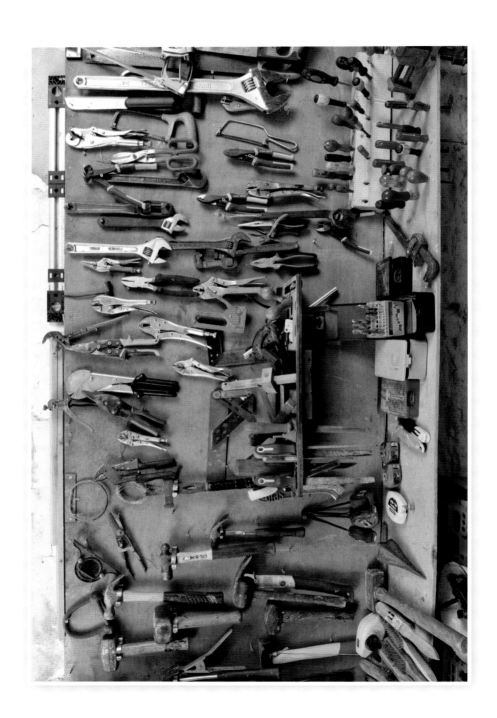

MEDIUM

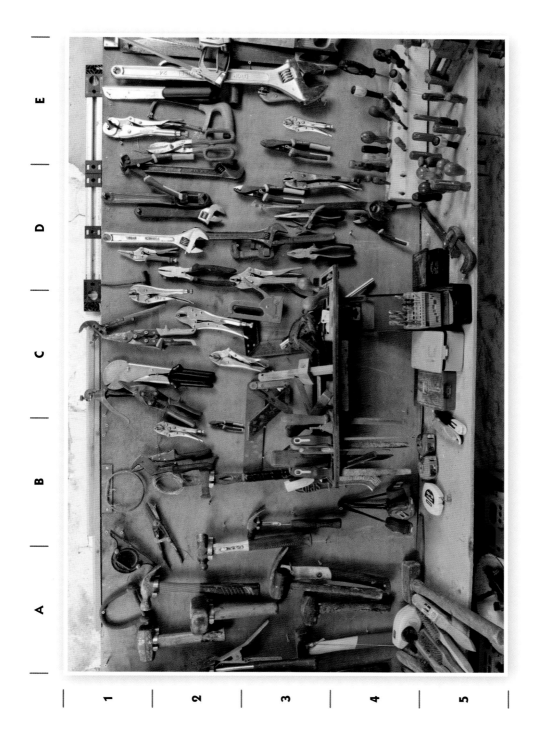

SCORE

A B C D E

1 2 3 4 5

New York, New York

It's up to you to find all the changes!

HARD

A

B

C

D

E

1   2   3   4   5

SCORE

Along the Canal

Time for a relaxing boat ride. Just don't fall in the water!

SCORE

Enjoying the Plaza

There's more than meets the eye in this artsy downtown setting.

HARD

A

B

C

D

E

1   2   3   4   5

161

Platform Predicament

The commute doesn't look too bad this morning!

A

B

C

D

E

1 2 3 4 5

Stuck Dockside

All tied up and no place to go.

All Locked Up

Now if I could only remember where I left my keys!

SCORE

A

B

C

D

E

1   2   3   4   5

Paper Clip Conundrum

Can you get a hold of the change?

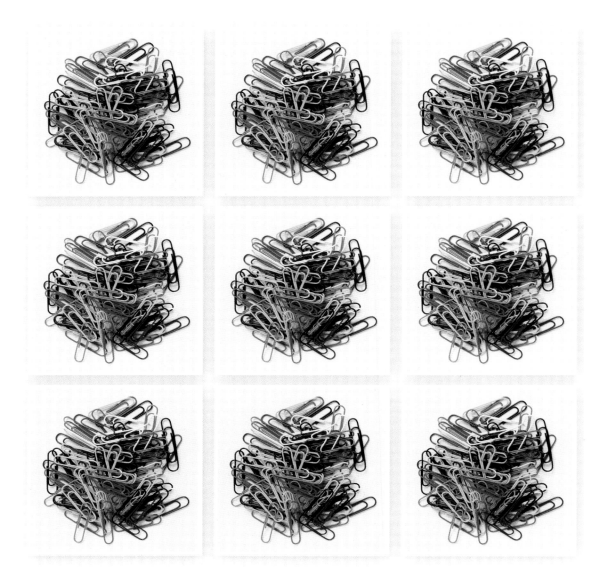

Wacky Windows

Look out to find what changed.

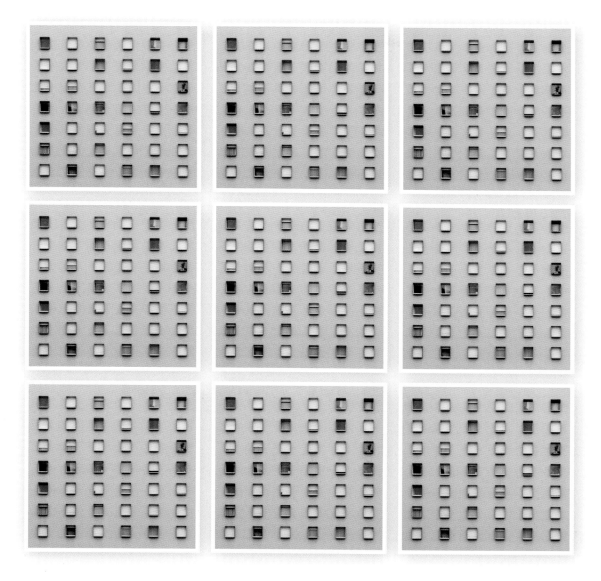

Stylish Ride

What a festive way to get around town!

HARD

SCORE

171

Bottled Up

So many different bottles and caps and liquids …

SCORE

Red Herrings

Has this puzzle got you seeing red?

A

B

C

D

E

1   2   3   4   5

Shop 'Til You Drop

Or at least until you find all the changes!

SCORE

Stamp Champ

This confounding puzzle has our stamp of approval!

HARD

A

B

C

D

E

1   2   3   4   5

SCORE

179

Cherry, Cherry

Can you put these juicy fruits in the right order?

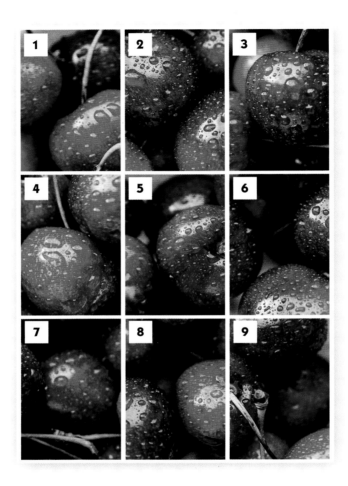

SCORE

EASY

Child's Play
Dave King

(A1) Paintbrush shortened; **(A3)** Green abacus bead added; **(B1)** Blue pencil added; **(B5)** White dot removed; **(C2)** Pink "6" now "9"; **(C2–C3)** Apple drawing removed; **(C4)** Green star now orange; **(D3)** Stick figure's arms moved; **(D4)** Panda now has two ears; **(D4)** Mouse's tail lengthened; **(E3)** Chalk shortened; **(E5)** Red pie section now blue.

Hearts and Crafts
Dave King

(A1) Dot removed; **(A2)** Purple ribbon now green; **(A4–A5)** Orange heart now purple; **(B1)** Small blue flower now green; **(C1)** Button added to orange heart; **(C2–D2)** Pink heart now orange; **(C3)** Purple ribbon removed; **(C4)** Small blue flower removed; **(D3–D4)** Dot removed; **(D4)** Yellow ribbon now pink.

Domo Arigato
Ian O'Leary

(A2) Antenna shortened; **(A5–B5)** Yellow balloon added; **(B3–C3)** Robot's smile now smaller; **(B4–B5)** Orange stripes on box now green; **(C1)** Blue shoulder now dark orange; **(C4–D4)** Yellow icing now green; **(D2)** Blue and green buttons switched; **(D3)** Purple, yellow, and green circles moved; **(D3)** Red button removed; **(E4–E5)** Red platform edge now purple.

Outfox the Toy Box
David Handley

(A3–A4) Green bead added and string lengthened; **(B1)** Monkey's arm lengthened; **(B2)** Red abacus bead added; **(B2)** Yellow abacus bead moved; **(B5)** Metal hook removed; **(C2)** White string removed; **(C3)** Pink and green beads switched; **(C4)** Reflections on box removed; **(C5)** Red marble added; **(D3)** Blue bead added to string; **(D4)** Door replaced with window; **(D5)** Blue cord wrapped three times around train; **(E1)** Blue kaleidoscope lengthened.

You've Gotta Be Kitten Me
Tracy Morgan Animal Photography

9	4	7
2	6	3
8	5	1

Day at the Beach
Dave King

3	8	5
7	2	9
4	1	6

Hail to the Chef
Dave King

(A1) Green frame now pink; **(A3)** Wallpaper apple leaf flipped horizontally; **(A3–B3)** Yellow flower added; **(A4)** Hook removed; **(A5–B5)** Blue keychain now green; **(B2–B3)** Hour hand moved; **(C1)** Apple on wallpaper no longer has a bite in it; **(D2)** Black knob on orange cookware now larger; **(D2)** White dots removed; **(D3)** Grape added; **(E3–E4)** White bristles on brush now blue.

Fun in the Kitchen
Dave King

(A4) Clock added; **(B1)** Blue bowl now melon colored; **(B2–B3)** Apples added to bowl; **(B5)** Jar and bowls switched; **(C1–C2)** Arrow on scale moved; **(C4–D4)** Red lines on apron now blue; **(C5)** Lemons now limes; **(D2)** Milk level higher; **(D4)** Peeled apple now whole; **(E3)** Apple added.

ANSWERS

ANSWERS

Practical Pantry 18–19

Will Heap

(C1–C2) Jar now taller; **(E3)** Pecan jar shortened; **(A4–A5)** Wood block removed; **(E1–E2)** Yellow jar now dark brown; **(C4–C5)** Nut jar shortened; **(A1–A2)** White jar now fuller; **(A3–B3)** Two jars removed.

Creative Space 20–21

James Merrell

(A1–B2) Picture flipped horizontally; **(A2–A3)** Brush moved; **(A5–B5)** Tassel removed; **(B1)** White square object added; **(B3–C2)** Red dots removed; **(D1–D2)** Green yarn now pink; **(D4)** Handle removed; **(E1)** Pen laying on book; **(E2)** White eraser added.

Building Blocks 22

Dave King

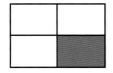

Art Project 23

Dave King

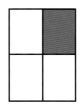
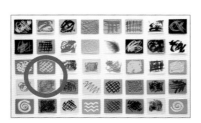

Getting Organized 24–25

Dave King

(A1–B2) Image inside green card rotated; **(A2)** Green line removed; **(B2)** Half moon cut into white circle; **(B2–C3)** Dark blue card rotated; **(C2)** "UNIONE" now "UNION"; **(C4)** Red stitching added; **(D4)** Yellow star added to blue card; **(E3)** Bar code shortened; **(E3)** Ticket seat "26B" now "6B."

Wrap It Up 26–27

(A1–A2) Cookie removed; **(A3)** Roll of tape added; **(A3–A4)** Handle removed; **(A5)** Ribbon shortened; **(B1–B2)** Lemon removed; **(B2)** Writing removed; **(B5–C5)** Bracelets removed; **(C1–D2)** White tablet now black; **(D1)** Silver fingernail now pink; **(D3)** "Thank You" now "Thanks."

Working From Home 28–29

Carolyn Barber

(A2) White bowl added; **(A5)** Wheels removed; **(B2)** Labels moved on pink boxes; **(D2)** Pink cylinders now dark purple; **(D4)** Knob added to desk drawer; **(E2)** Black lamp now taller.

The Dark Room 30–31

Steve Gorton/John Hedgecoe

(A1) White tag moved; **(A2)** Red clips removed; **(B1)** Two beakers added to shelf; **(B2–B3)** Two tools switched; **(C1)** White cap now blue; **(C4)** Door handles changed; **(D3)** White spray can flipped horizontally; **(D5–E5)** White trash bin moved; **(E2)** Shelf lowered; **(E4)** Scissors removed.

Flag Day 32

Dave King

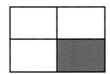

Put a Pin in It 33
Peter Anderson

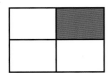

If You Can't Take the Heat … 34–35
Carolyn Barber

(A2–A3) White cord removed; **(A3)** Button removed; **(B2–B3)** Wall outlet switches flipped vertically; **(B4)** Toaster now plugged in; **(C1)** Blue kettle now gold; **(C2)** Time on clock changed; **(C2–C3)** Frying pan flipped horizontally and moved; **(C2–D2)** Blue lines removed; **(C3)** Coffee level higher; **(C3–C4)** Blue jar added; **(D2–E2)** White grate extended.

Without a Shadow of a Doubt 36–37
Dave King

(A2–B3) Frame moved; **(C1)** Woman flipped horizontally; **(C4–C5)** Silhouette different; **(D1)** Woman's arm moved; **(D1–D2)** Frame shortened; **(D4–D5)** People now farther apart.

The Moon Party Fizzled Out............................... 38–39
Will Heap

(A1–B1) Brown and white stars switched; **(A5)** Gray star added; **(B3–B4)** Silver band removed; **(C3)** Red ball added; **(C4)** Astronaut's visor now white; **(C5)** Big gray star flipped horizontally; **(D2)** Rocket exhaust now larger; **(D3)** Gray star added; **(E1)** Star now has four "prongs"; **(E3)** White star now brown; **(E4–E5)** Small star added.

Garden Games.. 40–41
Dave King

(A4) Ladybug and flower switched; **(B2)** Middle tine in red tool removed; **(B3)** Yellow flower now red; **(B3–C3)** Purple stick lengthened; **(B5)** Green caterpillar now pink; **(C1)** Face removed; **(C3)** Dirt removed; **(C4)** Ladybug added to brown pot; **(D1)** String shortened; **(D3–D4)** Frog enlarged; **(E2)** Leaves added; **(E5)** Red lines removed.

Tile Style 42
Jeff Carroll

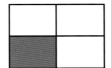

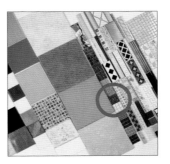

All Buttoned Up... 43
Andy Crawford

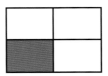

Duly Noted.. 44–45
Claire Cordier

(A2–A3) Yellow paper now overlaps green paper; **(B4–C4)** Red paper lengthened; **(B5)** White pin moved; **(E2)** Red paper now overlaps yellow paper; **(E4)** Red pin now yellow.

ANSWERS

Row, Row, Row Your Boat 46–47
Anna Mockford

(A2) White line removed; **(A3)** Window now open; **(B4)** "PASQUALE" now "PASQUALI"; **(B5)** Chimney removed; **(C4)** Red backpack now green; **(C5)** Window removed; **(D1)** Blue bar removed; **(C2–D2)** Red pants now blue; **(D2)** "DANFE" now "DANF"; **(E5)** Wood lengthened.

A Batch Made in Heaven 48–49
Will Heap

(B3–B4) Half moon cookie now a full circle; **(C1)** Orange candy piece added; **(C2–D3)** Icing removed; **(C2–D3)** Yellow necklace now blue; **(C4)** Pocket protector removed; **(C5)** Raisin removed; **(D1)** Yellow candy piece now red; **(D5)** Cookie now has brown hair; **(E4)** Icing drips removed.

They Say You Can't Take It With You 50–51
James Tye

(A3) Pole behind board now wider; **(B2–C2)** Magnet flipped horizontally; **(B3)** Red magnet removed; **(C2)** Red magnets now closer together; **(C5)** "65" now "35"; **(D1–E1)** Tower now taller; **(D2)** Small red window removed; **(D3)** Third green window added; **(D4–D5)** White string removed.

Little Drummer Boys 52
Ruth Jenkinson

7	1	5
9	4	2
8	6	3

All The World's a Stage 53
Alessandra Santarelli/Joeff Davis

8	1	3
5	9	7
4	2	6

We Had a Joke for This One 54–55

(A2–A3) Grape added; **(B1–C1)** Pretzel flipped vertically; **(B3–C3)** Cheese slice removed; **(B5–C5)** Red handle lengthened; **(C5)** Acorn added; **(D1–D2)** Circle cracker added; **(D3–D4)** Cheese square added; **(D5)** Herbs lengthened; **(E3)** Pretzel removed.

Pencil Power 56–57
Dave King

(A1) Yellow pencil lengthened; **(A3)** Blue pencil moved; **(B3)** Dark purple clip now light purple; **(B5)** Light blue pencil now purple; **(C2)** Blue horizontal lines changed; **(C4)** Orange dots removed; **(D1)** Orange pencil shortened; **(D1)** Pencil sharpener removed; **(D2)** Pink paper edge now light blue; **(D3)** Red stars moved/removed; **(D5)** Yellow pencil lengthened; **(E4)** Pink pencil shortened.

Wool Pile 58–59

(A1) Light blue ball now purple; **(B2)** Pink ball now purple; **(B5)** Yellow ball now orange; **(C3)** Red ball now light blue; **(C5)** Purple ball added; **(D2)** Green ball now purple; **(E3)** Light blue ball now light green; **(E5)** Yellow ball added.

Newspaper Caper 60–61
Andy Crawford

(A1–B1) Picture frame now larger; **(A5)** Vertical line in background moved; **(B3)** White pot removed; **(C2)** Girl's braid removed; **(C2–D2)** Pink dots on apron now blue; **(C3)** Newsprint inside bowl changed; **(C5–D5)** Purple paintbrush added; **(D3)** Pink paper now green; **(D5)** Orange part of newspaper now green; **(E1–E2)** Crumpled newspaper added.

MEDIUM

Quilt Quandary 62–63

Andy Crawford

(A2) Yellow flag flipped vertically; **(B4–C4)** Small white dots now large white dots; **(C1)** Blue flag now orange; **(C3)** Blue square now green; **(C5)** Blue mast now yellow; **(C5–D5)** White dots removed; **(D1–D2)** Green sails now dark blue; **(E3)** Yellow square now orange; **(E5)** Tag moved.

Sew Much to Do 64–65

Penny Wincer

(A1) Cup added to shelf; **(A2)** Photograph removed; **(A3–B3)** Color swatches flipped vertically; **(A5)** Red flowers now purple; **(B1–B2)** Yellow and red pattern flipped horizontally; **(B2)** White line now thinner; **(B5)** Two triangles in pattern now red; **(C2)** Colored squares reordered; **(C4)** Photograph added; **(C4)** White knob removed; **(D1)** Purple spool of thread removed; **(D5–E5)** Table leg removed.

Music Boxes 66–67

(A1–B1) Label removed; **(A3–B3)** Brown box now purple; **(C1)** Small brown box added; **(C5)** Silver handle removed; **(D2)** Bow added; **(D3)** "4" now "1"; **(E1)** Small circle removed; **(E2)** Label on blue box moved; **(E2–E3)** Brown box now green.

Clean Up Your Toys! 68–69

Steven Greaves/Prospect Park Audubon Center

(A3) White fixture removed; **(B2–C3)** Air conditioner now taller; **(C1)** Steering wheels removed; **(C3)** Red book now blue; **(D3)** Fish moved; **(D3)** Red plastic tile added; **(D3–E3)** Circular outlets removed; **(E2)** Moose added.

Be Creative 70–71

Steven Greaves/Make Meaning

(A1) Writing removed; **(B2–C2)** Crossword puzzle replaced with teddy bear; **(B3)** Security light removed; **(B4)** White circle added; **(C1)** Green circle added; **(C4)** Small green circle now orange; **(D5–E5)** Chair leg removed; **(E1–E2)** Green chair now blue.

You Can Paint It Any Color 72–73

Alex Robinson

(B2) Clock removed; **(B4)** Small window removed; **(B4–B5)** Tower now taller; **(B5)** "RESTAURANTE" removed; **(C1)** More palm leaves added; **(C2)** Window flipped horizontally; **(C4)** Red blanket now wider; **(C5)** Open window now closed; **(D2)** Small window added; **(E4)** Round sign on door moved; **(E4)** "CARROSSA" now "CARPOSSA"; **(E5)** Light added to building.

Dollhouse Delight 74–75

Dave King

(A3) Cat moved; **(B3)** Towel on pink rack lengthened; **(B5)** Panda now has two black eyes; **(C1)** Hinge added; **(C2)** Purple drawing flipped horizontally; **(C2–C3)** Blue door and window switched; **(C4–C5)** Wooden piece removed; **(D3–D4)** Red heart added; **(D4)** Pink broom handle lengthened; **(E2)** Red car now blue; **(E4)** Pink fabric now green; **(E4)** Plastic hedges added.

Hong Kong at Night 76

Nigel Hicks

4	9	3
7	5	1
3	6	8

ANSWERS

Stuck in Traffic 77
Mike Good

9	5	3
1	7	4
8	6	2

X Marks the Spot 78–79
Lorraine Johnson

(B2) Whale flipped horizontally; **(B3)** Island removed; **(B4)** New hill added; **(B4)** Palm tree added; **(B4)** Shark fin added; **(C3)** "X" moved; **(C4–C5)** Ship windows now black; **(D2–E2)** Compass arrows shading switched; **(D3)** Water splashes changed; **(D4–E4)** New peaks added.

Rumpus Room 80–81
Vanessa Davies

(A1–B3) Picture frames moved; **(B1)** Red box removed; **(B3–B4)** Clock time changed; **(B4)** Extra peg on rack; **(B5–C5)** Green jacket now pink; **(C2–D2)** Book now taller; **(D1–D2)** Middle pole added to basket; **(D3–E3)** Green and white stripes removed.

Toys, Toys, Toys! 82–83
Andy Crawford

(A3–B3) Blue die "3" now "4"; **(A4)** Coupling removed; **(B1–C1)** Red car now purple; **(B2)** Small tree removed; **(B3–C3)** Red car now blue; **(B5)** Yellow star now orange; **(C2)** Yellow "6" replaced with blue "2"; **(D3)** Spot removed; **(D4–D5)** Basketball rotated; **(E1)** Two blue dots removed.

Did You Hear the Story About the Bed? 84–85
Penny Wincer

(A1) Plane on wallpaper flipped horizontally; **(A1)** Hinge moved; **(A3–B3)** Bunny moved; **(A4–B5)** Lamp moved; **(C2)** Black area added; **(C4–C5)** More book pages added; **(D1–D2)** Outlets removed; **(D3)** Blue diamond now green; **(D4–E5)** Base of bed now all one piece; **(D5)** Red bus now green; **(E2–E3)** Blue light now red.

Idyllic Iceland 86–87
Nigel Hicks

(A2) Chimney added; **(A3)** Sign removed; **(A5)** Window removed; **(B2–C2)** Red roof now green; **(B5–C5)** Trees added; **(C2)** Two windows added; **(D2)** Yellow symbol removed; **(D3)** Two windows now one window; **(D5)** Car removed; **(E5)** Car added.

Moroccan Mementos 88–89
(A1) Red plate added; **(A4)** Light fixture changed; **(B4–C4)** Flower pattern now light green design; **(B5)** Red plate now green; **(C2–D3)** Light green feather duster now pink; **(C5–D5)** Red plate now blue; **(D3)** Man's shoes darkened; **(E1)** Yellow candle holder now blue; **(E2–E3)** Black cat added; **(E4)** Dark blue tajine now light blue.

Sunday in Slovenia 90–91
Linda Whitwam

(A1) Pipe removed; **(A2)** Triangle-shaped window removed; **(A3–A4)** Black design removed; **(A4–A5)** Bicycle wheel rotated; **(B3–B4)** Blue helmet now red; **(B4–B5)** Red item removed; **(C2)** Small square window removed; **(C5)** Woman lost her shadow; **(D2)** Flag removed; **(D4–D5)** Orange shirt now blue; **(E1–E2)** Yellow band added; **(E3)** Small oval sign removed.

Lamp Rays 92

8	1	2
6	5	3
4	7	9

Gift Decorations 93
Dave King

Any Port in a Storm 94–95
(A1) Blue tarp now orange; **(A4)** Yellow flotation devices removed; **(B2)** Boat flipped vertically; **(B3)** Boat removed; **(B5)** Boat moved; **(C1)** Boat added; **(C4)** Boat added; **(D2)** Dock section removed; **(D4–D5)** Boat switched; **(E1)** Boat removed; **(E3)** Orange boat removed.

It Looks Like Rain 96–97
James Tye

(A1) Brown handle removed; **(A2)** Tip removed; **(A5–B5)** Handle and pole removed; **(B1)** White strap flipped horizontally; **(C1)** Solar panel rotated; **(C3)** Drawing on sign changed; **(D1)** Yellow handle flipped horizontally; **(D1–D3)** Blue umbrella now orange; **(D3)** Blue strap removed; **(D5)** Yellow handle now brown; **(E2)** Brown handle flipped horizontally; **(E4)** Brown handle flipped horizontally.

On-Street Parking 98–99
(A5) Manhole added; **(A5)** Red car now purple; **(B1)** White rectangle added around car; **(B3)** Silver car moved; **(B3)** White bar extended; **(D1)** Black car removed; **(D2)** Blue car now red; **(D2–D3)** Tree added; **(D4)** Black and white car added; **(D5)** Silver car moved.

Hitting the Shops 100–101
Tony Souter

(A1) Chimney removed; **(A5)** Bent wire now straight; **(B2–B3)** Brown sign now taller; **(B3)** Exclamation point removed; **(B4)** White necklace removed; **(B4)** Yellow license plate now white; **(B4)** Yellow strap removed; **(C2–D2)** Orange sign now purple; **(D1–D2)** Dark gray banner now white and aquamarine; **(D5)** Stripes removed; **(E2)** Sign changed; **(E5)** Silver pole now blue.

Holiday Gifts 102–103
(A2–B3) Pink gift now green; **(A4–A5)** Ribbon and bow now darker; **(B1)** White bow removed; **(B3–B4)** String added; **(B5)** Pink candy wrapper now brown; **(C3–D3)** Long box now has three bows; **(C5)** Circular orange box rotated; **(D1)** Bow on maroon box changed; **(D4–E5)** Maroon-colored gift flipped vertically; **(E3)** Orange box now pink.

Too Many Towels 104–105
Philippe Giraud

(B1) Blue stripe removed; **(B2–C2)** Yellow stripe now blue; **(C3)** "Coton" removed; **(C3–C4)** Blue-green stripe now yellow; **(C4)** Price tag removed; **(D2–E2)** Light green stripe now blue; **(D3)** White stripe filled in with blue; **(E1)** "850" now "550"; **(E3–E4)** "RAMUNTXO" now "RAMUNTRO"; **(E4)** Yellow hook now red.

Market Madness 106–107
Linda Whitwam

(A2–A3) Tower now taller; **(B1)** Small dormer removed; **(B3)** Small window now larger; **(B2–C2)** White umbrella removed; **(C2–C3)** Beige umbrella added; **(C4)** Blue-gray umbrella added; **(C5)** People added; **(C5)** White banner removed; **(D3)** Yellow structure now green; **(D4–D5)** Red and green umbrellas switched; **(E1)** Small square light removed; **(E3)** People added.

ANSWERS

ANSWERS

Out of the Office
Steve Gorton

Matching Mosaics
Dave King

Raise the Roof
(A2–B2) Pointed green tile now rounded; **(A4)** Broken light blue tile now rounded; **(B3)** Orange tile now green; **(C1)** Green tile now gray; **(C1)** Rusted green tile now bright yellow; **(C4)** Pointed brown tile lengthened; **(D1)** Orange tile now blue; **(D2–D3)** Brown tile now green; **(D5)** Pointed blue-green tile now brown; **(E2–E3)** Light blue tile lengthened.

All Aboard!
Ian O'Leary

(A1) Striped flag now polka dots; **(A3–B3)** Green ribbon design now purple; **(B3–B4)** Small box added; **(B3–C3)** More chocolate sticks added; **(D1)** Orange candy now yellow; **(D3)** White marshmallow smokestack removed; **(E3)** Wheel removed; **(E5)** Orange flag now green.

Oh Sugar!
Tim Ridley

(A1) Heart-shaped candy rotated; **(A5)** Striped candies moved; **(B2)** Candy now has more purple showing; **(B4)** Yellow gummy bear moved; **(C1)** Yellow gummy bear now orange; **(C2)** Red and orange candies switched; **(C5)** Purple candy lengthened; **(D4)** Heart-shaped candy colors switched; **(D4)** Red candy now light green; **(E1)** Pink egg now blue.

Shields Up!
Christine Webb

(A1) Chimney removed; **(A4–A5)** Sign changed; **(B4)** Red part of shield now blue; **(B4)** Sign moved; **(B4–B5)** Column now has four metal bands; **(C2)** Small brown square added; **(C3)** Blue shield changed; **(C4)** Yellow shield flipped horizontally; **(D4)** Sign removed; **(E2–E3)** White shield and green shields switched.

What a Crock!
Martin Hladik

(A1) Red cup now blue; **(A2)** Upside-down cup removed; **(A3)** Missing section of wood replaced; **(A4)** Green and purple cups switched; **(A5)** Yellow bowl now green; **(B1)** Price tag removed; **(B2)** Price tag added; **(B3–B4)** White and brown cups switched; **(B5)** Price tag added; **(B5)** Price tag removed; **(C1–D1)** Price tag added; **(E2–E3)** Price tags removed.

Unbearable
Dave King

(A4) Dark brown bear's arm changed; **(B1)** Bear's blue tie now purple; **(B2)** Pink bear now blue; **(B3)** Cream-colored bear now has no mouth; **(B3–C3)** New bear added; **(B4–B5)** Bear's blue tie now green; **(C1–D1)** White bear now has two eyes; **(C3–D3)** Light bear's tie removed; **(C4)** Orange bear now has two ears; **(D4)** Tie added; **(E1–E2)** Brown bear's tie changed; **(E4)** Bear's darker paw area removed.

Birds of a Feather …

Simon Rawles

(A2–B2) Lights turned off; **(A4)** Piece of bread removed; **(A4)** Pigeon added; **(A4)** Pigeon removed; **(C1)** Window closed; **(D2–D3)** Blue badge removed; **(E4)** Pigeon flipped horizontally; **(E2–E3)** Blue sign now gold; **(E5)** Pigeon flipped horizontally.

Andy Crawford

James Tye

Anna Mockford

(A1–B1) Building now taller; **(A3)** House removed; **(A4–B4)** Three trees now taller; **(B3–B4)** Window added; **(C3–C4)** Gray boat removed; **(D1)** Orange ring now blue; **(D3)** Small yellow sticker removed; **(D4)** Orange buoy removed; **(E3)** Black bucket removed; **(E4–E5)** Rope removed; **(E5)** Blue part of boat now brown.

James Tye

(A3) "ARBALETE" now "ARBALET"; **(A4)** Red stick added; **(B1)** Blue plastic piece added; **(B3)** Bull's-eye now 12; **(C1)** White part of flag moved; **(C3)** White sign added; **(C5)** Blue arrow tip now red.

Tamara Thiessen

(A2) Chimney now taller; **(A2)** Small window removed; **(A4)** Green lighthouse now blue; **(C2–C3)** Blue boat now green; **(D1)** Green buoy removed; **(D1)** Orange and white raft removed; **(E1–E2)** "833303" now "83330"; **(E5)** Green buoy moved.

Will Heap

(B1) Blue card now red; **(B3–C3)** Red card now blue; **(C1)** Blue card added; **(C4–D4)** Two aces switched suits; **(D1)** Red card now blue; **(D2)** White die "3" now "2"; **(D3)** Two of diamonds now has three diamonds.

Dave King

(A3) Red spool of thread moved; **(B3–C3)** Fish and red bucket flipped horizontally; **(B4–C4)** Yellow star now pink; **(B5)** Red dots removed on star; **(B5)** Red ladybug now green; **(D1)** Silver key now has two holes; **(D2–E2)** Orange pencil now pink; **(D3)** Green marble now blue; **(D4–D5)** White-and-yellow-striped button rotated; **(E5)** Blue die "4" now "5."

(A1) Cowboy and horse switched; **(A2)** "208" now "200"; **(A4–B4)** "CMV" now "OMV"; **(B1)** "USA" removed; **(B3–C3)** Dark blue plate now maroon; **(C1–C2)** Red numbers and letters now black; **(C5–D5)** "C205" now "C2C5"; **(D2–E2)** "LAFAYETTE" now "FAYETTE"; **(D4)** "972" now "927"; **(E2)** "2002" now "2012"; **(E3)** Circular gray object removed; **(E4)** New plate added.

ANSWERS

Domino Distraction...138–139
(B2) Dot removed; **(B3)** Dot added; **(C3)** Dot removed; **(C4)** Dot removed; **(D2–E3)** Domino rotated; **(E3)** Dot added.

Marching Band..140
Steven Greaves

4	6	1
7	3	9
8	5	2

Cycling Chaos...141
John Davis

6	3	9
1	5	8
4	7	2

Finding Fossils...142–143
Colin Keates
(A3) Chisel now shortened; **(B2)** Hammer handle shortened; **(B2–C3)** Tools switched; **(B4–B5)** Brush flipped vertically; **(C2)** Pencil shortened; **(C2–C3)** Brown brush removed; **(D1)** Fossil added; **(D3)** Small stone added; **(D4–D5)** Cloth strands removed; **(D4–E4)** Book removed; **(D4–E4)** Pentagon-shaped fossil drawing removed; **(E3)** Wooden slide removed.

Jelly Bean Bonanza...................................144–145
(A2–A3) Red jelly bean now purple; **(A4)** Speckled brown jelly bean removed; **(B1–C1)** Light blue jelly bean now light green; **(B2–B3)** Bright green jelly bean now purple; **(B3)** Orange jelly bean now red; **(D1)** Light blue jelly bean now purple; **(E4)** Red jelly bean added.

Flower Power...146–147
(A2) Purple flower now red; **(A3)** Pink flower added; **(A5)** White flower added; **(B1)** Red flower now purple; **(B4)** Bumblebee added; **(C4)** Green bud added; **(D2–D3)** Red flower now yellow; **(D4)** Closed bud now a yellow flower; **(E1)** Pink flower added; **(E2)** Pink flower now yellow.

It's in the Mail..148–149
(A1) Words switched; **(A4)** "FORSTER" now "FOSTER"; **(A4)** Hole removed; **(B2)** Gold label added; **(B2)** Label moved; **(B4)** Protruding paper removed; **(C3)** White letters removed; **(D1–E2)** Green box now purple; **(D2–E2)** Writing removed; **(D5)** Label added.

P Is for …...150–151
Geoff Dann
(A2) Picture of parrot flipped horizontally; **(A3)** Picture of dog moved; **(B3–B4)** "P" moved; **(C1)** Puppet's purple eye patch now black; **(C1)** Red bottle of paint added; **(C4–C5)** Green clips now purple; **(D2)** Red paint circle now dark blue; **(D3–D4)** Green paint bottle now purple; **(E3–E4)** Extra puzzle piece added; **(E4)** Wooden leg removed.

A Real Mind-Number...................................152–153
Dave King
(A2) Stick figure removed; **(A2–B2)** White stars removed; **(B3)** Rainbow removed; **(B4)** Red circle removed; **(C1)** Paper "30" removed; **(C3)** Two peas removed; **(C4)** "3" billiard ball now "8"; **(C5)** Red dot added; **(C5)** Two planets switched; **(D1–D2)** "6" now "9"; **(E1–E2)** Red pen shortened; **(E4)** Planet moved.

Tool Time..154–155
Peter Anderson
(A2) Yellow hammer now orange; **(A2–B2)** Hammer top flipped horizontally; **(A4)** Red part of handle now higher; **(A5–B5)** Metal spike removed; **(B2)** Blue and yellow pliers added; **(B5)** Green tape measure now orange; **(C2–C3)** Orange stapler now blue; **(D1)** Black piece on ruler moved; **(D5)** Green screwdriver handle added; **(E3–E4)** Silver saw replaced with wrench.

HARD

New York, New York 156–157
(A3) Tree added; **(B1–B2)** Tree added; **(B3)** Silver car added; **(B4)** Black car removed; **(C1)** Silver car added; **(C1–D2)** All people removed; **(C2)** Silver car added; **(D2–E2)** Yellow taxi moved back; **(D3)** Motorcyclist removed; **(D5)** Yellow car now light blue; **(E3)** Blue car moved one lane over; **(E4)** Yellow car added.

Along the Canal 158–159
Robert Schweizer

(A2) Lamps removed; **(B1)** Rooftop dormer removed; **(B2)** Closed umbrella added; **(B2)** Window altered; **(B4)** Blue pillow added; **(C3)** Neon sign moved; **(C3)** Sign removed; **(C5)** Orange section of pole now blue; **(D3)** Yellow shirt now pink; **(D4)** Blue bag now green; **(D4)** Logo removed; **(E4)** Girl's shorts lengthened.

Enjoying the Plaza 160–161
(A1–B1) Flag removed; **(B5)** Street lamp removed; **(C1)** Black square emblem removed; **(C2–D2)** Blue shirt now red; **(C3)** Person added; **(C4)** Yellow fire hydrant now red; **(C4–C5)** White car moved; **(C4–D4)** Jaguar on obelisk flipped horizontally; **(C5)** Red part of car now blue; **(D2–D4)** Handrail removed; **(D4)** Small light removed.

Platform Predicament 162–163
Chris Stowers

(A2) "5" removed; **(A3–B3)** Yellow flag now orange; **(B2)** Bird moved; **(B5)** White text and logo removed; **(C3)** Pole removed; **(C5)** Light pole now taller; **(D2)** Circle on ground moved; **(D3–E3)** Man flipped horizontally; **(E2)** Person added; **(E4)** Orange shirt now blue.

Stuck Dockside 164–165
Anna Mockford/Nick Bonetti

(A1) Boat now has two engines; **(A4–A5)** White buoy moved; **(B3–C2)** Wooden plank now yellow; **(C1)** White pillow removed; **(C4)** Red area of boat now white; **(D2–E2)** White pillow added; **(E4–E5)** Duck added.

All Locked Up 166–167
(A1–B1) Blue lock now green; **(A3)** Large blue heart now pink; **(A5)** Silver lock now larger; **(B2)** White heart removed; **(C1)** Writing removed; **(C4)** Writing added; **(D3–E3)** "858" now "88"; **(D4)** Pink lock now yellow; **(D5)** Bright red lock now purple; **(E1)** Cartoon drawing replaced with white heart.

ANSWERS

Paper Clip Conundrum 168
Steve Gorton

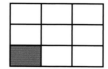

Wacky Windows 169

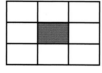
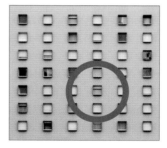

Stylish Ride 170–171
Steve Gorton

(A4–B4) "On" now "in"; **(A5)** Words removed; **(B3)** Orange flowers now pink; **(D2)** Orange reflector now blue; **(C1)** Green painted tree removed; **(C1)** Orange flower added; **(C2)** Red reflector removed; **(D5–E5)** Leaves added to ground; **(E2)** Crack removed; **(E4)** Cigarette removed.

ANSWERS

Bottled Up..172–173

Andy Crawford

(A2) Small white bottle removed; **(A3)** Dark bottle replaced with lighter brown one; **(A4)** Faucet removed; **(A5)** Cabinet knobs moved; **(B3)** Woman's hair lengthened; **(C4)** Clear plastic funnel removed; **(C5)** Button removed; **(D1–D2)** Bottle added; **(D4)** Plastic bottle less full now; **(D4)** White cap now black; **(E3)** Liquid level higher in last bottle; **(E4)** Pestle removed.

Red Herrings.....................................174–175

(A1) Die "2" flipped horizontally; **(A4)** Red "7" now "1"; **(B3)** Berry removed; **(B3)** Figure's face changed; **(C3)** Die "6" now "4"; **(C4)** Magnet now has two flowers; **(C4–D4)** Black dot removed; **(D2)** Extra bus window on lower level; **(D5)** Purple cap now green; **(E2)** Vertical line of four jelly beans now five.

Shop 'Til You Drop 176–177

(A3) Metal pole added; **(A5)** Purple banner now orange; **(B1)** Green trash can added; **(B3–B4)** Escalator removed; **(B3)** Orange chair now green; **(C2)** Green plant added; **(C3)** Trash can moved; **(C5)** Green sign now blue; **(C5)** Man flipped horizontally; **(D5–E5)** Woman moved; **(E1)** Person removed.

Stamp Champ.....................................178–179

Demetrio Carrasco

(A1) Bird on green stamp flipped horizontally; **(A4–B4)** Man's arm now bent; **(A5)** "PIURA" removed; **(C1)** Dark blue stamp moved; **(C2)** "50"s now "55"s; **(C5)** Background image extended upward to cover text; **(D1–E2)** Orange stamp now purple; **(D3)** Cent symbols removed; **(D4–D5)** "PERU" removed; **(E2)** "30" removed; **(E3–E44)** Yellow section on blue stamp now blue.

Cherry, Cherry 180

1	5	9
3	7	4
6	2	8

BICYCLE RIDES
Orange County

•• **58 Rides With Detailed Maps & Elevation Contours** ••

BY DON AND SHARRON BRUNDIGE

Books by Don and Sharron Brundige:
Bicycle Rides: Los Angeles and Orange Counties (Out of Print)
Bicycle Rides: San Fernando Valley and Ventura County (Out of Print)
Bicycle Rides: Orange County
Bicycle Rides: Los Angeles County
Bicycle Rides: Inland Empire
Bicycle Rides: San Diego and Imperial Counties
Bicycle Rides: Santa Barbara & Ventura Counties
Mountain Biking L.A. County (Southern Section)
Outdoor Recreation Checklists

Published by B-D Enterprises
122 Mirabeau Ave.
San Pedro, California 90732-3117
e-mail: bnyduk@aol.com

Most recent printing by Advantage Printing in Northridge, California
First Printing - September 1988
Second Printing (revised) - April 1990
Third Printing (revised) - August 1993
Fourth Printing (revised) - November 1996
Fifth Printing (completely revised and expanded) - February 2001

Photography by Don and Sharron Brundige (unless noted otherwise)
Custom Photo Work by The Foto Factory in Torrance

We want to hear from you!

Corrections and updates will make this a better book and are gratefully appreciated. Publisher will reply to all such letters. Where information is used, submitter will be acknowledged in subsequent printing and given a free book (see above) of choice.

Front Cover: Dana Point Harbor Inside Title Page: Irvine's South Lake
Back Cover: Walnut Canyon Reservoir in Anaheim Hills (upper); Galaxy Park in Newport Beach (lower)

TABLE OF CONTENTS

51 Trips and 58 Rides

———
* Major Revision of Previous Edition

DEDICATION

To our family
....Who we love very much

George, Bernice, Don, Pat, Kathie, Jim, Stevie, Rich, Pon,
Eric, Greta, Greg, Mark, Pete, Michelle, Diane and Bradley

ACKNOWLEDGMENTS

We offer our thanks to family, friends and bicycling acquaintances who gave us ideas, advice and plenty of encouragement while developing this biking book. This includes a "thank you" to the state, county and city agencies and individuals who offered their services and publications. Kudos to Sam Nunez, Robert Simms and the folks we met on the road, for sharing the tours. We also show particular gratitude to our venerable crew that was kind enough to review and comment on our original manuscript: Jill Morales, Al Hook and Walt Bond. We also thank Bernice Palmquist for her updates to our previously published book. Thank you Jacqui Broom and Alex Moi for helping us through so many computer crises.

We specifically wish to acknowledge the following individuals and/or organizations who provided some excellent ideas for bicycle trips in the original book: Donald K. Jensen and Toshio Kuba of the City of Buena Park; the Community Services Departments of Huntington Beach and Tustin; the Citizen's Advisory Committee of Newport Beach; the City of Costa Mesa; CALTRANS District 07: Public Transportation and Ridesharing Branch: Sherri Miller and Richard Sherry of the Orange County Environmental Management Agency: Transportation Planning; and Mary Shimono of the City of Rancho Santa Marguerita.

Finally, we want to thank contributors to our 2000 edition: Richard Sherry, Sherri Miller and Harry Persaud of the County of Orange Planning and Services Department; Will and Kathi Decker of the *Southern California Bicyclist* magazine for keeping us on our toes to update our tours; and Dick Farrar, Dave Monshaw, Mandie Loren, Bill Barr, Mary Beth Grigg, Gene Adler, Steven Izumi and Cheryl Denson, all local cycling enthusiasts, for providing corrections/updates to some of our previous ride descriptions.

INTRODUCTION

As with all our books, we wanted to provide a trip guide that concentrates on trip navigation, contains a large number of well-documented trips, provides the necessary trip maps and elevation contours, and is reasonably priced. Hopefully, again, we have succeeded!

This guide has been developed based on biking trips developed or revisited in 2000. It is a total update/revision of *Bicycle Rides: Orange County*. Because of addition of new bikeways, new construction, new or modified traffic flow, changes of park and facility names and other effects of time, this book has over 30 completely new maps and both map and route description changes to a majority of the original trips. Also, 16 new trips spread between the coastal zone, river/creek trails and the county interior have been added. Finally, there are numerous new photos in highly scenic areas scattered throughout.

There are over 800 <u>one-way</u> bike miles described! The document identifies 51 on-road trips which blanket Orange County. Trips of exceptional length or complexity are broken down into segments or "rides." There are a total of 58 rides described. Each ride is written to be as complete and self-standing as possible. The authors and riding buddies used 18-speed bicycles, although the vast majority of trips can be ridden with bikes having a lesser number of gears. The few rides which are more amenable to hybrid and or fat-tire ("balloon-tire") bikes are noted. In no cases are mountain bikes required.

A cross section of trips is provided. There are some short-length family trips on separated bikepaths, many longer exploratory and workout trips for more experienced bikers on various quality bike routes, and a few "gut-buster" trips on open roadway for the most physically fit and motivated cyclists. The trip domains include cities, parks, beaches, harbors, rivers, lakes, valleys, canyons and mountains. The trips vary from extremely scenic to somewhat monotonous (e.g., certain stretches of the high-mileage concrete "wastelands" along the Class I river routes). There is a little something for everybody!

The strong emphasis in this book is "getting from here to there." This navigation is provided using detailed route descriptions in terms of landmarks, mileage, elevation contours and a quality set of trip maps. Scenery, vistas and scenic or historic landmarks and sightseeing attractions are regularly noted for each trip, although detailed information about these features must be sought out in other publications. Public restrooms and sources of water are identified on those few trips where these facilities are available. Pleasant rest spots are also pointed out. Finally, "wine and dine" spots are noted for two specific circumstances: 1) where places to eat along the route are scarce; and 2) where the establishment is too unique or exceptional not to mention.

HOW TO USE THIS BOOK

There are two ways to use this book: one way is for the person who wants to enjoy the research along with enjoying the bike ride, and another way for the biker who is just anxious to get out there "amongst em."

For the "anxious biker," follow Steps I through 5 below and split!

1. Check the "BEST RIDES BY CATEGORY" trip summary noted on the inside cover for candidate trips or use the "Master Trip Map" in the "TRIP ORGANIZATION" section to select areas of interest for the bike ride. Note the candidate trip numbers. (Another option is to select a trip based on landmarks and sightseeing attractions referenced in the "INDEX.")

2. Go to the "Master Trip Matrices" in the "TRIP ORGANIZATION" section and narrow down the number of candidate trips by reviewing their general features.

3. Read about the individual trips and select one. Make a photocopy of the trip(s) of interest subject to the copyright limitations noted on page ii.

4. Read and understand the safety rules described in the "GENERAL BIKING CONSIDERATIONS" section and review the "CHECKLIST" section.

5. See you later. Enjoy the ride!

For the more methodical folks, continue reading the next chapter. By the time you're through, you'll understand the trip description and maps much better than the "anxious biker."

TRIP ORGANIZATION

This bike book is organized by trip number. Extended length trips are broken down into trip segments by ride number, which is the trip number plus a letter. Thus, Trip #17 is the "Santa Ana River Trail," while Ride #17A is the "Green River Road to Yorba Linda Park" segment. Trip numbers are in a general sequence governed by whether the tours are coastal, river, inland or special tours. Refer back to the "TABLE OF CONTENTS" for the entire trip list.

The "Master Trip Maps" show the general trailhead location of trips using a circled reference number (i.e., ⑦ refers to Trip #7). Extended length trips are identified by circled numbers at both beginning and terminal points.

The "Master Trip Matrices" provide a quick reference for selecting candidate trips and for more detailed reading evaluation. The matrices are organized by trip number. The key trip descriptors provided in those matrices are briefly explained in the footnotes at the below of the last matrix (page 9). A more detailed explanation of those descriptors is provided in the "TRIP DESCRIPTION/ TERMINOLOGY" section which follows.

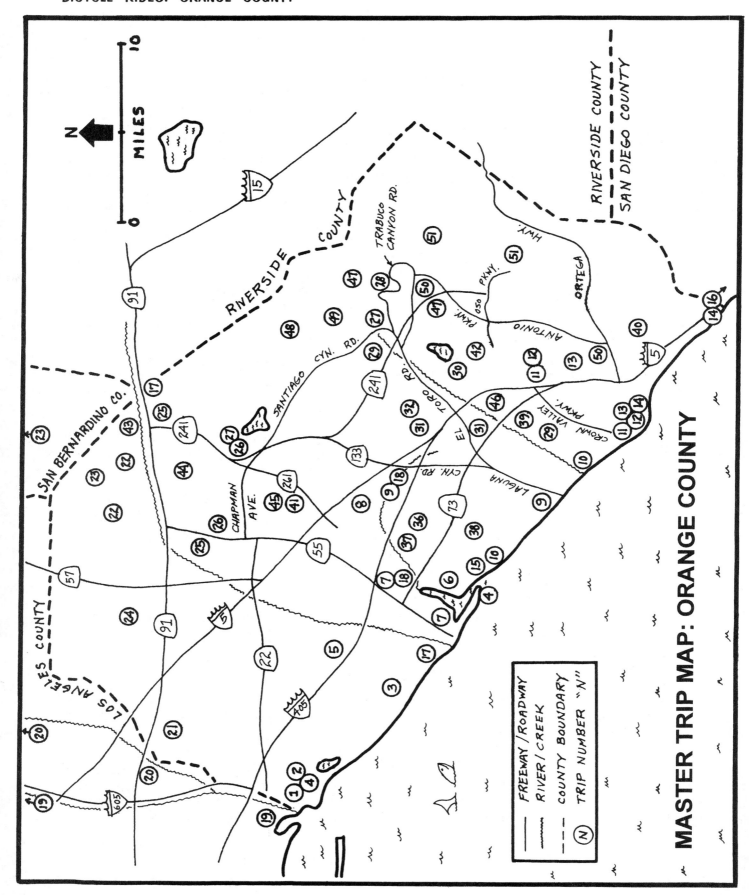

MASTER TRIP MAP: ORANGE COUNTY

FREEWAY / ROADWAY
RIVER / CREEK
COUNTY BOUNDARY
(N) TRIP NUMBER "N"

MASTER TRIP MATRIX

TRIP NO.	GENERAL LOCATION	LEVEL OF DIFFICULTY			ROUTE QUALITY			TRIP CHARACT.²	COMMENTS
		L.O.D.¹	MILES	ELEV.	BIKE TRAIL (%)	BIKE LANE (%)	OTHER (%)		
1	Seal Beach-Sunset Beach	E (r/t)	4.3 (1-w)	Flat	-	60	40	S, L, S/A	Seal Beach to Sunset Beach
2	Huntington Beach	E(1-w) M(r/t)	12.0 (r/t)	Flat	-	30	70	S, N, L, S/A	Sunset Aquatic Park/ Huntington Harbor
3	Huntington Beach	E	4.7	Flat	100	-	-	S, N, L, S/A	Huntington Central Park Loop
4	Sunset Beach-Newport Beach	E(1-w) M(r/t)	13.8	Flat	90	10	-	S, L, S/A	Sunset Beach to Newport Beach Strand
5	Fountain Valley	E	7.6	Flat	100	-	-	S, L, S/A	Mile Square Park Loop
6	Newport Beach	M	6.2	Mod.	-	90	10	S, N, S/A	Upper Newport Bay Loop
7	Newport Beach, Irvine	M	24.4	Mod.-Steep	15	80	5	S, N, L, S/A	Newport Beach/Irvine City Loop
8	Irvine, Tustin	M(r/t)	15.6	Flat	-	100	-	S, L	Irvine Bikeway (Loop) + Numerous Spur Trips
9	Irvine, Laguna Canyon, Laguna Beach	M(1-w) M-S(r/t)	10.6	Mod.	-	10	90	S, L, S/A,	Laguna Canyon Road
10	Corona Del Mar - Laguna Beach	M (1-w) M-S (r/t)	9.1 (1-w)	Mod.-Steep	-	70	30	S, L, E	Laguna Beach City Tour
11	Mission Viejo, Laguna Beach	M (1-w) M (r/t)	7.0 (1-w)	Mod.	-	100	-	S, E	Laguna Niguel Bikeway (+ various return options)
12	Mission Viejo-San Juan Capistrano	E (1-w) E-M (r/t)	6.9 (1-w)	Flat	50	50	-	S, L, S/A	Doheny Bikeway
13	San Juan Capistrano-Dana Point	M	17.2	Mod.	60	40	10	S, N, L, S/A	Del Obispo Bikeway, San Juan Creek Loop

1,2 See footnotes on page 8

5

MASTER TRIP MATRIX

TRIP NO.	GENERAL LOCATION	LEVEL OF DIFFICULTY			ROUTE QUALITY			TRIP CHARACT.[2]	COMMENTS
		L.O.D.[1]	MILES	ELEV.	BIKE TRAIL (%)	BIKE LANE (%)	OTHER (%)		
14	Dana Point-San Clemente	M	17.1	Mod.	20	70	10	S, L, S/A	Doheny Beach-San Clemente Loop
15	Newport Beach-Corona Del Mar	M	10.1	Mod.	-	40	60	S, L, S/A	Newport Beach-Corona Del Mar Beach Loop
16	San Clemente-Oceanside-San Diego	S (1-w) VS(r/t)	67.2 (1-w)	Mod.-Steep	20	80	-	S, N, L, S/A, E, M	San Clemente-San Diego Bicentennial Bike Route
17	Santa Ana Canyon-Huntington Beach	M (1-w) S(r/t)	30.6 (1-w)	Flat	90	5	5	S, N, L, M	Santa Ana River Trail (Santa Ana Canyon-Ocean)
17A	Santa Ana Canyon-Yorba Linda	M (1-w) M (r/t)	7.4 (1-w)	Mod.	100	-	-	S, N	Green River Road to Yorba Regional Park
17B	Yorba Linda-Placentia-Orange	E(1-w) M(r/t)	10.0 (1-w)	Flat	100	-	-	S, L	Yorba Regional Park to El Camino Real Park
17C	Orange-Garden Grove-Huntington Beach	E(1-w) M(r/t)	13.4 (1-w)	Flat	100	-	-	S, N	El Camino Real Park to Huntington State Beach
18	Newport Beach-Irvine	E(1-w) M(r/t)	9.9 (1-w)	Flat	90	10	-	S, N	San Diego Creek
19	Seal Beach-Azusa	M-S S (r/t)	39.0 (1-w)	Flat	100	-	-	S, N, L, S/A, M	San Gabriel River (shore to mountains)
19A	Seal Beach-Long Beach	E (1-w) E (r/t)	5.6 (1-w)	Flat	100	-	-	S, N, S/A, M	Ocean to El Dorado Park
19B	Long Beach-Downey	E (1-w) M (r/t)	9.7 (1-w)	Flat	100	-	-	S, N, S/A, M	El Dorado Park to Wilderness Park
19C	Downey-Pico Rivera	E (1-w) M (r/t)	7.7 (1-w)	Flat	100	-	-	S, N, L, M	Wilderness Park to Whittier Narrows/Legg Lake
19D	Pico Rivera-Inwindale	E (1-w) M (r/t)	11.4 (1-w)	Flat	100	-	-	S, N, L, M	Whittier Narrows/Legg Lake to Santa Fe Dam

1,2 See footnotes on page 8

MASTER TRIP MATRIX

TRIP NO.	GENERAL LOCATION	LEVEL OF DIFFICULTY			ROUTE QUALITY			TRIP CHARACT.[2]	COMMENTS
		L.O.D.[1]	MILES	ELEV.	BIKE TRAIL (%)	BIKE LANE (%)	OTHER (%)		
19E	Irwindale-Azusa	E (1-w) M (r/t)	7.5 (1-w)	Flat	100	-	-	S, N, L, M	Santa Fe Dam to San Gabriel Canyon
20	Long Beach-Cerritos	E (1-w) M (r/t)	14.0 (1-w)	Flat	100	-	-	S, L, M	San Gabriel River-Coyote Creek
21	Cypress, La Palma, Buena Park	E-M	14.9	Flat	15	80	5	S, L	Cypress City Tour (loop)
22	Yorba Linda	E (1-w) M (r/t)	8.2 (1-w)	Mod.	80	-	20	S, N	El Cajon Trail
23	Brea, Chino Hills, Brea, Diamond Bar	S	23.3	Steep	-	20	80	S, N, E, M	Chino Hills Loop
24	Fullerton	M-S	15.4	Mod.-Steep	-	80	20	S, N	Fullerton Tour (loop), Craig Park, Tri-Cities Park
25	Anaheim Hills	E (1-w) M (r/t)	7.6 (1-w)	Mod.	-	100	-	S, M	Santa Ana Canyon Road
26	Orange	M (E)	10.2 (3.9)	Mod. (Flat)	10 (100)	80	10	S, N, L (S, N, L, S/A)	Orange/Irvine Park Loop (Irvine Park)
27	Santiago Canyon	S (1-w) S (r/t)	12.6 (1-w)	Mod.-Steep	-	-	100	S, N, E,	Santiago Canyon Road
28	Rancho Santa Margarita	E	7.4 (r/t)	Flat-Mod.	100	-	-	S, N	O'Neill Regional Park Tour
29	El Toro-Laguna Niguel	E (1-w) M (r/t)	15.9 (1-w)	Mod.	100	-	-	S, N, L	Aliso Creek Bike Trail
29A	El Toro-Lake Forest	E (1-w) E-M (r/t)	7.7 (1-w)	Mod.	100	-	-	S, N, L	Aliso Creek Bike Trail, Northern Segment
29B	Lake Forest-Laguna Niguel	E (r/t)	8.2 (1-w)	Mod.	100	-	-	S, N	Aliso Creek Bike Trail, Southern Segment

1,2 See footnotes on page 9

MASTER TRIP MATRIX

TRIP NO.	GENERAL LOCATION	LEVEL OF DIFFICULTY			ROUTE QUALITY			TRIP CHARACT.[2]	COMMENTS
		L.O.D.[1]	MILES	ELEV.	BIKE TRAIL (%)	BIKE LANE (%)	OTHER (%)		
30	Mission Viejo, El Toro, Laguna Hills	M-S	15.6	Mod.	30	70	-	S, N, L	Mission Viejo Bikeway (loop)
31	Laguna Hills, Irvine, Laguna Beach	M-S	14.3	Mod.-Steep	-	30	70	S, L, S/A	Laguna Hills Loop
32	Lake Forest	E	5.3	Flat-Mod.	20	80	-	S, N	Lake Forest Loop
33	San Gabriel Rvr.-Coyote Creek-Santa Ana River	S	63.5	Mod.	70	20	10	S, N, L, M	Western Orange County Loop
34	Santiago Cyn.-Aliso Crk.-PCH-Santa Ana Rvr.	VS	76.9	Mod.-Steep	30	60	10	S, N, L, S/A, M	Eastern Orange County Loop
35	Santiago Cyn.-Aliso Crk.-PCH-San Gabriel Rvr.-Coyote Crk.-El Cajon Trail-Villa Park	M	105	Mod.-Steep	40	30	30	S, N, L, S/A, M	Orange County "Century"
36	Irvine	M	4.3	Mod.	-	100	-	S, N	Turtle Rock Road (loop) + Class I spur trip
37	Irvine	E (E)	1.9 (2.4)	Flat (Flat)	100 (100)	-	-	S, N (S,N)	Mason Regional Park (west) (east grounds)
38	Orange County/ Newport Coast	S	8.1	Mod.-Sheer	-	45	55	S, E	Pelican Hill & Signal Peak (loop)
39	Laguna Niguel	S	8.4	Mod.-Steep	-	100	-	S, N, E	Laguna Niguel Tour (loop)
40	Capistrano Beach, San Clemente	M / M-S	9.7 / 15.1	Mod. / Mod.-Steep	30	60 / 50	10 / 50	S, L / S, N, L	Hillside San Clemente (two loops)
41	Tustin	M	8.0	Mod.	-	100	-	S, S/A	Tustin Ranch Loop + Peters Canyon Bikeway

1,2 See footnotes on page 9

MASTER TRIP MATRIX

TRIP NO.	GENERAL LOCATION	LEVEL OF DIFFICULTY			ROUTE QUALITY			TRIP CHARACT.[2]	COMMENTS
		L.O.D.[1]	MILES	ELEV.	BIKE TRAIL (%)	BIKE LANE (%)	OTHER (%)		
42	Mission Viejo	M	4.4	Mod.	100	-	-	S, N, L	Pavion, Jeronimo Gnbt., Oso Viejo & World Cup Parks
43	Yorba Linda	VS	23.6	Steep-Sheer	25	5	70	S, N, E	Yorba Linda Tour (three hill climbs)
44	Anaheim Hills, Orange	S	14.2	Steep-Sheer	-	10	90	S, E	Anaheim Hills Loop(s)
45	Lemon Heights	M-S	6.1	Steep	-	15	85	S, L, E	Lemon Heights Loop
46	Aliso Viejo	M	8.2	Mod.	-	100	-	S	Aliso Viejo Double Loop
47	Mission Viejo, Trabuco & Live Oak Canyons	S	13.2	Mod.-Steep	-	50	50	S, N, E	Cities and Canyons Loop
48	Silverado Canyon (Cleveland Nat. Forest)	M-S	11.3	Mod.	-	-	100	S, N	Silverado Canyon (up and back)
49	Modjeska Canyon (Cleveland Nat. Forest)	M-S	6.2	Steep-Sheer	-	-	100	S, N, S/A	Modjeska Canyon (loop)
50	Mission Viejo. Rancho Santa Margarita, SJC	S	27.1	Mod.-Steep	10	65	25	S, N, L, E, M	Arroyo Trabuco Loop
51	Coto De Caza	M	11.2	Mod.	-	-	100	S, L	Coto De Caza Loop (private: residents & guests only)

[1] **L.O.D.** - Overall trip level of difficulty: **VS**-very strenuous; **S**-strenuous; **M**-Moderate; **E**-easy;
1-w-one way; r/t-round trip or up and back

[2] **TRIP CHARACTERISTICS** - General trip features and highlights: **S**-scenic; **N**-nature trail; **L**-landmark(s);
S/A-sight-seeing attractions; **E**-elevation workout; **M**-mileage workout

TRIP DESCRIPTION/TERMINOLOGY

The trip descriptors in the "Master Trip Matrices" are described below in further detail. Several of these same descriptors are also used in the individual trip writeups.

GENERAL LOCATION: The general location of the bike trail is provided in terms of a city, landmark or general area description, as applicable. The "Master Trip Map" may be useful in conjunction with this general locator.

LEVEL OF DIFFICULTY: The rides are rated on an overall basis with consideration for elevation gain, trip distance and condition of the bike route.

A *very strenuous* trip can be of any length, has very steep grades and is generally designed for bikers in excellent physical condition. Trips are well enough described such that the biker might plan to ride the easier part of a stressing trip and link up with other easier trips.

A *strenuous* trip has some steep grades and/or relatively long mileage (on the order of 50 miles total). The trip is of sufficiently long duration to require trip planning and strong consideration of weather, water, food and bike spare parts. Some portions of the trip may be on surfaces in poor condition or on shared roadway.

A *moderate* trip may have mild grades and moderate mileage, on the order of 15-30 miles. The trip is typically of several hours duration and is generally on well-maintained bike route.

An *easy* trip is on the order of 10 miles or less, is relatively flat and is generally on well maintained bike trails or bike paths.

TRIP MILEAGE: Trip mileage is generally computed for the one-way trip length for *up and back* trips and full-trip length for *loop* trips. *Up and back* is specifically used for trips that share a common route in both outgoing and return directions. *Loop* specifically means that the outgoing and return trip segments are on predominantly different routes. *Round trip* is used without distinction as to whether the trip is an *up and back* or *loop* trip. In the trip writeups, the mileage from the starting point or "trailhead" is noted in parentheses to the nearest tenth mile, for example, (6.3).

Obviously, the one-way trips listed can be exercised with a planned car shuttle, ridden as an *up and back* trip, or biked in connection with another bicycle trip listed in this book. Connections with other trips are noted in the trip text or in a separate subsection for that trip titled, "Connecting Trips."

TRIP ELEVATION GAIN: The overall trip elevation gain is described in a qualitative fashion. *Flat* indicates that there are no grades of any consequence. Steepness of upgrades is loosely defined as follows: 1) *light* indicates limited slope and very little elevation gain; 2) *moderate* means more significant slope requiring use of low gears and may be tens of feet of upgrade; 3) *steep* indicates workout-type grades that require low gears and high physical exertion; 4) *sheer* indicates gut-buster grades that require extreme physical exertion (and a strong will to live!).

The frequency of upgrades is divided into the following categories: 1) *single* for flat rides with a single significant upgrade; 2) *periodic* for flat rides where uphill segments are widely spaced; 3) *frequent* where narrowly spaced upgrades are encountered (e.g., rolling hills).

Elevation contour maps are provided for trips with significant elevation change. A reference 5% (*steep*) grade is shown on all such maps.

BIKE ROUTE QUALITY: The trip is summarized with respect to route quality in the "Master Trip Matrices" and a more detailed description is given in the individual trip writeups. The following route terminology (which is similar to that used by CALTRANS) is used:
- *Class I* - off-roadway bike paths or bike trails
- *Class II* - on-roadway, separated (striped) bike lanes
- *Class III* - on-roadway, signed (but not separated) bike lanes

If the route is on-roadway and not signed (i.e., not marked as a bike route), it is arbitrarily referred to as *Class X*. All routes are paved unless otherwise noted.

TRIP CHARACTERISTICS: The overall highlights of the bike trip are provided in the "Master Trip Matrices" to assist in general trip selection. The trip may be scenic (*S*), with sweeping vistas, exciting overlooks or generally provide views of natural or man-made attractions such as cities. Alternatively, the trip may be a nature trail (*N*) or a path through areas which have an abundance of trees, flowers and other flora. The nature trips or portions thereof are generally on Class I bike routes. The trip may highlight historical or well-known landmarks (*L*) or may have one or more sightseeing attractions (*S/A*). An example of the former is the Prado Dam on the Santa Ana River (Trip #22C) while the latter might be the Laguna Museum of Art (Trips #9 and #10). Finally, some trips are potentially good workout trips in that there is significant elevation change (*E*) or lengthy mileage (*M*) if the entire trip is taken. Some trips may provide a mix of these characteristics and are so noted.

Several descriptors are unique to the individual trip writeups. Those descriptors are defined below.

TRAILHEAD: The general location of the start of the bike path is provided for a single starting point. Driving directions to that trailhead and/or directions for parking are included where there is a possibility of confusion. Always check to ensure that parking is consistent with current laws.

Note that for most trails, there are multiple points of entry beyond the primary point listed. For some of the trips in this book (particularly the river routes), alternate bicycle entry points are noted on maps by arrows (↗) along the bike route. Alternate trailheads may be found using information obtained from other bikers, or from state or local publications for more popular routes.

WATER: In the "Trailhead" description, general statements are provided about water needs. In the "Trip Description," available water along the route is noted where water is scarce. Particular emphasis is placed on public facilities for water and use of restrooms. Stores, shopping centers and gas stations are sometimes noted, although the availability of water or other facilities in these instances is subject to the policies of those establishments.

CONNECTING TRIPS: Where bike trips can be linked, they are so noted. *Continuation* trips are those where there is direct linkage at the beginning or end of the trip being described. *Connection* trips are either not directly linked (i.e., a Class X connector is required) or the linkage occurs at the interior of the trip being described. A brief "connector" route description is provided.

BIKE TRIP MAPS: Each ride in the book has an accompanying detailed bike map. A summary of symbols and features used in those maps is provided below.

— — — —	Bike trail in trip description (unless otherwise noted).		
· · · · · ·	Alternate bike route (unless otherwise noted).		
SANTA ANA RIVER 〜〜〜〜	River or creek when it is a major trip focus.	MAIN ST	Roadway
〃〃〃〃 IRVINE 〃〃〃〃	Nearby City	▨ Park	☐ 5 ▨ 5	Landmark #5
W	Public Water Source	P Parking	↗	Entry Point to Trail
•—•	Locked Gate/ Limited Entry	┼┼┼┼┼ Railroad Crossing or Overcrossing	⊿	School (as a trip point of interest)
⊕	Mission	✗ Gravel Pit	△5%	Reference 5% grade

MAP SYMBOLS AND FEATURES

GENERAL BIKING CONSIDERATIONS

These are a collection of the thoughts that we've had in the hundreds of miles of biking that we have done:

SAFETY: Use common sense when you are biking. Common sense when combined with courtesy should cover most of the safety-related issues. The four safety "biggies" are: 1) understand bike riding laws; 2) keep your bicycle in safe operating order; 3) wear personal safety equipment as required (helmet is a must, bright or reflective clothes, sunglasses); 4) ride defensively--always assume that moving and parked car inhabitants are not aware that you are there.

Common courtesy is to offer assistance to bikers stopped because of breakdowns. Point out ruts, obstructions, and glass to bikers behind you.

TRIP PLANNING/PREPARATION: We are absolute believers in advance planning. You minimize nasty surprises and have the joy of two trips for one (the anticipated trip and the physical trip itself). Familiarize yourself with the trip ahead of time -- start by reading recent tour guides and talking to people who have been there before. For long-distance and/or more remote adventures, we do not recommend going alone.

Plan bicycle trips that are within your (or your group's) physical and technical abilities. Start with less-demanding trips and work your way up the difficulty ladder. Work on physical fitness and technical skills between trips to maintain or improve your abilities. Take rides with professional leaders and/or learn the necessary skills with an accomplished veteran in that activity area. As part of the training, learn first-aid techniques and use of the kit as appropriate for your activity.

The discussion which follows is applicable to both high-difficulty and/or extended-mileage day trips and multi-day tours: Look over the topographic maps and get a feel for the key areas of elevation change and locate the key road junctions. Where relevant, check that the roads/river trails are open and available for public travel by making advance inquiries. Identify contingency routes if there is any doubt as to your ability to follow the nominal plan or if adverse weather or road conditions could require trip alteration.

Once you have identified your outdoor adventure, assess your gear needs for the trip. Work with your group to define individual responsibilities for group gear items. Ensure that you know how to use each piece of activity gear before departure. Maintain your gear, particularly that most critical to safety, and perform a pre-trip check that gear is in design-operable condition.

EQUIPMENT: This subject is covered in great depth in B-D Enterprises' recent publication, *Outdoor Recreation Checklists*. That reference covers gear needs for about every major outdoor activity, including on-road and mountain biking for both daytime and multi-day trips. Refer to the last page of this book for more information.

The discussion which follows focuses on day trips: The minimum biking equipment includes a water bottle or two, tire pump, tool kit (typically tire irons, wrench(s), screwdriver(s), patch kit, and (sorry to say) bike lock. For longer day trips add a spare tube and bike repair manual. We recommend a bike light even if there are no plans for night biking.

Necessary cyclist apparel includes a helmet, sunglasses, and clothes which will fit pessimistic weather conditions (particularly for longer trips). On all-day, cool or wet winter outings, we carry a layered set of clothes (this includes long pants, undershirt, long-sleeve shirt, sweater, and a two-piece rain suit). Padded cycling pants and biking gloves are a must for long trips. Modern day, warm-when-wet clothes are light and extremely functional. For cool and dry days, we may drop the rain suit for a windbreaker (look for a windbreaker that folds up into a fanny pack). For other conditions, our outfits are normally shorts, undershirt, long-sleeve shirt and windbreaker. Laugh if you must, but wait until you find yourself biking home at night, in mid-winter, along a beach with a healthy sea breeze after you spent the day biking in the warm sun (an example of poor trip planning, we admit).

Bring a first-aid kit. For urban tours, our packaged, baggie-sealed kit has the following: sunscreen (15 SPF or greater), lip salve, aspirin and band aids. For trips where help may not be so readily available, we add gauze (roll), ace bandage (roll) and butterfly clips, small scissors, moleskin, needle and an antiseptic such as hydrogen peroxide or iodine. Think about insect repellent if you think conditions may warrant.

If you are going to get your money out of this book, **get an automobile bike rack**! The cost of bike racks is cheap compared to most bikes. Besides, it just doesn't make sense to bike fifty miles to take the planned twenty-mile bike trip.

THE COAST

From Dana Dr. in Dana Point Harbor

TRIP #1 - SEAL BEACH/SUNSET BEACH TOUR

GENERAL LOCATION: Seal Beach, Sunset Beach

LEVEL OF DIFFICULTY: Up and back - easy
Distance - 4.3 miles (one way)
Elevation gain - essentially flat

HIGHLIGHTS: A pleasant tour which concentrates on the beach community setting, this trip starts at the end of the Long Beach Marina, passes along the Seal Beach beachfront, transits a section of highway along the Anaheim Bay National Wildlife Refuge, and ends with a short cruise through the small beach community of Sunset Beach. The trip terminates at Bolsa Chica State Beach (see Trip #4 for the continuation route). This route is Class X through lightly traveled Seal Beach and Class II for about a 1-1/2 mile stretch of Pacific Coast Highway (PCH), as well as within Sunset Beach.

TRAILHEAD: Free public automobile parking is available at the Long Beach Marina along Marina Dr. in Long Beach or along First St. in Seal Beach. From PCH in Seal Beach, turn west on Marina Dr. (just west of Main Street) and continue roughly 1/2 mile to First Street. In another 1/4 mile, cross the San Gabriel River and drive a short distance to the marina parking area near Seaport Village.
   Public sources are scarce, however only a light water supply is needed for this short trip.

TRIP DESCRIPTION: Seal Beach. Leave the marina area and Seaport Village, cross the Marina Ave. bridge over the San Gabriel River (0.1) and turn right at First St. Bike parallel to the San Gabriel River and take in the beautiful view of the marina breakwater and the fleet of pleasure craft. At the end of First St. (0.3), turn left on Ocean Ave. and cruise along the beachfront residences to the Seal Beach Pier and Eisenhower Park (0.8). Join the fishermen on the pier or take in the ocean view from the strand.
   Pedal on Ocean Ave. until it begins curving to the left (northeast) and becomes Seal Beach Blvd. Take a right at PCH (1.7) and start a small upgrade on a bridge with Anaheim Bay on the right and the U.S. Naval Weapons Station on the left. With some fortune, a large naval ship might be docked in Anaheim Bay. Cycle a second upgrade to another bridge and at (2.5) admire the vista from the highest point. Another excellent view of Anaheim Bay is to the right and Anaheim Bay National Wildlife Refuge to the left.
   Surfside - Sunset Beach. Follow PCH past the private community of Surfside and the cluster of small eateries, making a right turn at Anderson St. in Sunset Beach (3.0). In a few hundred feet turn left at S. Pacific Ave. and bike along the long, snug row of beach residences. Coast on this Class II bike lane for about 1.3 miles to its terminus at Warner Ave.

CONNECTING TRIPS: 1) Continuation with the Sunset Beach to Newport Beach Strand ride (Trip #4) - continue this trip south into Bolsa Chica State Beach; 2) connection with the bike route to the Anaheim Bay National Wildlife Refuge (Trip #2) - pedal east (away from the beach) on Warner Ave.; 3) connection with the PCH portion of Trip #4 to the Bolsa Chica Ecological Preserve - continue southward on PCH beyond Warner Ave.; 4) connection with the Belmont Shore/Naples area - from the parking area, take Marina Dr. northwest and turn left (west) at 2nd St.

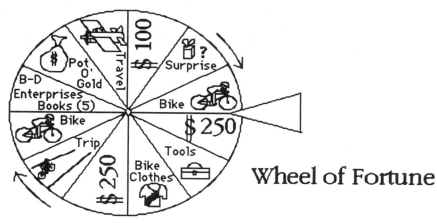

Wheel of Fortune

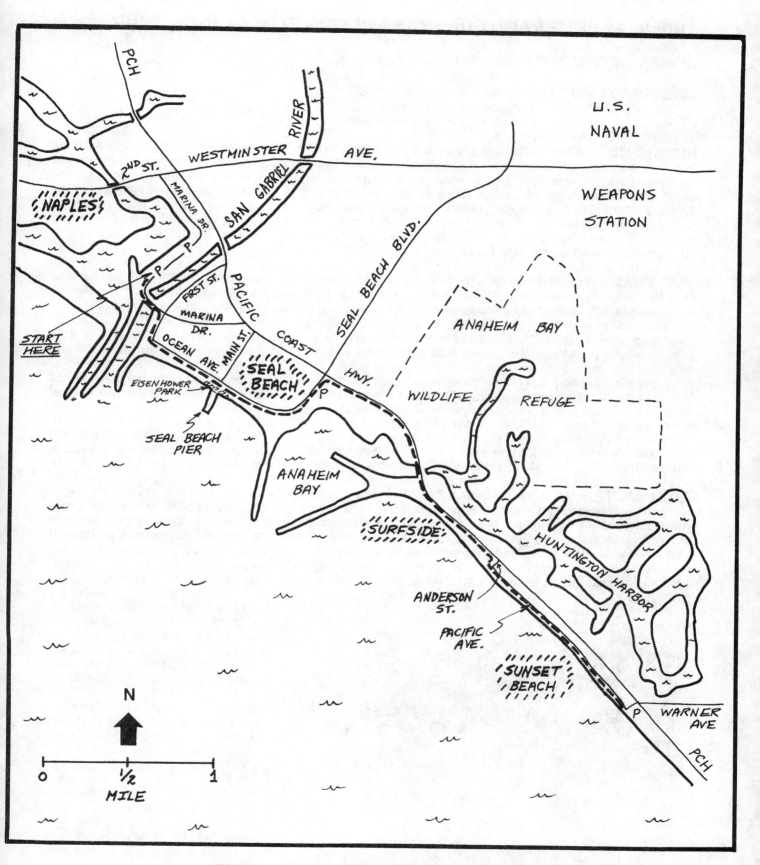

TRIP #1 - SEAL BEACH/SUNSET BEACH TOUR

15

TRIP #2 - SUNSET AQUATIC PARK/HUNTINGTON HARBOR TOUR

<u>GENERAL LOCATION</u>: Huntington Harbor (Huntington Harbour)

<u>LEVEL OF DIFFICULTY</u>:　One way - easy; loop - moderate
　　　　　　　　　　　　　　　Distance - 12.0 miles (loop)
　　　　　　　　　　　　　　　Elevation gain - essentially flat

<u>HIGHLIGHTS</u>: The trip starts with a visit to the natural setting of Sunset Aquatic Park. From here, this free-form bike ride has only a suggested route which explores the "nooks and crannies" of the northern Huntington Harbor area. Cyclists can meander through housing areas set along lovely canals, enjoying many great views of the main channel and boat marinas, and visiting such enjoyable places as little Trinidad Island. There are opportunities to stop and rest at any one of several small parks along the way. The trip through Huntington Harbor is mostly Class X, but the roadway is generally lightly traveled. There is an option to return to Sunset Aquatic Park via a route along Saybrook Ln. and Edinger Ave., which is primarily Class II.

<u>TRAILHEAD</u>: From Pacific Coast Highway (PCH) turn east on Warner Ave., drive about 1-1/2 miles, then turn left (north) on Bolsa Chica St. Continue about 1-1/4 miles to Edinger Ave., turn left (west), then proceed 1-3/4 miles and cross a small bridge (1.8). Stay on the road now named Sunset Way East for about 0.2 mile to the marina <u>public</u> parking area at Sunset Aquatic Park. Do not use the permit parking spaces on Park Circle. (If the public lot is full, park along Edinger Ave. Another option is to start from near the Huntington Harbor Mall. Park in the shade on the frontage road along Davenport Dr. near Courtney Ln.)
　　From the San Diego Fwy., exit west at Westminster Ave. and go about 1-1/2 miles to Bolsa Chica Rd. Turn left (south) and drive two miles to Edinger Ave. Turn right and continue as described above. From the Garden Grove Fwy., exit south at Valley View St./Bolsa Chica Rd. and motor about three miles to Edinger Ave. Continue as described above.

　　Public restrooms are located near the Harbor Patrol building in the park. Beyond this point, there is water at the three well-spaced Huntington Harbor parks noted on the trip map.

<u>TRIP DESCRIPTION</u>: **Sunset Aquatic Park.** From the parking/picnic area (a couple of open sites with benches and barbecues), bicycle through the boat launch entry (auto pay gate) on Park Circle that you passed when driving in. Cycle to the Harbor Patrol building and the boat launching area. Stop and watch the small cars pulling out big boats and burning up their tires! Ride just beyond the launch area, lock your bike to the nearby fence and take a walking tour of the natural (unimproved) Sunset Aquatic Park. There are numerous tide pools, interesting vegetation and birds of many types. Return to the parking area and pedal across the bridge over the Bolsa Chica Channel (0.9) to Edinger Ave.

Huntington Harbor (northwest)

Huntington Harbor (northwest). For this reference ride, turn right on Countess Dr. (1.0) and make the first left turn, passing through the pedestrian fence onto Sparkler Dr. Pass Sea Bridge Park (water, restrooms shade) and follow a loop which goes between a cozy network of quaint two-story homes. Just before returning to Edinger Ave., turn right on Bravata Dr. (1.8), then immediately right again on Windspun Dr. Cycle on that street to Trinidad Ln. and turn right (2.4). In about 0.1 mile, take in the striking view of the long, home-surrounded canal.

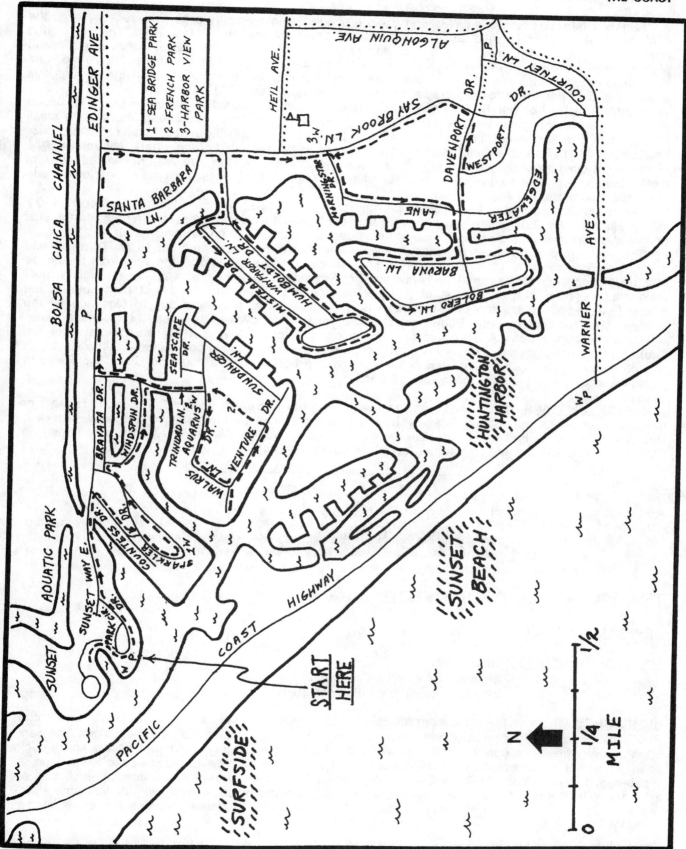

TRIP #2 - SUNSET AQUATIC PARK/HUNTINGTON HARBOR TOUR

Trinidad Island. Cross a small bridge, pass a shaded swimming/play area (with restrooms) to the right, and look head-on into the southern extremity of small, meandering French Park. This is Trinidad Island. Turn right on Aquarius Dr. and cycle to the tiny grassy area at the western point of the island (2.9). A small path along the periphery of the island heads in either direction at this point. Turning left, the path proceeds along the main channel. Bike about 0.5 mile to French Park and wind through this grassy, compact park back to Trinidad Lane. Return to Edinger Ave. (4.5).

Huntington Harbor (east). Turn right on Edinger Ave. and right again on Saybrook Ln. (5.7). Cruise about 0.3 mile on this pleasant, but busy roadway to Humboldt Dr. Turn right (west) and cross a small bridge; there is a fine view from atop the bridge of the harbor, the nestled harbor "castles" and a cozy little beach (6.1). Tour the quiet island loop following Wayfarer Ln. (to the right), Mistral Dr., the westernmost inner loop and return to the bridge via Humboldt Dr. (7.7). There are only limited views of the harbor on this loop as the large and sometimes beautiful residences are packed in side-by-side along the bay shore.

Return across the bridge to Saybrook Ln. and turn right (south). Follow Class II Saybrook Ln. 0.2 mile to Harbor View Park where there is water and shade (recreation/play areas and tennis courts). Just beyond the park and on the opposite side of the street, turn right (west) on Morningstar Dr. (8.1).

The route returns to quiet residential streets and heads to Edgewater Ln. (8.2). Turn left and continue to Davenport Dr. (8.5). Turn right (west) and ride over a small bridge; the view from the bridge is almost a copy of that seen from Humboldt Dr. The island loop tour is a cruise through a quiet residential neighborhood on Baruna Ln., around to Bolero Ln. and back to the starting point at the bridge (9.5). Again, there are only scattered harbor views from the island due to blockage by the tightly-packed residences. From Edgewater Ln., one option is for cyclists to repeat the incoming route.

Direct Return Route. A more direct return option is to follow Davenport Dr. east to Saybrook Ln. (9.8). Turn left (north), pass along the western edge of the Huntington Harbor Mall and follow Saybrook Ln. 0.9 mile to Edinger Ave. Turn left again and make a beeline of 1.3 miles on Class II bikeway to your parked car. The total trip mileage is 12.0 miles.

CONNECTING TRIPS: Connection with the beach bikepath to Sunset Beach/Seal Beach (Trip #1) or to the Sunset to Newport Beach Strand (Trip #4) - near the one-way trip terminus (Edgewater Ln. and Davenport Dr.), turn right (south) on Edgewater Ln. and bicycle to Warner Ave. Turn right (west) on Warner Ave., cross PCH and turn north (Trip #1) or south (Trip #4).

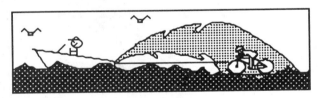

TRIP #3 - HUNTINGTON CENTRAL PARK

GENERAL LOCATION: Huntington Beach

LEVEL OF DIFFICULTY: Loop - easy
Distance - 4.7 miles
Elevation gain - periodic light grades

HIGHLIGHTS: This short and pleasant trip takes in both east and west sections of Huntington Central Park, which has over four miles of fine Class I touring without even biking the innermost trails. The park offers a lovely treed area on the east side with Lake Talbert, the Huntington Central Library and a duck pond. The west side has less tree cover, but is an equally nice area which sports Lake Huntington, a "Frisbee-golf" course and the Donald D. Shipley Nature Center. There is a nice eatery on each side of the park, with Breakfast-in-the-Park on the west side providing lakeside dining under sun umbrellas. (We're suckers for this type of environment.) Also provided is a pleasant diversion trip around Lake Huntington.

TRAILHEAD: From the San Diego Fwy., exit south at Goldenwest St. and drive 3-1/2 miles to Slater Ave. Continue another l/4 mile and turn left into the east section of Huntington Central Park. From Pacific Coast Highway (PCH) southbound, drive four miles past Warner Ave. (Huntington Harbor), and

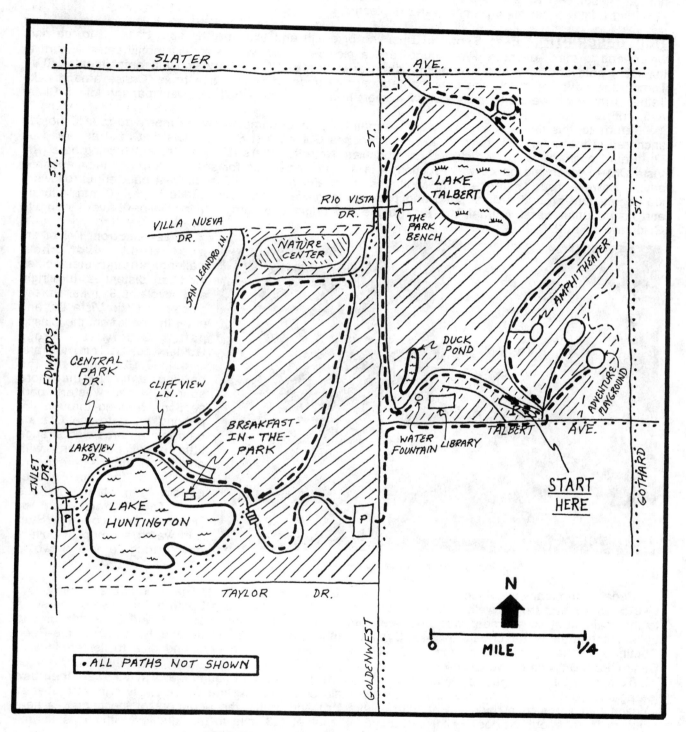

TRIP #3 - HUNTINGTON CENTRAL PARK

turn left at Goldenwest St. Go 2-1/2 miles north passing Talbert Ave. In another quarter mile, turn right into the park. From PCH northbound, drive two miles past Beach Blvd. (Huntington Beach) and turn right at Goldenwest St. Proceed as described above.

Bring a light water supply since water is plentiful.

TRIP DESCRIPTION: **East Section.** Enter the bikepath and examine the spur trails off to the right which lead to the "Adventure Playground" and a picnic area above the small amphitheater. Return to the main path and bike into a relatively open area between the library and the amphitheater (0.4). Turn to the right and follow the park's outermost trail under the tall shade trees. Cruise around Lake Talbert (dry when we visited) and follow a short upgrade to the small loop and parking lot on Slater Ave. (1.6).

Return to the flat and bicycle past a small play area complete with "merry-go-round" horses anchored in the sand. Just beyond, the path reaches Goldenwest St., parallels that road and reaches The Park Bench, a nice little rest stop for munchies. Note that there is a testy street crossing here (Rio Vista Dr.) to reach the park's west section; it is not recommended for small children or inexperienced adults. However, our reference route continues south and reaches the southwest park edge, follows a 180-degree turn around a duck pond and passes alongside and below the Huntington Central Library and its beautiful water fountain. Return to the trip origin and turn right on Talbert Ave., biking to Goldenwest St. (2.7).

Lake Huntington and Breakfast in the Park

West Section. For bikers who aren't wild about walking/carrying their bikes for short distances, turn right and cycle 0.3 mile to the crossing at Rio Vista Dr. and enter the park from the Class I path. Otherwise, cross Goldenwest St., turn left and pedal 0.15 mile to the parking entry to the more sparsely treed western park section. Proceed through the parking lot onto the Class I path into an area with strange little metal stanchions with chains on them -- these are the "holes" that the Frisbee-golfers "sink" their Frisbees into. This is "disk golf" or "Frisbee-golf" country. Stop and watch a group of golfers drive through a hole or two.

Pedal to the stairway which leads to the lower level of the park (3.2). The options are to carry your bike down the steps or to walk it down a steep incline. Follow the Class I path at the base of the steps to the main western segment loop and veer left. (The option to turn hard left and do a ride around Lake Huntington is described below.) Cycle 0.15 mile to the lakeside and Breakfast-in-the-Park. Continue on the main path another 0.15 mile to Cliffview Ln., turn right and bike to its terminus at Central Park Dr., one of two westside park entries.

Turn right into a lengthy parking area, bike to the nearest northbound walkway/bikeway, then turn left again at the intersection. Just short of the Donald D. Shipley Nature Center, stay right at a shaded junction (left leads to a park exit at Villa Nueva Dr.) and cruise the periphery of the center, a neat place to learn about the local wildlife (3.8). Bike another 0.3 mile to the junction with the spur trail which heads north to Rio Vista Dr. Stay on the shaded main trail another 0.2 mile, pass a large children's play area and return to the Lake Huntington area just beyond.

Return Segment. Return via the reference route which means a bike carry up the steps and crossing at Talbert Ave. The total trip distance is 4.7 miles. The alternative is to take the spur trail mentioned above and return via the Rio Vista Dr. crossing and repeat the eastern park ride segment. This adds about 1/4 mile to the trip length.

Excursion: Lake Huntington Spur. There are patches of packed dirt and sometimes short, soggy stretches on this 0.4-mile spur. At the base of the steps described above, turn left and pedal around the eastern side of the lake. Follow the treed lakeshore below Taylor Dr. on the south side, swing north and reach the trail's end at Inlet Dr. Bike on the sidewalk alongside the lake as the road curves left and becomes Lakeview Dr. The roadway veers further left, then changes name to Cliffview Ln., meeting the trail from Breakfast-in-the-Park.

CONNECTING TRIPS: Connection with the Sunset Beach to Newport Beach Strand (Trip #4) - pedal 2-1/2 miles on Goldenwest St. to PCH. Bike on the highway or the beachside Class I path just beyond in either direction.

TRIP #4 - SUNSET BEACH TO NEWPORT BEACH STRAND

GENERAL LOCATION: Sunset Beach, Huntington Beach, Newport Beach

LEVEL OF DIFFICULTY: One way - easy; up and back - moderate
Distance - 13.8 miles (one way)
Elevation gain - essentially flat

HIGHLIGHTS: Orange County's answer to L.A.'s South Bay Bike Trail, this trip is entirely along the beach and almost entirely a Class I route. This is a very pleasant tour which mixes open areas with great ocean views along the well-populated strand. The trip passes three piers, scattered surfing areas, several state or local parks and beaches, and has numerous locations for food/water/rest stops. Parts of the trip are well populated, particularly near the piers and especially in summertime. The Bolsa Chica State Beach portion of the route is lighted for those folks who like "moonlight" bike rides. An optional partial loop trip is possible by riding portions of Pacific Coast Highway (PCH) on the return leg. This optional leg passes near the Bolsa Chica Ecological Reserve.

TRAILHEAD: Limited free public parking is available along Pacific Ave. in Sunset Beach, or if one is willing to pay, at Bolsa Chica State Beach. To park at Sunset Beach, turn off of PCH toward the ocean on Warner Ave. and turn right a short distance later at N. Pacific Ave. The state beach entrance is almost 1-1/2 miles further south from Warner Ave. on PCH, across from the Bolsa Chica Ecological Preserve.

TRIP DESCRIPTION: **Bolsa Chica State Beach to Huntington Beach Pier** (5.2 miles). The Class I Bolsa Chica State Beach portion of the bike trip begins at Warner Ave. within the state park. Immediately, one has open beach area and a view across San Pedro Channel to Long Beach, L.A. Harbor, and on a clear day, Santa Catalina Island. The roomy bikepath passes the state beach entrance at (1.6) and continues to an area where beach sand has been piled high on either side of the path (2.2). This should give some hint as to what high tide means in this area during heavy storms!

Next, the route climbs gradually for a short distance to the Huntington Beach Cliffs above Huntington City Beach (2.3). Take a break and hike to the cliff edge for a guaranteed view of surfer heaven, morning to evening. The bikepath stays on the bluffs and includes a palm tree-lined portion of path, as well as a small park/rest stop.

At (4.7) the path heads downhill and returns to the beach. For the next mile, this area is occupied year round by bathers, swimmers, bikers, walkers and other folks who are interested in being near the Huntington Beach Pier. At (5.2) the trail reaches the pier. A short walk to its end leads to some excellent views of the surrounding beach areas, plus the camaraderie of ever-present fishermen. On

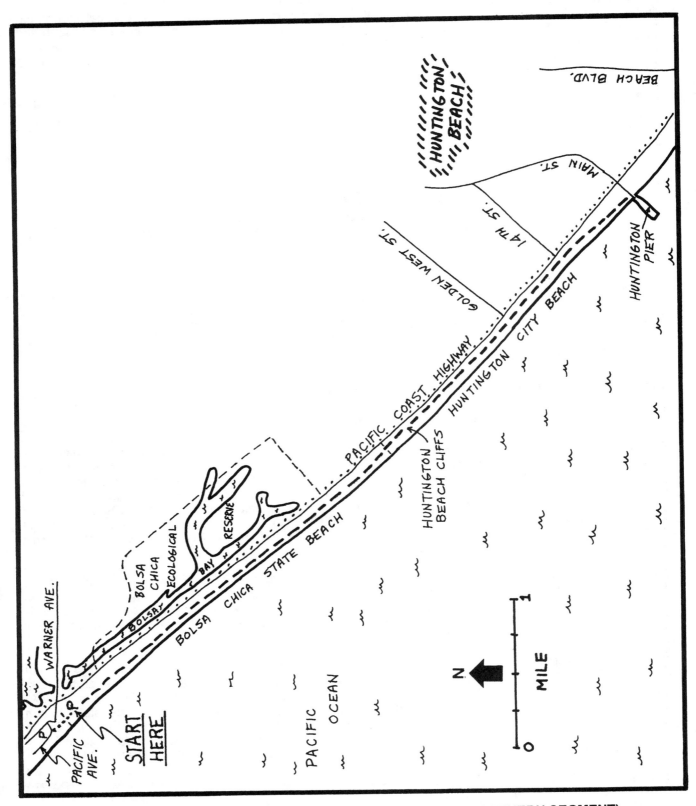

TRIP #4A - SUNSET BEACH TO NEWPORT BEACH STRAND (NORTHERN SEGMENT)

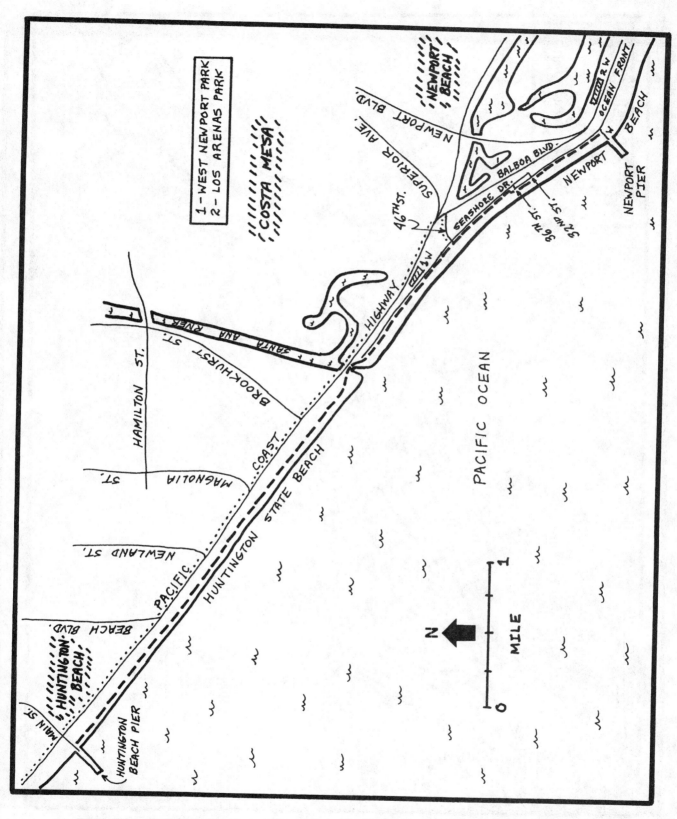

TRIP #4B - SUNSET BEACH TO NEWPORT BEACH STRAND (MIDDLE SEGMENT)

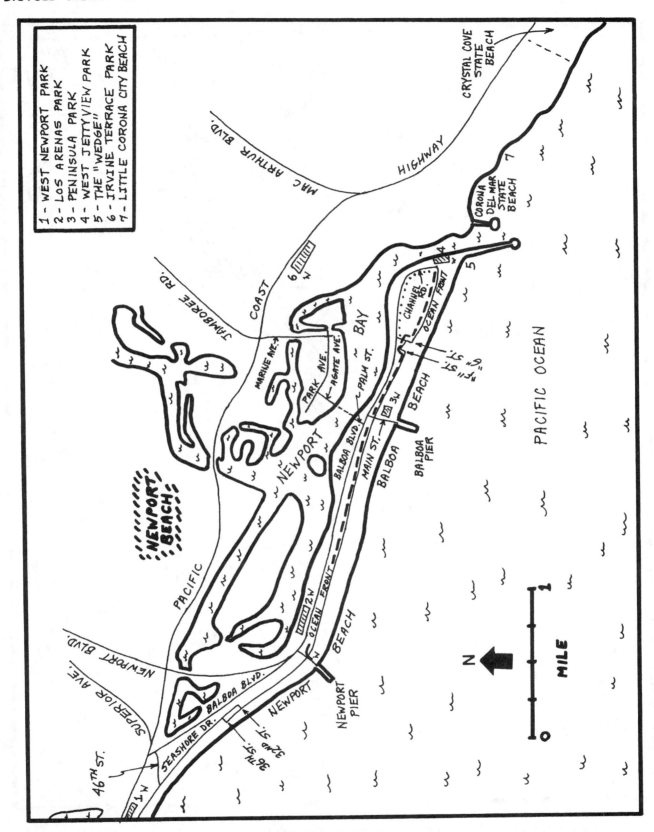

TRIP #4C - SUNSET BEACH TO NEWPORT BEACH STRAND (SOUTHERN SEGMENT)

the other side of the pier, stop and check out the surfers riding the waves to the beach, and sometimes under the pier.

Huntington Beach Pier to Newport Pier (5.4 miles). Cycle south through Sunset Vista Beach to the Huntington State Beach entrance at Beach Blvd. (Hwy. 39) (6.1). In about two miles, the state beach ends and the route reaches the Santa Ana River. This is the junction with the Santa Ana River bike route (see Trip #17). Cross the wooden foot bridge and take the right branch of the bikepath a short distance to Seashore Dr., then travel a Class II path along the beachside community homes.

West Jetty View Park

At (9.0) pass the eastern edge of West Newport Park (water, restrooms, children's playground and athletic courts) at 56th. St. and at (9.9) reach 36th St. Take a right turn (toward the beach) and ride a short distance to a Class I bikepath along the strand. On this part of the trip to the end of the bikeway, bikers effectively share the living rooms of all those beach folks living along the strand. The strand path reaches the Newport Pier at (10.6). Try the shops at the pier for some excellent munchies (We are fans of Charlie's Chili.) or take a tour down the pier. Another option is to watch the surfers just north of the pier.

Newport Pier to Balboa Peninsula Point (3.2 Miles). Bicyclists who bypass Newport Pier have another chance for a break at Balboa Pier (12.4). In addition to good munchies and a tour of the pier, there are the additional options of shopping at the nearby mall or laying in the grass at Peninsula Park (rest rooms, picnic benches and children's playground). Another 0.4 mile further down the path, the route ends abruptly at the wall of a beach house. Return a short distance to "F" St. and turn away from the beach. Pedal a short distance to Balboa Blvd., turn right soon after at "G" St., then continue as "G" St. fuses into Ocean Front.

Cruise on this pleasant little street on Class X roadway until it ends at West Jetty View Park near Balboa Peninsula Point (benches, grass and water fountain) (13.8). This is the scenic highlight of the trip! Take in the views across the channel to Corona Del Mar State Beach, Little Corona City Beach or across Newport Bay. A short walk out toward the ocean to the West Jetty provides a great view down the coast. Just north of the jetty is "The Wedge," an area with unusual and dangerous currents and tides -- and one of the prize areas for surfers who want to challenge "Mother Nature."

Alternate Return Route: From West Jetty View Park, take Channel Rd. toward Newport Bay to its end at Balboa Blvd. Bike on Balboa Blvd. until it meets "F" St., roughly 3/4 mile from the park. There are frequent "peeks" between the residences into Newport Bay and of Balboa Island. Reverse the incoming bike trip along the strand. Turn northwest (inland) on 46th St. and bicycle several blocks to Balboa Blvd. Turn left and in a few hundred feet make a left turn onto PCH.

The remaining return trip can be made on PCH, which is a mix of Class II and Class X routes. This is the choice for more experienced cyclists who are looking to "air it out." However, the Class X portion of PCH, for a several mile stretch surrounding the city of Huntington Beach, is a narrow roadway with high-speed traffic. To bypass this segment, use the strand bikepath described on the "up" leg between Huntington State Beach (at the Beach Blvd. entrance) and the Huntington Beach Cliffs.

On the PCH return leg, stop at the Bolsa Chica Ecological Reserve, which is just 0.4 mile from the trip origin at Warner Ave. The Reserve is entered via a walking bridge (no bikes) across Bolsa Bay and contains an abundance of bird wildlife over miles of walkways.

CONNECTING TRIPS: 1) Continuation with the Seal Beach/Sunset Beach Tour (Trip #1) - go north from the trailhead; 2) connection with Sunset Aquatic Park/Huntington Harbor Tour (Trip #2) - cycle east on Warner from the trailhead; 3) connection with the Newport Beach/Corona Del Mar Tour (Trip #15) and Upper Newport Bay route (Trip #6) - from the junction of PCH and Balboa Blvd., proceed southeast on PCH to Tustin Ave. and Jamboree Rd., respectively; 4) connection with the Santa Ana River Trail (Trip #17) - from Huntington State Beach, take the bike trail from the north side of the Santa Ana River which passes under PCH.

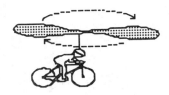

TRIP #5 - MILE SQUARE PARK

GENERAL LOCATION: Fountain Valley

LEVEL OF DIFFICULTY: Loop - easy
Distance - 8.7 miles (outer plus inner loops)
Elevation gain - essentially flat

HIGHLIGHTS: This trip is a family delight! L.A. County has El Dorado Park, but Orange County has Mile Square Park, and there's no major roadway to divide it. As advertised, it is about a mile on each of its four sides. Along with great Class I bike trails are picnic grounds with covered picnic sites, small lakes, playgrounds, sports courts, baseball diamonds, soccer fields, and separated archery and nature areas. The park also sports two adjoining golf courses, one of which has a coffee shop.

The mileage shown is for a fixed route consisting of a tour around the exterior boundary of the park, followed by two "inner loops." The route is actually free-form and at the discretion of individual bikers. The bikeways throughout are lightly used and generally in excellent condition.

TRAILHEAD: From the San Diego Fwy., exit at Warner Ave. and head north about 1/2 mile. For the trip as described here, turn left at Brookhurst St. and drive about 1/2 mile to Heil Ave. There is free parking within the park in this area. There are also numerous places to park free on the periphery (see the map). Finally, there is pay parking within the eastern section, accessed through the entries across from Los Rivas Ave. and Camellia Ave.

Bring a light water supply. There are water and restroom facilities throughout the park.

TRIP DESCRIPTION: **Outer Loop.** Return to Brookhurst St. and turn right (north) on the bikepath. Pass the handball courts, tennis courts, and the western edge of the Baker Golf Center. There is a fine view of both Mt. San Antonio and Mt. Saddleback from this area on a clear day. Turn right at Edinger Ave. (0.5) and cruise along the golf center. Cross a blocked auto entry at Los Rives Ave. (1.2) and follow the bikeway/walkway past the auto entry. For the outer loop, stay to the left at each trail junction on the park's eastern side.

Enjoy this grassy, tree-studded section while passing a long string of picnic kiosks and scattered park benches. Cycle to the western edge of a small lake with several bridges over to a small island playground. Then pedal along the outside park path to Euclid Ave. and turn right (1.6). In the next 0.9 mile along Euclid Ave. are many picnic areas, grassy knolls and plentiful tree cover, a second lake near the park's southeastern edge and the Euclid St. auto entry.

There is a gradual turn around the southernmost lake and the bike trail begins to parallel Warner Ave (2.6). Bicycle past a collection of soccer fields, pass through a small parking area, go by the maintenance yard and then hug Warner Ave. In about 0.6 mile, the path crosses the Ward Ave. entry to the Mile Square Golf Course and a coffee shop. The bikeway continues along the golf course all the way to Brookhurst St. (3.5). Turn right, bike along the course's western edge (noting the "reference junction" to the right) and return to the parking area entrance at Heil Ave. (4.0).

Westside Inner Loop. Reverse direction and head back to the "reference junction." Make a sharp left onto that path and pedal alongside the fenced-in golf course. Follow a wide semi-circle which encloses numerous baseball fields and cruise alongside the fence which encloses a future addition to the golfing areas. (This region used to contain an old airstrip which was used for radio-controlled

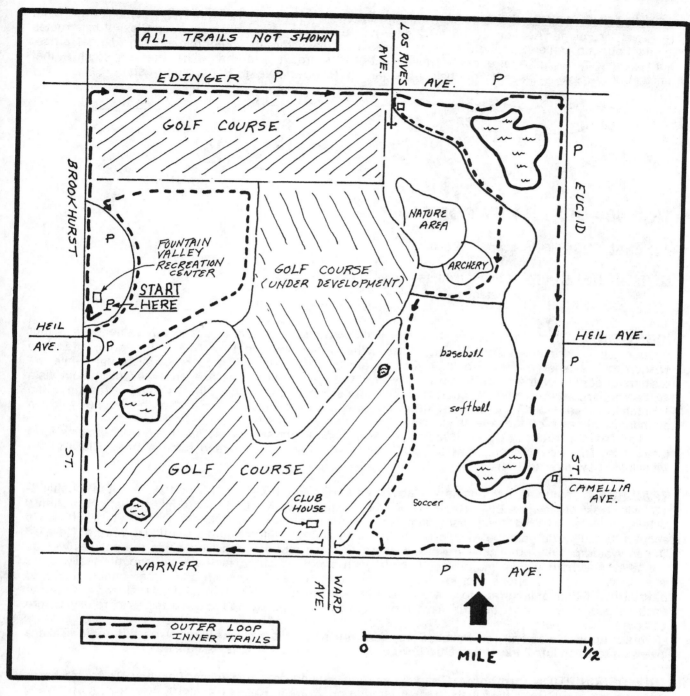

TRIP #5 - MILE SQUARE PARK

model cars, high-speed aerodynamic bicycles, and the middle area between strips was used for model airplanes. Though a national focal point for these activities, it lost out to "progress.")

Near the northernmost point, work back toward Brookhurst St, using both trails and roadway. (Our preference was to take an existing path eastward to Los Rivas Ave. and the east side of the park, but it was gated when we passed through.) Return to the Heil Ave. trip start point at (5.2).

Eastside Inner Loop. Repeat the outer loop, turning right again at the Edinger Ave. auto entry. Follow the entry road alongside the fenced Nature Area, pass through a parking lot and find the bikeway/walkway at the lot's southeastern edge. (From this point, keep the main auto roadway to your left.) Bike alongside the archery range, then steer toward the separator fence, passing to the west of a succession of baseball, softball and soccer fields, in that order. Pass through the parking lot to Warner Ave. again, then repeat the exterior park circuit along Warner Ave. and Brookhurst St. (8.7).

CONNECTING TRIPS: 1) Connection with the Santa Ana River Trail (Trip #17C) - take Warner Ave., Heil Ave., or Edinger Ave. east (1 to 1-1/2 miles); 2) Spur trips - there are numerous Class II bike routes in the Fountain Valley/Huntington Beach area which pass through predominantly residential areas. For example, take Heil Ave. about 1/2 mile west to Bushard St. and head either north or south at that junction. Ward Ave is Class II from below the park to Yorktown Ave. in Huntington Beach.

TRIP #6 - UPPER NEWPORT BAY

GENERAL LOCATION: Newport Beach

LEVEL OF DIFFICULTY: Loop - moderate
Distance - 6.2 miles
Elevation gain - periodic moderate grades

HIGHLIGHTS: This is a pleasant loop trip with a highlight of natural scenery together with a tour through some varied residential areas. It visits the Upper Newport Bay Wildlife Preserve, offering a chance to see a large variety of bay scenery and wildlife. The bay area roadway is flat, while the residential portion of the trip offers a couple of challenging uphills. There is an excellent lookout vista at the northern end of Upper Newport Bay. The trip is almost completely Classes I and II if taken in the counterclockwise direction as written. There are also two excellent spur trips off of this "looper" with an abundance of parks off those excursions.

Note that the Newport Dunes Waterfront Resort itself might serve as a fine base of operations for a family ride. The area is scenic, has a nice Class I path at its periphery and a much larger Class I area with light, slow-moving traffic.

TRAILHEAD: Jamboree Rd. begins at Pacific Coast Highway (PCH) in Newport Beach. It is roughly 2-1/2 miles east of Newport Blvd. (the outlet of the Costa Mesa Fwy.) and 1-1/4 miles west of MacArthur Veteran's Memorial Blvd. Take Jamboree Rd. 1/4 mile northeast to Backbay Dr. and turn left. Drive about 100-200 yards past the Newporter Inn grounds and turn left into the pay parking area at Newport Dunes Waterfront Resort. There are picnic, recreation and restroom facilities within the park as well as a market. Nearby is a boat marina and a pedestrian bridge which crosses a local lagoon. Finally, there is a Class I path on periphery of the eastern and northern sections which goes from Jamboree Rd. to Bayside Dr. Other options are to use the very limited free parking in surrounding residential areas, at Fashion Island or to start the trip from the Eastbluff Dr. area. (Read the roadsigns carefully before parking.)

Load up with water at the trailhead as there are no public facilities directly on this route. Take a diversion to Eastbluff Park or Eastbluff Village Shopping Center if water is needed.

TRIP DESCRIPTION: **Jamboree Road.** Leave the parking area and follow Backbay Dr. to Jamboree Rd. Turn left (north) onto the Class I path and head up a grade, passing Santa Barbara Dr. (0.4). This is an entrance to Fashion Island Shopping Center. Continue uphill to a plateau at San Joaquin Hills Rd. (0.9), then navigate a steep downhill, followed by another moderate-to-steep uphill. Near the top of the grade, turn left at Eastbluff Dr. (1.4) and pedal through a pleasant residential neighborhood. Pass a large recreation field at Corona Del Mar High School, Vista Del Sol (an entry to Eastbluff Park which has restrooms, athletic fields, children's play areas) and then cruise by Eastbluff Shopping Center (2.1). The route passes along a pleasant palm tree-lined bluff, then heads downhill. Part way down this grade is Backbay Dr. (2.9).

Backbay Drive. At this junction stop and enjoy one of the premier views of the north end of Upper Newport Bay. Bike down a moderate to steep grade on Backbay Dr. and travel along the bay itself. There is a one-way bike lane on the west side of the road only (thus, our counterclockwise route), which continues to the starting point. The route passes a large, open, marshy flat with thousands of

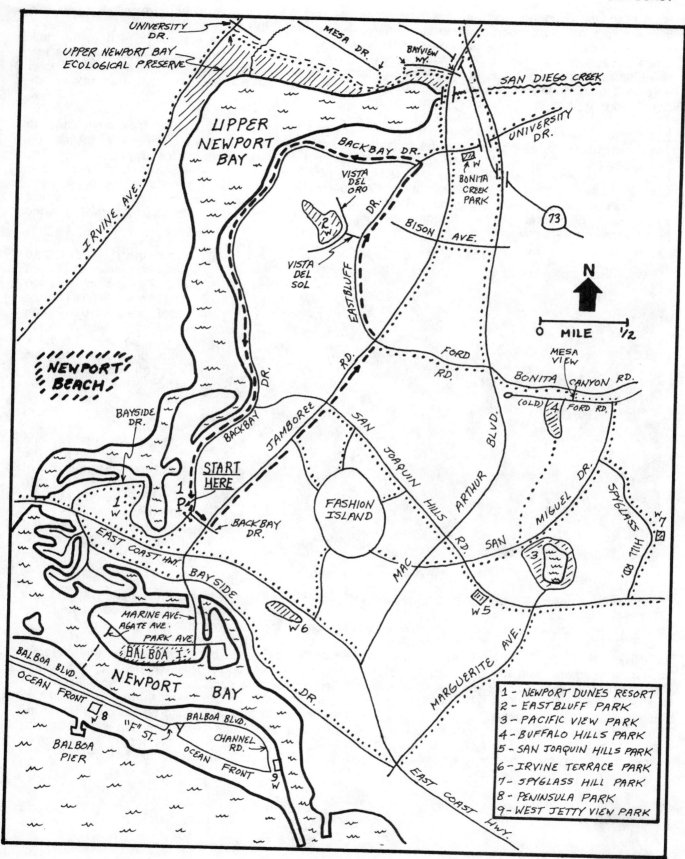

TRIP #6 - UPPER NEWPORT BAY

birds (3.2) and continues to twist and wind along the bay. There are continuous excellent views into the mud flats, marshes, open bay and the bluffs on both sides of the bay.

In 3/4 mile, the view opens into an expansive sweep, including the high bluffs across the bay. There are numerous turnouts along the way, some of which are occupied by bird watchers and a few tame ducks. There is a series of light "ups and downs" in this area with signs to indicate that the road may be flooded during storms (4.7). The route snakes past a relatively low, but scenic turnout/overlook (5.6), and returns to the aquatic park entry (6.2).

Excursions: **Upper Bay Excursion.** At Eastbluff Dr. and Backbay Dr. go east on the former street to Jamboree Rd., Turn left (north) onto the Class I connector on the road's west side, follow that path on the bridge across San Diego Creek and cycle alongside the eastern edge of the Upper Newport Bay Ecological Preserve. The trail swings west alongside Bayview Wy. then passes a junction which goes north to the end of that street in 0.2 mile from Jamboree Rd. Note that the path is shared by walkers, bikers and equestrians, with the horse people using the paralleling dirt path. There are numerous foot trails below and nearer the water's edge, as well as walking and horse trails coming from the rustic hillside residences above.

Pass the junction, continuing west, and enjoy the views to the left of the upper bay and the distant bluffside residences. Pedal by an entry from Mesa Dr. (0.4), cruise another 0.6 mile, then use the extensive wooden footbridge to cross this sometimes marshy area of the bay. Go over the Delhi Channel on a less-spectacular bridge and bike parallel to the western segment of University Ave. The path reaches Irvine Ave. in another 0.4 mile (about two miles total from the Eastbluff Dr./Backbay Dr. junction.)

Backbay Drive in Upper Newport Bay

Special Scenic Connection: Connection with the Sunset Beach to Newport Beach Strand tour (Trip #4) - bike south on Jamboree Rd., cross PCH and follow the roadway onto Balboa Island. Take the ferry from the south end of Agate Ave. across the bay to the Balboa Peninsula.

CONNECTING TRIPS: 1) Continuation with the Newport Beach/Irvine Tour (Trip #7) - the tours share a common segment from the trip origin; 2) connection with the Newport Beach/Irvine Tour (Trip #7) - take the **Upper Bay Excursion** described above to Irvine Ave. and continue south; 3) connection with the San Diego Creek Trail (Trip #18) - at the scenic overlook at Backbay Dr. and Eastbluff Dr., continue downhill on Eastbluff Dr. (use the sidewalk on the north side) to Jamboree Rd. Turn left at the trail sign at that intersection and bike to the creek entry near the bridge.; 4) connection with William R. Mason Regional Park (Trip #37) - at Eastbluff Dr. and Backbay Dr., follow the former street across Jamboree Rd. where it becomes University Dr. and bike 1-1/2 miles to the park main entrance.

TRIP #7 - NEWPORT BEACH/IRVINE LOOP

GENERAL LOCATION: Newport Beach, Irvine

LEVEL OF DIFFICULTY: Loop - moderate
Distance - 24.4 miles
Elevation gain - periodic moderate-to-steep grades

HIGHLIGHTS: This jim-dandy biking experience on mixed Class I/II/III bikeway takes a "slice" out of several different Newport Beach and Irvine areas. The tour leaves from inviting Newport Dunes Waterfront Resort, visits the Fashion Island area, tours posh and scenic Spyglass Hill, and passes over San Diego Creek. Next is an eight-mile circuit through a modern light commercial area (into Irvine), a cruise alongside John Wayne Airport, a westside tour of Upper Newport Bay, visits to sightseer's Galaxy Park and sportsman's Mariner's Park, and a scenic return on Dover Dr. and Pacific Coast Hwy (PCH). The Spyglass Hill area climb and the collection of moderate upgrades throughout the route place this trip at the upper end of a moderate rating.

TRAILHEAD: Jamboree Rd. begins at PCH in Newport Beach. It is roughly 2-1/2 miles east of Newport Blvd. (the outlet of the Costa Mesa Fwy.) and 1-1/4 miles west of MacArthur Blvd. Take Jamboree Rd. 1/4 mile northeast to Backbay Dr. and turn left. Continue alongside the Newporter Inn grounds and turn left into the pay parking area at Newport Dunes Waterfront Resort. There are picnic, recreation, and restroom facilities within the park, as well as a market. Nearby is a boat marina and a pedestrian bridge which crosses a local lagoon. Other (free) options are to use Fashion Island, the very limited free parking in the surrounding residential areas or the Eastbluff Dr. area. (Pay close attention to local parking laws.)

   Bring a full water bottle. There are scattered water sources throughout the route, although no public water sources were found in the 8.3-mile northern industrial segment.

TRIP DESCRIPTION: **San Joaquin Hills Rd.** Leave the park, return to Jamboree Rd. and turn left (north). Bike on the sidewalk (marked Class I) through a series of workout roller-coaster grades and turn right at San Joaquin Hills Rd. near the top of the grade (1.1). Pass the gas station and bike on this wide road with plenty of shoulder or use the sidewalk where marked. (There are numerous areas in Newport Beach where signs designate bikeable sidewalks.) The uphill route passes Santa Cruz Dr. (an entry to the Newport Harbor Art Museum), then several impressive buildings in the Fashion Island complex, and reaches a crest soon after (1.5). There is an excellent view into the canyons to the northeast, as well as a long-distance view to Mt. Saddleback.

Cruise through a residential area and pass Santa Rosa Dr., MacArthur Blvd. and San Miguel Dr. Next is an uphill pedal which takes riders to Crown Dr. and lawn bowler's paradise at San Joaquin Hills Park. Shortly, the road passes Marguerite Ave. and begins a steep upgrade. During this workout, bikers are treated to the well-manicured and flowered Pacific View Memorial Park Cemetery (3.1) to the left. The path flattens in a short distance.

Spyglass Hill Road

Spyglass Hill Rd. Turn left onto Spyglass Hill Rd. and enjoy the prestigious and well-maintained neighborhood while heading uphill. Use the Class I sidewalk or the wide road. Near the crest at El Capitan Dr. is cozy Spyglass Hill Park (actually a children's play area with grass, light shade and a water fountain). Just beyond is a downgrade that leads to an area with an expansive view to the west near Ridgeline Dr. Spread out before you are Fashion Island, Newport Bay, the surrounding Orange County flatlands, and a long-distance view to Catalina Island. Follow a steep downhill that flattens near San Miguel Dr. and turn right (north) (4.5).

Upper Newport Bay-East. Follow Class II San Miguel Dr. 0.5 mile to its terminus, turn left on mixed Class I (Old) Ford Dr. Turn right at Mesa View, left at Bonita Canyon Dr. and follow what is a general downgrade through mixed residential/light commercial area to Jamboree Rd. (6.5). Cross Jamboree Rd. on the Class II street now named Eastbluff Dr. and bike I.3 miles through a well-groomed residential neighborhood, passing Vista Del Sol (entry to Eastbluff Park which has restrooms, athletic fields and children's play areas) and the Eastbluff Shopping Center. The bikeway transits a pleasant tree-lined bluff, then heads downhill and returns to Jamboree Rd.

Across Jamboree Rd., Eastbluff Dr. becomes University Dr., which leads shortly to super Bonita Creek Park (restrooms, snack shop, recreation fields/courts and limited tree cover.) However, the reference game plan is to bike across the bridge over San Diego Creek on the west side of Jamboree Rd. and to note the Class I bike trail just north of the bridge at Bayview Wy. Turn left and follow that path along the northern periphery of the bay if you desire to take the shorter I4.8-mile Newport Bay Loop. (See the **Upper Bay Excursion** in Trip #6.) However, our reference route continues north on Jamboree Rd. and turns left at Bristol St. (north direction of that divided road) (8.1).

Irvine. At the first intersection, turn right at Dove St. and begin an 8.3-mile arc that passes through light industrial/high-tech territory with plenty of biking room. This portion of the tour is more scenic than expected, particularly for "building watchers" and "sidewalk superintendents." Note that Class I sidewalk biking is allowed where posted. Pedal 0.4 mile to Newport Place Dr. and cross MacArthur Blvd. onto what is now Von Karmen Ave.

Bike northwest on the Class I sidewalk past a variety of interesting building architectures and clever landscaping. In succession cross the main intersections at Campus Dr. (transition to Class II), Michelson Dr., pass over the freeway, and cruise to Main St. The number of stoplights on this industrial area tour are limited to the major intersections. The density of industrial complexes tails off north of the freeway and this bee-line route stays on lightly used roadway to Barranca Pkwy. (12.1). The gigantic blimp hangers of the now-closed Marine Corps Air Facility are clearly visible from here. Turn left and bike on the Class II road 0.7 mile to Red Hill Ave. and turn left again. Pedal past a gas station at MacArthur Blvd. Cycle 2.7 miles on the Class II route through an array of modern, light commercial complexes, passing over both the San Diego Fwy. and the San Joaquin Transportation Corridor (State Hwy. 73). Along this segment are stowed aircraft and support facilities, as well as the arriving and departing flights of the John Wayne Airport.

Upper Newport Bay-West. Turn left at S. Bristol St. (16.8) and bike 0.4 mile to Irvine Ave., then turn right and pedal downhill past the Newport Beach Golf Course. Near University Dr. on the Class II road is the first peek into Newport Bay. (Note that there is a Class I path on the east side of the road below University Dr. This is the outlet of the **Upper Bay Excursion** in Trip #6.) Irvine Ave. winds through some small rolling hills and in 1.3 miles from Bristol St. reaches an open area with a view across the bay with Mt. Saddleback in the background that will "knock your socks off."

Pedal a short distance to Santiago Dr. through more small rolling hills. One option is to continue 0.7 mile south to Mariner's Park on Irvine Ave. However, the reference route turns left at Santiago Dr., left again at Galaxy Dr. and proceeds on the latter road through a quiet residential neighborhood. In just short of a mile is little Galaxy Park with a fountain, benches and a dynamite view of Upper Newport Bay.

Continue on winding Galaxy Dr., turn left on Polaris Dr., and bike past Northstar Ln. (this road leads to a small marina and little Northstar County Beach) (20.2) and Westcliff Park (grassy scenic site at the end of Westwind Wy.). The road turns sharply right and follows a short and steep uphill to Westcliff Dr. Follow this road 0.4 mile and veer left onto a short spur that leads to Dover Dr. Follow this street as it bends to the left and returns to Irvine Ave. at Mariner's Park (recreation fields, playgrounds, shade and water).

Return Segment. Turn left (south) and bike 0.7 mile to 17th St./Westcliff Dr. Turn left, pass Westcliff Plaza (shopping center) and turn right at a "T"-intersection back onto Dover Dr. Free-wheel another 0.4 mile of mostly downhill to PCH (23.2). Follow the Class I path on the east side of Dover Dr. under the west end of the bridge to reach PCH eastbound (got that ?!). The territory on the return segment changes from residential to a mix of open and commercially-developed land and higher density traffic on PCH.

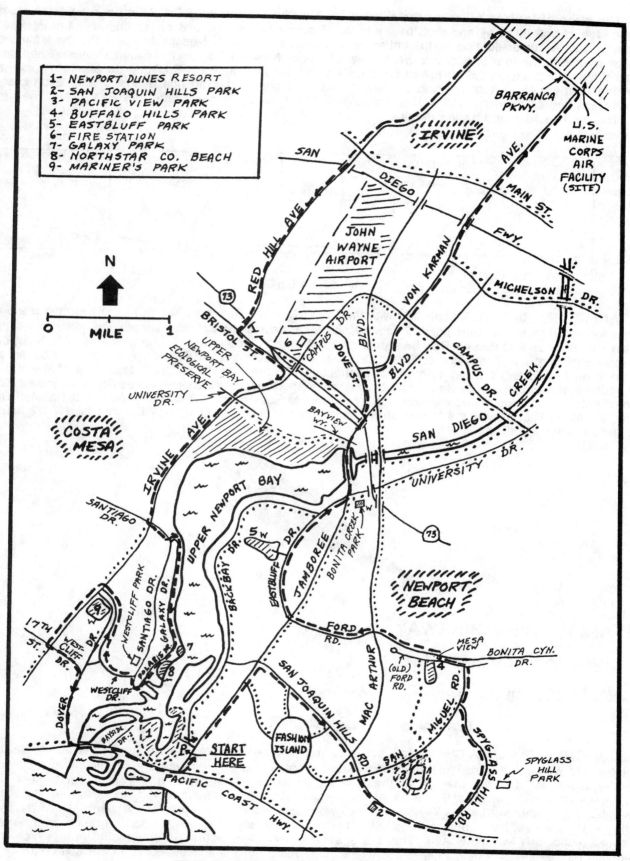

1- NEWPORT DUNES RESORT
2- SAN JOAQUIN HILLS PARK
3- PACIFIC VIEW PARK
4- BUFFALO HILLS PARK
5- EASTBLUFF PARK
6- FIRE STATION
7- GALAXY PARK
8- NORTHSTAR CO. BEACH
9- MARINER'S PARK

TRIP #7 - NEWPORT BEACH/IRVINE LOOP

Cross the bridge eastbound on the sidewalk or the Class II path on PCH. There is a fine view from the bridge of both the bay and the boaters below. Docked at the east end of the bridge is the Pride of Newport sternwheeler floating restaurant/nautical museum. The path crosses Bayside Dr., then follows a 0.4 mile upgrade that provides a grand view of Upper Newport Bay and Newport Dunes Waterfront Resort from the crest. In 0.6 mile, turn left on Jamboree Rd., left again at Backbay Dr. and return to the parking area (24.4). (A turn north at Bayside Dr. at the signal and short ride almost to the resort entry booth provides a "backdoor" Class I alternate entry to Newport Dunes Waterfront Resort and the trip origin. The Trip #6 map has the detail.)

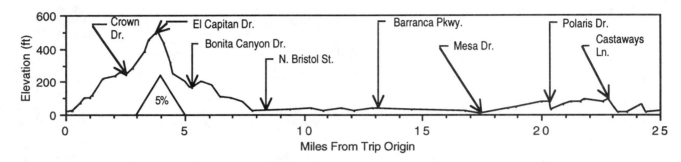

CONNECTING TRIPS: 1) Continuation with the Upper Newport Bay tour (Trip #6) - the two trips share a common route from the start point; 2) connection with the Newport Beach/Corona Del Mar Tour (Trip #15) - at PCH and Jamboree Rd., bike east on PCH; 3) connection with the Sunset Beach to Newport Beach Strand route (Trip #4) - at Dover Dr. and PCH, bike west on PCH, turn toward the ocean at Balboa Blvd., and turn right at 46th St.; 4) connection with the San Diego Creek tour (Trip #18) - at the south side of the bridge over San Diego Creek, follow the Class I trail on the west side of Jamboree Rd. down below the bridge; 5) connection with William R. Mason Regional Park (Trip #37) - at Easbluff Dr. and Jamboree Rd., follow the former street east where it becomes University Dr. and bike 1-1/2 miles to the park main entrance.

TRIP #8 - IRVINE BIKEWAY

GENERAL LOCATION: Irvine

LEVEL OF DIFFICULTY: Loop - easy to moderate
Distance - 15.6 miles
Elevation gain - essentially flat

HIGHLIGHTS: This 100% Class II, all-residential multi-looper explores a community that has to be the bikers and walkers dream. Wide sidewalks, Class II paths and public parks are seemingly everywhere. Add three Class I paths that cross the locale and two pristine lakes, and you've got to feel like somebody actually planned this area to be lived in! This is a pleasant, flat, moderate-mileage trip which takes in the Northwood-Westwood-Southwood-Eastwood Loop north of the Santa Ana Fwy. and the West Yale-East Yale Loop to the south. There is a multitude of spurs that can be taken off the main route, particularly off Yale Ave. There are several excellent spurs off the main route which are provided as excursion rides. Finally, there are many excellent marked bikeways in the adjacent city of Tustin.

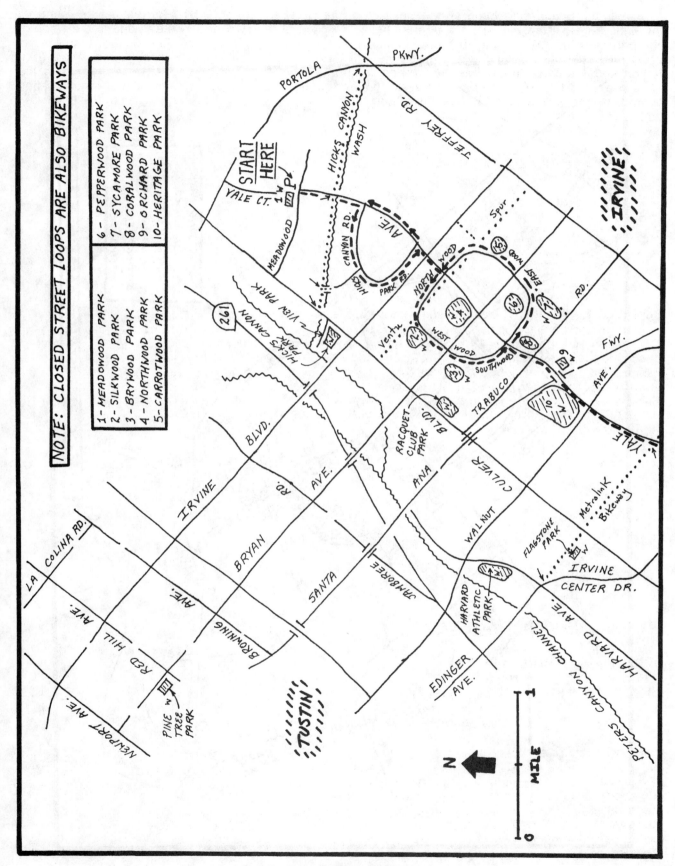

TRIP #8A - IRVINE BIKEWAY

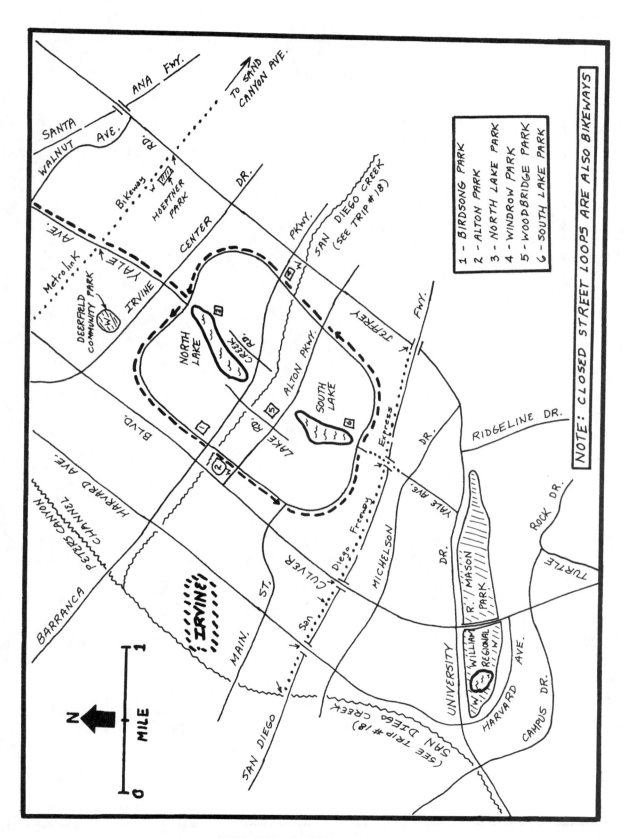

TRIP #8B - IRVINE BIKEWAY

36

TRAILHEAD: From the Santa Ana Fwy., exit at Culver Dr. and head northeast about 1-3/4 mile to Portola Pkwy. Turn right and drive 0.6 mile to Yale Ct. Turn right (south) and drive to street's end at Meadowood Park. The park is equipped with a small community center, restrooms, trees, children's playground, as well as picnic and barbecue facilities.

From the San Diego Fwy., exit northeast at Culver Ave. and motor 5-1/4 miles to Portola Pkwy. Continue as described above. From the Eastern Transportation Corridor (State Hwy. 261), go southeast at the Portola Pkwy. off-ramp and motor 1-1/2 miles to Yale Ct. Turn right as described above.

Only a light ration of water is needed since there are many parks, gas stations, and shopping centers along the way.

TRIP DESCRIPTION: **The Northern Half-Section.** Proceed down Class II Yale Ave. and cross over Hicks Canyon Wash and the Class I Hick's Canyon Bikeway, turning right at Hick's Canyon Rd. (0.3) Follow the arc through a nicely-landscaped residential area to it's half-way point where the street name becomes Park Pl. Return to Yale Ave. (1.3) and turn right, cross Irvine Blvd. then pass a shopping center. At (1.7), turn right on Northwood and follow this semi-circle 0.3 mile to Silkwood Park. The park has a water fountain, trees, grass, a children's playground, picnic area with barbecue facilities and a section of the Class I Ventu Spur Trail.

As the road swings southwest it's name changes to Westwood and it passes Brywood Park at (2.5). There is water near the baseball field and a restroom on the side of the elementary school facing the park, as well as limited picnic and barbecue facilities, treecover, children's play area and other sports fields. In about 0.4 mile, the roadway is now Southwood and it returns to Yale Ave. at (3.1). Turn right, bike 0.3 mile and pass Orchard Park (just off of Roosevelt), then cross over the Santa Ana Fwy. soon after. The park has limited tree shade, restrooms, grass and a children's playground.

The Southern Half-Section. Just after the freeway crossing is the area's granddaddy, Heritage Park. Besides all the amenities of the prior parks, it also has an aquatic park, library, fine arts center and community center. Pedal past Walnut Ave. (3.8) and reach Presley Park, with facilities like those at Silkwood Park, then follow a bridge over the OCTA Metrolink railroad tracks with their paralleling Class I bikeway.

At (4.8) Yale Ave. ends at the northern tip of North Lake and cyclists head right onto West Yale Loop. Almost the entire loop is through residential environs with scattered parks and open grassy areas with single-family residences and some townhouse complexes. A mile-plus of pedaling leads across Warner Ave., a passby of Birdsong Park (numerous facilities, but no water) (6.4), followed by Barranca Pkwy. and a shopping center. At (6.7), pass over San Diego Creek (see Trip #18) and the northern edge of Alton Athletic Park (trees, water, restrooms and numerous athletic fields).

Soon, cross Alton Pkwy. followed by Main St. (7.3). Note that, below Alton Pkwy., all parks we investigated are off the main loop and private. Bicycle around to the southern edge of the loop to the tip of South Lake and pass a small segment of Yale Ave. to the south. Nearby is Springbrook on the north side, which is an entry to South Lake (8.4).

East Side of South Lake

Closing the Loops. Not far beyond, cyclists find themselves on East Yale Loop, heading northeast past Alton Pkwy. and a couple of shopping complexes (9.8). In 0.2 mile recross San Diego Creek and look for the signed entry to Windrow Park. (See Trip #18 for the park description.) Cross Barranca Pkwy. and follow the loop as it arcs 0.8 mile before returning to Yale Ave. (11.0). Nearby is a shopping complex and Ruby's, an upscale burger, fries and milkshake diner with a North Lake vista.

Retrace the incoming route across Irvine Center Dr. (11.2), Walnut Ave. (12.3), the Santa Ana Fwy. (12.6) and then cruise 0.4 mile to Southwood. Turn right and follow the semi-circle back around to Yale Ave. (14.4), then bike north 0.3 mile to Irvine Blvd. (Near where Southwood becomes Eastwood on the semi-circle, look to the right for Sycamore Park with a water fountain on the park's southern edge and tree cover, covered picnic areas, barbecues, park benches and a children's playground.) All that remains is a 0.9-mile pedal on Yale Ave. back to Meadowood Park (15.6).

Excursions: Hicks Canyon Bikeway. The Class I path is enclosed within a pristine shaded and nature-surrounded swath along the Hicks Canyon Wash. It starts at the intersection of View Park and Central Park at the western edge of Hick's Canyon Community Park and goes east to Portola Pkwy., a distance of about two miles. Access from the south-side residential area is at Culver Blvd., Yale Ave. and Portola Pkwy., all of which also have street underpasses. There is one walkway/bikeway over the wash off of Hicks Canyon Rd. In addition to the underpass accesses, there are numerous gated entries from the private community on the north side.

Cyclists planning an up-and-back ride should consider starting from the west in order to tackle the steady, but mild uphill on the outbound leg. The natural start point is Hick's Canyon Community Park, which has a small community center, water, restrooms, Class I bikeway/walkways throughout the park, children's play area, covered and uncovered picnic facilities and sports fields.

Ventu Spur Trail. This Class I mini-trail is used by local walkers and bikers to access both sides of the northern loop area. It meanders between residences from just east of Culver Blvd. at Matera and continues southeast 1.5 miles to Jeffrey Rd. It passes through the north end of both Silkwood Park and Pinewood Park near the western and eastern ends of the trail respectively. There are marked street crossings at Westwood, Yale Ave. and Eastwood.

Metrolink Bikeway. The western and eastern entries to this three-mile Class I path alongside the OCTA Metrolink railway are off of Harvard Ave., just north of Irvine Center Dr. and Sand Canyon Ave., just south of Burt Rd. respectively. There are also entries at Culver Rd., Yale Ave. and Jeffrey Rd. Though removed from traffic elsewhere, there is a single road crossing at Jeffrey Rd.

Yale Loop North-South Connector Trail. This 1.7-mile Class I path cuts through the heart of the Yale Loop heading roughly north-south. The northern and southern entries are near the northern and southern Yale Ave./Yale Loop intersections, respectively. The trail skirts the western periphery of North Lake and the eastern side of South Lake. It bypasses Barranca Pkwy. on a walker/biker overpass, cruises through Woodbridge Village Center (eateries, shopping), crosses San Diego Creek on a walkway/bikeway bridge, cuts through Woodbridge Community Park and follows a second overpass on Alton Pkwy.

San Diego Freeway Express. This Class I trail (name unknown) parallels the San Diego Fwy. on its north side, going uninterrupted 1.1 miles from Jeffrey Rd. to Culver Blvd. Reaching the straight-through 0.8-mile west side segment requires crossing Culver Blvd. at a marked, signal-lighted intersection. The entire path follows beneath the power towers/transmission lines through brush-lined (east side) or grass-surrounded (west side) environs. The entries to the east side are at Jeffrey Rd., Yale Ave and Culver Blvd., and to the west side are Culver Blvd., Reed Ave., Harvard Ave. and the path terminus at San Diego Creek.

CONNECTING TRIPS: 1) Connection with the San Diego Creek ride (Trip #18) - at the creek crossings, look for the entry on the north side of Alton Park or south side of Windrow Park; 2) connection with the Turtle Rock Drive (Trip #36) and William R. Mason Regional Park (Trip #37) tours - follow Yale Ave. south of Yale Loop and take the pedestrian/bike crossing over the San Diego Fwy. Continue on Yale Ave to its end at University Dr., cross the street and take the Eastern Mason Park Bikeway westbound to "The Triangle Junction." Turn east or west for the Mason Park tour or south to reach Turtle Rock Dr.; 3) connection with the Tustin Ranch Loop (Trip # 41) - from the Irvine Blvd. intersection, bike northwest 1-3/4 miles to Jamboree Rd.

TRIP #9 - LAGUNA CANYON ROAD

GENERAL LOCATION: Irvine, Laguna Canyon, Laguna Beach

LEVEL OF DIFFICULTY: One way - moderate; up and back - moderate to strenuous
Distance - 10.6 miles
Elevation gain - frequent moderate grades

HIGHLIGHTS: This sun-exposed canyon route starts from Irvine in the Orange County interior and dumps out at breezy Laguna Beach. The first 1.9 miles is on Class II roadway which passes through light-industrial complexes, followed by a 1.2-mile ride through open agricultural area on Class X roadway. The remaining Class III portion within Laguna Canyon traverses a series of rolling hills through 3.1 workout miles before cruising downhill into the City of Laguna Beach. The highlights of the trip are the canyon vistas and the points of interest near Laguna Beach. The latter include Irvine Bowl and Irvine Bowl Park, as well as Laguna's Main Beach. Just to the north off of Pacific Coast Hwy. (PCH) are Heisler Park and the Laguna Art Museum.

TRAILHEAD: From the Santa Ana Fwy., exit southwest at Jeffrey Rd. and drive 1-1/2 miles to Barranca Pkwy. Turn right and then left at Yale Loop East (the first street) and motor about 200 yards. Turn left at the signed entrance to Windrow Park and drive to the park's edge on Jeffrey Rd. From the San Diego Fwy., exit northeast at Jeffrey Rd./University Dr. and go one mile to Barranca Pkwy. Turn left and follow the directions above. The park has water and restrooms near the athletic fields (cross the wooden pedestrian bridge for access), shade trees and gymnasium.
Bring a filled water bottle, two if you are doing an up-and-back ride. There are public water sources at Windrow Park and in Laguna Beach, with nothing in between.

TRIP DESCRIPTION: **Windrow Park to Laguna Canyon Road.** From the park's eastern edge, follow the Class I San Diego Creek Bikeway under Jeffrey Blvd. Continue along the creek for a 1.3-mile amble to Laguna Canyon Rd. or leave the creek and bike roughly the same distance along the light-industrial complexes on Class II Barranca Pkwy. Turn right onto Class II Laguna Canyon Rd., which becomes Class X at Pasteur. Bike over the San Diego Fwy. and cycle through agricultural environs.
Laguna Canyon Entry. Laguna Canyon Rd. fuses with the Laguna Fwy. outlet traffic in an area surrounded by open fields (2.8). In 0.1 mile, the bikepath starts heading into the canyon opening; the Laguna Reservoir is high on the hillside to the left. There are rolling hills and a small creek along the roadway as the route proceeds into the canyon proper. The roadway becomes a signed Class III at (3.1).
The Canyon Tour. Follow a moderate upgrade (3.7) and reach the crest in an area with a few small shade trees (4.0). In another 0.4 mile, pass a small hamlet to the left (east); to the right are small tree stands and overgrowth. In about 1.3 miles of light rolling hills and nearly treeless roadway, pass over the outlet creek from North Laguna Lake (5.7). This creek parallels the road through much of the canyon.
Bike over the rolling hills within the canyon and head up a grade with a "Laguna Beach City Limit" sign near the summit (6.1). At the time of our initial trip, there were a large number of hawks circling the area. In 0.3 mile, pass under the San Joaquin Hills Transportation Corridor, then observe the interesting rock formations just beyond and to the right. Pass the El Toro Rd. terminus (7.2) and, soon after, a small community to the left (east).
In succession, the uphill-downhill route passes Stan's Ln. (7.6), opens up to a view of a ridge-top community to the east, and then passes through a small roadway community with an adjacent cattle grazing area near Raquel Rd. (8.1). The terrain flattens out and passes a park-like area to the east, meets another small community (8.4), then proceeds through a 1.2-mile narrow canyon segment with no other cross-streets. Just beyond Canyon Acres Dr., the canyon opens up to some strong indications that the "big city" is near.
Laguna Beach. The now flat route begins to exit the canyon and passes through heavier residential/commercial areas, the site of the seasonal Sawdust Festival, then meets the turnoff to the Irvine Bowl and Irvine Bowl Park (10.2). Just beyond is a view into the commercial heart of Laguna Canyon Rd. and a "peek" at the local beach. At (10.6) from the trip start, the bikepath ends at PCH and enticing Laguna Beach's Main Beach.
Return Route Options: The options at this point are to return directly back up the canyon, take a lengthy tour of the City of Laguna Beach or plop down at the beach. The Laguna Beach tour might

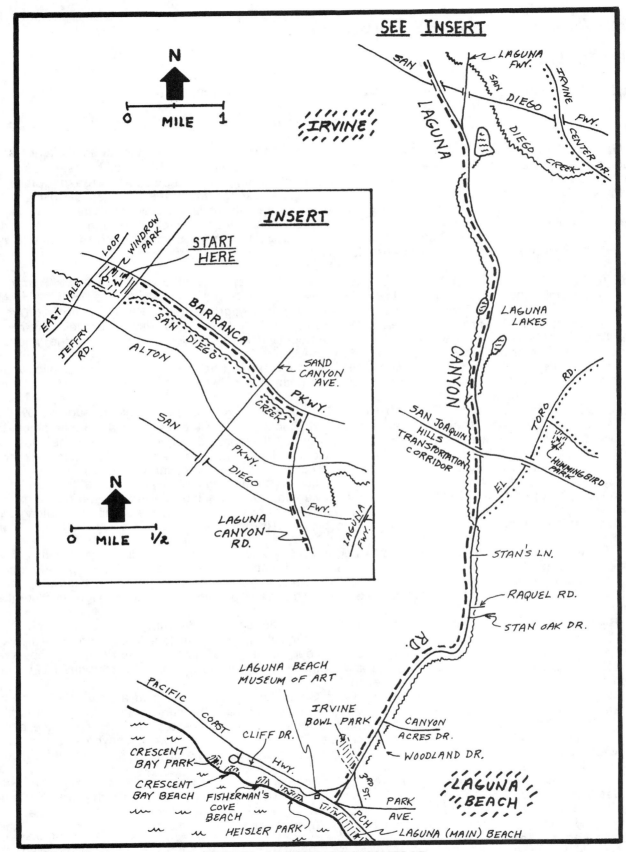

SEE INSERT

N
0 MILE 1

IRVINE

SAN

LAGUNA FWY.

LAGUNA

SAN DIEGO

IRVINE FWY.

DIEGO CREEK

IRVINE CENTER DR.

CANYON

Laguna Lakes

TORO RD.

INSERT

LOOP

WINDROW PARK

START HERE

EAST YALE

BARRANCA

JEFFRY RD.

SAN DIEGO

ALTON

SAND CANYON AVE.

PKWY.

CREEK

SAN

PKWY.

DIEGO

FWY.

LAGUNA CANYON RD.

LAGUNA FWY.

N
0 MILE 1/2

San Joaquin Hills Transportation Corridor

EL

HUMMINGBIRD PARK

STAN'S LN.

RAQUEL RD.

STAN OAK DR.

RD.

LAGUNA BEACH MUSEUM OF ART

IRVINE BOWL PARK

CANYON ACRES DR.

PACIFIC COAST

CLIFF DR.

HWY.

WOODLAND DR.

CRESCENT BAY PARK

CRESCENT BAY BEACH

FISHERMAN'S COVE BEACH

HEISLER PARK

3RD ST.

PARK AVE.

PCH

LAGUNA (MAIN) BEACH

LAGUNA BEACH

TRIP #9 - LAGUNA CANYON ROAD

include a trip to Heisler Park and the Laguna Art Museum; they are reached via Cliff Dr., just north on PCH. A shadier option is to return to Irvine Bowl Park.

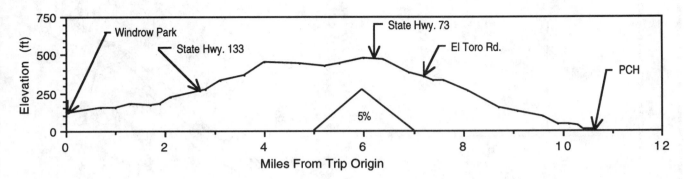

CONNECTING TRIPS: 1) Continuation with the Laguna Beach Tour (Trip #10) - at the trip terminus take PCH to the right (northwest) towards Crystal Cove State Park or left towards Aliso Beach Park; 2) continuation with the San Diego Creek route (Trip #18) - from the trip origin, bike east as described in the tour description or west toward the Yale Loop; 3) connection with the Irvine Bikeway (Trip #8) - from the trip origin, bike west to the Yale Loop on the San Diego Creek bikeway, Barranca Pkwy. or Alton Pkwy.; 4) connection with the Laguna Hills Loop (Trip #31) - at the junction with El Toro Rd., head northeast on that road.

TRIP #10 - LAGUNA BEACH TOUR

GENERAL LOCATION: Corona Del Mar - Laguna Beach

LEVEL OF DIFFICULTY: One way - moderate; up and back - moderate to strenuous
Distance - 9.1 miles (one way)
Elevation gain - frequent moderate-to-steep grades

HIGHLIGHTS: This is one of the finer beach tours, provided that a continuous diet of hills and limited stretches of "tight" biking quarters on Pacific Coast Highway (PCH) aren't a turnoff. There are excellent beach vistas spread throughout the route, including the Crystal Cove State Beach area, at Crescent Bay Point Park and Heisler Park. The route passes through pleasant Laguna Beach and some of the local hillsides and ends at pocket-sized, scenic Aliso Beach. Most of the route is Class II or III, although there is a short section near the center of Laguna Beach that rides more like a Class X route.

TRAILHEAD: Proceed south from Newport Beach on PCH. Roughly 1-1/4 miles from MacArthur Blvd., turn right (south) on Seaward Rd. and find parking in that residential neighborhood. From Laguna Beach continue 3/4 mile north beyond the northern boundary of Crystal Cove State Beach to Seaward Rd. (If you pass Poppy Ave., you've gone too far.)

TRIP DESCRIPTION: **Crystal Cove State Park.** Return to PCH and turn right (south). This is the start of a Class II route through residential areas. Just beyond Cameo Shores Rd./Cameo Highlands Dr. (0.3) the development thins. There are hills to the left (northeast) and the bluffs of Crystal Cove State Park on the ocean side. (At the park's western edge is a Class I trail which, when connected with the park

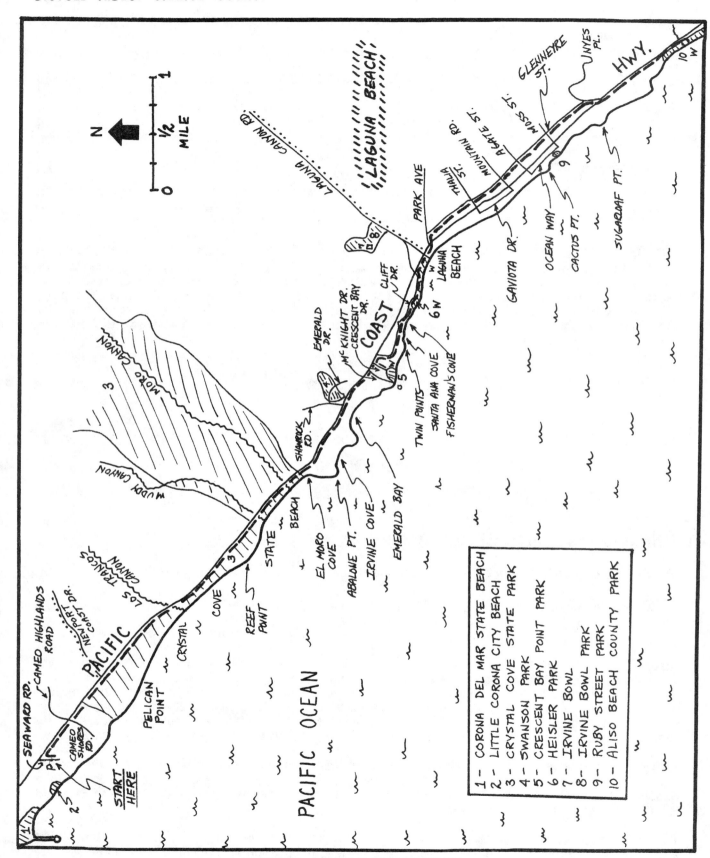

TRIP #10 - LAGUNA BEACH TOUR

1 – CORONA DEL MAR STATE BEACH
2 – LITTLE CORONA CITY BEACH
3 – CRYSTAL COVE STATE PARK
4 – SWANSON PARK
5 – CRESCENT BAY POINT PARK
6 – HEISLER PARK
7 – IRVINE BOWL
8 – IRVINE BOWL PARK
9 – RUBY STREET PARK
10 – ALISO BEACH COUNTY PARK

roads, covers almost three miles alongside PCH.) Pass the park entrance near Newport Coast Dr. (1.0), Los Trancos Canyon (1.5), and then start a steep downhill. In another 0.1 mile is another entry to the park near the Crystal Cove area followed by a short, steep upgrade. There is a nice peek at one of the many coves in the area near the crest (2.1).

The Hills. In another 0.5 mile, cyclists pass near Reef Point. Head steeply downhill and enjoy a spectacular view into El Moro Cove. (Stop and admire the cove surroundings.) Near the bottom of the grade, there is a roadside snack stand, just at the point where another short, steep upgrade starts (3.3). (Those clever devils!) Work through steep rolling hills, pass Irvine Cove Wy., Bay Dr., and reach a crest at McKnight Dr. (4.7). Just beyond is Crescent Bay Dr. where cyclists can divert 0.1 mile to the right (toward the ocean) to take in Crescent Bay Point Park and one of the great vistas along the coast. There is also a water fountain here.

Cliff Drive. In less than 0.2 mile, the bikepath leaves PCH and turns toward the beach on Class III Cliff Dr. The short tour along this lightly-traveled, mild roller-coaster residential street is one of the premier parts of this trip. Bikers pass large groups of scuba divers preparing for the trip down to the coves, get periodic peeks down to those coves, then pass on the city side of Heisler Park (5.7).

View From Heisler Park

This pleasant, long and thin park has a number of fine vista points supplied with benches. Walkways are distributed across the grounds. Stop and watch the scuba divers and scuba school in Diver's Cove. There are nice picnic spots with barbecues and water, too. Beyond is the Laguna Lawn Bowling Green, more park benches with a beach overlook, beach access at the south end of Heisler Park (a great view to the south beaches), and the Laguna Beach Museum of Art (5.8).

Central Laguna Beach. The route returns to PCH in 0.1 mile and heads downhill to the busiest part of town (and some of the tightest Class III bikeway we've seen). Pass Laguna Beach at the foot of Broadway, which is the local sunbather's Mecca. There is water here and also pleasant outdoor dining at Greeter's Corner Restaurant next to the beach.

Paralleling PCH. Shortly, the path again leaves PCH and follows Park Ave. two blocks to Glenneyre St. (another block east on Catalina St. is the marked Pacific Coast Bicentennial Bike Route). We do not recommend riding PCH in the next mile or two because of the heavy traffic and absence of a usable shoulder! Instead, turn right on Glenneyre St. (6.3) and return southbound through a commercial district with light traffic and plenty of bike room. Pass through rolling hills past Thalia St. (6.7) and Cress St. (7.0). The road tightens down into a small one-lane road through more rural area near Calliope St. (7.1).

Beyond Agate St. (7.4) is a steep upgrade and, in another 0.3 mile, the path reaches Diamond St. and a decision junction. Continue on Glenneyre St. if you want some challenging uphill and exciting downhill, turning right at Alta Vista Wy., left at Solana Wy., left at Victoria Pl. then right at Nyes Pl., to return to PCH (8.2). The easier option is to turn right toward the ocean and return to PCH at Diamond St.

Aliso Beach State Park. Beyond Nyes Pl., head downhill past a mobile home park in the hillsides and Aliso Creek Plaza (8.3). Pass Wesley Dr. (8.8) then coast a steep downhill to the Aliso Beach entrance (9.1). Aliso Beach State Park sports a pavilion with seasonal snack stand and restrooms, a fine and lightly-used beach, children's playground, scattered palm trees, fire pits and a real, live creek that runs through the park to the beach.

Return Route Options. On the return trip, follow the bikeway/walkway along the north side of Aliso Creek under PCH. Return by the same route unless there is a desire for some fun diversions. They are as follows: 1) at Moss St. and PCH, turn west on Moss St. to Ocean Wy.; follow that pleasant street up on the ocean bluffs to Agate St. Cross PCH there and return to Glenneyre St., then proceed to Mountain St.; 2) turn west and recross PCH to Gaviota Dr. (a little road behind a bunch of garages that has limited, but classy ocean views). Continue on Gaviota Dr. to Thalia St. and again cross PCH, returning to Glenneyre St. The remainder of the trip is a backtrack to the starting point.

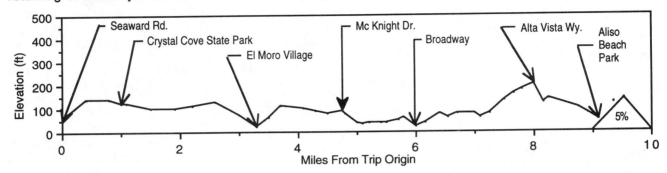

CONNECTING TRIPS: 1) Connection with the Laguna Canyon Road tour (Trip #9) - turn inland (north) in Laguna Beach proper at Broadway (State Hwy. 133) and continue north; 2) connection with the Newport Beach/Corona Del Mar Tour (Trip #15) - go two streets north on PCH beyond Seaward Rd. to Poppy Ave. Turn toward the coast and bike 0.3 mile to Ocean Blvd. above Little Corona City beach; 3) connection with the Signal Peak and Pelican Hill ride (Trip #38) - turn north at Newport Coast Dr.

TRIP #11 - LAGUNA NIGUEL BIKEWAY

GENERAL LOCATION: Mission Viejo, Laguna Niguel

LEVEL OF DIFFICULTY: One way - moderate; up and back - moderate
Distance - 7.0 miles (one way)
Elevation gain - frequent moderate grades

HIGHLIGHTS: This tour explores territory ranging from the dryer interior hills to the breezy west-facing beaches. The route has an initial exposed section followed by a lengthy lush, tree-lined segment. There are scattered undeveloped sections, as well as large shopping centers at the trip origin, middle segment and terminus. The one constant of this trip is mildly hilly terrain. There are several excellent vista points, particularly late in the trip.

There is an excellent spur trip off the main Class II Crown Valley Pkwy. route. It is a Class I hillside trail along the lower part of the Salt Creek Trail, reached via Camino Del Avion, that winds alongside the Monarch Beach Golf Links and lets out at Salt Creek Beach Park. There is additional (directly connected) fun biking near the beach below the awesome Ritz Carton Hotel, within the upper park and across PCH at Sea Terrace Community Park.

For round-trip riders, there are several classy return options which use some combination of Camino Del Avion, the Salt Creek Trail, Niguel Ave. and the Street of the Golden Lantern (SGL). All are more difficult than the basic up-and-back tour, but offer some interesting return trip variety. The **Salt Creek Trail to Street of the Golden Lantern** is a particularly appealing, sight-filled option.

TRAILHEAD: From the San Diego Fwy., exit east on Crown Valley Pkwy and proceed about 1/2 mile to Medical Center Rd. (El Regateo to the north). Turn right (south) and find parking within the Mission Viejo Mall. From the San Joaquin Transportation Corridor (State Hwy 73), exit at Greenfield Dr. and

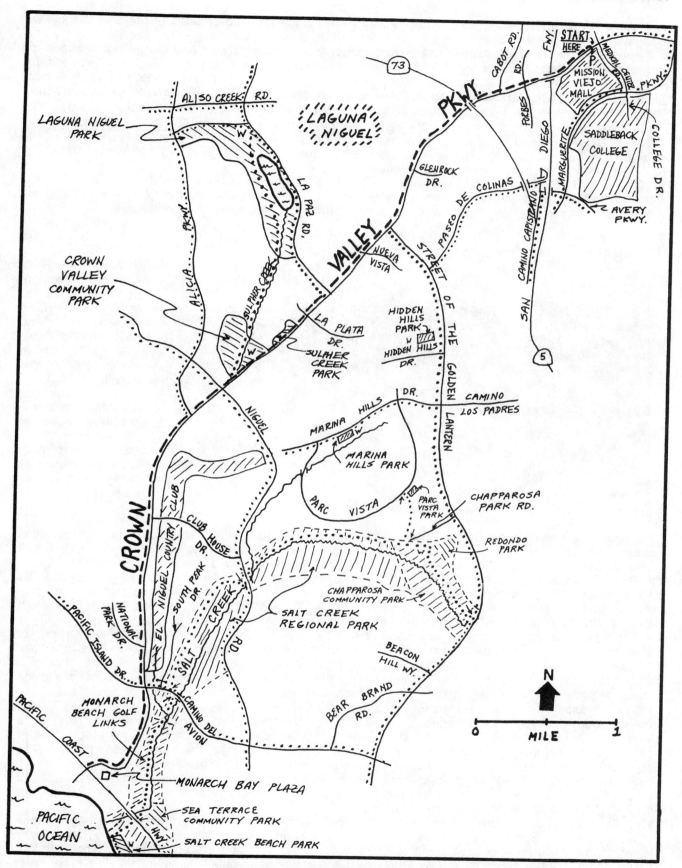

TRIP #11 - LAGUNA NIGUEL BIKEWAY

45

turn south. In about 1/3 mile, take Crown Valley Pkwy. left (east) and cross over the San Diego Fwy. Continue as described above.

Bring a moderate water supply and plan to resupply at Crown Valley Community Park near the trip midpoint and/or Salt Creek Beach Park at the spur trip end point.

TRIP DESCRIPTION: **Mission Viejo.** Exit the Mission Viejo Mall and turn left (west) on Crown Valley Pkwy. For the next 1/4 mile the Class II route remains alongside the mall, heading downhill with residences in the hills to the right. Just beyond the passage over the San Diego Fwy. (0.2), the road becomes Class III and the surrounding territory begins to transition to a drier, less-developed look. The route passes Forbes Rd., crosses over Oso Creek (0.3), goes under State Hwy. 73 just beyond Cabot Rd. (0.7), then passes The Center at Rancho Niguel.

The Foothills. Cycle uphill, reaching the top of the upgrade in about another 0.5 mile. This is Class II roadway, as it will stay for the trip's remainder. There is a nice view out of the small canyon, (back toward Mission Viejo proper) which includes the distant mountains and foothills.

Proceed through this partially-developed, hill-enclosed section, pass Glenrock Dr. (1.7) and head downhill to Moulton Pkwy./SGL (2.1). Crown Valley Pkwy. has paralleled Sulphur Creek for the last 1/2 mile and will continue to do so for another 1-1/2 miles. There is a Class I bikeway along the creek for most of this stretch.

Lower Salt Creek Trail

Laguna Niguel. In another 0.2 mile, bike past Nueva Vista where there are newer residential developments in the hills to the right (northwest) and a small shopping center to the left. Cross Adelanto Dr. (2.6), continue uphill to La Paz Rd., then follow a long downgrade past La Plata Dr. to the Sulphur Creek Reservoir (3.1), where Sulphur Creek pulls away from the roadway. In another 0.3 mile is Crown Valley Community Park. This is a nice shade park with water and restrooms, which is a great place for a rest break. Pedal up to Niguel Rd. (3.7) to a flat, reaching Alicia Pkwy. In this 0.3 mile is a multitude of places to stop and snack, including "The Village" and the Crown Valley Mall.

The hilly route continues uphill just north of Alicia Pkwy. and the surroundings change from one of the dryer interior to more coastal and treed. The road curves to the south in this area. Bike in a tree-lined section which crests at a point above the El Niguel Country Club and Golf Course (4.5). Follow a roller-coaster stretch by Club House Dr. (4.9) and Laguna Woods Dr. (5.2), then enjoy the views into the surrounding hills. Crown Valley Pkwy. meets Camino Del Avion (east)/Pacific Island Dr. (west) at (6.1).

The Coast. There is an exceptional spur trip off of Camino Del Avion which is described below. However, our reference route continues on a workout upgrade to a crest near Sea Island Dr. (6.5). As a diversion, cross the roadway for a vista that takes in a wide coastal area. Begin a long steep descent from this crest and enjoy the periodic "peeks" at the ocean. In 0.35 mile, the route passes the Monarch Bay Plaza entrance and, in another 0.15 mile, meets PCH (7.0) at the plaza's southern edge.

Return Route Options for Up-and-Back Riders. Retrace the incoming Crown Valley Pkwy. route to Class II Camino Del Avion (7.7). At this juncture, cyclists can simply retrace the incoming ride or turn right (east) and take one of the alternates below:

Surface Street Return. (See the elevation contour below for the "Alternate Return Leg.") Cross the bridge over Salt Creek and make a short climb, then coast to Niguel Rd. (8.4). A short easy pedal is followed by a serious climb to Class II SGL. Turn left (north), coast another short stretch, then pump a steep grade for the next mile past a succession of gated communities. The initial crest is reached just after Old Ranch Rd./Bear Brand Rd., followed by Beacon Hill Wy. in 0.3 mile (9.9).

Pass a fire station and the Salt Creek Trail outlet just south of Sardina/St. Christopher (10.6). Reach another local crest near Dunes in 0.4 mile, cruise to Marina Hills Rd., then tough out a final climb to the trip high point near Duchess St. (12.5). (Note that, on the way up at the northwest corner of Hidden Hills Rd., is Hidden Hills Neighborhood Park. The cozy park has a water fountain, picnic benches, gazebos, limited shade and children's play area.) Pass the sign noting the pending 10% downgrade, then glide by Paseo De Colinas in 0.4 mile and reach Crown Valley Pkwy. at (13.4). Turn right and retrace the outgoing route back to Medical Center Rd. (15.5). Of the three return options, this is the hardest and the full loop is rated strenuous.

Salt Creek Trail to Niguel Ave. Look for the trail at street level to the west side of the bridge on the north side of Camino Del Avion. (It is just east of private South Peak Dr.) This up-and-down trail stays part way up the western side of the canyon. The canyon bottom is in a relatively natural state and both east and west ridgelines are topped with upscale residences.

In one mile, coast downhill to Niguel Ave. and find the street's undercrossing. Parallel the street and take the Niguel Ave. return trail exit, heading northeast. Once on Niguel Ave. northbound, climb steeply to a false crest in 0.3 mile (just beyond Club House Dr.), then resume a less testy 0.95 mile pull to a second summit just near La Hermosa Ave. A 0.25-mile steep coast leads to Crown Valley Pkwy. Turn right and just reverse the incoming route from Niguel Ave. to Medical Center Rd. The total loop is 14.1 miles. The return via this route makes for a moderate-to-strenuous round trip.

Salt Creek Trail to Street of the Golden Lantern. Follow the Salt Creek Trail as described above. However, rather than taking the fork northeast to Niguel Ave., take the trail eastward into San Juan Canyon. A steady light upgrade on the canyon's northern face leads to a large sports complex at the western edge of Chapparosa Community Park in 1.1 miles, which has restrooms, several baseball diamonds, athletic courts and fields, picnic facilities and children's playground.

Skirting the park on its northern edge leads to a steep exit path north to scenic Parc Vista Park and Parc Vista (a roadway) near Minori. Continuing past this exit path leads to the auto outlet at Chapparosa Park Rd. on the park's eastern edge. Cross the road and look for an entry gate heading uphill to the right. A 1/4-mile section of steep uphill leads to a milder, winding, canyon-hugging grade where the views back down the incoming Salt Creek Trail just get better with altitude. In 1.1 miles from Chapparosa Rd. is the trail's end at SGL just south of Sardina/St. Christopher. (Note there is parking just across the small canyon at SGL for Dog Park users and bikers who want to explore upper Salt Creek Trail.) The SGL segment (left) to Crown Valley Pkwy. is described in the **Surface Street Return** above. The total loop is 16.0 miles and is rated strenuous.

Excursion: Salt Creek Beach via Salt Creek Trail. On the incoming route, turn east on Camino Del Avion and bike 0.1 mile, then look for a steep Class I trail on the west side of the bridge over Salt Creek. (There is also an entry on the north side of the street at the east end of the bridge.) Take the trail down to Salt Creek Regional Park and head south. There is a great view to the ocean and surrounding classy residential territory at this point. Bike the Class I path another 1.3 miles down a winding canyon path alongside the Monarch Beach Golf Links, pass under Pacific Coast Highway (PCH), and cruise to Salt Creek Beach.

Once at the coast, the trail proceeds southeast about 20-30 feet above the beach and reaches Bluff Park (picnic tables, barbecues and supreme view). A short distance beyond is the steep (private) trail to the Ritz Carlton Hotel and a second steep (public) trail that heads north toward PCH. The latter trail passes under Ritz Carlton Dr. and reaches a parking area with restrooms, tree shade and an adjacent landscaped park area. Biking further north leads under PCH to Sea Terrace Community Park with its grassy knolls, picnic benches and library. (Bikers who follow the full spur tour can return to Salt Creek most conveniently via PCH.)

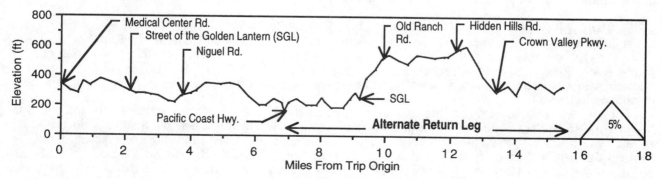

47

CONNECTING TRIPS: 1) Connection with the Aliso Creek Trail (Trip #29) - Option A: Exit Crown Valley Pkwy. at La Paz Rd. or, Option B: Exit Crown Valley Pkwy. at Crown Valley Community Park and ride north on the bike trail.; 2) Connection with the Mission Viejo Bikeway (Trip #30) - from the Mission Viejo Mall, turn right (east) on Crown Valley Pkwy., continue about 1/2 mile to Marguerite Pkwy. and turn left (north); 3) connection with the Westside Laguna Niguel tour (Trip #39) - the two trips share a common segment on Crown Valley Pkwy.; 4) connection with the Aliso Viejo Figure "8" (Trip #46) - at Crown Valley Pkwy. and La Paz Rd., bike north on the latter street to Aliso Creek Rd.; 5) connection with the Arroyo Trabuco Loop (Trip #50) - at Crown Valley Pkwy. and Medical Center Rd., bike southwest on the latter street to Marguerite Pkwy.

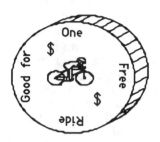

TRIP #12 - DOHENY BIKEWAY

GENERAL LOCATION: Mission Viejo, San Juan Capistrano

LEVEL OF DIFFICULTY: One way - easy; up and back - easy to moderate
Distance - 6.9 miles (one way)
Elevation gain - essentially flat

HIGHLIGHTS: This is a pleasant trip on mostly Class I and Class II bikeways along Oso, Trabuco and San Juan Creeks. Included is a segment which passes near historic San Juan Capistrano Mission and a ride terminus at scenic Doheny State Beach, which has plentiful facilities. The route starts at the southern edge of Mission Viejo and cruises the periphery of Laguna Niguel, then visits San Juan Capistrano, Dana Point and Capistrano Beach. There are several pleasant parks for rest spots south of Junipero Serra Rd.

TRAILHEAD: From the San Diego Fwy., exit at Avery Pkwy. One option is to drive west a short distance to the end of Avery Pkwy., turn left (south) and find parking on Camino Capistrano. A second option is to drive east on Avery Pkwy., cross Marguerite Pkwy. and proceed steeply 0.2 mile up to Los Ondas Ave. Turn left and drive 0.1 mile to Coronado Park. There are scattered trees, park benches and barbecues, as well as a children's playground, but no water.

From the San Joaquin Hills Transportation Corridor (State Hwy. 73) southbound, continue onto the San Diego Fwy. transition and exit east at Junipero Serra Rd. Turn north onto Rancho Viejo Rd. and drive two miles to Avery Pkwy. Proceed as described above.

Bring a light water supply. There are commercial water stops near the Avery Pkwy. western terminus and public sources at several parks along the way.

TRIP DESCRIPTION: **Camino Capistrano.** From Coronado Park, return to Class II Avery Pkwy. and coast on a steep downhill past Plata Pl. (an entrance to Saddleback College) to Rancho Viejo Rd. (0.2). Cross that street and go under the San Diego Fwy. on a short Class X stretch, turning left (south) at the Avery Pkwy. terminus. Proceed south on Class III Camino Capistrano under Hwy. 73, passing numerous roadside businesses and fast food stops into a more open countryside (0.5). Here the route transitions to Class II.

For the next couple of miles, the surrounding backdrop is the hills to the right (west) and the San Diego Fwy. to the left. There is a short stretch of highway which has been blocked to auto traffic for several years, but is passable by bikers and pedestrians. Beyond the road closure, cyclists pass the Rancho Capistrano Cemetery (0.7) and orange groves, then cross over the Arroyo Trabuco (1.4). South of the confluence of Oso and Trabuco Creeks, the waterway takes the name of the latter. The route

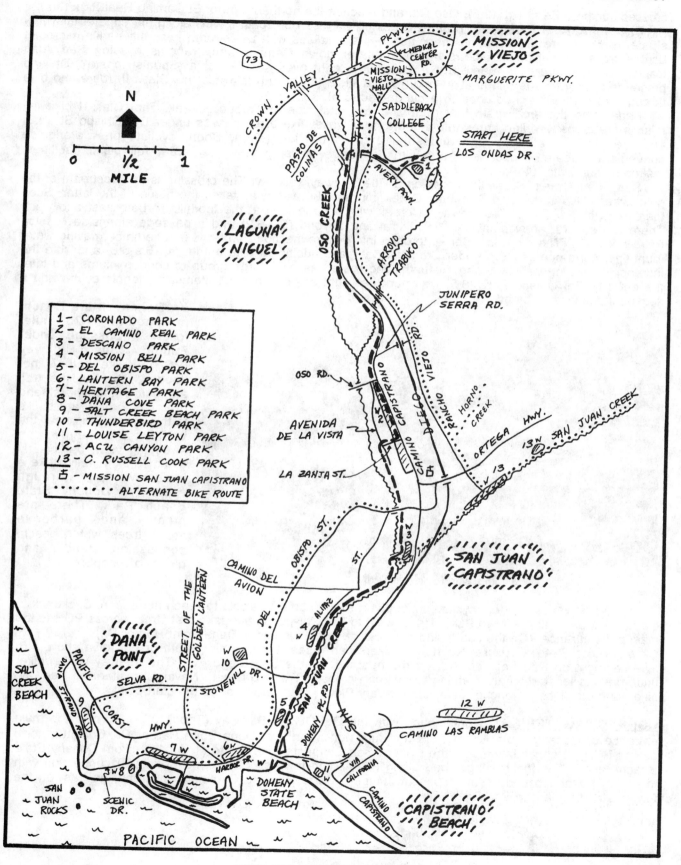

TRIP #12 - DOHENY BIKEWAY

crosses Junipero Serra Rd. (2.3), Oso Rd. and reaches the northern end of El Camino Real Park (2.7).

El Camino Real Park and Trabuco Creek. The Class I bikepath travels along the edge of this well-shaded park. There are scattered park benches and tables with a restroom near the park's mid-point across from Calle Bonito. About 1/4 mile further down Camino Capistrano is Mission San Juan Capistrano. However, the marked bike route turns right (west) at La Zanja (Spanish pasta?) St. and proceeds shortly to a terminus at Avenida De La Vista (3.3). Turn left onto this Class III route and bike through residential neighborhood to a cul-de-sac (3.5).

Pedal onto the small path that returns to the east side of Trabuco Creek. That Class I bikeway follows the cement-walled creek into a more open valley-like area, passes under Del Obispo St. (4.0) and then cruises along a light industrial area to the left (east). Soon, cyclists pass alongside conveniently-located Descanso Park with its shade trees, grassy rest area, full picnic facilities, restrooms and water (4.4).

San Juan Creek. Cross the creek on a little bikeway/walkway. The crossing is just upstream of the point where Oso Creek and San Juan Creek join and the waterway takes the name of the latter. Soon there is a long-distance view down the creek with a good look at the foothills to both east and west. There are several entry points at Via Mistral and beyond (5.0-5.2) and a passage alongside Mission Bell Park (5.5). (The long, thin park is broken into several sections, with the southernmost having water fountains, porta-potties.) Dip under Stonehill Dr., pass additional bike entries at (5.9-6.0) and note the increasing housing density along the path. The route passes a large group of condominiums and later the entry to Del Obispo Park (6.5).This park has light shade, baseball diamonds, tennis courts and a seasonal concession stand.

San Juan Creek Outlet at the Ocean

Doheny State Beach. In another 0.25 mile, follow a passage under Pacific Coast Highway (PCH). If the path is not flooded, stay on the trail alongside the marshland (frequently there are ducks in this area). Stop near the beach and enjoy the sweeping view, particularly south (6.9). Finally, take a leisurely spin through expansive Doheny State Beach Park. There are picnic and barbecue areas, trees, water, beach, concession stands, and plenty of people.

If the bikeway is flooded, cyclists must divert to the surface streets to reach the ocean. Backtrack to the nearest trail entry point to PCH. Travel west to Del Obispo St. and take that street across PCH to the main park entrance. (On the south side of PCH, the street's name is Dana Point Harbor Dr.)

Alternate Return Route. Round-trip bikers can repeat the incoming route or opt for a short, 1.5-mile segment on Rancho Viejo Rd. on the east side of the San Diego Fwy. The freeway walker/biker underpass is located where Camino Capistrano crosses Trabuco Creek. Having transited the freeway, bike north on Class II Rancho Viejo Rd. to Avery Pkwy., then return to the trip start point.

CONNECTING TRIPS: 1) Continuation with the Del Obispo Bikeway (Trip #13) - return to the main entrance of Doheny State Beach/Park and turn right (north) at Dana Point Harbor Dr. Continue north across PCH; 2) continuation with the Doheny/San Clemente Bike Route (Trip #14) - from Doheny State Beach/Park, follow the frontage road along PCH south towards Capistrano Beach; 3) connection with the Arroyo Trabuco Loop (Trip #50) - at Junipero Serra Rd. and Camino Capistrano, go east on the former street under the San Diego Fwy.

TRIP #13 - DEL OBISPO BIKEWAY

GENERAL LOCATION: San Juan Capistrano-Dana Point

LEVEL OF DIFFICULTY: Loop - moderate
Distance - 17.2 miles
Elevation gain - periodic light upgrades; single, short and steep upgrade

HIGHLIGHTS: This is a "must do" adventure! The outbound leg is built around the Del Obispo Bikeway with an alternate return leg provided for variety. Most of the trip is on Class I or Class II bikeway. Far and away, the tour highlight is the Dana Point Harbor tour at the end of the outbound leg. The route also passes next to historic Mission San Juan Capistrano. In addition, there is a pleasant cruise on Del Obispo St., several park visits and a tour into the "far reaches" of San Juan Creek. Finally, there are fine scenic views from atop Lantern Bay Park and some super-duper vista points from a very strenuous spur trip off of Scenic Dr.

TRAILHEAD: From the San Diego Fwy., exit at Ortega Hwy. and head west about 1/4 mile to Camino Capistrano. Turn right (north) and continue 1/4 mile to El Camino Real Park. Find a turn-around point north of La Zanja St. and pick a spot alongside the shaded park. (The park also has benches, grass and a restroom near the park's mid point across from Calle Bonita.) From Pacific Coast Hwy. (PCH), turn north at Del Obispo St. (Dana Point Harbor Dr. to the south) and drive 0.5 mile to the park.

Bring a moderate water supply. There are shopping centers and parks with water scattered about this bike route. For additional detail on the parks along San Juan and Trabuco Creeks, refer to Trip #12.

TRIP DESCRIPTION: **Trabuco Creek.** Ride south and turn right (west) on La Zanja St. Follow the marked Class III route a short distance to Avenida De La Vista and turn left (south). Pedal about 0.2 mile through a residential neighborhood to a cul-de-sac (0.4). (Do not even think about those private swimming pools you see along the roadway!) Bike onto a small path that leads to the east side of Trabuco Creek. Follow the creek about 0.4 mile on a Class I path and exit at Del Obispo St., heading right (southwest) (0.8).

Del Obispo St. Cruise on the Class II bike route through a residential area, passing Alipaz St. and Paseo Terraza (1.2). The roadway curves southward and follows a light upgrade just beyond. There are nearby hills with homes to the right (west), with residential below and the more distant hills, both to the left. This type of scenery continues for more than a mile. Pass the mammoth "Farm to Market" produce outlet (1.8), Via Del Avion (2.2), and Blue Fin Dr. (2.6). The residential density increases on both sides of the street beyond this point.

In 0.4 mile, bike across Stonehill Dr., passing a large shopping center. At (3.5), the route meets Quail Run, where there is a large condominium community across the road and an entry into Del Obispo Park just beyond. (This park has light shade, baseball diamonds, tennis courts and a seasonal concession stand.) At (3.9) is the busy PCH intersection with its collection of small eateries.

Dana Point Harbor. After crossing PCH, the road name becomes Dana Point Harbor Dr. (also referred to as Harbor Dr.). Pass the Doheny State Park main entrance (left) and the Street of the Park Lantern, with its steep road entry to Lantern Bay Park. Bike on Class II Harbor Dr. and pass below the steep bluffs to the landward side of the road. Then turn left toward the harbor on the Street of the Golden Lantern (4.3). (Is this a great name or what?!) Proceed to the wharf area and eyeball the row-on-row of pleasure craft tied up there. A short tour to the westernmost edge of the wharf area leads to such places as Harpoon Harry's, a fun cafe with outdoor seating under sun umbrellas and picture-postcard harbor view.

Return to the boat slips and proceed west on the sidewalk alongside the harbor. Turn left onto Island Wy. (5.2) and bike on the bridge over to the central island in the harbor. At the island entrance is the Dana Statue, which sits in the middle of a long, thin park on the island's seaward side. The park has benches, grass, barbecue facilities, little roofed picnic shelters, water and restrooms. Grab a bench and watch the boats sail the harbor.

A tour to the east leads to The Beach House and the Harbor Patrol Building. There is a nice southward view from the eastern edge of the island (5.9). Heading back across Island Wy. to the western edge of the island, cyclists observe the fisherman on the breakwater as well as take in the super view west and north to the seaside bluffs (6.7). Next, bikers recross the harbor on Island Wy. and return to Harbor Dr. at (7.3).

51

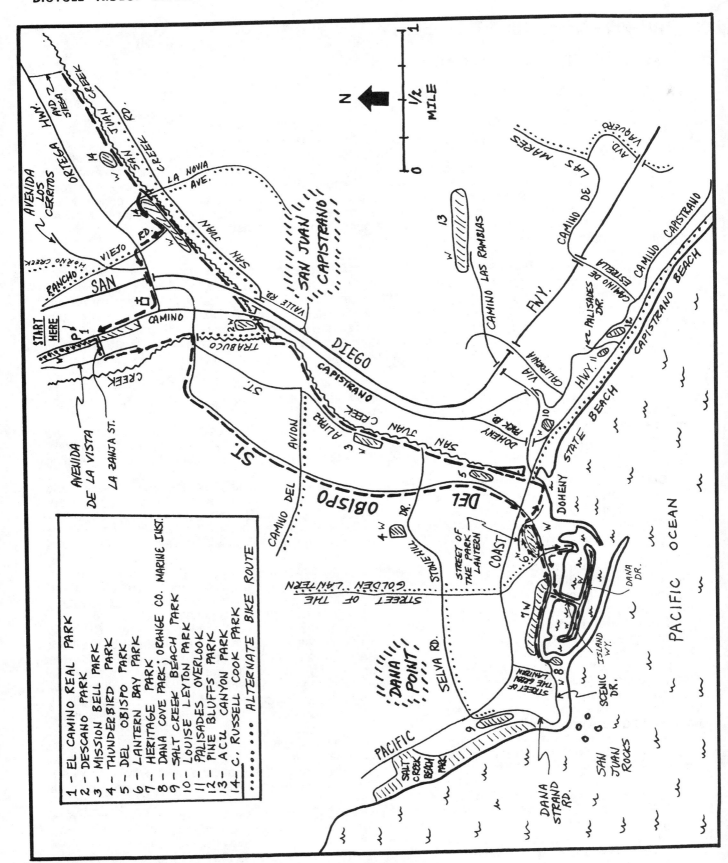

1 – EL CAMINO REAL PARK
2 – DESCANSO PARK
3 – MISSION BELL PARK
4 – THUNDERBIRD PARK
5 – DEL OBISPO PARK
6 – LANTERN BAY PARK
7 – HERITAGE PARK
8 – DANA COVE PARK; ORANGE CO. MARINE INST.
9 – SALT CREEK BEACH PARK
10 – LOUISE LEYTON PARK
11 – PALISADES OVERLOOK
12 – PINE BLUFFS PARK
13 – ACU CANYON PARK
14 – C. RUSSELL COOK PARK
•••••• ALTERNATE BIKE ROUTE

TRIP #13 - DEL OBISPO BIKEWAY

Turn left and pass sandstrewn Heritage Park. It has all the amenities of the park on the island plus trees, recreation/play area, and a bonified windsurfer area. Bicycling westward leads to Dana Cove and the foot of Cove Rd. (7.8). (A diversion on this sheer Class X road leads up to some great vista points on what becomes Scenic Dr. The view of Dana Point harbor from these heights is unparalleled!)

Stay on Harbor Dr. and pass the Ocean Institute (marine studies) within Dana Cove Park. Consider a sidetrack to the pedal tour and visit the old sailing ship docked there. The Harbor Dr. route ends just beyond, at the beginning of the outer breakwater. One can walk onto the breakwater or hike northward along the tight coves from this point.

Lantern Bay Park. Return to the Street of the Golden Lantern (9.0). At the northeast corner of the intersection, follow the short, steep Class I switchback trail up to Lantern Bay Park. There is a 360-degree view from the top of the bluff that takes in the hills to the east, harbor to the south, homes on the bluffs to the west (including a wedding chapel) and condomania to the north. The park has water, trees, picnic/barbecue facilities and children's playground. Continue along the south edge of the park on the bikeway/walkway to the Smyth Amphitheater (9.3). This is a mini-amphitheater with a great scenic view. There was a wedding here on the Saturday we passed through, complete with piccolo players in tuxedos!

San Juan Creek. Bike east to the Street of the Park Lantern and follow that steep roadway downhill past a restroom to the intersection with Harbor Blvd. Cross the street into the Doheny State Beach/Park entrance and follow the path nearest the beach to the San Juan Creek outlet (9.8).

Stay to the west side of the creek and pedal north under PCH. (If this marshy area is flooded, take the diversion route described in Trip #12.) Pass the entrance to Del Obispo Park (10.3) and then cycle uninterrupted along San Juan Creek past the Mission Bell Park entrance (11.1). In another 1.2 miles, the path crosses a bike bridge over Trabuco Creek just south of the creek junction. Dead ahead is small Descanso Park with shade, water, restrooms, grass, and picnic benches/barbecues.

The bikepath branches at this juncture, left along Trabuco Creek, and right to stay on San Juan Creek. Take the right branch, pass under Camino Capistrano (12.6) and ride along a wide, green, natural riverbed on continued Class I bikeway. Pass under the San Diego Fwy. and, in 0.4 mile from Camino Capistrano, meet the Paseo Triador cul-de-sac. Follow that road to Calle Arroyo and turn right onto a Class II bikepath.

Dana Point Harbor from Dana Cove Park

Shift over to the Class I path along Calle Arroyo or take the small Class I walkway/bikeway off to the right that runs through C. Russell Cook Park paralleling Calle Arroyo (13.2). The entry to the path is just beyond a large equestrian staging area and it stays near and parallel to San Juan Creek. There are trees, picnic benches and barbecues scattered along this greenbelt. Pass Rancho Viejo Rd. (13.6), then bike along a more-developed recreation area which has restrooms, scattered trees, picnic tables, children's playground and sports fields and courts.

At the recreation area's eastern edge is La Novia Ave. where Cook Park's western edge ends. The path jogs to the left (north) and goes alongside Calle Arroyo, crosses La Novia Ave., then continues as a Class I trail along the creek. There is heavy residential development to the north and open fields across the creek to the south. There are horse trails which parallel the bikepath and several bike entry points in this area (13.8, 14.1). At (14.2), enter the unconnected east segment of C. Russel Cook Park, which has a small shady playground area. In 0.3 mile, skirt some athletic fields with restrooms and a water fountain near Via Solana. Return to Calle Arroyo at Via Estenaga, the main park entry at Cook

Park's eastern edge. The bikeway next passes a large area of horse stables and ends at Avd. Siega (14.8). (The dirt road on the creekside of Avd. Siega may serve as a bikeway extension in the future.)

Mission San Juan Capistrano. Return to Rancho Viejo Rd. (16.0), turn right, and ride 0.3 mile to Ortega Hwy. Go left and take a 0.4 mile Class X segment that requires careful biking because of fast-moving traffic. At Camino Capistrano, turn right (north) and pass Mission San Juan Capistrano. Stop and visit this venerable Spanish mission or continue biking another 0.5 mile to the parking area (17.2).

Excursions: Horno Creek Trail. At the Marbella Golf and Country Club entrance at Rancho Viejo Rd., the Class I path along Golf Club Dr. follows the rough contour of Horno Creek. The one-way distance is 1.2 miles. Admittance is a courtesy -- the implicit understanding is that cyclists will respect the standard cycling rules of good conduct.

La Novia Ave. A fun loop in the hills, bike across San Juan Creek from the Calle Arroyo/La Novia Ave. intersection, cross San Juan Creek Rd. and cycle on the wide-shouldered Class X road or pick up the Class I path on the street's east side. Pass Via Entrada (0.6) and begin a steep climb for 0.2 mile before the grade moderates. Enjoy the views eastward into San Juan Capistrano up to and beyond the crest, which is 0.25 mile beyond Via Cerro Rebal. The road transitions to a wide-shouldered Class X, passes the San Juan Hills Golf Course and continues downhill to Valle Rd. (2.0).

Turn right and bike 0.3 mile alongside the San Diego Fwy., then right again at San Juan Creek Rd. Follow that Class II road 1.2 miles on the south side of San Juan Creek to La Novia Ave., turn left and return to the excursion start point (3.7).

CONNECTING TRIPS: 1) Connection with the Doheny Bikeway (Trip #12) - at the Descanso Park junction, take the westernmost bike trail along Trabuco Creek; 2) connection with the Doheny/San Clemente Bike Route (Trip #14) - follow the roadway from the Doheny State Beach/Park entrance over San Juan Creek and link up with the bikeway heading south along the beach; 3) connection with the Arroyo Trabuco Loop (Trip #50) - at Ortega Hwy. and La Novia Ave., go either direction on the former road.

TRIP #14 - DOHENY/SAN CLEMENTE BIKE ROUTE

GENERAL LOCATION: Dana Point-San Clemente

LEVEL OF DIFFICULTY: Loop - moderate
Distance - 17.1 miles
Elevation gain - periodic moderate grades in San Clemente area

HIGHLIGHTS: This trip is a mix between a beach route and a city tour. The first half follows Pacific Coast Highway (PCH) and provides numerous views of surf and sand. The second half is a loop tour through the heart of San Clemente on El Camino Real (ECR). The return trip includes an alternate return leg on a number of connecting residential roadways.

Highlights of the tour are Doheny State Beach and Capistrano Beach Park near the trip origin, the San Clemente City tour in general, and the pleasant out-of-the-way beach at San Mateo Point at the trip's southernmost point. The route is a mix of Classes I, II and III biking with a limited stretch of Class X. There are some moderate rolling hills in the San Clemente area and some segments of ECR where there is very limited bike room.

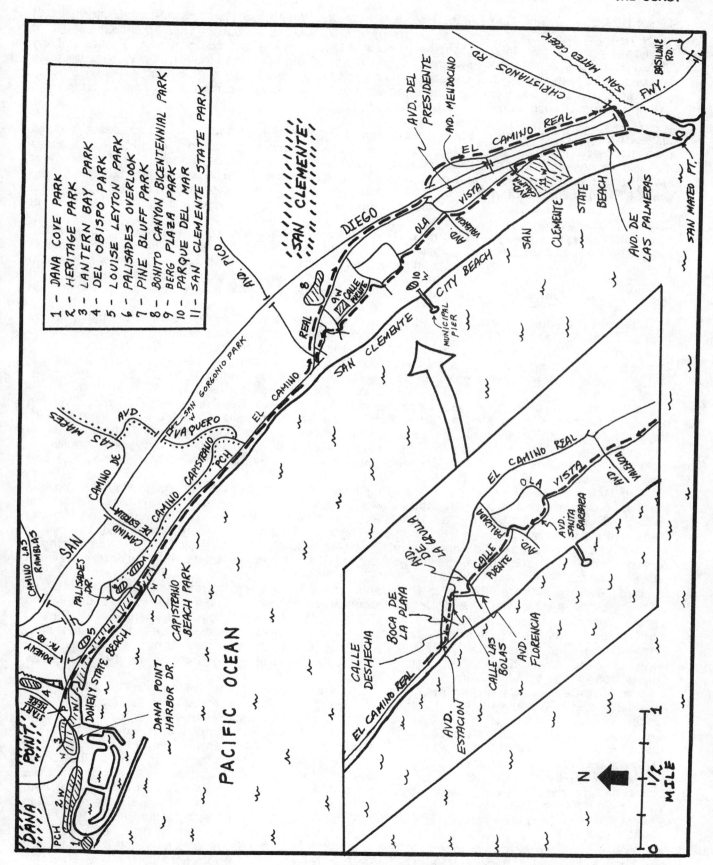

TRIP #14 - DOHENY/SAN CLEMENTE BIKE ROUTE

TRAILHEAD: From the San Diego Fwy., exit west on Camino Las Rambles and continue until that roadway fuses with PCH. Continue about 1/4 mile to Dana Point Harbor Dr. (named Del Obispo St. at the northern end of the intersection) and turn left. Drive a short distance and turn left into Doheny State Beach Park. A free parking alternative is to motor up the hill across from the park's gate entrance and park at Lantern Bay Park. That roadway is named the Street of the Park Lantern.

Bring a moderate water supply. There are scattered public water sources as noted on the trip map, and other sources such as gas stations in the city proper.

TRIP DESCRIPTION: **Doheny State Beach.** Take the entrance road south which becomes a frontage road alongside PCH and pass over San Juan Creek. Follow the path to the right which passes alongside a camping area and then enters the north end of Doheny State Beach (0.3). This pleasant stretch has clear ocean views and passes directly alongside the sunbathing area (get our drift?). The Class I path parallels the beach, transits Capistrano Beach Park, and exits at Beach Rd. (1.1) where it then follows PCH on a Class II path. (Note that there is a restroom and water just south of Beach Rd. at Capistrano Beach Park.)

Pacific Coast Highway - El Camino Real. The next 1.7 miles is along a stretch of highway with low bluffs to the east and rows of bushes which block the sea view to the west. At this point, PCH meets Camino Capistrano where a nice ocean view opens back up. The road name becomes El Camino Real at this point. There is a small shopping center to the east and a snack bar on the beachfront (2.8). The route returns to the surrounding cliffs for another 0.6 mile, then enters the San Clemente City limits at Avd. Estacion.

The roadway changes to Class III at this juncture. Begin a long, steady upgrade through a heavy trafficked commercial district (4.1). There are portions of the next two miles where bike room on ECR is very restricted. Pass the entry to Bonito Canyon Bicentennial Park at El Portal (tree shade, some facilities, but no water) (4.6), reach a level before Avd. Palizada and gain the crest near Avd. Del Mar (5.1). There is a view of the lovely hillside residential community from this area. After another more moderate upgrade, the route reaches its highest point near Paseo De Cristobal (5.7).

In 0.2 mile at Avd. Valencia, the road splits into ECR and Avd. Del Presidente. Our route forks left on ECR and passes under the San Diego Fwy. onto a short, limited-shoulder, Class X section (6.0). Beyond here to the ECR terminus, the route is more residential, has lighter traffic, and offers more bike room. (If this is not your forte, use Avd. Del Presidente on both outgoing and return legs.). Parallel the freeway on small rolling hills with predominantly downhill riding. Pass Avd. Mendocino (6.5) and reach ECR's terminus at Christianos Rd. (8.0).

San Mateo Point. The trip route follows Christianos Rd. west over the San Diego Fwy. Just beyond the southbound on-ramp is a small path/roadway entrance that is blocked to automobiles. Follow that route south and downhill 0.3 mile and take the junction west at that point. (The southbound bikeway leads to the south gate of Camp Pendleton per Trip #16.) Pedal this junction path another 0.4 mile to a lovely and lightly-used beach and an overlook/vista near San Mateo Point (8.7). If your timing is right, you may even see one of the high-speed AMTRAK passenger trains whiz by on the elevated railway near the beach.

Avd. Del Presidente. Return to Christianos Rd. and turn left (toward the ocean). This is the southern terminus (or origin) of Avd. Del Presidente (9.4). Follow the Class II roadway moderately and generally uphill past Avd. De Las Palmeras (9.7), the entry to a posh private residential area. Parallel the San Diego Fwy. on the seaward side and head uphill past Avd. Vista De Oceano (9.9), then pass alongside the north edge of San Clemente State Park. There is a bike entry from this roadway into a large, pleasant, forested park (with campsites) (10.4). Our route stays along Avd. Del Presidente through rolling hills to Avd. Califia.

San Vicente Residential Route. One option here is to pedal another 0.7 mile on Class II Avd. Del Presidente and turn south on Avd. Valencia. However, our reference route turns left (south) at Avd. Califia and soon turns right at Ola Vista, a pleasant, quiet residential street through rolling hills. At Avd. Valencia, our tour mainly follows the old Pacific Coast Bicentennial Bike Route (11.3). The marked route (as shown on the detail map) follows in order: Ola Vista, left on Avd. Santa Barbara, right on Calle Seville, right on Avd. Palizada, left on Calle Puente, left and downhill on Avd. De La Grulla, right and downhill on Avd. Florencia, left on Calle Los Bolas, left on Boca De La Playa, right on Calle Deshecha, and right on Avd. Estacion, returning to ECR (13.7). Along the way is a market near Avd. Victoria and S. Ola Vista and the road access to the Municipal Pier on Avd. Del Mar near Calle Seville. Also there is a cozy rest and water stop at Max Berg Plaza Park along Calle Puente.

El Camino Real - Pacific Coast Highway. The return route is Class III along ECR until the automobile roadway narrows to one lane and the bike lane expands. It remains Class II until the left turn entry at Beach Rd. back into San Clemente Beach Park (16.0). From here the path reverses the outgoing route and returns to Doheny State Beach (17.1).

CONNECTING TRIPS: 1) Connection with the Doheny Bikeway (Trip #12) - from Doheny State Beach, bike to the outlet of San Juan Creek and follow the bikepath on the north side of that creek; 2) connection with the Del Obispo Bikeway (Trip #13) - return to the Doheny State Beach entrance, turn right (north) on Dana Point Harbor Dr. and continue across PCH; 3) continuation with the San Clemente to San Diego ride (Trip #16) - continue south beyond the San Mateo Point turnoff discussed in this trip text; 4) connection with the Hillside San Clemente ride (Trip #40) - turn north at Camino Capistrano (Northern Loop) or Avd. Pico (Southern Loop).

TRIP #15 - NEWPORT BEACH/CORONA DEL MAR TOUR

GENERAL LOCATION: Newport Beach, Corona Del Mar

LEVEL OF DIFFICULTY: Loop - moderate
Distance - 10.1 miles
Elevation gain - periodic moderate grades

HIGHLIGHTS: This is a great coastal tour that provides a number of vistas and other scenic attractions. It is a mixed class route with a significant amount of Class X on relatively lightly-traveled roadways. The outgoing bikepath travels Pacific Coast Highway (PCH) just north of Lower Newport Bay, then ducks inland to visit Ocean Blvd. on the bluffs above the Corona Del Mar beaches. The return leg is on Bayside Dr. directly alongside the bay. There are numerous spur tours into the islands along the bay, the Newport Strand or Upper Newport Bay.

TRAILHEAD: From PCH heading south, drive about 1/2 mile beyond the Newport Blvd. overpass and turn left at Riverside Ave. Bike a short, modest uphill to the southern junction with Cliff Dr. and turn left to stay on Riverside Ave. Turn left again at Cliff Dr. (honest!) and find parking. Cliff Drive Park sports a grassy area with modest picnic facilities, a couple of palm trees, water and a super view of the Newport Beach local area. From PCH northbound, go about one mile beyond Dover Rd., turn right at Riverside Ave. and continue as described above.

Bring a light water supply. There is water at Irvine Terrace Park and on Ocean Blvd. near the trip mid point.

TRIP DESCRIPTION: **Pacific Coast Highway/ Lower Newport Bay.** Before starting the trip, take in the vista from Cliff Drive Park. Following this, bike back to PCH and turn left (east). The next half-mile is Class X and best spent riding very carefully on PCH or using the wide sidewalks if the car traffic gets tough. The path soon becomes Class II. Pass the exclusive Balboa Bay Club (0.8) and enjoy the long-distance view of Fashion Island which opens up soon after. In 0.3 mile, cross Bayshore Dr. and bike to the bridge over Newport Bay. There is a diversion under the bridge which takes riders to Dover Dr. on the opposite side of PCH.

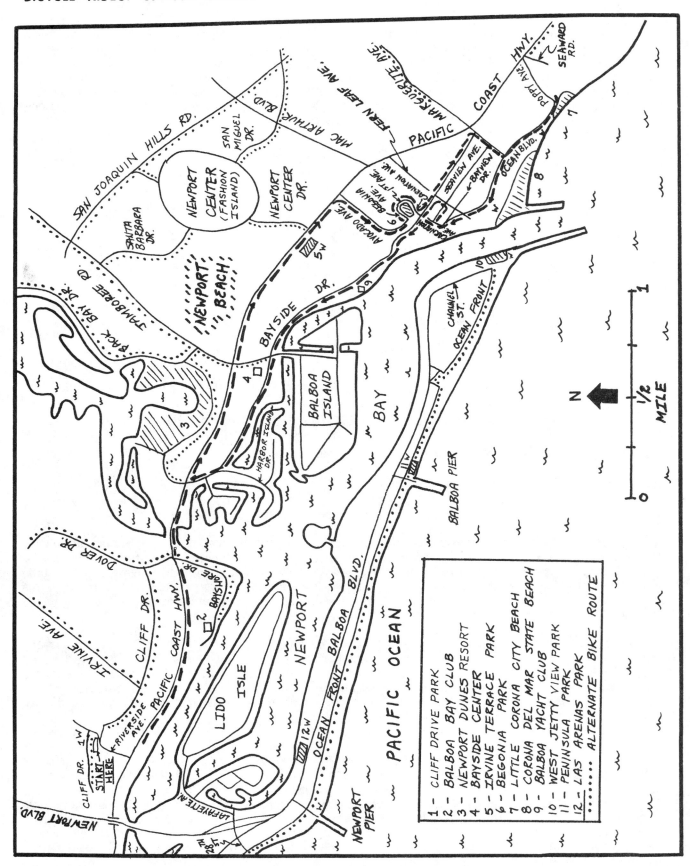

TRIP #15 - NEWPORT BEACH/CORONADEL MAR TOUR

Cross the bridge on the sidewalk or on the Class II path on PCH. Stop and observe the boat traffic and the Pride of Newport (sternwheeler) floating restaurant/nautical museum, which is docked near the bridge on the east end. Next cross Bayside Dr. (1.8) and start uphill. Near the crest is a grand view of Upper Newport Bay and Newport Dunes Waterfront Resort (2.2).

Pass private Promontory Dr., then Jamboree Rd. In this tree-lined section of bikeway, there is a choice of using the marked sidewalk path or the Class II bikeway on PCH; this option continues for about 0.5 mile. Cross Malabar Dr., which is one access to Irvine Terrace Park (restrooms, modest tree cover, barbecue facilities, sports fields, athletic courts and children's playground) (3.0). In about 300 yards (near the Newport Center Dr. access to Fashion Island across PCH) is a gated entry to walled-off Irvine Terrace Park. Cycle another 0.2 mile and turn right (south) on Avocado Ave. This is the beginning of a Class X segment on lightly-traveled roadway -- this will be typical of the biking conditions up to the loop return to PCH.

Corona Del Mar. In 0.2 mile, at the start of a small upgrade, cross the road and ride up the sidewalk in this short, one-way section. The road curves left and becomes Pacific Dr., proceeds a short distance, curves right and becomes Begonia Ave. (3.9). There is a park bench here and a captivating view down a small canyon to the ocean.

Soon, the route swings around Begonia Park (Begonia Ave., right on First St., right on Carnation Ave.). Begonia Park, appears to be the home of the Itsy-Bitsy Bathing Suit Frisbee Throwers Society (I.B.S.F.T.S.)! Coast downhill on Carnation Ave. and turn left (southwest) at Bayside Dr. (4.1). To the right are bluffs and an overlook to be visited later. Pedal another 0.5 mile with some uphill through a residential neighborhood and turn right on Marguerite Ave., then go 0.2 mile to Ocean Blvd. This begins the highlight segment of the trip (4.8).

Corona Del Mar State Beach from Ocean Blvd.

Ocean Blvd. Turn left (southwest) on Ocean Blvd. and ride 0.2 mile to a small grassy vista point that has a fabulous overlook of Corona Del Mar State Beach, the Newport Harbor breakwater and Catalina Island. There is a water fountain here. Bicycle another 0.2 mile to the end of Ocean Blvd. at Poppy Ave. There is an equally fine view into Little Corona City Beach and southward.

Return to Marguerite Ave. (5.5) and cruise past Jasmine Ave., the entry to the state beach. In another 0.1 mile is Heliotrope Ave. with a grassy overlook point which is directly above hillside residences. Just beyond is another mini-park (with water fountain) and vista point, this one with an excellent view down the breakwater and into Lower Newport Bay (5.8).

Soon, Ocean Blvd. fuses into Bayview Dr. which turns right and becomes Carnation Ave. Bike to the north end of this street for an interesting overlook of the harbor, Begonia Park and lower Carnation Ave. (6.1). The two Carnation Ave. segments used to be at the same level until that "terrible quake of '38" (just kidding!). Backtrack to Seaview Ave., turn left on Fern Leaf Ave. and follow a steep downhill to Bayside Dr. (6.4).

Bayside Drive. Turn left (northwest) and glide downhill a short distance on a tight roadway with the coastal bluffs to the right. The first view of the marina is at (7.1), followed by a transition back to a residential area (7.3), then a return to a marina setting near the classy looking Bahia Corinthian Yacht Club. The area returns to residential, now with bayside berths and classy boats, as the route passes Jamboree Rd. (7.7). Here is the Newport Beach Yacht Club and the Bayside Shopping Center, complete with a market and a classy restaurant at it's western edge.

59

Pass alongside a canal with the lovely Balboa Island homes, each with its own boatslip, across the water. In 0.3 mile is the Balboa Yacht Basin road entry and at (8.5) the route returns to PCH. Bike across the bridge and carefully ride the narrow Class X segment back to Riverside Ave. and the trip starting point (10.1).

CONNECTING TRIPS: 1) Connection with the Sunset Beach to Newport Beach Strand tour (Trip #4) - continue northwest past Riverside Ave. on PCH and take the southside walkway up to Newport Blvd. Cross the bridge and pedal to Ocean Front; 2) connection with the Upper Newport Bay ride and Newport Beach/Irvine Loop (Trips #6 and #7, respectively) - turn north on Jamboree Rd. and go 1/4 mile to Backbay Dr.; 3) connection with the Laguna Beach Tour (Trip #10) - follow the end of Ocean Blvd. as it curves north and becomes Poppy Dr. and bike 0.3 mile to PCH. Turn right (southeast) and go 0.15 mile to Seaward Rd.

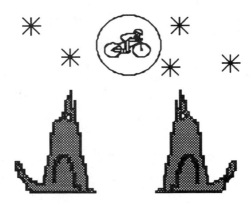

TRIP #16 - SAN CLEMENTE TO SAN DIEGO

GENERAL LOCATION: San Clemente, Camp Pendleton, Oceanside, Carlsbad, La Jolla, San Diego

LEVEL OF DIFFICULTY: One way - strenuous
Distance - 67.2 miles
Elevation gain - periodic moderate-to-steep grades;
sheer grade at Torrey Pines Reserve

HIGHLIGHTS: Few trips that we've ridden have the variety and natural scenic beauty of this coastal classic. The entire tour described follows the Pacific Coast Bicentennial Bike Route, predominantly on Class I and Class II roadway. This classic visits the seaside bluffs of San Onofre State Beach, the hilly roads through Camp Pendleton and cruises along the beaches of cities from Oceanside to Del Mar. Next is a breathtaking scenic ride into the Torrey Pines State Beach area followed by a breathtaking (huff-puff) sheer climb into the lovely woodlands of the Torrey Pines State Reserve. The trip winds up with a brief La Jolla City tour, a pedal on the periphery of both Mission Bay and San Diego Bay, and ends near the Cruise Ship Terminal area of downtown San Diego.

An option is to start this trip from Santa Ana or Oceanside and take the AMTRAK on the return leg. Refer to **The AMTRAK Option** at the end of the trip description.

TRAILHEAD: From the San Diego Fwy. exit at Christianos Rd. and drive north of the freeway to El Camino Real (ECR). Find parking subject to local traffic laws. If an over-night trip is planned, do not park on El Camino Real; an option is to park in a nearby residential area, subject to posted laws. AMTRAK riders can use the parking lots at or near the station.

Bring a couple of filled water bottles, particularly on hot days. There are public water sources at parks and commercial businesses scattered along the entire route.

TRIP DESCRIPTION: **San Onofre.** Return to Christianos Rd. and pedal to the Class I trail entry just west of the southbound freeway on-ramp. Follow the Class I road along the rolling terrain of the oceanside bluffs. In one mile, pass through a fence and follow a Class II frontage road, then cross over the northernmost Camp Pendleton entry at Basilone Rd. Bike on a bridge over the railroad tracks (2.5),

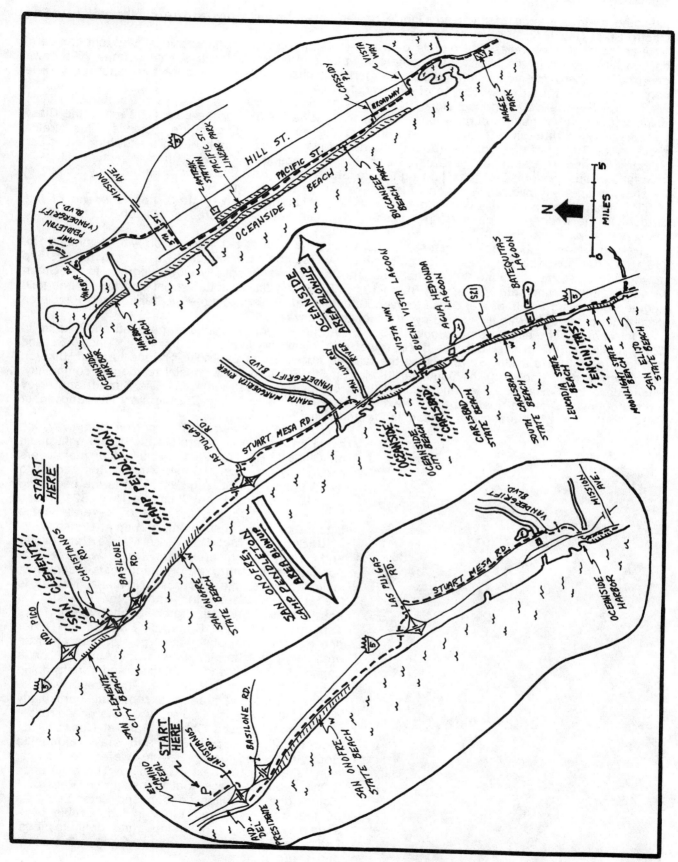

TRIP #16A - SAN CLEMENTE TO SAN DIEGO

pass the main entrance of the San Onofre power generating station, and reach the entry to San Onofre State Beach (4.0).

For the next three miles, the bicycle path bee-lines through the park, passing RV's, tent campers, canyon hiking trails to the beach, and numerous water and restroom stops. If time permits, hike down one of the marked, scenic canyon trails. At the park's southern end, pass through the motorized vehicle barrier and ride on the Class I section of old Hwy. 1.

Camp Pendleton. Continue along the top of the ocean bluffs, pass below an automobile vista point, and follow the path through a tunnel under the freeway (9.3). For the next 1-1/2 miles, the Class I roadway goes through flat and arid terrain with the freeway fading in the distance. This stretch provides the feeling of real isolation (barring the numerous passing bikers). At trail's end, turn left at Las Pulgas Rd. and check in at the Camp Pendleton entrance gate (11.2). (Bring a picture ID as a precaution.) Just beyond the gate, turn right onto Stuart Mesa Rd., pass Camp Flores (Boy Scouts of America) in one-half mile, and stay on Stuart Mesa Rd. by turning right.

The next three miles is on rolling hills with a particularly tough upgrade near the end of this stretch. In the middle section, the road passes the main Los Flores area at Nelson Dr. (Avoid the menacing tank parked there!)

Pass the road to the Cook overcrossing and stay to the right at the intersection with Hammond Rd. (16.1). Pedal past the large fields of cultivated flowers, continue alongside a canyon on a steep downgrade, pass the surrounding salt marshes, and then pump an equally steep upgrade to the Stuart Mesa Rd. intersection with Vandergrift Blvd. (19.1). Turn right on the latter street and bike a one-mile upgrade of varying levels of steepness to Wire Mountain Rd. Pass that street, exit the Camp Pendleton main gate, cross San Rafael Dr., and cycle under the freeway (20.7).

Oceanside. The street name is now Harbor Dr. At the first intersection turn hard left and bike up to Class II Hill St. (the prettier but less direct route is to follow the winding Harbor Dr. to Pacific St. and turn left), go 0.8 mile to 6th St. and cross the railroad tracks. Pedal to Pacific St. and turn left. Bike on that Class III road (including the southward jig-jog at 5th St.) through a coastal residential community. Pass above the Oceanside Pier and Pacific Street Linear Park (restrooms and The Strand) and enjoy the periodic views of the nearby beach. Next, pedal 1-1/4 miles to Morse St. and cozy little Buccaneer Beach Park, which has restrooms, limited shade and a tiny snack stand.

Oceanside Beach

Turn left on Cassidy St., right on Broadway, left again on Vista Wy. (all are Class III), and right again on Class II Hill St. (25.1). This set of maneuvers occurs over a short 0.6-mile stretch, but serves to avoid a busy Hill St. segment. This is the beginning of a 16-mile stretch on California Hwy. S21. Cross Buena Vista Lagoon, the first of several scenic lagoons on this trip segment, and enter Carlsbad.

Carlsbad to Del Mar. Pass Magee Park (water and shade), and cruise an area with several popular, but contrasting, dining establishments, including venerable and posh Neimans. Nearby is the stately Carlsbad Inn and Hotel. Next is the entrance to Carlsbad State Beach (water). Pass Tamarack Ave. and Tamarack Surf Beach (water and a great surfer observation point.), then enter an area with the fisherman working the Agua Hedionda Lagoon to the left and sunbathers and surfers doing their thing on the ocean side. The scenery in the southern Carlsbad area is exceptional, particularly because the bikeway is directly on the oceanfront.

The road passes Cannon Park at Cannon Rd., then Palomar Airport Rd., and stays alongside South Carlsbad State Beach (water, restrooms, camp sites) for the next 2-1/2 miles. The main entry to this beautiful beach is at Poinsettia Ln. Pass over picturesque Batiquitos Lagoon and enter Leucadia as the tree-lined road turns inland. Cruise by a series of inviting lunch stops and delicatessens, Leucadia Blvd. (33.6), Leucadia Park (with water), and enter Encinitas.

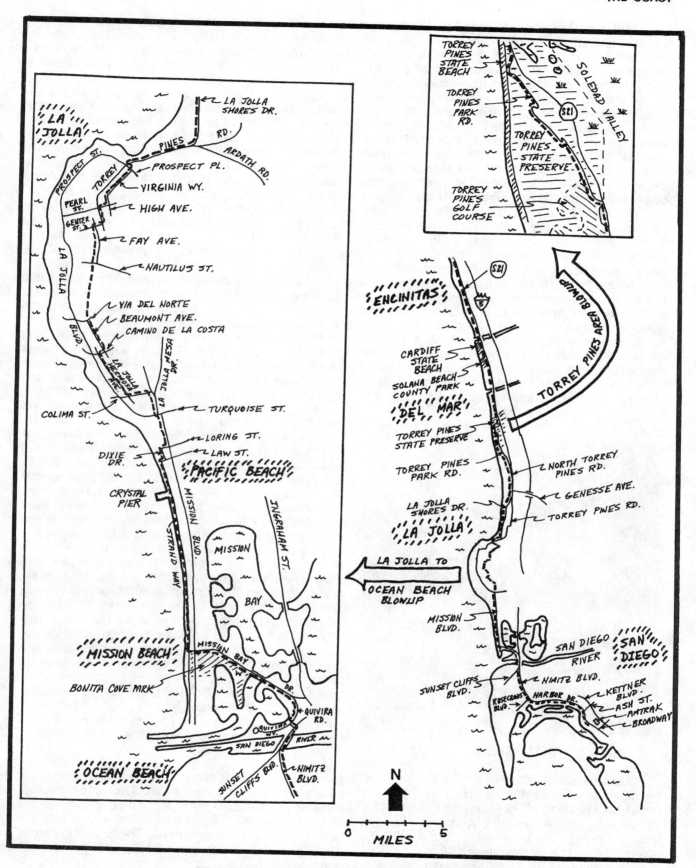

TRIP #16B - SAN CLEMENTE TO SAN DIEGO

The Class II road passes the Moonlight State Beach entry at Encinitas Blvd. (water), the interesting Lumberyard shopping area and the palatial Indian grounds of Swamis City Park. Hwy. S21 returns to the beachfront and passes San Elijo State Beach (water) at Cardiff-by-the-Sea. There is an exceptional view of the coastal cliffs to the south from this area. The bikeway is two-way, Class II, although there is a Class I path on the opposite side of the street.

Bike on the bridge over the expansive San Elijo Lagoon with Cardiff State Beach on the opposite side. Follow a short upgrade away from the ocean to Solana Beach. Stop at one of the cyclist-oriented eateries along the highway in this area. Menu choices include such goodies as "power sandwiches " and "energy drinks." Cross over the lagoon created by the San Dieguito River, take in the postcard view of the Del Mar Racetrack just inland, and enter the city of Del Mar (40.5).

Just past 27th St., start a one-mile upgrade heading inland and enjoy the periodic views of the city below. The grade is steep for 1/4 mile, then lessens to a steady, mild uphill. The road passes several posh inns and Del Mar Heights Rd. (42.7), then reaches its local high point just beyond.

Now all the work pays off! Follow a steep downgrade that opens up to one of the trip's premier spectacles -- the view across Soledad Valley and the nearby small lagoon, as well as the forested hills of the Torrey Pines State Preserve in the distance. Return to sea level at the gigantic seaside-lagoon play area. Follow the bikeway into Torrey Pines State Beach. (An option is to stay on Hwy. S21 at this point; this option is faster, but far less scenic.)

Torrey Pines State Preserve. Follow a steep upgrade which gets even steeper beyond the first curve. In this segment is some very difficult sustained biking, particularly after the prior 44-plus miles. In 0.6 mile of sheer upgrade is the North Grove area with several foot trails leading into the surrounding forest. Continue a steep uphill through the lovely forested preserve, then pass the ranger station and a fantastic overlook of La Jolla. Start another upgrade (350 feet elevation gain in the first mile) which soon flattens significantly. The path angles back towards the highway and offers some excellent inland views. Pedal along the Torrey Pines Memorial Golf Course and reach the top of this extended pull 1.9 miles from the beach. Return to S21 (North Torrey Pines Rd.) and follow the rolling hills along the golf course past Science Park Rd., the Scripps Clinic and reach Genesee Ave. (47.0).

Torrey Pines State Preserve

La Jolla. Veer right and bike downhill on the Class II tree-lined road. Pass Torrey Pines Scenic Dr. (the turnoff to the San Diego Glider Port and the Salk Institute), bike alongside the University of California, San Diego campus, and in 0.9 mile turn right again at La Jolla Shores Dr. In 0.6 mile on this Class III road, pass Horizon Wy. and begin a steep and winding downgrade on the lovely treed highway. There is a fine vista just beyond Horizon Wy. Pass the Scripps Aquarium and Museum and in 0.3 mile reach a flat (49.7).

In 0.6 mile, turn right at Torrey Pines Rd. and follow a workout Class II uphill for 0.9 mile to the crest at Prospect Pl. Turn left and bike a short, steep uphill to Virginia Wy. (The route described for the next 2.6 miles is the low-traffic option.) The well-marked Class III route passes through a residential neighborhood and in succession turns left on High Ave., right on Pearl St., left on Girard Ave., right on Genter St., left on Fay Ave. and right on Nautilus St. Ride a short distance to a Class I path, cruise 3/4-mile on that rural bikeway and turn left at Beaumont Ave. Pedal to Camino De La Costa, turn right and then left again on La Jolla Hermosa Ave.

Pacific Beach. To reach the beach, turn left on Colima St., right at La Jolla Mesa Dr. (which becomes Mission Blvd.), right on Loring St., left on Dixie Dr., and right on Law St. This places cyclists at the northern end of the Class I Strand Wy. on the ocean (56.4).

Bike south 1.9 miles to Ventura Pl. on this scenic and well-populated path. The strand bikeway passes Crystal Pier and cruises both the Pacific Beach and Mission Beach areas. There are numerous commercial stops in this stretch. A word of caution! On one trip, we arrived at 5:00 PM on Saturday night; we had to leave the super-crowded strand (walkers, bikers, skaters, skate boarders, wind surfers ---- OK, just kidding!) and followed the back alley known as Strand Wy. (58.8).

64

Mission Bay. Bike on Ventura Pl. past the amusement park and continue east on what is now Mission Bay Dr. Turn left into Bonita Cove Park (water, restrooms, shade, scenic harbor views) and pedal on the Class I trail that parallels Mission Bay Dr. to a point just short of the bridge over Mission Bay Channel. Follow the small road up to the bridge. The scenic views from all bridges in this area are exceptional. Reenter the main road and follow the Class II route over the bridge, turning right into Quivira Rd. Glide around Quivira Basin to the junction where the road becomes Quivira Wy. and turn left onto Sunset Cliffs Blvd.

Ocean Beach to Point Loma. Bike on the bridge over the San Diego River and observe the myriad of bikepaths through the area (60.7). Stay with the fast-moving traffic for the few hundred yards needed to turn left at Nimitz Blvd. (We found no easy or low traffic route to this intersection.)

Follow this Class II divided roadway about two miles through primarily residential territory being very wary of cars entering and exiting Nimitz Blvd. north of Tennyson St. The route turns sharply left at North Harbor Dr. at the Nimitz Blvd. terminus.

San Diego Bay. Pedal on the sidewalk next to the Fleet Anti-Submarine Warfare School (where in Don's younger Navy days, he learned that, "A collision at sea can ruin a man's entire day"), then observe the cement-bound U.S.S. Recruit "floating" majestically along the north side of the highway. Pass over the bridge and on the opposite side, follow the Class I bikepath that meanders through the cozy mile-long thread of Spanish Landing Park. There are scattered water sources and restrooms, tree shade, and benches from which to observe the comings and goings in the bay.

Proceed around the Sheraton Hotel (65.2) and cross Harbor Island Dr., returning to a Class I path along the harbor. Pedal alongside the San Diego International Airport, pass the U.S. Coast Guard Station, cross Laurel St. and take in the view of the San Diego City skyline. The bikeway rounds the bend of the harbor heading south, passes by the old windsailer, Star of India (now a museum), and reaches the trip's end point at the Cruise Ship Terminal (and a few eateries) just beyond. (67.2).

Excursion: **The AMTRAK Return Trip Option.** Park at either the Santa Ana or Oceanside AMTRAK stations (these have baggage stops), bike to San Diego, and take the train on the return trip. The San Diego station is near the intersection of Kettner Blvd. and "C" St. The biker's "special" presently leaves San Diego twice daily on the weekend (be there 45 minutes early). Call AMTRAK at 800-872-7245 for the latest information before starting the trip.

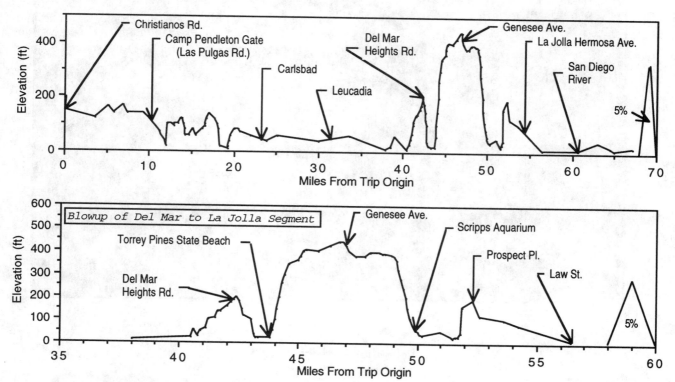

CONNECTING TRIPS: Continuation with the Doheny/San Clemente Bike Route (Trip #14) - at the trip origin, bike north on El Camino Real.

RIVER TRAILS

San Diego Creek Outlet to Upper Newport Bay

TRIPS #17A-#17C - SANTA ANA RIVER TRAIL

This moderate-to-strenuous level Santa Ana River trip from Prado Dam to Huntington Beach (61.2 strenuous miles round trip) is broken up into three sections. The general area map for the entire trip is provided below. Almost the entire route is Class I path with horse trails paralleling much of the bikeway. There are two places where the bikepath crosses the Santa Ana River bottom (Katella Ave. and 17th St.) and several areas where the path is very near the water (e.g., Orangewood Ave.). In high water situations, the nominal route is blocked by locked fences. Cyclists must return to and cross highways, as necessary, in these instances.

Trip #17A explores the most northerly section of the bikepath starting below Prado Dam, visiting Featherly Park and ending at Yorba Regional Park. Trip #17B starts at Yorba Regional Park, goes through a short, scenic treed section early in the route and terminates at Anaheim Stadium or El Camino Park. Trip #17C starts at El Camino Park, passes along Centennial Regional Park and the Mesa Verde Country Club and lets out at the Pacific Ocean in Huntington Beach.

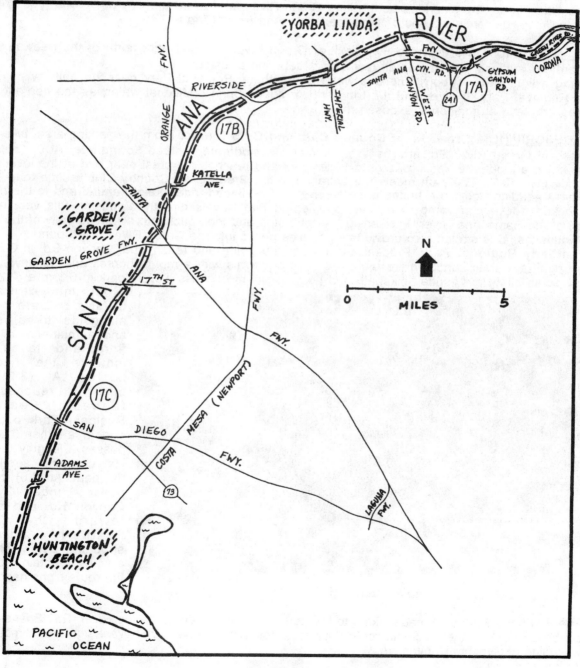

TRIP #17A - SANTA ANA RIVER: GREEN RIVER ROAD TO YORBA PARK

GENERAL LOCATION: Prado Dam, Anaheim Hills, Yorba Linda

LEVEL OF DIFFICULTY: One way - moderate; up and back - moderate
Distance - 7.4 miles (one way)
Elevation gain - periodic moderate grades

HIGHLIGHTS: At the top end of the Santa Ana River Trail, this predominantly Class I route starts just south of the Prado Dam at Green River Rd. and ends at Yorba Regional Park. Along the way are a few rolling hills, a horse corral, a mini-motorcross area for children, inviting Featherly Regional Park, and a short tour of La Palma Ave. Allow time for bicycle tours of Featherly and Yorba Regional Parks, which have an abundance of bikepaths or bikeable roadways. For cyclists interested in a more lengthy workout, the trip can be extended north along Green River Rd. toward the City of Corona (see Trip #17 Extension map) or continued south along the Santa Ana River (Trip #17B).

TRAILHEAD: From the Riverside Fwy., exit at Green River Rd. and park north of the freeway where there are gas stations, a mini-market, fast-food outlets and a restaurant.
     Bring a light water supply. There is water at Featherly Regional Park near the halfway point and Yorba Regional Park. If extending the trip north or south, bring additional water, as the nearest water supplies are several additional, exposed miles away.

TRIP DESCRIPTION: **Green River Country Club and Golf Course.** From the parking area, bike south on Class III Green River Rd. and begin an immediate moderate-to-steep downgrade. At 0.3 mile, the route begins a moderate uphill, passes a trailer park and reaches the crest near and at the level of the Riverside Fwy. (0.7). The path meets the entrance to the Green River Country Club, a little road (taboo to bikers) heading right on a bridge over the river (1.0). Instead, ride straight ahead and to the right of the blocked freeway on-ramp to a Class I bikepath that travels directly alongside this very narrow stretch of the Santa Ana River. Further up the trail, stop and look back into a framed view of the Santa Ana Mountains. This stretch also provides some nice peeks into the Green River Golf Course.
     Featherly Regional Park. Proceed up a moderate grade and reach Coal Canyon Rd. in 0.2 mile. To the right is a small ranch where there are several corrals with a mix of horses and donkeys. Cycle directly south along the asphalt bikepath and pass a mini-motorcross bicycle park in 0.3 mile (2.2).

Near Yorba Regional Park

For the next mile, the Class I path stays alongside trees, scrub, and a multitude of other flora and fauna that indicate the river is nearby. At (3.2), the bikeway reaches the fenced Featherly Regional Park boundary and in another 0.2 mile, passes a lengthy tent and RV camping section of the park. At (3.6) the trail passes under Gypsum Canyon Rd. and swings toward the large Featherly entrance structure, below which is a water fountain. Look for the route signs near here.

     The *Featherly Park* sign leads bikers to the park's main entrance, while the *River Trail East* sign just directs bikers back to the incoming route. Our route follows the *River Trail West* sign and climbs up to the west side of Gypsum Canyon Rd.

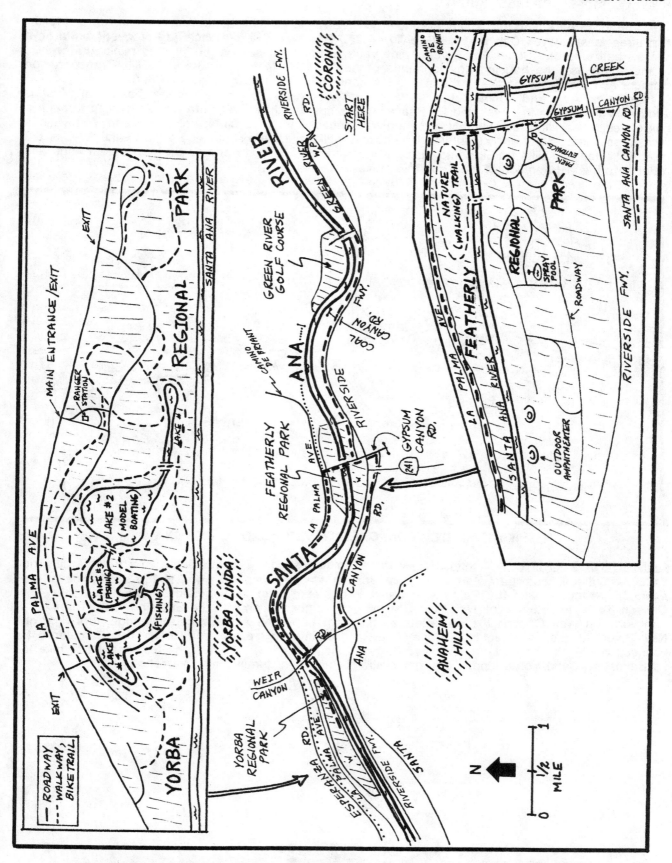

TRIP #17A - SANTA ANA RIVER: GREEN RIVER ROAD TO YORBA REGIONAL PARK

One option here is to turn south, go under the freeway to Class II Santa Ana Canyon Rd. and follow that street east to Weir Canyon Rd. (See Trip # 25.) However, the reference ride proceeds north on a Class I path over the Santa Ana River, a fine vantage point for viewing the gypsum mining in the hills to the southeast, the housing developments of Anaheim Hills, the San Joaquin Hills Transportation Corridor and the classy homes in the hills to the north. Bike 0.3 mile to road's end (4.0).

La Palma Ave. and Yorba Regional Park. Turn left (west) and proceed on the Class I trail which is sandwiched between the river and La Palma Ave. Enjoy the thick river flora while bicycling through a mix of residential, light commercial and industrial sections for 3.1 uninterrupted miles to Yorba Linda Blvd. Cross that street and pedal along the narrow walkway on the south side of La Palma Ave. for 0.3 mile. Take the first bike trail left into Yorba Regional Park, then ride around the park's east edge and return to a riverside portion of the Santa Ana River Bike Trail (7.4).

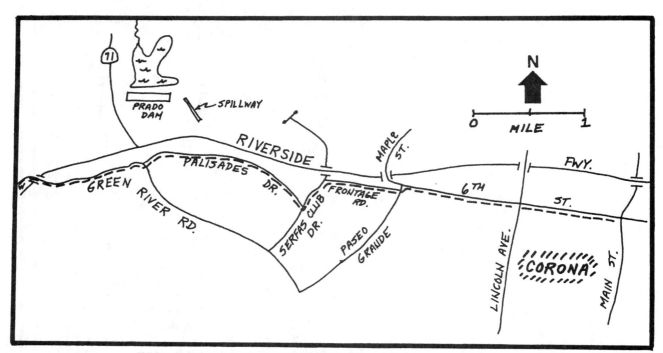

TRIP #17A EXTENSION: GREEN RIVER ROAD TO CORONA

CONNECTING TRIPS: 1) Continuation with the middle segment of the Santa Ana River Trail (Trip #17B) - continue south past Yorba Regional Park and across Imperial Hwy. to the south side of the river; 2) connection with the Santa Ana Canyon Rd. route (Trip #25) - continue west on Santa Ana Canyon Rd. at its intersection with Weir Canyon Rd.; 3) connection with the El Cajon Trail (Trip #22) - turn north on Weir Canyon Rd. at its intersection with La Palma Ave. Cross the bridge, turn right on New River Rd. then right again at Esperanza Rd. Continue to the trail entry near Avd. Barcelona; 4) connection with the Yorba Linda Bits and Pieces Tour (Trip # 43) - from Yorba Regional Park, bike to La Palma Ave. and Yorba Linda Blvd. going straight ahead or turning left, respectively.

TRIP #17B - SANTA ANA RIVER: YORBA TO EL CAMINO REAL PARK

<u>**GENERAL LOCATION**</u>: Yorba Linda, Placentia, Orange

<u>**LEVEL OF DIFFICULTY**</u>:   One way - easy; up and back - moderate
Distance - 10.0 miles (one way)
Elevation gain - essentially flat

<u>**HIGHLIGHTS**</u>: This section of the river ride starts at Yorba Regional Park which, in itself, could serve as a nice area for a family biking excursion. The trip joins the Santa Ana River Trail at any one of several points from within the park, passes through a lovely area of trees and grassy knolls for several miles, and then transitions into an open and exposed route for the remainder of the ride. In the latter section are a gigantic open mining pit, Anaheim Stadium, and the terminal point at shaded El Camino Real Park.

<u>**TRAILHEAD**</u>: From the Riverside Fwy., take the Imperial Hwy. exit and drive 1/4 mile north to La Palma Ave. Turn right (east) and travel about one mile to free parking at the baseball diamonds/soccer fields south of the roadway. Better yet, pay a small fee and park within Yorba Regional Park itself; the entrance is about another 3/4 mile further northeast on La Palma Ave.

Only a moderate water supply is needed. There are both water and restroom facilities at the beginning of the trip (at the park) and near the end (at a small restroom directly on the bikeway). There is also a small market stop along the way.

<u>**TRIP DESCRIPTION**</u>: **Yorba Regional Park to "The Rest Stop."** There are bikepaths around the lakes and throughout Yorba Regional Park (see the detailed map accompanying the prior ride). Follow the park bikepath nearest the river and take one of the many paved or direct paths across to the river trail. Within the first mile from the main parking area within the park, there is marshland along the river with many birds.

Bicycle along the natural riverbed and cross from the north to the south levee at Imperial Hwy. (2.1). Pass through a pleasant area with grassy knolls, trees, bushes, a few joggers, and even a few horseback riders (on a paralleling path). At (3.9), pass under Lakeview Ave. and at (4.9) the Riverside Fwy. Stop and check out the man-made water holding basins in the riverbed -- they're cleverly constructed. At (5.1), pass an exit through a fence which leads to a little market that has soft drinks and other "stuff" on ice. Do the entire Santa Ana River and you will know why we call this "The Rest Stop!"

Anaheim Stadium and El Camino Real Park. The river bends in a more southerly direction in this area. Pass under Glassell St. (6.2) and ride alongside a gigantic open mining pit in another 0.3 mile. Next the path crosses under Lincoln Ave. (7.0) and Ball Rd. (8.3) while traveling through an industrial area.

At (9.1), there is a small restroom stop (with water) alongside the bike trail. Soon, the route crosses the river bottom at Katella Ave. (9.3). Shortly after, the bikepath travels alongside Anaheim Stadium and under the Orange Fwy. (9.7). In 0.3 mile is Orangewood Ave.; a nearby exit to the north and a right turn at Stadium Wy. will lead to Anaheim Stadium. For our reference trip, however, an exit to the south and an additional 0.4 mile pedal leads to El Camino Real Park. (See Trip #17C for a discussion of park facilities.)

<u>**CONNECTING TRIPS**</u>: 1) Connection/continuation with Trips #17A or #17C along the Santa Ana River Trail - follow the described route to the Santa Ana River and turn north (Trip #17A) or continue south from the trip terminus (Trip #17C); 2) connection with the Santa Ana Canyon tour (Trip #25) - at the trip origin, ride to Weir Canyon Rd. (east) or Imperial Hwy. (south) on the Santa Ana River Trail. Cross the Riverside Fwy. and head in either direction on Santa Ana Canyon Rd.; 3) connection with the Anaheim Hills ride (Trip #44) - exit the river at Lincoln Ave. and bike east across the river to Santiago Blvd.

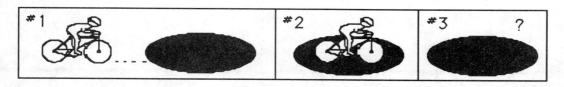

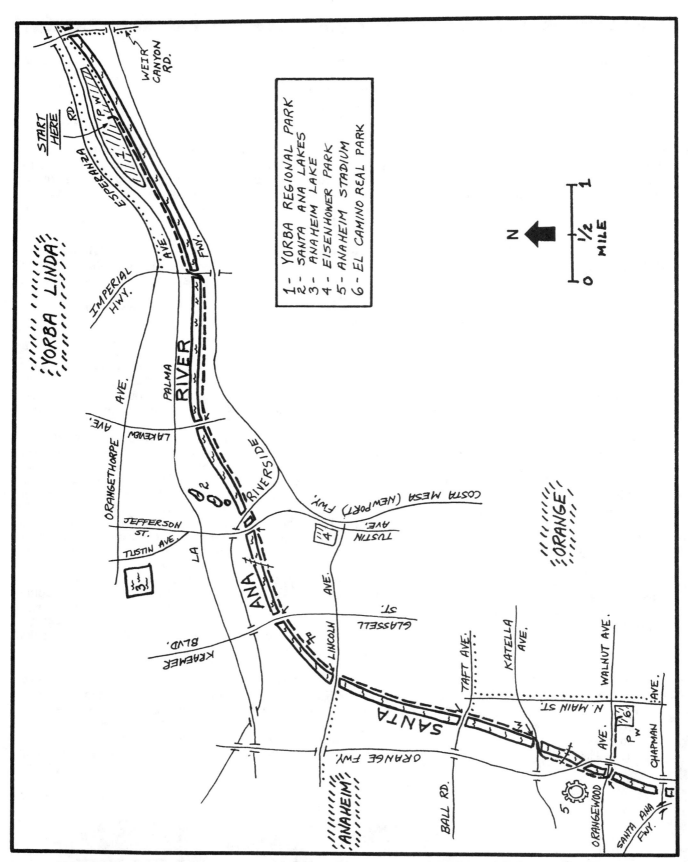

TRIP #17B - SANTA ANA RIVER: YORBA REGIONAL PARK TO EL CAMINO REAL PARK

TRIP #17C - SANTA ANA RIVER: EL CAMINO PARK TO PACIFIC OCEAN

GENERAL LOCATION: Orange, Garden Grove, Costa Mesa, Huntington Beach

LEVEL OF DIFFICULTY: One way - easy; up and back - moderate
Distance - 13.4 miles (one way)
Elevation gain - essentially flat

HIGHLIGHTS: Initially, this Santa Ana River Bike Trail segment is a tree-lined route along a portion of the riverbed that is lush meadowland. The Class I bikeway passes near several golf courses, as well as a couple of small parks and the large and pretty Centennial Regional Park. In between some of these lovely sights is a lot of concrete and industry backed up along the river. The trip lets out at a pleasant stretch of beach at the southern end of Huntington State Beach.

TRAILHEAD: From the Santa Ana Fwy., exit at Katella Ave. and head east 3/4 mile to State College Blvd. Turn right (south) and make a left turn in 0.4 mile at Orangewood Ave., then continue one mile to El Camino Real Park. The park has water, limited shade, children's play area and varied sports facilities. There is parking closer to the river on the side streets off Orangewood Ave.; however, read the parking signs carefully if you park here. From the Orange Fwy., exit at Orangewood Ave. and proceed east about 0.5 mile. From the Garden Grove Fwy., exit at Main St. and proceed north about 1-1/4 mile to Orangewood Ave. and turn left.

Fill a water bottle at the park. There are facilities at a couple of nearby stops along the trip south, or travel one mile north (see Trip #17B) where there is a restroom and water along the bikeway.

TRIP DESCRIPTION: **Lower Santa Ana River Meadowland.** From El Camino Real Park, bike 0.4 mile west on Orangewood Ave. to the entrance point on the west side of the river. Cruise south and pass Chapman Ave. (1.0), the Santa Ana Fwy. and the Garden Grove Fwy. (1.8).

Near the Warner Ave. Overpass

Just beyond this point is one of the most refreshing stretches of the trip. The river bottom is a rich meadowland for the next 1-2 miles and the bikepath meanders through a surrounding mini-forest. Pass Garden Grove Blvd., which is an exit to luscious River View Golf Course (2.2). Soon after is Alona Park with a children's play area, barbecue facilities and a biker's rest stop (water, restroom).

Centennial Regional Park. At 17th St., the bikepath crosses the river bottom (3.4). From this point to the ocean, the river is one long concrete waterway. Pass under Fairview St. (3.8), 5th St., McFadden Ave. and Edinger Ave. (6.0). Shortly after Edinger Ave. and about 200 yards off the bikepath is inviting Centennial Regional Park with its little lakes, birds and shady gazebos. There is a maze of bikeways/walkways throughout the park, as well as restroom facilities. (The park circuit by itself might serve as a grand locale for family bike outing.)

Cycle south past Harbor Blvd. (6.9), Warner Ave. and pass one of the steepest underpasses of the river bikeway system at Slater Ave. (7.6). Then cross under Talbert Ave. and, at (8.1), traverse a tunnel under the San Diego Fwy. (be watchful for broken glass) and pass a grassy rest area next to the path. The route becomes more scenic as it cruises alongside the Mesa Verde Country Club (9.4), passes under Adams St., and by the site of Fairview Regional Park (10.7).

73

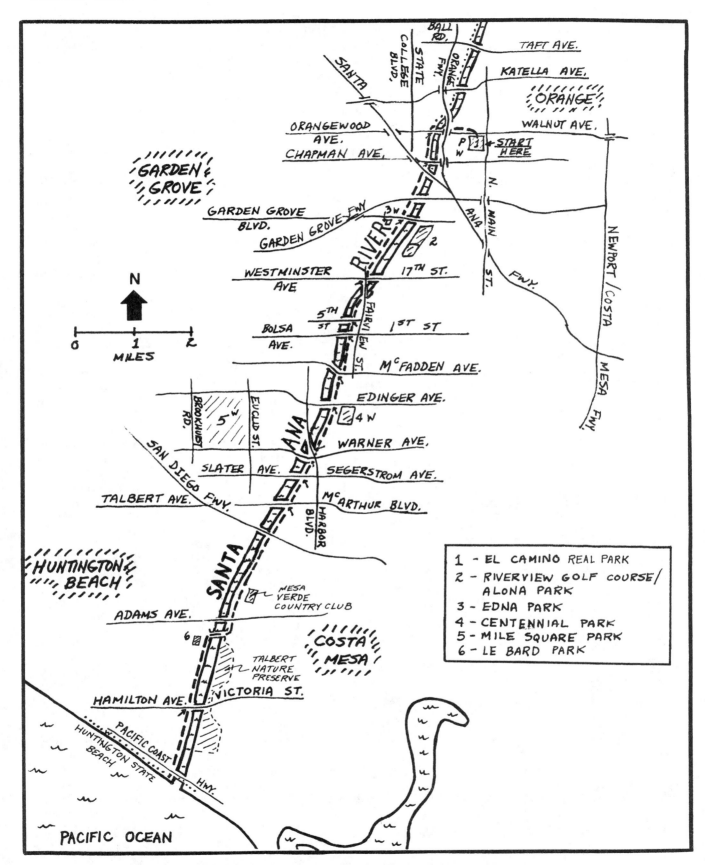

TRIP #17C - SANTA ANA RIVER: EL CAMINO PARK TO PACIFIC OCEAN

The Coast. In about a mile, follow the wooden bike bridge across the river to the west side; there is a small park/playground a few hundred yards beyond the crossing and off the trail at Le Bard Park (water) (10.9). Across the river is the Talbert Nature Preserve. Proceed south and pass Victoria St./Hamilton Ave. (11.9), the "fragrant" Orange County Sanitation Treatment Plant (12.9) and a small bridge over a separate channel just north of Pacific Coast Highway (PCH) (13.3). In another 0.1 mile, pass under PCH and enter Huntington State Beach at the junction with the Sunset Beach-Newport Beach Strand bikepath.

CONNECTING TRIPS: 1) Continuation with the Sunset Beach-Newport Beach Strand route (Trip #2) - at the terminus of the Santa Ana River Trail, turn south and pass over the bridge/bikeway toward Newport Beach or turn north and head towards Sunset Beach; 2) connection with Mile Square Regional Park (Trip #5) - turn west at Edinger Ave. or Warner Ave. and turn into the park in about one mile at Euclid St.

TRIP #18 - SAN DIEGO CREEK

GENERAL LOCATION: Newport Beach, Irvine

LEVEL OF DIFFICULTY: One way - easy; up and back - moderate
Distance - 9.9 miles (one way)
Elevation gain - generally flat; periodic light grades in Yale Loop area

HIGHLIGHTS: This pleasant trip follows San Diego Creek upstream starting from its confluence with upper Newport Bay. The creek is soil-lined for the most part and contains marshes, water pools, and mud flats at low water, particularly along the lower creek segment. The route passes near a state wildlife preserve, the University of California, Irvine Campus, two parks and the attractively-developed Yale Loop residential area. The 2.1-mile end segment beyond Jeffrey Rd. transits less-developed territory, terminating at the Laguna Fwy. There are numerous spur trips off the main route. The trip is nearly 100% Class I on well-maintained bike surfaces.

TRAILHEAD: From the intersection of Pacific Coast Highway (PCH) and Jamboree Rd. in Newport Beach, drive north on Jamboree Rd. for 1-1/2 miles to Eastbluff Dr. Turn left, proceed 3/4 mile to Vista Del Sol and turn left again. At Vista Del Oro, the next street, find parking subject to local traffic laws. From the San Diego Fwy., take the Hwy. 73 exit in Costa Mesa and continue to the S. Bristol St. turnoff. Follow this one-way street 1/4 mile further to Jamboree Rd., turn right (south) and drive one-half mile to Eastbluff Dr. Turn right on Eastbluff Dr., then head up the hill 3/4 mile to Vista Del Sol and find parking as described above. From the Costa Mesa Fwy., exit southeast at State Hwy. 73 and continue as described above.

Bring a moderate water supply. There are well-placed public water stops near the bikeway up to Jeffrey Rd. The remaining 2.1-mile segment is waterless.

TRIP DESCRIPTION: **Upper Newport Bay to U. C. Irvine.** From the intersection of Eastbluff Dr. and Jamboree Rd., follow the bikepath on the west side of Jamboree Rd. down to San Diego Creek. Follow the trail sharply right and parallel to the creek on its south bank, passing under Jamboree Rd. (0.3). Proceed into the quiet, open, natural area above the soil-lined river bed and go over a small wooden bridge (0.5). Pass an outlet to the University Dr./S. Bristol St. intersection (See the **Bonita Creek Trail**

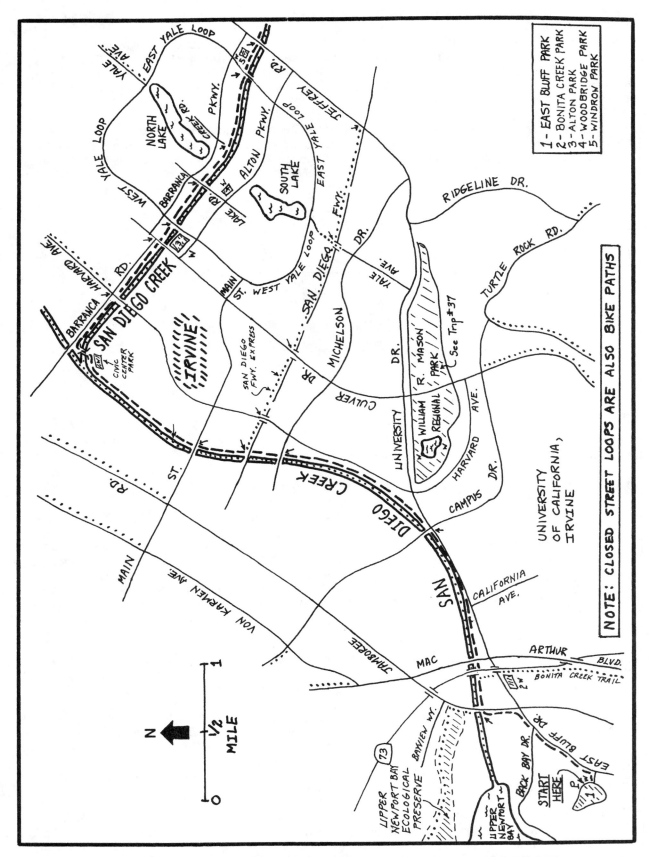

TRIP #18 - SAN DIEGO CREEK: JAMBOREE ROAD TO JEFFREY ROAD

Excursion below.) and bike under the San Joaquin Hills Transportation Corridor. In another 0.1 mile is the MacArthur Trail junction which leads to MacArthur Blvd. There is a sign with a map of the local streets and trails, one of several along the route.

Windrow Park

Cycle under MacArthur Blvd and then meet the California Rd. junction (1.1). To the left, on the other side of the creek bank, are the man-made ponds of the State Wildlife Preserve. To the right is the California Rd. entry along the periphery of the U.C. Irvine campus. Our reference route passes under Campus Dr. (1.6) and begins a slow turn to the north away from University Dr. There is a junction off to the right which leads to the William R. Mason Regional Park.

The Marshlands to Peters Canyon Channel. On the San Diego Creek route, there is a marshy area that seems to be a favorite for a variety of birds and even a few ducks (1.8). Cycle alongside the Rancho San Joaquin Country Club/Golf Course and then jig-jog on a bridge over a small wash (2.8). In turn, pedal under Michelson Dr., the San Diego Fwy., and Main St. (3.5) through some of the more open territory of the trip. There are trail exits from each of these undercrossings, with the exit along the San Diego Fwy. described in the **San Diego Freeway Express** Excursion in Trip #8.

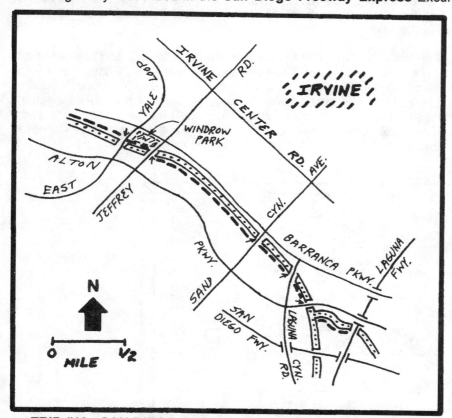

TRIP #18 - SAN DIEGO CREEK: JEFFREY RD. TO TRAIL'S END

In a mile from Main St., the bike trail skirts the Irvine Civic Center, passes through Civic Center Park (sports fields and a water fountain), then crosses a bridge to the opposite side of San Diego Creek (4.4). The waterway heading north is the Peters Canyon Channel, while our route takes us right (east) paralleling Barranca Pkwy. The gigantic airship hangers at the now-closed U.S. Marine Corps Air Facility are to the northeast.

Alton Park. In about 0.7 mile, cross Harvard Ave. at the signal, then return along the channel. There is a steep undercrossing at Culver Dr. (may be flooded during storms) and, in 0.2 mile, another at West Yale Loop (5.9). To the right (south) is little Alton Park with restrooms, water fountain, trees and baseball fields. Nearby and accessible West and East Yale themselves are part of a four-mile-plus circular bike loop. (Refer to Trip #8.)

Condomania to Jeffrey Road. Cruise through an area where condominiums are built up alongside the creek with a lovely church across the water (6.2). In 0.2 mile, cross under Lake Rd. (a short spur takes bikers to North Lake) and enter another condo area alongside the creek. Next, pass under Creek Rd. (6.8), pedal along a pleasant eucalyptus-lined stretch, pass the East Yale Loop bikepath, and go under Jeffrey Rd. through a small tunnel (7.8). (The tunnel floods during rainy periods and collects a layer of dirt afterwards. If it is impassable, bike to Barranca Pkwy. or Alton Pkwy. and cross at the light.)

Jeffrey Road to the Laguna Freeway. Turn right and bike to the south creek levee. (Though paved, the north side has road crossings at Valley Oak Dr., Sand Canyon Ave. and Laguna Canyon Rd.) The initial section is residence-surrounded until the cement-block-lined creek creeps up beside Barranca Pkwy. Beyond Sand Canyon Ave., trees lining the bikeway hide Barranca Pkwy. and filter out many of the industrial complexes on the south side (8.9). The creekbed transitions to a natural bottom.

Follow the tree-lined path under Laguna Canyon Rd. (9.2) and Alton Pkwy. (9.5), noting that these under-road sections can flood during Winter rains. Beyond Alton Pkwy., the trail leaves the creek levy and passes next to a modern industrial complex, becoming the Alton Regional Bikeway. Return to creekside in a short distance and cruise to the trail terminus (both north and south side paths) in 0.5 miles from Alton Pkwy. At this point are the steep berms that supports the fenced-off Laguna Fwy. (9.9).

Alternate Return Routes. There are many ways for completing the return trip. The fastest return to Windrow Park is via Alton Pkwy. southbound, then north at Jeffrey Rd. After a return to the creek, there are options to divert south on East Yale Loop and ride to Main St. or to exit the loop at Alton Pkwy. and bike east. The sneakiest and fastest return is to bike south from Windrow Park on Jeffrey Rd. and take the Class I path just to the north side of the San Diego Fwy 1.9 miles to the creek. (See the Trip #8 **San Diego Freeway Express** spur trip.)

Excursion: Bonita Creek Trail. Leave the San Diego Creek and bike to the University Dr./S. Bristol St. intersection. Cross the street and look for the Class I trail on the left (east) bank of brush- and tree-strewn Bonita Creek. Parallel the San Joaquin Transportation Corridor on a mild, steady upgrade 0.7 mile and turn right at its end. In about 20 yards is a junction. Biking south leads to the end of the separated trail at Bison Ave. and MacArthur Blvd. in another 0.5 mile. Taking the junction westbound across the creek leads to a Class I trail which returns downhill alongside Bonita Creek Park. The park, whose entry is at Milano Dr. and La Salud, has restrooms, limited shade, snack shop, recreation fields, sports courts and children's playground. Bypassing the entry leads back to University Dr. The round-trip distance from San Diego Creek to Bison Ave. is 2.8 miles.

CONNECTING TRIPS: 1) Connection with the Upper Newport Bay route (Trip #6) and the Newport Beach/Irvine Loop (Trip #7) - these trips share a common segment on Eastbluff Dr.; 2) connection with the Irvine Bikeway (Trip #8) - exit the creek trail at either West or East Yale Loop; 3) connection with the Laguna Canyon Road tour (Trip # 9) - use the creek outlet at Laguna Canyon Rd.; 4) connection with the Turtle Rock Road ride (Trip #36) leave the creek at Campus Dr. and bike west to street's end; 5) connection with the William R. Mason Regional Park ride (Trip #37) - leave the creek at Campus Dr., turn northeast at University Dr. and cycle 1/2 mile to the park's main entrance.

Bike Sweet Bike

TRIPS #19A-#19E - SAN GABRIEL RIVER TRAIL

The San Gabriel River Trail is probably the premier single river trail in this book. It is heavily plied by bikers from both Orange and Los Angeles Counties, since it starts from the border between the two. The route captures Southern California from the sea through the inland valley to the mountains, all in one continuous 39-mile shot. Taken in the winter after a cold storm, this trip is one of the best in every sense. The general area map is provided below.

The first segment (#19A) explores the river outlet near Seal Beach, a wildlife area to the north and ends at super El Dorado Park. The connection segment (#19B) visits no less than five parks and finishes at Wilderness Park in Downey. The next northerly segment (#19C) leaves Wilderness Park, travels alongside some fine San Gabriel river bottom and ends at one of the tour highpoints, the Whittier Narrows Recreation Area. Trip #19D starts at that fabulous recreation area and ends at another, the Santa Fe Dam Recreation Area. The most northerly segment (#19E) leaves from that dam and ends in the foothills at the entrance to San Gabriel Canyon.

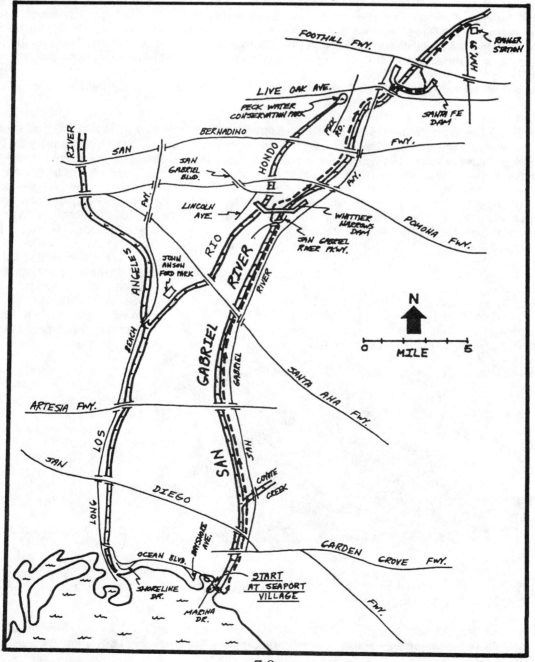

TRIP #19A - SAN GABRIEL RIVER: SEAL BEACH TO EL DORADO PARK

GENERAL LOCATION: Seal Beach - Long Beach

LEVEL OF DIFFICULTY: Up and back - easy
Distance - distance - 5.6 miles (one way)
Elevation gain - essentially flat

HIGHLIGHTS: This is the starting segment of one of the most varied and interesting trips in this book. This is a completely Class I bike route that starts at the scenic lower section of the Gabriel River Trail near the Long Beach Marina and winds up at El Dorado Park. The early part of the trip provides a look at "recreation city" with water, boats, water skiers and jet skiers. The trip transitions into a nature area rich in wildlife and ends in a park that is so inviting that it could serve as a separate family excursion.

TRAILHEAD: Free public parking is available at the Long Beach Marina along Marina Dr. in Naples or along First St. in Seal Beach. From Pacific Coast Highway (PCH) in Seal Beach, turn west on Marina Dr. (2-3 blocks from Main Street in Seal Beach) and drive roughly 1/2 mile to First St. In 1/4 mile, cross the San Gabriel River and continue a short distance into the marina near Seaport Village for parking. The trailhead is at Marina Dr. at the east end (Seal Beach side) of the bridge over the San Gabriel River.

Only a light water supply is needed for this short trip. There are public water sources at the trip origin and terminus.

TRIP DESCRIPTION: **The Scenic Lower River Segment.** The first part of the trip provides views of boaters, water skiers and an interestingly-developed shoreline. The natural river basin passes PCH (0.4), the Westminster Ave. access, and the Haynes Steam Plant (electricity generation). At (2.2), a small alternate Class I bikepath leads off to the east along a 1.2-mile shaded route to Seal Beach Blvd. In this stretch of the river, up to the concrete portion (3.5), cyclists have views of the large bird population that includes pelicans, egrets and the ever-present seagulls. The bikeway passes under the Garden Grove Fwy. (2.3); just beyond is an exit which takes cyclists to College Park Dr. and Edison Park. Next is the San Diego Fwy. undercrossing (3.5). In this part of the bikepath are many "freeway orchards" -- those freeway-locked areas under the power poles filled with containerized plants.

Coyote Creek Bridge Crossing

The Creek Crossing and El Dorado Park. In 0.4 mile, take the signed bikeway/walkway bridge across the river. Do not miss the bridge unless you've decided to change plans and see Coyote Creek (Trip #20). Once over the bridge, there are views across the river to the El Dorado Golf Course and El Dorado Park West. At 0.7 mile from the bridge crossing, reach Willow St. and skirt the edge of the Nature Study Area which is the south end of El Dorado Park East (5.0). Shortly afterward, the bikepath reaches Spring St. and the entry to Areas I and II of the park (5.6).

There are a myriad of bike trails within the park. This portion of the trip is worth a good exploration effort in itself, particularly for family riding.

CONNECTING TRIPS: 1) Continuation with the San Gabriel River Trail (Trip #19B) - bike north beyond El Dorado Park toward Wilderness Park; 2) continuation with the Seal Beach/Sunset Beach tour (Trip

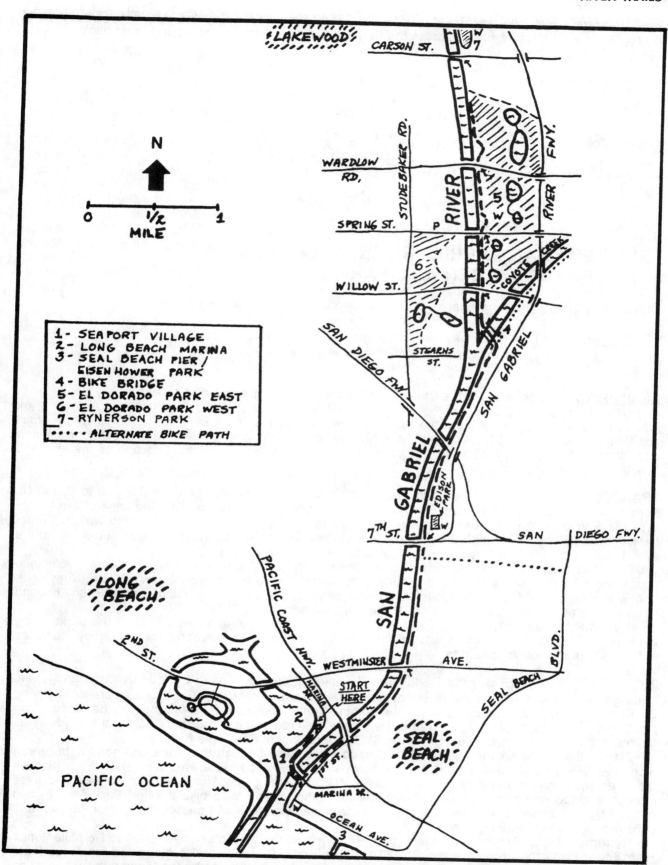

TRIP #19A - SAN GABRIEL RIVER: SEAL BEACH TO EL DORADO PARK

#1) - at the trip origin, bike east on Marina Dr.; 3) connection with the Coyote Creek Trail (Trip #20) - at the eastern end of the bike bridge across the San Gabriel River, stay on the eastern river bank.

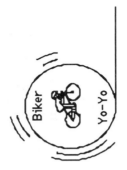

TRIP #19B - SAN GABRIEL RIVER: EL DORADO PARK TO WILDERNESS PARK

GENERAL LOCATION: Long Beach, Lakewood, Cerritos, Norwalk, Downey

LEVEL OF DIFFICULTY: One way - easy; up and back - moderate
Distance - 9.7 miles (one way)
Elevation gain - essentially flat

HIGHLIGHTS: This segment of the Class I San Gabriel River Trail has direct access to five major parks. In particular, this trip should not be completed without a tour of El Dorado Park. Rynerson Park provides a pleasant diversion from the river route and Wilderness Park is a fine rest stop with a small pond/lagoon to dip the toes into before returning to the trip origin. There are horse corrals and equestrian trails beside the bike route in some sections. This is a good workout section as the bike and foot traffic is relatively light.

TRAILHEAD: From the San Diego Fwy., turn north on Palo Verde Ave. and drive 0.9 mile to Spring St. Turn right (east) and continue about 0.8 mile to free parking along Spring St., just west of the bridge over the San Gabriel River. Other options are to head over the bridge and park in the Nature Center parking area (turn south at the park entrance), or to drive up Spring St., make a U-turn and return to the Area II park entrance to the north (right). The latter two options are pay parking.

From the San Gabriel Fwy., turn west on Willow St. (Katella Ave. in Orange County), continue about one mile to Studebaker Rd. and turn right (north). Drive 0.3 mile to Spring St. and turn right. Follow the parking instructions above. For direct entry at Area II (pay parking) from the southbound freeway, exit at Spring St. and turn right at the park entrance.

Bring a light water supply. There is plenty of water and many restroom facilities at the parks along the way. El Dorado Park is a particular delight! Bring some food for the barbecue and enjoy munchies at the park after a tough" bike ride.

TRIP DESCRIPTION: **El Dorado Park.** From the parking area on Spring St., ride over the bridge and turn right (south) at the Nature Center entrance. Make another sharp right and pedal parallel to Spring St. (but in the opposite direction) along the Nature Center roadway. Bike 0.2 mile to the fence along the San Gabriel River Bike Route. Rather than passing through the fence entry, follow the roadway as it turns to the right and passes under Spring St. The road enters Park Area II.

Stay to the left rather than bike into El Dorado Park. Pass through the fence and head right (north) along the San Gabriel River Trail (0.6). The first part of the trip parallels Park Area II. The path leaves the river again and follows the roadway under Wardlow Rd. (1.1). Again, stay to the left and pass through a fence which returns to the river trail (the other option is to bike through Park Area III and rejoin the trail 1/2 mile later). The path stays beside a stand of trees and passes the end of Park Area III (1.6) near the weapons firing range.

Rynerson Park. Pass a pedestrian bridge (a diversion route which crosses over to De Mille Junior High School) and then pass Carson St. (2.0). For the next 0.7 mile, cruise alongside fun River Park, which boasts tree cover, horse stalls and corrals, horse trails, a little footbridge leading to a connecting

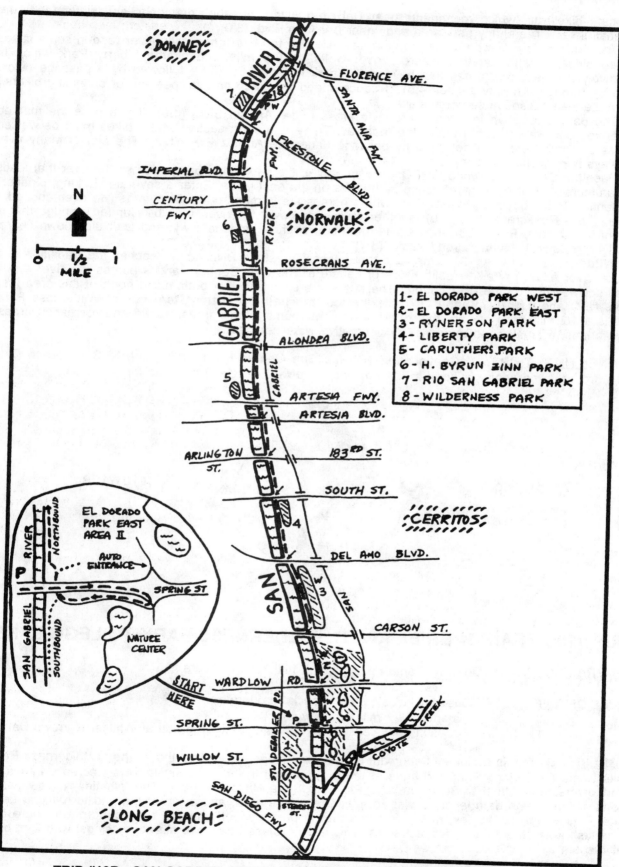

TRIP #19B - SAN GABRIEL RIVER: EL DORADO PARK TO WILDERNESS PARK

alternate bike trail (which reconnects near Del Amo Blvd.), baseball diamonds and water (near the baseball fields). The shady park area ends near Del Amo Blvd. (3.0).

The Middle Trip Section. For the next half mile, the trip highlight is the clever (and in some cases not so clever) graffiti on the concrete river walls. In 0.8 mile, reach little Liberty Park which is effectively a grassy rest area. Just beyond the park is South St. (3.8), followed by a passage below 183rd St. through a narrow tunnel (4.5). (Reduce speed and keep an eye "peeled" for oncoming bikers.) The route then passes more horse stalls.

The path dips down into the riverbed to cross under Artesia Blvd. (4.9). If you miss the marked route, you can walk (crouch) under the roadway. There is a short section where bikes must be walked across a railroad crossing, followed by passage under the Artesia Fwy. (5.3). The first of many river spillways is near this junction.

Pass the Cerritos Ironwood Golf Course; nearby is the pedestrian bridge across the river that leads to Caruthers Park (5.6). Our reference path stays on the east levee. Enter a several-mile long, pleasant residential stretch beyond Alondra Blvd. where horses are in many of the backyards (we even spotted a llama). Pass Rosecrans Ave. (7.0), another walk bridge over the river, then bike under a bridge that is part of the Century Fwy. (7.8). In 0.3 mile, the path reaches Imperial Hwy. and later dips down nearer the river, passing below a railroad trestle (8.7).

Wilderness Park. At (9.0), the bike trail passes Firestone Blvd., then reaches the transition to a natural river bottom after 11 solid miles of concrete. Rio San Gabriel Park is across the river and a small spillway graces the river bottom. There is some excellent river bottomland north of this area (see Trips #19C and #19D). In about 0.7 mile the tour reaches a refreshing terminus at Wilderness Park. This is a 1/2-mile strip of park that offers water, restrooms, shade trees, sports and recreation areas, playgrounds, a small pond and a lovely decorative water fountain.

CONNECTING TRIPS: 1) Continuation with the San Gabriel River Trail south to Seal Beach (Trip #19A) from the trip origin, or north to the Whittier Narrows (Trip #19C) from the trip terminus.

Biking   Worldwide

TRIP #19C - SAN GABRIEL RIVER: WILDERNESS PARK TO LEGG LAKE

GENERAL LOCATION: Downey, Santa Fe Springs, Whittier, Pico Rivera

LEVEL OF DIFFICULTY: One way - easy; up and back - moderate
Distance - 7.7 miles (one way)
Elevation gain - essentially flat (single steep grade at Whittier Narrows Dam)

HIGHLIGHTS: This is a pleasant segment of the San Gabriel River Trail that starts at Wilderness Park, visits Santa Fe Springs Park and ends at the trip highlight in the Whittier Narrows Recreation Area. A short diversion at Whittier Blvd. leads to Pio Pico State Historical Park. The Whittier Narrows area sports a ride on the dam levee, a visit to a wildlife refuge area, and a trip at the end to relaxing Legg Lake. This is one of the few river segments that is predominantly natural river bottom and there are some lush areas that beckon for rest stops. This is 99% Class I trail (two street crossings) with light bike traffic south of the Whittier Narrows Dam.

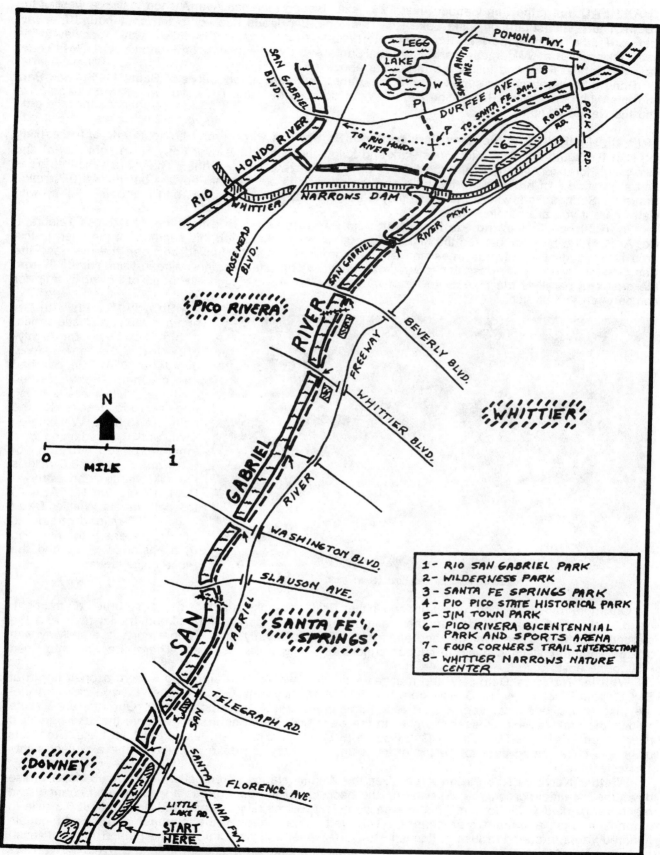

Legend:

1 — RIO SAN GABRIEL PARK
2 — WILDERNESS PARK
3 — SANTA FE SPRINGS PARK
4 — PIO PICO STATE HISTORICAL PARK
5 — JIM TOWN PARK
6 — PICO RIVERA BICENTENNIAL PARK AND SPORTS ARENA
7 — FOUR CORNERS TRAIL INTERSECTION
8 — WHITTIER NARROWS NATURE CENTER

TRIP #19C - SAN GABRIEL RIVER: WILDERNESS PARK TO LEGG LAKE

TRAILHEAD: From the San Gabriel River Fwy., exit west on Florence Ave. A short distance west of the freeway, turn left (south) on Little Lake Rd. This road also leads back onto the southbound freeway; therefore, in a few hundred feet, turn right onto Little Lake Rd. proper. Continue on this roadway to the free parking area at Wilderness Park. From the Santa Ana Fwy., exit west on Florence Ave. Pass under the San Gabriel Fwy. and follow the directions above.

Bring a moderate water supply. There is no enroute water supply between Santa Fe Springs Park and the Whittier Narrows Recreation Area. (Water sources near the recreation area are at Legg Lake and the Nature Center.)

TRIP DESCRIPTION: Wilderness Park to Santa Fe Springs Park. From the south end of the parking lot, skirt the south edge of Wilderness Park and follow the path to the river entry. Turn right (north) and bike past Florence Ave. (0.2) and the first of many spillways 0.2 mile further. There are scattered trees and a great deal of brush along the path and the riverbed is built up into holding basins. At (0.7) reach Santa Fe Springs Park where there are play areas, shade, recreation fields and restrooms. Fill up with water here if you are running low.

The Railroad Route and Pio Pico Historical Park. About 0.4 mile from the park, cross Telegraph Rd. At (1.4) the bikeway passes the highest (about six feet) spillway on this segment of the river. In this area is a stand of eucalyptus trees and a collection of horse stalls tucked between the river and the San Gabriel Fwy. At (2.1) pass under a railroad trestle. Soon after, another railroad track comes in from the east and parallels the bike route for several miles. There is a high likelihood of having a train for company on this stretch.

Four Corners Trail Intersection (Susan Cohen Photo)

Shortly, pass under another railroad trestle which, in turn, lies below the highly-elevated Slauson Ave. overpass (2.3). The riverbed and greenery in the riverbed continue, while there is brush and railroad tracks to the right. At (3.0) is Washington Blvd. and the beginning of a long exposed stretch of bikeway. In about 0.6 mile is the biker/pedestrian entry at Dunlap Crossing Rd. At (4.7) the path meets Whittier Blvd.; it is a 0.2-mile diversion to the right (east) to visit Pio Pico Historical Park and the Pio Pico Museum.

Our route transits a short tunnel under Whittier Blvd. and passes alongside dense brush on the right. At (5.3) the path heads under another railroad trestle; the paralleling railroad tracks fuse and the merged track leaves the river heading east. In 0.2 mile is Beverly Blvd. Further north is a spillway with a large enough collecting basin to support a flock of young water frolickers. There is a view into Rose Hills to the east.

Whittier Narrows Dam. The trip reaches a junction where the trail changes from asphalt to dirt at San Gabriel River Pkwy. (6.1). The dam is viewable at this point. Continue ahead if you have a wide-tire bike and a desire to see Pico Rivera Bicentennial Park and Sports Area. Our reference route follows the parkway and crosses the river to the west side. Pedal north and observe the lush tree-filled river bottom. Pass the Pico Rivera Golf Course (6.7) and make a hard left at the dam base. From this point is a short, steep path to the top of the dam (6.9). Stop and take in some of the excellent sights viewable here.

Whittier Narrows Recreation Area. (See the Whittier Narrows Recreation Area Detail Map.) Cruise down the meandering concrete bikeway on the backside of the dam, cross a water run-off channel and reach the marked Four Corners Trail Intersection (7.2). Bike straight ahead and pedal about 0.3 mile to a junction near another water channel. Turn left, crossing over the channel and bike a couple hundred yards through the lush bottomland to Durfee Ave. and pass through the gate. Turn right (east) and cruise a few hundred feet to the Legg Lake parking area entry within the Whittier Narrows Recreation Area (7.7).

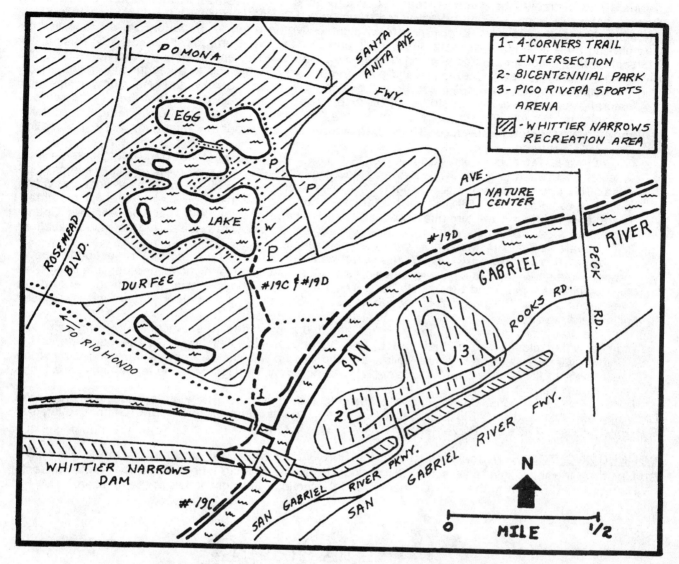

WHITTIER NARROWS RECREATION AREA DETAIL MAP

Excursions: Legg Lake. (See Whittier Narrows Recreation Area Detail Map.) The entire lake trip is on well-compacted dirt and is easy to ride with any type of bike. However, some care is needed in a couple of fine gravel and wet areas. Leave the parking lot and head north toward the lake. Veer right for the counterclockwise tour. Pass a roofed picnic area, a little spillway into the lake and visit a giant sandy play area with a ten-foot high cement octopus (0.2).

Shortly the route passes a food stand and boat rental area. There are numerous ducks and geese in the area. Further on is a "rocket" playground and some lovely shaded picnic sites situated at the lake edge (0.4). Just beyond is a trail junction. Diverting to the left leads to a bridge crossing between the northernmost lake and the main lake. The reference trip heads right and passes around the north lake through the green, natural, tree-covered surroundings. On this southbound segment the path meets the other end of the junction route between the lakes at (1.6). This area is one of the fishermen's favorites.

In 0.1 mile, pass a spillway near the lake's western end of the lake, one of the few lake areas where motor traffic is visible. We passed a group of ducks sleeping on the grass six feet away from a busy fisherman near here. The route turns eastward later and roughly parallels Durfee Ave. (2.1). The final stretch continues to wind along the lake edge and returns to the trip origin in another half mile (2.6).

Upper Rio Hondo and Lario River Trails. Exit the parking lot and cross Durfee Ave. a few hundred feet to the west. Pass through the signed gate and retrace the incoming route back to the Four Corners Trail Intersection (0.5). The route to the left (east) goes to the San Gabriel River and heads north, while the route dead ahead (south) heads back towards the dam and returns to the southerly San

Gabriel River segment (the incoming route). Our tour goes right (west) and roughly parallels the dam, passing alongside some striking vine-covered trees. In a 1/2 mile is a view back into Rose Hills (1.0). Cross a small footbridge over a wash and reach Durfee Ave. in 0.1 mile. Pedal on Class I road and go 0.2 mile to the intersection of Rosemead Blvd. and Durfee Ave./San Gabriel Blvd. (1.3). Cross the intersection to the north side and bike on Class I San Gabriel Blvd. until reaching the bike entry to the Rio Hondo River (just before the bridge and on the east levee) (1.5). This is a key junction point.

    Upper Rio Hondo Trail (northbound). Drop down from the road and ride along a pleasant, natural tree- and brush-lined stretch of the river. The growth is so dense that the river view does not open up for a 1/4 mile or so. Pass under the Pomona Fwy. (3.3), veer to the right, then parallel that freeway at road level for 0.6 mile before reaching the northern recreation area (Recreation Area "A") entrance.

    Whittier Narrows Recreation Area "A." The bike entrance to the park is at its south end. Cyclists can cruise both the bikeways and slow-moving, lightly-traveled roads within the recreation area. The park dimensions are roughly 1/2 mile north-south and 1/4 mile east-west, providing plenty of room to roam. The park is moderately treed and has restrooms and water, picnic areas, recreation fields, model airplane flying and model car racing areas. This Los Angeles County recreation area, combined with Legg Lake, is certainly on par with recreation/biking areas such as Mile Square, William R. Mason or Irvine Regional Parks.

    Upper Rio Hondo and Lario Trails (southbound). At the key junction point mentioned above, proceed over the river 0.1 mile to Lincoln Ave. (1.6). Turn left and make another immediate left turn onto an asphalt road blocked to cars. The trail follows above and at some distance from the west bank of the Rio Hondo. This section has scrub brush, an oil well pump or two and low eroded hills to the west.

    The trail pulls away from the river at about 0.2 mile from the Lincoln Ave. entrance and comes within close view of that street. Just beyond are the first views of the backside of the Whittier Narrows Dam. In 0.2 mile, follow a steep trail up the backside of the dam and summit the west levee of the Whittier Narrows Dam (2.1). As noted by the sign near the levee entry, this is the start of the Lario Trail.

For the detailed discussion and maps associated with the Upper Rio Hondo and Lario Trails, the Los Angeles River and the "Big Banana" ride which connects them all to the San Gabriel River, see B-D Enterprises' publication, *Bicycle Rides: Los Angeles County*.

CONNECTING TRIPS: 1) Continuation with the San Gabriel River Trail south to El Dorado Park (Trip #19B) - from the trip origin, bike south; 2) continuation with the San Gabriel River Trail north to Santa Fe Dam (Trip #19D) - from the Four Corners Trail Intersection, turn right (east) at the junction.

TRIP #19D - SAN GABRIEL RIVER: LEGG LAKE TO SANTA FE DAM

GENERAL LOCATION: Whittier Narrows, El Monte, Baldwin Park, Irwindale

LEVEL OF DIFFICULTY: One way - easy; up and back - moderate
                Distance - 11.4 miles (one way)
                Elevation gain - essentially flat (short, steep grades at Santa Fe Dam
                        and at Whittier Narrows Dam for up-and-back ride)

HIGHLIGHTS: This is one of our favorite segments of the river trips. The San Gabriel River in the Whittier Narrows region is river stomping at its best; there are trees, thickets, clear running water and readily visible wildlife in all. The Whittier Narrows Recreation Area offers a wildlife sanctuary, Legg Lake, vista points from the top of the dam and a diversion trip to the Pico Rivera Bicentennial Park and Sports Area. The Santa Fe Dam Recreation Area offers an expansive, pleasant picnic and recreation area at the edge of the lake, as well as superb lookout points from the top of the dam. Set aside a few hours and fully explore these territories. The best time to take this trip is within several days of a cold winter storm when the snow level in the nearby mountains is low. The route is nearly 100% Class I (one street crossing).

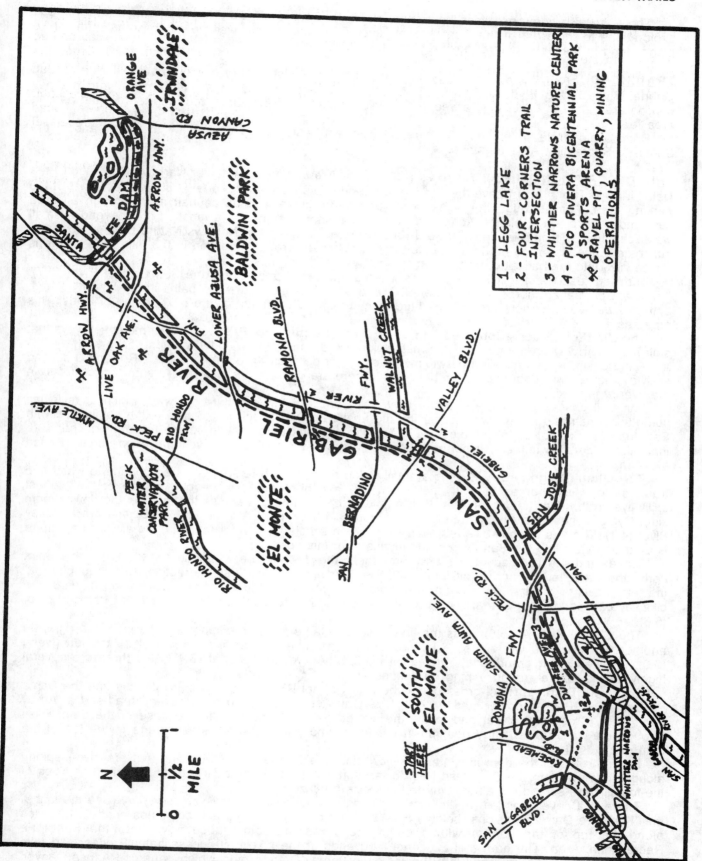

TRIP #19D - SAN GABRIEL RIVER: LEGG LAKE TO SANTA FE DAM

There are also some excellent trip excursions in the Santa Fe Dam area. They range from on-road explorations to the west of the San Gabriel River Fwy. and on the west levee to some fat-tire bike meandering in the flood control basin behind the dam.

TRAILHEAD: From the Pomona Fwy., exit at Rosemead Blvd. south, travel about 0.8 mile to San Gabriel Blvd./Durfee Blvd. and turn left. Drive on Durfee Ave. 0.6 mile and turn left into the pay parking area at Legg Lake. Find a tree under which to park your car. Bring four quarters for the parking area fee.

Bring a moderate water supply. There are rest and water stops directly on the route and at the Santa Fe Recreation Area terminus.

TRIP DESCRIPTION: **Whittier Narrows Recreation Area.** (See the Whittier Narrows Recreation Area Detail Map in Trip #19C.) Leave the parking area and cross Durfee Ave. a few hundred feet west of the parking area. Pass through the signed gate and pedal down a small asphalt road through an area surrounded by bushes, plants, trees and brush. In a short distance is a junction just beyond a small water channel. The path left leads toward (but bypasses) the Whittier Narrows Nature Center. However, our route proceeds to the right and meets the Four Corners Trail Intersection in 0.3 mile (0.5). There is a nice view into the backside of the Whittier Narrows Dam from this area.

Turn left (east) and follow the path as it turns northward and rejoins the San Gabriel River (0.7). There are permanent horse trails to the left (west) and also "find-your-way" paths in the lush river bed; both are well used by horse riders, the latter accompanying our path for the next couple of miles. This area has excellent views of Rose Hills to the east.

The Unofficial Recreation Area/San Jose Creek Confluence. Pass the first of many spillways that stair-step their way up the river (1.4). Small children slide down the rounded portion of the spillway into a holding basin below and even a swimming dog might be seen. In 0.4 mile is Peck Rd. and a second spillway with a large pool backed up behind it. (There are gas stations and restaurants not too far from the river at this exit.)

The trail passes under the Pomona Fwy. (2.0) and reaches the third spillway, which usually has some fishermen and a few swimmers using the upstream water pool. In 0.3 mile is the confluence with San Jose Creek and one of the most well-used of the unofficial recreation spots on the river. There are inner-tube riders, swimmers, fishermen, horses with riders crossing the river and even some off-road bicycling.

The Middle Segment. At (2.7) is a small rodeo ring where bikers have a free chance to watch the trainers work with horses or, with luck, to watch a mini-rodeo. Just beyond is one of the highest spillways on the river (about ten feet) with a holding basin stretched across the river on the downstream side. Cycle alongside residential areas, pass Mountain View High Athletic Field (3.9) and reach Valley Blvd. (4.1). There is a small bike rest stop here with a simple pipe water fountain. On a clear day, there is a striking view into the San Gabriel Mountains from this point.

Travel under a railroad bridge and later meet the Walnut Creek junction (4.3). From this point north, the water level drops significantly and the river bed is much less interesting. At this junction, to the left (west) of the trail, is a corral that holds Brahma bulls and a buffalo. Continuing onward, the bikeway passes the San Bernardino Fwy. (4.7) and then meets another biker rest area at Ramona Blvd. (5.6).

The Gravel Pits. At (6.5), pass the first of several large gravel dredging operations (to the right). In another 0.2 mile is Lower Azusa Rd. There is a large, open, water-filled gravel pit to the left (west) (5.9), followed by a "granddaddy" gravel pit across the river to the right (6.4). Also there are several highly visible above-ground mining operations.

Santa Fe Dam. At (7.5), cross under the San Gabriel River Fwy. and stare directly into the Santa Fe Dam face. Pass a power station (7.0), Live Oak Ave. and bike to an apparent dead-end at Arrow Hwy. (8.8). Cross that street and follow the signed path left and bike to the base of the dam. Pass through the walker/biker entry opening in the fence and pump a short, steep grade to the top of the dam (9.2).

From the top of the dam in winter are views into the San Gabriel Mountains that are awe-inspiring along with views into the San Jose Hills to the southeast and Puente Hills to the south. The cities of the foothills are spread out all the way to the western horizon.

There is a paved trail left (northwest) that ends just below the west levee terminus. (See the last of the "Santa Fe Dam Excursions" below.) However, our route goes right and continues another 1.9 miles along the top of the dam providing other fine views, including those down into the Santa Fe Recreational Area. The dam trail descends and ends at the bike trail access gate. Proceed 0.2 mile further to the auto access road into the recreation area (Orange Ave. which is named Azusa Canyon Rd. south of Arrow Hwy.). The mileage at this point is (11.4).

Santa Fe Dam Recreation Area. The recreation area behind the dam is a charmer. To get there, make a hard left onto the automobile roadway access just downhill of the auto pay gate. There are bikepaths and a low-speed-limit, lightly-traveled paved road that can be linked into a couple of miles more biking. The entire park is built alongside a lake and comes equipped with water and restrooms, picnic areas, swimming area with a sand beach, playgrounds, fire pits, shaded pagodas (group area at the western end of the lake), boat rental and a snack bar.

Atop Santa Fe Dam with Recreation Area Below

There are also bicycle roadways beyond the west end of the lake. In periods of low water, fat-tire bikes can be ridden through this maze of dirt trails to the westside dam levee access. (See the last of the "Santa Fe Dam Side Trips" below.)

Excursions: Santa Fe Dam Side Trips. At the west base of the dam, just before beginning the climb to the top, there is a trail heading north and west to a tunnel under the San Gabriel River Fwy. On the west side of the freeway is a "T"-junction. The south fork transitions to dirt in 0.5 mile and follows the Buena Vista Channel west almost to Buena Vista St. -- a fence prevents access to that street. The north fork climbs a small levee in 0.8 mile to San Gabriel Fwy. level, then drops down to the Santa Fe Dam Flying Area (model airplanes). Climbing to the opposite levee leads to a ride extension of 0.5-mile, paralleling Duarte Rd., to the levee's terminus. At the terminus, the packed-dirt road leading west towards Duarte Rd. is blocked by the City of Duarte Maintenance Yard, while the eastern path leads into the dirt areas of the main flood control basin. The path south parallels the freeway and loops back to the incoming route in 0.5 mile. The north fork route totals three miles round trip.

Another choice, once on top of the Santa Fe Dam, is to bike northwest and explore the one-mile west levee, which parallels the San Gabriel River Fwy. The outlet is a downhill into the main flood control basin behind the dam. There are dirt paths winding over the entire basin, including routes leading across to the lakeside recreation area or under the San Gabriel River Fwy. and Foothill Fwy. (Do not attempt to bike in this area during rainy periods!)

CONNECTING TRIPS: 1) Continuation with the southbound San Gabriel River Trail to Wilderness Park (Trip #19C) - from the Four Corners Trail Intersection, head south and over the Whittier Narrows Dam; 2) continuation with the northbound San Gabriel River Trail to the San Gabriel River Canyon (Trip #19E) - at the recreation area auto access, bike north (nearly straight ahead). Follow the trail signs.

TRIP #19E - SAN GABRIEL RIVER: SANTA FE DAM
TO SAN GABRIEL CANYON

GENERAL LOCATION: Irwindale, Azusa

LEVEL OF DIFFICULTY: One way - easy; up and back - moderate

Distance - 7.5 miles (one way)

Elevation gain - essentially flat (single short, steep grade at Santa Fe Dam)

HIGHLIGHTS: This 100% Class I trip starts downstream of the Santa Fe Dam, then climbs onto and follows the dam levee. The route cruises from the dam upstream to the end of the San Gabriel River Trail at the L.A. National Forest Information Center in San Gabriel Canyon. Along the way, the path traverses the Santa Fe Dam Nature Area which has a natural river-bottom cactus garden. There are spectacular close-up views of the foothills and surrounding mountains. These views are absolutely great after a cold winter storm. The stretch north of the dam is little used and makes a good work-out trip.

TRAILHEAD: From the San Gabriel River Fwy., exit east on Live Oak Ave. and continue 0.9 mile to the junction with Arrow Hwy., making a U-turn onto Arrow Hwy. Drive in the reverse direction about 0.8 mile to free parking near the dam outlet.

An option is to use pay parking in the Santa Fe Dam Recreation Area. This is particularly useful if you wish to avoid riding up onto the dam and want to start from the recreation area. Exit on Live Oak Ave. (east) as above, but continue one mile past the junction of Live Oak and Arrow Hwy. Turn left (north) at the Recreation Park entrance at Orange Ave. (named Azusa Canyon Rd. to the south).

TRIP DESCRIPTION: **Santa Fe Dam.** From the free parking area on Arrow Hwy., pedal to the bike entry through the fence (to the west of the spillway near the dam base). Follow the bike trail signs and pump the steep roadway to the top of the dam (0.2). At the top is a great 360-degree view. Most prominent are the San Gabriel Mountains to the north and the San Jose Hills and Puente Hills to the southeast and south, respectively. The view into the mountains is a real "heart grabber" when the snow level is down to low elevations and the sky is clear.

There is a paved trail left (northwest) that ends just below the west levee terminus. (See the last of the "Santa Fe Dam Excursions" in Trip #19D.) However, our route goes right and continues another 1.9 miles along the top of the dam providing other fine views, including those down into the Santa Fe Recreational Area. The dam trail descends and ends at the bike trail access gate. The route then proceeds 0.2 mile further to the auto access road into the recreation area (Orange Ave. which is named Azusa Canyon Rd. south of Arrow Hwy.). The mileage at this point is (2.3).

Head downhill and turn sharply left below the pay gate to visit the developed park (southern) section of the Santa Fe Dam Recreation Area (see Trip #19D). Our reference route follows the signed bikeway and keeps straight ahead.

Northern Santa Fe Dam Recreation Area. Follow the road to the dead-end at a little walled park-like area (2.8). Turn left and continue tracking the well-marked road 0.2 mile until it turns right (north) again. In 0.2 mile reach the Wildlife Interpretive Center which has both picnic and tent camping areas near the roadway intersection (3.2). Turn left again and pedal a few hundred feet to the ranger station. There are two bike route options at this point, plus marked walking/nature trails which tour the wildlife area. All routes head west and shortly meet an old north-south asphalt road. Follow the bike trail marker and turn right (north) on that old road.

The roadway passes through an interesting ecological area which is surrounded by a wide variety of cactus. At (3.8) reach the top of a small rise; from here is a nice view which includes a good look at the surrounding bottomland, the backside of the Santa Fe Dam and a view north to the Foothill Fwy. In 0.4 mile, the path returns to the San Gabriel River and passes under the Foothill Fwy. just beyond (4.3).

The Gravel Pits. At (4.8) pass a trans-river passenger cable car. In 0.1 mile is Huntington Dr./Foothill Blvd. Next is the Santa Fe Equestrian Staging Area which has restrooms and water (5.2). There is a large above-ground gravel mining/processing works in the background. The river bed is boulder- and brush-filled with a low spillway breaking the continuity of the scene every half-mile or more.

At (5.5), the path goes by an old closed-off railroad bridge. There is a residential area across the river with the homes continuing up into the nearby foothills. There are more gravel operations along the roadway to the right (east) with one sand and gravel operation lying right next to the trail (6.1). The route also passes a large water-filled gravel pit (6.5).

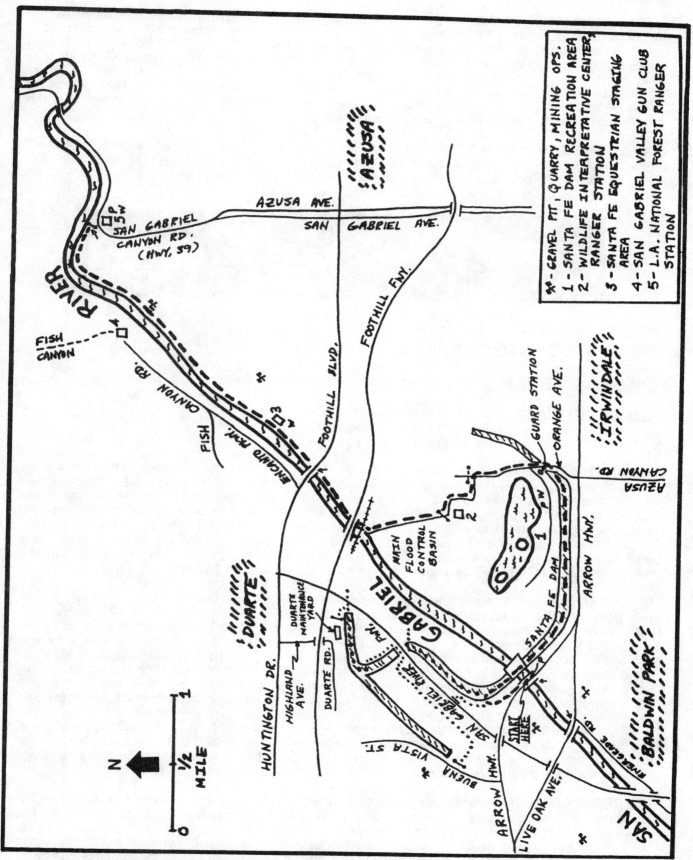

TRIP #19E - SAN GABRIEL RIVER: SANTA FE DAM TO SAN GABRIEL CANYON

San Gabriel Canyon Entrance. The trail heads into a progressively more well-defined canyon environment. At (6.8), pass Fish Canyon in the hills to the left (west). There is an exquisite series of waterfalls (wintertime) several miles back into the canyon called Fish Falls. (Sorry, this is hiking country only.) At this point on the bike trail, there is also a firing range, the San Gabriel Valley Gun Club. The hills echo the sounds, providing a "Gunfight at the OK Corral" aura.

Just beyond, the trail dead-ends at a fence (7.5). A small trail to the right leads to Hwy. 39 and the L.A. National Forest Ranger Station. There is water and parking here if you want to start from this direction or to use this as a pickup or turnaround point.

CONNECTING TRIPS: 1) Continuation with the San Gabriel River Trail south to Whittier Narrows (Trip #19D) - cross Arrow Hwy. and bike east a few hundred feet (in front of the spillway); 2) continuation with a very strenuous Class X "gut-buster" up San Gabriel Canyon Rd. - we <u>observed</u> a few hearty bikers working their way up the several miles of continuous steep grade.

TRIP #20- COYOTE CREEK TRAIL

GENERAL LOCATION: Long Beach, Seal Beach, Cerritos, Santa Fe Springs

LEVEL OF DIFFICULTY: One way - easy; up and back - moderate
Distance - 14.0 miles (one way)
Elevation gain - essentially flat

HIGHLIGHTS: Another of the river trails, this is a 99.44% pure Class I route. It starts at the scenic lower section of the San Gabriel River outlet near the Long Beach Marina and proceeds to the Coyote Creek junction. The Coyote Creek path is well maintained, but lightly used. The 10.1-mile Coyote Creek section is not highly scenic, unless one enjoys "window shopping" into backyards of the adjoining homes and apartments. It is a fine workout bikeway, however. The trip passes alongside Cerritos Regional County Park, which is a convenient and pleasant rest point near the center of the Coyote Creek segment. Beyond the Artesia Fwy. is the 2.5-mile (most recent) extension through commercial area to a terminus at Foster Rd. A short ride from here leads to shaded Frontier Park.

TRAILHEAD: Free public parking is available on Marina Dr. in Long Beach or along First St. in Seal Beach. From Pacific Coast Highway (PCH) in Seal Beach, turn west on Marina Dr. (2-3 blocks from Main Street in Seal Beach) and continue roughly 0.5 mile to First St. In another 1/4 mile, cross the San Gabriel River and continue a short distance along the marina for parking. The trailhead is located at Marina Dr. at the east end of the bridge over the San Gabriel River (across from Seaport Village).

An alternate start point is Edison Park, which starts cyclists much nearer to the Coyote Creek/San Gabriel River junction. From Studebaker Rd. in South Long Beach, turn east on E. 9th St. and right (south) immediately after. Continue on that unnamed road to its end at College Park Dr., cross the San Gabriel River, and turn left just beyond into the park. Carefully observe posted parking signs.

Bikers should have a filled water bottle since the trip is waterless up to Cerritos Regional Park. Riders starting at Seal Beach can cycle south about 0.3 mile from the trailhead to use restrooms at the beach. The side trip may also serve as a very pleasant scenic diversion. After the ride, Seaport Village at the marina edge may serve as a nice dining spot, watering hole, or place to shop.

TRIP DESCRIPTION: **The Scenic Lower Segment.** (See Trip #19A for a map of this segment.) The first part of the trip provides views of boaters, water skiers, and an interestingly-developed shoreline. The natural river basin then passes the PCH access, the Westminster Ave. entry (1.2), and the Haynes Steam Plant (electricity generation). At (2.2), a small diversion Class I path leads off to the east along a 1.2-mile shaded route to Seal Beach Blvd. In this stretch of the river, up to the concrete portion at about (3.5), cyclists have views of a large bird population that includes pelicans, egrets, and the ever-

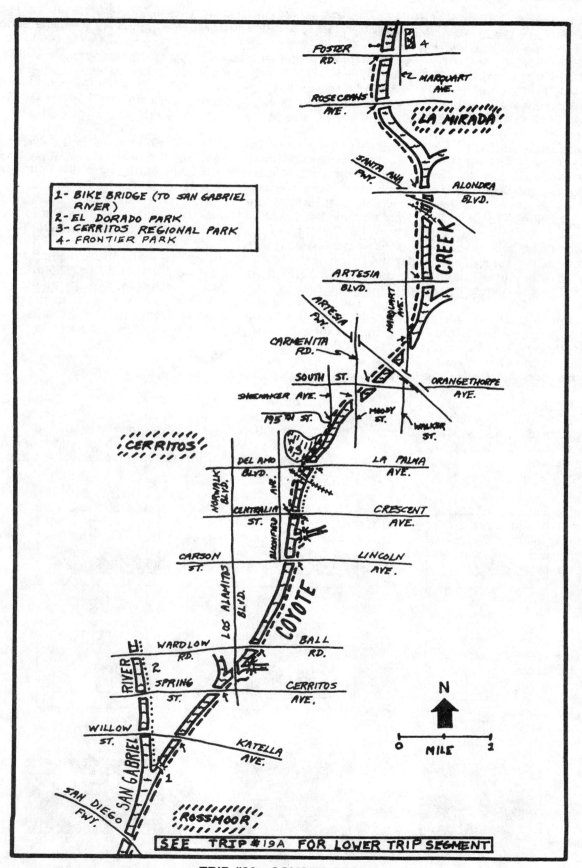

1- BIKE BRIDGE (TO SAN GABRIEL RIVER)
2- EL DORADO PARK
3- CERRITOS REGIONAL PARK
4- FRONTIER PARK

TRIP #20 - COYOTE CREEK

present seagulls. The path goes under the Garden Grove Fwy. (2.3), passes Edison Park, then ducks below the San Diego Fwy. (3.5). In this portion of the path are many "freeway orchards" -- those freeway-locked areas under the power poles which are used for growing containerized plants.

Coyote Creek. At (3.9), a marked bridge over the river takes bikers to the connecting portion of the San Gabriel River Bike Trail (Trip #19A). However, at this junction, our route continues along the east side (stay to the right) of the channel and passes the Katella Ave. entry, the San Gabriel River Fwy., and the Cerritos Ave. access (5.2). Nearby, the channel junctions to the north (no easy access at this junction was found), although our reference route stays along the east side of the channel. Two additional small channel junctions to the east are encountered at (5.6) and (7.3). However, both junctions are closed off by locked gates and the main Coyote Creek path crosses those junctions via small overpasses. The Los Alamitos access is at about (5.6). Pass Ball Rd., a small walking-only bridge across the creek at (6.3), Lincoln Ave., and bike to Crescent Ave./Centrailia St.

Exit the bikeway and cross to the west bank. Continue 1/2 mile to La Palma Ave./Del Amo Blvd. and pass alongside Cerritos County Regional Park. There is water within sight of the bikeway plus a park complete with restrooms, recreational fields, and a limited amount of shade. Pedal along a residential area and pass under Moody St./Carmenita Rd., then South St./Orangethorpe Ave. (Note the fast food establishments and gas stations to the west.) (9.2).

In a short distance, bike under the Artesia Fwy. and pass alongside residential developments (with scattered shade trees), then cycle past Walker St./Marquart Ave. The path veers left (due north) along the La Canada Verde Creek fork (the main Coyote Creek fork branches northeast) and continues another 0.4 mile to Artesia Blvd. The channel dips under the Santa Ana Fwy. and Alondra Blvd. on the most recently-opened 2.5-mile path extension through a strictly commercial zone. The bikeway passes alongside the Santa Fe Springs Drive-in Theater (12.3), then beelines 1.7 miles to its end at Foster Rd.

A short ride east on Foster Rd. leads to Marquart Ave. and Frontier Park. The park has shade (a rare commodity on the ride), water, restrooms, a children's play area and barbecue facilities.

CONNECTING TRIPS: 1) Continuation/connection to lower and middle portions of the San Gabriel River tour (Trips #19A and #19B) - take major access streets west and cross the San Gabriel River Fwy., noting that distance between Coyote Creek and the San Gabriel River increases the further north cyclists go on Coyote Creek; 2) connection with the Cypress tour (Trip #21) - bike east from any exit street between Katella Ave. and La Palma Ave.; 3) connectors to the lower portion of this trip along the San Gabriel River are described in Trip #19A.

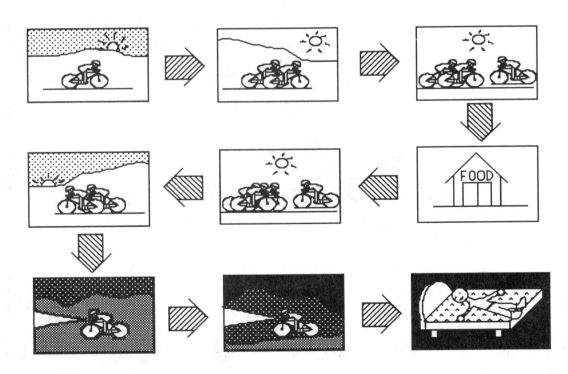

INLAND

Lake Forest

TRIP #21 - CYPRESS TOUR

GENERAL LOCATION: Cypress, La Palma, Buena Park

LEVEL OF DIFFICULTY: Loop - easy to moderate
Distance - 14.9 miles
Elevation gain - essentially flat

HIGHLIGHTS: This is a pleasant cruise primarily on Class II city streets that explores several inland Orange County cities. The tour leaves pleasant and tiny Eucalyptus Park and follows a lightly-traveled loop through mostly residential and some light industrial areas. There are two enjoyable Class I loops within the larger tour. Other highlights are Cypress College, El Rancho Verde Park and Bicycle Path and the numerous exceptional parks spread throughout. The route described can be linked with numerous other Class II and III routes in the area.

TRAILHEAD: From the Garden Grove Fwy., exit north on Valley View St. and drive 1-3/4 miles to Orangewood Ave. Turn left and motor a short distance to Eucalyptus Park. From the San Gabriel River Fwy., exit east at Katella Ave./Willow St. Continue east three miles to Valley View St., turn right and drive one-half mile to Orangewood Ave. Turn right again and continue to the park.
Bring a light water supply. There are numerous well-placed water sources scattered along the way.

TRIP DESCRIPTION: **Northbound.** Leave the park and bike east on Orangewood Ave. Once across Valley View St., pass Maplegrove Parks North and South (athletic courts, grass, shade, water) and in another 0.4 mile go past Manzanita Park (water fountain, trees, athletic courts and children's play area). Turn left (north) at Knott Ave. and bike 0.3 mile to the end of the housing tract. Turn left and bike 1.0 mile along a wash on the Class I path, returning to Valley View St. (2.5).
Turn right and cruise north on the sidewalk 0.5 mile to Cerritos Ave., turn left onto the Class II street, turn right shortly on Walker St. (the eastern edge of the Los Alamitos Race Course) and left again on Class II Ball Rd. There are small shopping complexes and a gas station at this intersection (3.9). Cycle west on Ball Rd. to Moody St. and begin a pleasant, sporadically-shaded 1.5 mile Class I partial loop on the large sidewalk. Along this stretch is Veteran's Park with restrooms, recreation fields, extensive lawns and a children's play area. The path turns right at Denni St. and right again at Orange Ave. passing Willow Park (restrooms, tree shade, picnic facilities, grass and a duckpond) and returning to Moody St. (5.4). Bike north on Moody St. for 1.8 miles. (Just south of Lincoln Ave on this stretch is Evergreen Park with restrooms, modest tree cover, benches and children's play area) Turn right just past Sharon Dr. onto the Class I bikepath below the power poles.
This is the westernmost edge of the El Rancho Verde Park and Bicycle Path, a laid-back two-mile stretch of mixed Class I path/grass, the last one mile (east of Valley View St.) for wide-tread tires only. Our reference route follows the (lighted) first mile; there are water fountains along the path at the baseball field near the half-way point and just across Walker St. Cruise to the end of the Class I path at Valley View St. (8.2).
Southbound. Follow Class X Valley View Ave. a short distance to La Palma Ave. and the La Palma Center (shopping). Turn right (west), left on Walker St. then right on Crescent Ave. All streets in this short I.8 mile zig-zag stretch are Class II. Stay on Crescent Ave. between the tennis courts to the right (north) and the sports complex of Arnold Park/Cypress Park to the left. (This fine park has stately trees, restrooms, barbecue facilities, park benches and children's playground.) At Moody St., turn left (south) (10.0).
Return on Moody St. to Orange Ave. and turn left, passing the Cypress Community Center/Oak Knoll Park with its recreation field, water and restrooms. At I.5 miles from the Moody St./Orange Ave. intersection, pass the expansive lawns of the Cypress College campus and turn right on Holder St. Follow Holder St. 0.5 mile to Ball Rd., turn right, pass Larwin Park (water fountain, scattered treecover, benches and children's play area) and return to Valley View St. (13.5). Bike I.4 mile south, turn right at Orange Ave., and return to Eucalyptus Park (14.9).

CONNECTING TRIPS: 1) Connection with the Western Orange County Loop (Trip #33) - at La Palma Ave. and Valley View St., bike east on the former street to Western Ave.; 2) connection with the Coyote Creek ride (Trip #20) - bike west on Lincoln Ave., Crescent Ave. or La Palma Ave. at the intersection with Moody St. and continue to the creek.

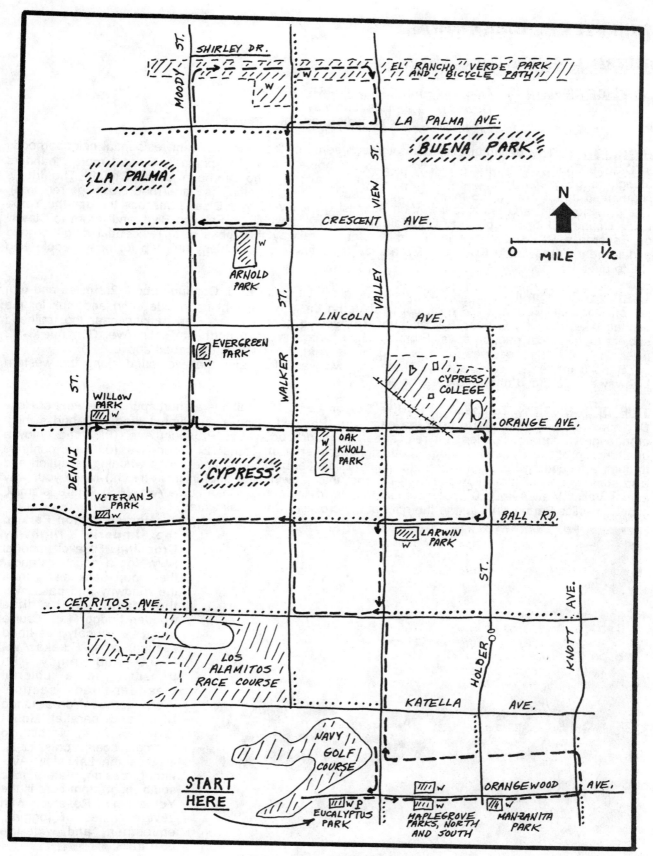

TRIP #21 - CYPRUS TOUR

TRIP #22 - EL CAJON TRAIL

GENERAL LOCATION: Yorba Linda

LEVEL OF DIFFICULTY: One way - easy; up and back - moderate
Distance - 8.2 miles (one way)
Elevation gain - periodic moderate grades

HIGHLIGHTS: This delightful trip roams through some of the most pleasant residential neighborhoods in Orange County, particularly for bikers who are horse lovers. The primarily Class I route meanders along the general route of the old El Cajon Canal (now the Anaheim Union Canal). The trip is segmented as follows: 1) 3.6 miles through a rural residential setting (several road crossings required); 2) a diversion onto a Class X roadway on Sunmist Dr. followed by a Class I passage through the Yorba Linda Country Club; 3) a climb to Lindafair Ln., Class X downhill on Fairlynn Blvd. and return to Class I on Esperanza Dr.; and 4) a final 1.8 mile Class I trailway through a rural residential neighborhood ending near Yorba Linda Blvd. and Esperanza Rd. This is a particularly fine trip for nosy people who like to peek into backyards.

TRAILHEAD: From the Orange Fwy., exit east at Yorba Linda Blvd. Continue about 2.2 miles and turn left on Rose Dr. Continue 0.6 mile just past Verna Ln. (on the right hand side only) and look for the asphalt bike trail. If you pass Bastanchury Rd., you've gone too far. Find parking near the trailhead subject to the local parking laws. From the Riverside Fwy., exit north at Tustin Ave. Continue 3-1/2 miles as Tustin Ave. becomes Rose Dr. and meets Verna Ln. Park as described above.

Bring a moderate water supply. There are two water fountains that we found along the western bikeway segment and one on the east side.

TRIP DESCRIPTION: **Trailhead to Hurliss Burton Park.** The trail has a short spur to the west of Rose Dr., however, our route starts from the east side. Proceed along a eucalyptus-lined path and a mini-orange grove through a pleasant residential neighborhood. Cross Prospect Ave. (0.3) and enjoy a quarter mile of "pure" horse country (both sights and smells). Transit El Cajon Ave. (0.6) and continue through a fenced trail area that borders many residential backyards. (We saw a wedding reception and also some young children jumping from the roof into a swimming pool in this stretch!) Make your way across Valley View Ave. (1.0), pass a small tank farm, then cross Casa Loma Ave. (1.3). There is small, shaded Hurliss Barton Park just to the right at the crossing which has water.

Near the Yorba Linda Golf Course

Hurliss Barton Park to the Imperial Highway Crossing. Parallel Imperial Hwy. for a short distance, then loop back away from the roadway and pass over the canal on a little wooden bridge (1.6). Cruise along a eucalyptus-lined section, cross Eureka Ave. (1.9), and enjoy the transition to a colorful oleander-lined section. Work across Yorba Linda Blvd. and parallel Mountain View Ave., climbing to a small, scenic crest (2.3). Next is the Lakeview Ave. undercrossing; half a mile south (right) from here is the Yorba Linda Reservoir with several miles of jogging, equestrian, and wide-tire bike trails.

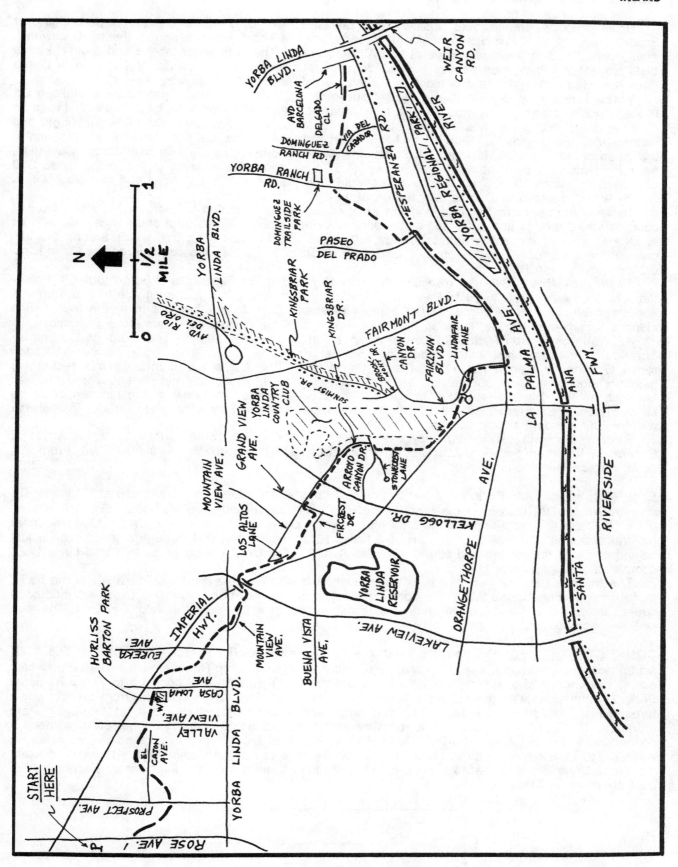

TRIP #22 - EL CAJON TRAIL

However, our reference route crosses under Lakeview Ave., turns right and passes on a bridge over Imperial Hwy. (2.5). Once across, follow the fenced trail (a short distance and to the right) downhill, then level off near a residential area at Los Altos Ln. (2.8). The path winds above and around Buena Vista Equestrian Park, then passes a small commercial zone near Fircrest Dr. At (3.0), cross Grand View Ave., turn left, proceed one block and continue right along Mountain View Ave. (3.4).

Yorba Linda Country Club and Golf Course. In 0.2 mile, the Class I path ends at Kellogg Dr. Proceed across that roadway onto a short, testy grade to Sunmist Dr. and turn right. Follow that road on a milder grade through a plush neighborhood to its terminus at Arroyo Cajon Dr. (4.1). Turn right and look for the little asphalt continuation trail in a short distance. Follow the path downhill while taking in the views of the Anaheim Hills and the Santa Ana River flood plain. At 0.3 mile from Arroyo Cajon Dr., the path reaches a point above Imperial Hwy. (4.3), then continues downhill to the Yorba Linda Golf Course and Country Club. Traverse the golf course near the fence, cross a small golf cart path (with a nearby water fountain), and pass over the canal on a little concrete strip.

There is a trail junction just beyond this point (4.8). The tree-shaded trail left travels along the golf course's western edge and is for golf carts. Our route goes straight ahead up a short, steep hill, with an expansive view to the south and southeast at the top of the grade. The trail winds around the hill, passes through a fence, and meets little Lindafair Ln. Cross that street and continue on the Class I trail 0.2 mile to Fairlynn Blvd.

Esperanza Road. Bike 0.3 mile downhill on Fairlynn Blvd. to Esperanza Rd. and turn left. Follow that Class I roadway 1.2 miles to Paseo Del Prado and turn left. Climb a short grade and turn right in about two blocks onto a perpendicular asphalt bikepath (6.9). In another 0.2 mile, the trail travels along a cactus-lined hillside, followed by a cruise alongside the backyards of numerous residences.

At (7.6) cross Yorba Ranch Rd., travel along a stately tree-lined section, pass through Dominguez Trailside Park (restrooms, water, swimming pool, tennis courts and children's playground) and soon reach Dominguez Ranch Rd. (7.8). Cross it and follow the Class I trail through this residential neighborhood passing in succession Via Del Conejo, Via Del Bisconte, Avd. Antigua, and the trail terminus at Avd. Barcelona, just above Avd. Granada (just north and west of the junction of Yorba Linda Blvd. and Esperanza Rd.) (8.2). If time permits, backtrack and try a freewheeling tour through the well-laid-out residential community.

Return Options. Round-trip bicyclists can modify the return route slightly by biking south to Esperanza Rd, then pedaling 2.2 miles west on that Class I route back to Fairlynn Blvd. From this point, retrace the incoming route.

Excursion: Kingsbriar Park. For up and back cyclists, start from the park's south end at Kingsbriar Dr. and Brookmont Dr., thereby doing most of the mild uphill on the outgoing leg. Bike north 0.7 mile on the quiet Class III road alongside the park and its small creek to Fairmont Blvd. Cross this busy street (no traffic signal) and look for the start of a Class I trail. Follow the trail through a treed section just behind a row of residences and bike 0.8 mile to Avd. Rio Del Oro. A short pedal to Yorba Linda Blvd. completes the signed tour (1.6).

The trip can be extended, but is not on a signed bikeway. Cross Yorba Linda Blvd. at the traffic signal, and continue along the park's northern reaches on a lightly-treed walkway. Cross neighborhood street Puesta Del Sol and bicycle another 0.35 mile to the greenbelt's end at Avd. Del Este. The total one-way distance is 2.1 miles.

CONNECTING TRIPS: 1) Connection with the Santa Ana River Trail (Trip #17A north or Trip #17B south) - continue east on Class I Esperanza Rd. under the Weir Canyon Rd. overpass and walk your bike across the open field to the right (south) to La Palma Ave. Turn right and continue to Yorba Regional Park; 2) connection with the Fullerton Tour/Craig Park route (Trip #24) - continue from the trip origin three miles west on Bastanchury Rd.; turn right (north) and proceed one mile to the Craig Park entrance. This road is on a Class X roadway with some sections having very narrow shoulder; 3) connection with the Carbon Canyon Workout (Trip #23) - at the trip origin, bike north I-I/2 miles on Rose Dr. to Valencia Ave., turn right, and continue 0.4 mile to Carbon Canyon Rd.; 4) connection with the Yorba Linda Bits and Pieces tour (Trip #43) - the trips share a common segment on Esperanza Rd. east of Fairmont Connector.

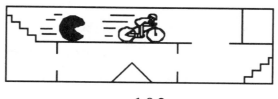

TRIP #23 - CHINO HILLS LOOP

<u>GENERAL LOCATION</u>: Carbon Canyon, Chino Hills, Diamond Bar, Brea

<u>LEVEL OF DIFFICULTY</u>:   Round trip - strenuous
Distance - 23.3 miles
Elevation gain - long moderate-to-steep grades on Carbon Canyon Rd.
and Grand Ave. in Chino Hills

<u>HIGHLIGHTS</u>: This three-county tour is for experienced bikers in excellent condition. Initially, cyclists pump a rugged uphill which starts from Carbon Canyon Park and proceeds to the Carbon Canyon Rd. summit, nearly 700 feet elevation gain in 5-1/2 miles. This segment is a canyon-watcher's delight with nice unobstructed views (which also means that there is little in the way of surrounding tree cover). A lengthy, sinuous, and scenic downhill dumps bicyclists into the developing City of Chino Hills with its myriad of parks. Once onto Grand Ave., bikers climb to a second scenic summit near Summitridge Dr., then essentially coast through Diamond Bar, Brea Canyon and the City of Brea. The finale is a nearly-flat four miles on State College Blvd. and Lambert Rd.

<u>TRAILHEAD</u>: Exit the Orange Fwy. eastbound at Lambert Rd., drive two miles and cross Valencia Ave. on what is now Carbon Canyon Rd. Continue one mile further to the Carbon Canyon Regional Park marked entry. There is an entry fee.

Bring a couple of quarts of water, particularly important for hot days. There are commercial stops on the rugged Carbon Canyon Rd. climb, if needed, plus numerous parks in the Chino Hills area and at the Grand Ave. summit (Summitridge Park). No on-route public water sources were found for the remaining (mostly downhill or flat) twelve miles of the trip, although there are commercial stops in Diamond Bar and Brea.

<u>TRIP DESCRIPTION</u>: Before leaving the park, explore the general area by using the roughly two miles of bikepath/roadway within. Families might consider using the park itself as a self-contained bike tour. There are also scenic hiking and equestrian trails in the area, with the most lengthy trail exploring the redwood tree stand at the southwestern park edge. The park has numerous water and restroom facilities, tree shade, playgrounds, sports grounds, tennis courts and picnic facilities.

Carbon Canyon Park to Olinda Village. Leave the park and turn right, immediately beginning a workout upgrade on a two-lane road with a modest biking shoulder. Pass through a pleasant forested area in this early segment, cycle by a large citrus grove and enter an area where the grade steepens (0.6). In 0.2 mile is an impressive canyon view looking north. The winding uphill road goes past a horse grazing area and reaches a flat at l.4 tough miles from the trip start. The vegetation transitions from lightly forested to more of a high desert appearance as the road climbs and heads further back into the canyon. Just beyond is Olinda Village with a restaurant and small market.

Olinda Village to Sleepy Hollow. Follow the steep downgrade which levels and passes the La Vida Mineral Springs (with resort). Pedal another winding upgrade through this short treed segment before reaching another flat (3.0). Proceed up again, cross the San Bernardino County Line, and soon reach the community of Sleepy Hollow. At Hillside Dr. is the "Party House," with liquid refreshment and a shaded terrace, as well as a grocery store (3.7).

Sleepy Hollow to the Carbon Canyon Rd. Summit. Continue on another difficult uphill on a 0.4-mile pull with scattered tree cover. (We didn't say that this was a picnic route!) Not far beyond the flat is Canyon Hills Rd. and Canyon Hills Stables (4.3). Bike alongside the Western Hills Golf Course, pass Valley Spring Rd. (5.0), and sweat out the quarter mile steep upgrade to a plateau. Pedal another 0.4 mile on the plateau, pass Carriage Hills Ln. and reach a crest at (5.6).

Summit to Summit. Carbon Canyon Rd. presents a dynamite S-curve almost immediately. The canyon vista below is gorgeous, as is the distant look at the eastern edge of the San Gabriel Mountains -- this is provided you stop and take a look! Just beyond Old Carbon Canyon Rd., the shoulder opens to a marked Class II bikeway (6.2). The curves moderate and the grade lessens as cyclists pass Fieldspar Dr. (6.4) and coast another mile into residential environs and meet Chino Hills Pkwy. Cucamonga Peak sits above the nearby homes to the distant north.

Turn left (northwest) onto the wide four-lane and pass a series of parks, each of which has water and restrooms, but offer very limited or no shade. Pass a shopping center just beyond Eucalyptus Ave. (7.7), continue coasting to Windmill Creek Rd. and climb mildly another 0.3 mile to a steeper uphill near Grand Ave. (8.9).

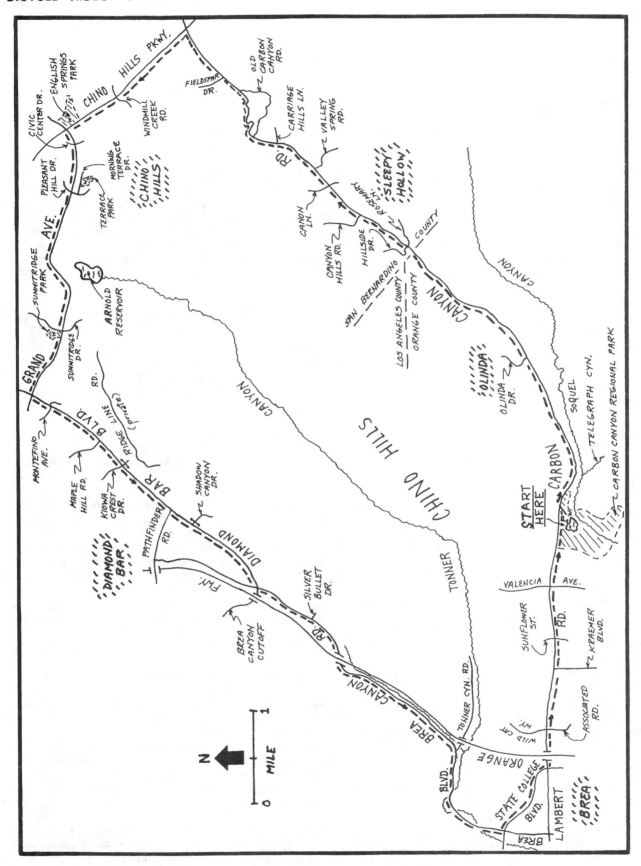

TRIP #23 - CHINO HILLS LOOP

A left here leads bikers along another wide four-lane road on a 2.4-mile, 300-foot upgrade to a crest at Summitridge Dr. On the climb through the surrounding residential area is Civic Center Dr., Pleasant Hill Dr. and Grand Ave. Park (9.8). Entering a relatively undeveloped area, cyclists are treated to a short downhill in another 0.4 mile, then more heavy-breathing uphill past the Arnold Reservoir (10.7). Longview Dr., just beyond the county border, is the beginning of a marked Class III in Diamond Bar), In 0.3 mile is Summitridge Dr. and Summitridge Park, which has water, restrooms, shade, an abundance of grass, picnic and sports facilities and a killer view west into the residence-filled canyon below (11.3).

Downhill into Brea. Life is good! The next eight miles into Brea is predominantly downhill. A steep downgrade leads to Diamond Bar Blvd. and a cluster of shopping centers in 0.9 mile. Turn left (south) and coast on a Class II roadway past shopping centers near Montefino Ave. (12.5) and Shadow Canyon Dr. (14.4), taking in the estates on the ridge to the left and above (Ridge Line Rd.). In another mile is Brea Canyon Rd. and a bevy of gas stations.

Brea Canyon

Turn left onto a Class X road with a narrowing shoulder and cross Silver Bullet Rd. (15.9). The next two miles plus is in a currently-undeveloped section of L.A. County. Pass under the Orange Fwy. at (16.2) and enter Brea Canyon proper. Just beyond the Orange County reentry (17.4), the road straightens on what is now Brea Blvd., passes Tonner Canyon Rd. (18.0), then takes a sweeping turn south. Canyon Country Dr. appears (19.1), the road leaves the canyon and State College Blvd./Central Ave. announces the City of Brea in another 0.3 mile.

The Final Lap. The return to dense residential area and the immediate array of shopping centers is a mild shock. Turn left onto State College Blvd., bike a short uphill on a wide four-lane, Class II road and reach Lambert Rd. in 0.8 mile (20.2). Make the final left turn of the trip (east) onto this wide Class X street and pedal back under the Orange Fwy. in 0.2 mile. Pass a large shopping complex on the left and enter an area with a mix of open residential areas mixed with gated communities. The road skinnies down to two lanes and takes some of the bike shoulder with it at (21.6). Pass a limited tree-lined stretch beyond Sunflower St. and reach Valencia Ave. at (22.3). The development thins as trip-hardened cyclists cruise the final mile to the Carbon Canyon Regional Park entry.

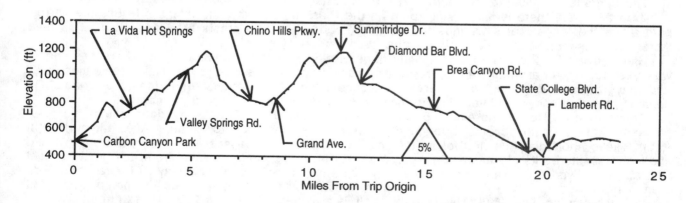

CONNECTING TRIPS: 1) Connection with the El Cajon Trail (Trip #22) - return to Valencia Ave., turn left (south) and continue 0.4 mile to Rose Dr. Turn left and follow that road I-I/2 miles to the trip origin.; 2) connection with the Fullerton Tour/Craig Park (Trip #24) - from the trip origin, bike west on Carbon Canyon Rd. (Lambert Rd. beyond Valencia Ave.) about four miles to State College Blvd. Turn south and cycle 3/4 miles to Imperial Blvd.

TRIP #24 - FULLERTON TOUR/CRAIG PARK

GENERAL LOCATION: Fullerton, Placentia, Brea

LEVEL OF DIFFICULTY: Full loop - moderate to strenuous
Distance - 15.4 miles (full loop)
Elevation gain - periodic moderate-to-steep grades

HIGHLIGHTS: This trip tours the rural, hilly portions of Fullerton and takes in pleasant Craig Park as well. Craig Park could serve as a family bike outing on its own. This tour has everything from Class I to Class X bike routes, but is mostly on signed motor vehicle roadways (Class III). The general area is scenic and the interspersed hill climbs provide a little extra variety. Well-stocked Ralph B. Clark Regional Park is an added bonus. Finally, a small family tour at Tri-City Park in Placentia is included.

TRAILHEAD: From the Artesia Fwy. (Riverside Fwy.) take Harbor Blvd. north into Fullerton. Drive about three miles to Valencia Mesa Dr. and turn left (west). Find parking near the intersection, but be sure to comply with the local parking regulations.

Bring a moderate water supply. The primary watering holes are in the shopping area near the starting point and at Ralph B. Clark and Craig Regional Parks. The latter two points are strategically located at the westernmost and easternmost ends of the trip, respectively. Although there are numerous parks with excellent grounds and facilities along the way, we found few which had a source of drinking water.

TRIP DESCRIPTION: Clark Park Loop. The trip starts southwest on Valencia Mesa Dr. traveling along a tree-lined route onto a moderate upgrade, then crossing over a small bridge near the crest (0.2). The route is Class III. For the next mile, cruise through a peaceful, rural residential neighborhood. The route crosses Euclid Ave. (0.9) and later follows a steep downhill to Bastanchury Rd. (1.5). A hard right, 0.2 mile of pedaling, and a left turn on Parks Rd. leads bikers past Edward White Park (1.8) along an upgrade through a residential area.

The upgrade continues to Rosecrans Ave. (2.4) where the tour heads left (west) and stays on an uphill. In this area, there is little biking room on the Class III roadway; an option is to use the narrow path along the fence that surrounds the neighborhood. The route crests at Gilbert St. (3.2), where there is a pleasant rest spot around the northeast corner at Coyote Hills Park.

Glide downhill 1.2 miles to significantly larger Ralph B. Clark Regional Park. There are shade, water, restrooms, an array of walkway/bikeways, picnic areas, barbecues, a small lake, recreation fields and playgrounds. The park could serve as a nice base of operations for a family bike ride. On departing the park, note the interesting formations of the East Coyote Hills to the north.

Return east on Rosecrans Ave. 0.5 mile to Sunny Ridge Dr. (4.7) and turn right (south). Follow a pleasant Class III path downhill through a residential neighborhood to Pioneer Ave. and turn right (6.2). Bike a short distance and follow the road as it turns left, passes little Emery Park (5.6), and suddenly recaptures its old name, Sunny Ridge Dr. The route winds downhill from this point to meet with Malvern Blvd. (6.0). Turn left (east) and go 0.8 mile on a Class III roadway to Bastanchury Rd., then turn left again. Cruise 0.5 mile to Valencia Mesa Dr. (7.3), then head up the steep grade and return to the starting point (8.8). This loop, by itself, is a moderate trip on a 100% Class III route.

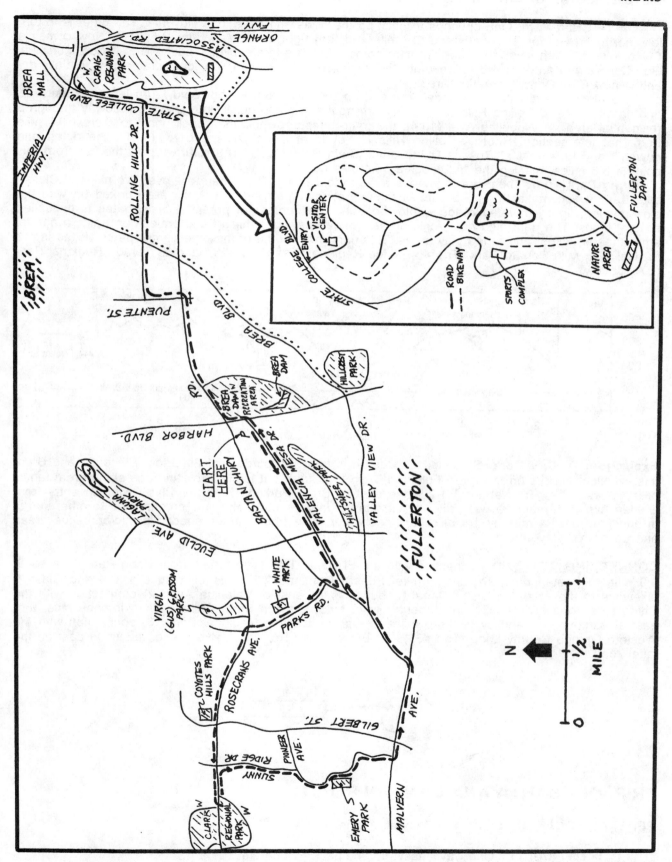

TRIP #24 - FULLERTON TOUR/CRAIG PARK

On To Craig Park. One option is to pack up the bikes and drive to Craig Park. The other is to turn left (north) on Harbor Blvd., proceed 0.2 mile and turn right on Bastanchury Rd. (9.0). Now comes a Class X route (with wide shoulder) through some moderate-to-steep hills past the Fullerton Municipal Golf Course and an area with a view into the backside of Brea Dam. The dam drainage is virtually dry and is now Brea Dam Recreation Area.

Bike along the reservoir drainage area and, in 0.6 mile from Harbor Blvd., turn left on Puente St. and ride 0.2 mile to Rolling Hills Dr. (10.1). Turn right and pump uphill on a Class II roadway through a residential area. At Woodline Ave. (10.4), the route heads downhill then back uphill to a crest 0.5 mile from that intersection. Shortly, Rolling Hills Dr. ends at State College Blvd. (11.5). Head left and downhill and turn right at Rosalia Dr. to enter Craig Park (12.1). The return trip to the car from this point is 3.3 miles, making the "full loop" a 15.4-mile ride.

Craig Park Tour. There are numerous ways to tour Craig Park. There are over two miles of Class I bike trails which make this an attractive family option. When the bike trails are hooked up with the slow-moving, lightly-traveled roads within the park, the number of potential bike routes is multiplied several times. The park also has picnic areas, shaded pavilions, hiking and equestrian trails, a natural amphitheater, lakes, and turfed play areas. This park rivals some of the other larger parks visited in our travels, e.g., Mile Square Park (Trip #5), Irvine Regional Park (Trip #26), and El Dorado Regional Park (L.A. County).

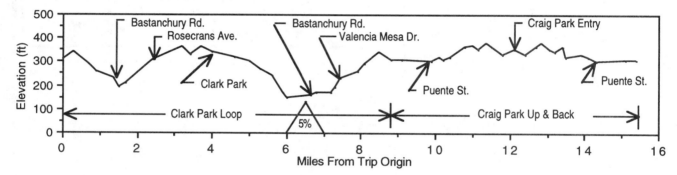

Excursion: Tri-City Park. So called because it is near the borders of Fullerton, Placentia and Brea, this excellent park is off the basic Fullerton/Craig Park tour, but is close by and has some great family biking possibilities. It is about 1-1/2 miles east of Craig Park on Kraemer Blvd., with an entry from Golden Ave. The main walkway/bikeway circuits the large central lake and is connected to other spurs. In addition, the 1/4 mile by 1/4 mile park has water, a restroom, trees, shaded picnic/barbecue areas and children's playground.

CONNECTING TRIPS: 1) Connection with the El Cajon Trail (Trip #22) - from Craig Park, bike south 0.9 mile to Bastanchury Rd. and turn left (east). Continue 2.7 miles on mild Class X and Class II bikeways to the Anaheim Union Canal (about 0.5 mile east of Valencia Ave.; 2) connection with the Chino Hills Loop (Trip # 23) - at Imperial Hwy., bike north on State College Blvd. for one mile, turn east at Lambert Rd. and cycle three miles to Carbon Canyon Regional Park.; 3) connection with the Western Orange County Loop (Trip #33) - at Bastanchury Rd. and Malvern Ave., continue east on the latter road.

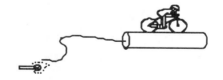

TRIP #25 - SANTA ANA CANYON ROAD

GENERAL LOCATION: Santa Ana Canyon, Anaheim Hills

LEVEL OF DIFFICULTY: One way - easy; up and back - moderate
Distance - 7.6 miles (one way)
Elevation gain - periodic moderate grades

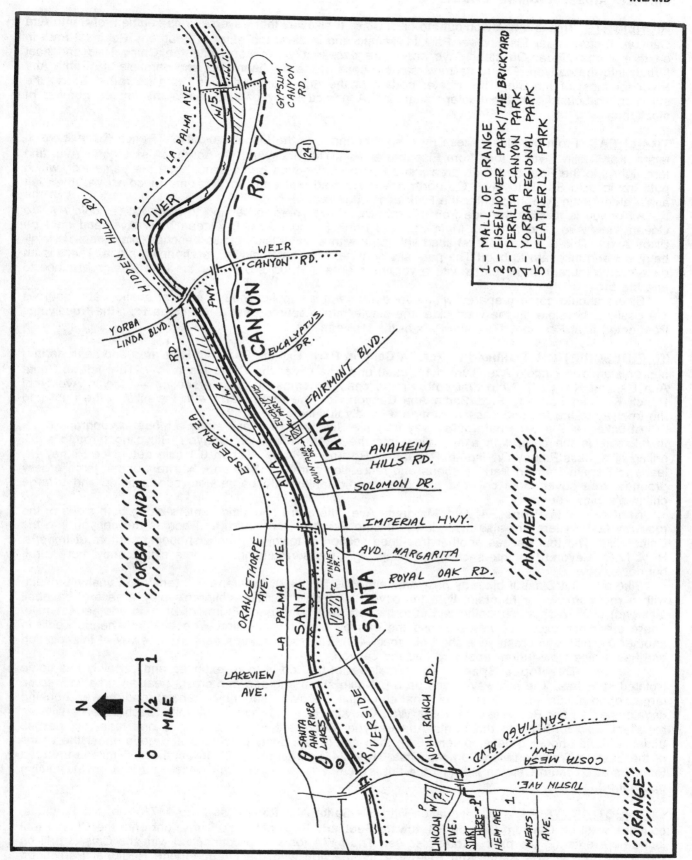

TRIP #25 - SANTA ANA CANYON ROAD

HIGHLIGHTS: This is a fine workout trip on a Class II bikeway that traverses one segment of Santa Ana Canyon. It starts near Eisenhower Park in Orange and ends at the entry to Featherly Regional Park in eastern Yorba Linda. On clear days, there are excellent views north into the Chino Hills and east further into the canyon. The route traverses the base of the Anaheim Hills and parallels the Santa Ana River for most of the trip. The greater portion of the trip is unshaded and can be rather hot in the summer, particularly on the eastern segment. A particular joy of this ride is the limited number of stoplights.

TRAILHEAD: From the Costa Mesa Fwy. southbound, use the Lincoln Ave./Nohl Ranch Rd. exit which lets out at Tustin Blvd. across from Eisenhower Park/The Brickyard. Go south, cross Lincoln Ave. and turn right into the Park and Ride area just beyond. Northbound traffic should use the same exit, which puts traffic onto Santiago Blvd. Go north a few hundred feet and turn left onto Lincoln Ave., then left again onto Tustin Ave. and enter the Park and Ride area.

An option is to start the ride from Eisenhower Park. There is parking to the west (Lincoln Ave. to Ocean View Ave. and right on Main St.) and north (Lincoln Ave. to Ocean View Ave. and right on Bixby Ave.). This is a pleasant, shaded little park with a small lake, picnic benches, play areas, a mini-barnyard and bikepath to boot! The park sits right next to The Brickyard, a shopping plaza. There is an excellent restaurant in the plaza with a verandah area that looks out over the lake -- a great place to end the trip.

Bikers should come prepared with a moderate water supply. Though several public water sources are easily accessible on the west side, the single public source east of Quintana Rd. (the Eucalyptus Park entry) is at Featherly Regional Park at the trip terminus.

TRIP DESCRIPTION: **Trailhead to Peralta Canyon Park.** Exit the Park and Ride area and head north a short distance to Lincoln Ave. Turn right (east) and bike under the Costa Mesa Fwy. Turn left on Santa Ana Canyon Rd. (0.2). Note that both streets change names at the intersection -- Lincoln Ave./Nohl Ranch Rd. and Santiago Blvd./Santa Ana Canyon Rd. The route starts with the hills to the right and the freeway to the left and passes through a eucalyptus-lined flat stretch.

At Lakeview Ave., the path pulls away from the Riverside Fwy. and starts a moderate upgrade (2.2). In 0.2 mile is the crest with a nice view into the Santa Ana River Canyon. Bicycling through small rolling hills, pass Pinney Dr. (south)/Royal Oak Rd. (north) (1.9). A short 0.1 mile detour on Pinney Dr. leads to Peralta Canyon Park, a sports and recreation paradise. The park has restrooms, large grassy grounds, tree cover, both covered and open picnic tables with barbecues, sports fields and a large children's playground.

Anaheim Hills Proper. At Avd. Margarita Ave., there are shopping centers along both sides of the roadway (2.4). There are also nice views into the Peralta Hills (south) and across the canyon into the Chino Hills. The tour passes another tree-lined section of town with more shopping centers at Imperial Hwy. (2.6). Beyond this intersection ten years ago, the surroundings become significantly more rural, but not so now.

Bike on a flat Class II bikeway past Anaheim Hills Rd. (3.2), Quintana Rd. (entry to Eucalyptus park, with a restroom, water fountain, light treecover, full picnic facilities children's play area and baseball diamond) (3.5), a small shopping center to the left (3.6), and reach Fairmont Blvd. in another 0.1 mile. There are more excellent views across the canyon near this junction. The bikepath heads uphill in another 0.4 mile and crests in a short distance (4.3). The route returns near the freeway at this location and has a nice view further eastward into the canyon.

The Less-Developed Spaces. The remainder of the trip is more exposed and certainly has some isolated stretches. The bikeway heads up a 0.2-mile steep upgrade and crests near an area with some large, open fields (4.7). Pass the Anaheim Hills Festival (shopping center) and newer housing developments near Roosevelt Rd. (5.5), Weir Canyon Rd. (5.7), and in 0.2 mile reach an area with an excellent view further into the Santa Ana Canyon. Soon, the route narrows to one lane and passes under a hillside housing development (6.1), then enters dry, dusty brushland and goes under the spans of the Eastern Transportation Corridor (State Hwy. 241) starting at (7.0). In another 0.6 mile is the road terminus at Gypsum Canyon Rd. (To the left is Featherly Regional Park while right is a private mining operation.)

CONNECTING TRIPS: 1) Continuation with the Santa Ana River Trail (Trip #17A) - at the terminus, continue west on Gypsum Canyon Rd. toward Featherly Regional Park. Turn right onto the Class I trail just before entering the park. (Note: also see Trip #17A for a loop connection with the Class I trail on the north bank of the Santa Ana River.); 2) connection with the Orange/Irvine Regional Park Loop (Trip #26) - near the trip origin, turn south on Santiago Blvd. from Lincoln Ave. and bike two miles on a Class II bikeway to Villa Park Rd.; 3) connection with the Yorba Linda Bits and Pieces tour (Trip #43)

- at Weir Canyon Rd. (becomes Yorba Linda Blvd.) or Gypsum Canyon Rd., bicycle north across the Santa Ana River to La Palma Ave.; 4) connection with the Anaheim Hills tour (Trip # 44) - at Nohl Ranch Rd. and Santiago Blvd., go east on the former street.

TRIP #26 - ORANGE/IRVINE PARK LOOP

GENERAL LOCATION: Orange

LEVEL OF DIFFICULTY: City of Orange Loop - moderate
Distance - 10.2 miles
Elevation gain - periodic moderate-to-steep grades

HIGHLIGHTS: A predominantly Class II loop through a rural section of Orange County, this route works its way through some lightly trafficked, pleasant residential areas after leaving Irvine Regional Park. There is a short challenging grade on Chapman Ave. and a longer workout on Santiago Canyon Rd., while the remainder of the tour is downhill or on light grades. There are several spurs off the primary route, with Orange Park Blvd. being most rural and scenic and Cannon St. being the most challenging. The park section is primarily Class I and could serve as a family trip in itself. The park has several miles of paved and dirt bikeway, as well as bike rentals, picnic areas, pony rides, small zoo, mini-train rides, lovely lagoon, and other attractions.

TRAILHEAD: From the Orange Fwy. or Costa Mesa Fwy., take the Chapman Ave. turnoff east. The distances to the Jamboree Rd. intersection are 4-1/2 miles and 7-1/2 miles, respectively. Turn left (north), get into the right-hand lane and go 1/3 mile to the signed Irvine Regional Park entrance at Irvine Park Rd. From the Eastern Transportation Corridor, exit at Chapman Ave./Santiago Canyon Rd. and drive west one mile to Jamboree Rd. Turn right and motor 1/3 mile to the park entrance.

Pay the entree fee and enjoy the park after the ride. (See the detailed map provided for park facilities.) An alternative is to start at Santiago Hills Park off of Trail's End Ln. The park has water, restrooms, walkway/bikeways, scattered tree cover, sheltered picnic/barbecue facilities and children's playground.

Bring a filled water bottle. This is a relatively exposed trip and there are no on-route public water stops after leaving the park. There is a concession stand at the park which might be a nice place to visit at ride's end.

TRIP DESCRIPTION: **City of Orange Loop.** Leave the park and return to Class II Jamboree Rd., turning left. (Note there is also a paralleling Class I bike path.) Bike to Class II Chapman Ave. and turn right (west), passing a shopping complex across the street. Observe the stately homes built high on the hillsides to the left while coasting to Newport Blvd. and another shopping center. Parallel a horse trail on the right which passes into an oak-shaded area next to a residential community and pump a gritty climb for 0.8 mile to a crest near Cliffway Dr. (1.8). Just before the crest is Orange Hill Ter. and a sheer trip up to the Orange Hill Restaurant with a spectacular view of the local Orange Country area.

There is an outstanding view into the canyon and back into the residential areas at this point. Cruise downhill past Cannon St./Crawford Canyon Rd., where the Class II section ends (2.6). Then coast on a moderating grade another 0.6 mile to Hewes St. Pedal on this quiet residential, Class X street to another at Spring St. and turn left (west). Cycle another 0.5 mile to Prospect St., turning right onto a Class II route, as it will remain for most of the trip's remainder. Bicycle on this curving roadway, taking a short Class I diversion alongside the Santiago Creek flood control basin. Across the street is an entry to the Class I bike trail along the creek. (See the **Santiago Creek Spur Trip** described below.)

A right on Class I Wanda Rd. (5.0) is followed by another right in 0.5 mile onto Class II Villa Park Rd. (Katella Ave. to the west). Bike through a tree-lined residential section to Lemon St. where hillside views open directly ahead. Climb modestly and cross Santiago Creek, then pass Cannon St. (7.1), where the road name is now Santiago Canyon Rd. In another challenging uphill 0.7 mile is Orange Park Blvd.; Windes Dr., the entry to Santiago Oaks Park, follows shortly.

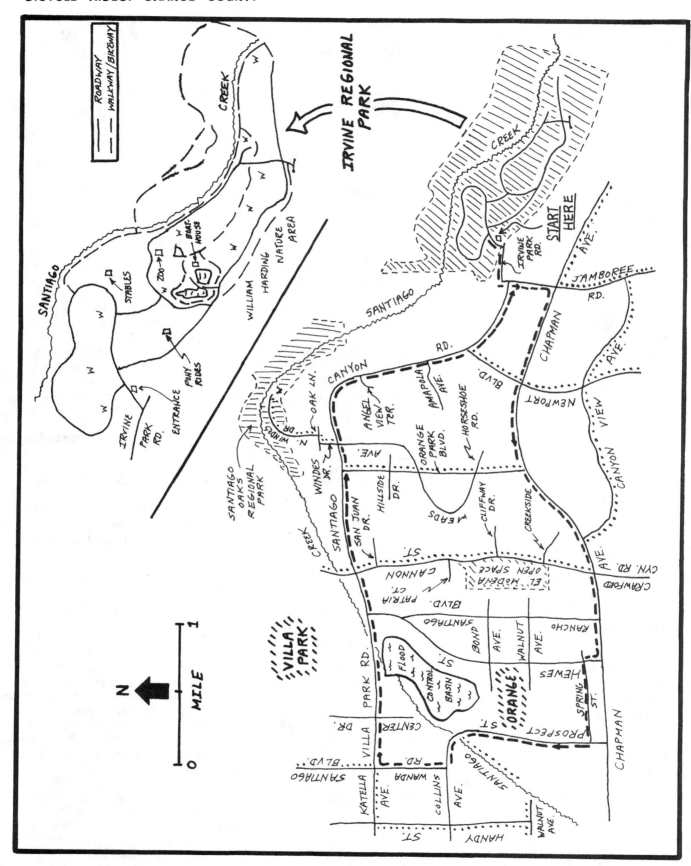

TRIP #26 - ORANGE/IRVINE PARK LOOP

Continue climbing past Angel View Ter. and reach the northern edge of the well-manicured lawns that are a part of the Holy Sepulcher Cemetery. Reach a crest near Amapola Ave. (9.2) and enjoy the striking hillside views to the left. Coast past Newport Blvd. and reach Jamboree Rd. in 0.5 mile. Turn left, then return to Irvine Park and look forward to your post-ride picnic (10.2).

Irvine Park. There is a multitude of ways to tour this park, which rivals Mile Square Park (Trip #5) and El Dorado Park (L.A. County) and which is certainly more in its natural state. Our tour started with a 1.9-mile ride around the bikepaths at the park boundaries and included a 2.0-mile interior tour.

The outside tour includes the route across (north of) Santiago Creek, a swingby of open expanses of the easternmost picnic and kite flying areas, and a pass-by of the William Harding Nature Area. The interior tour includes the Santiago Creek parallel path, middle park path through the playgrounds and group picnic areas, and a pedal around the lagoon and zoo areas. In addition, there is an equal amount of roads through the area that are lightly traveled and serve as excellent bikepath options for all but the most inexperienced bikers. In short, the Irvine Park tour could, in itself, serve as part of an all-day family picnic and biking outing.

Ocean Park Boulevard

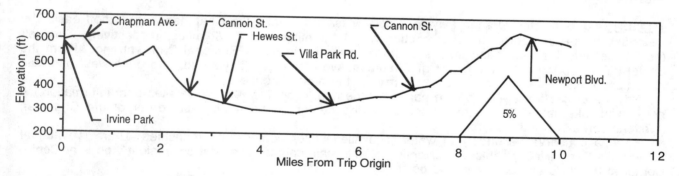

Excursions: **Orange Park Blvd. and Cannon St. Options.** The tour of Orange can be extended by connecting the reference tour with either or both of these roadways. Class II Orange Park Blvd. meanders through a rural residential area for 1.3 miles between Santiago Rd. and Chapman Ave. This moderate segment has horse trails, scattered tall trees and upscale homes. Cannon St. is a 1.6-mile mostly Class II roadway with a Class I segment along the El Modena Open Space. There is a very steep (0.7-mile, 300-foot) climb from the south and a steep (0.9-mile, 240-foot) pump from the north which bumps the overall ride to the moderate-to-strenuous category. The crest is near Cliffway Dr.

Canyon View Ave. From Chapman Ave., turn south on this lightly-developed residential street and pedal a Class II roadway on a 0.1-mile flat before taking a gritty 0.8-mile climb to a crest near Outrider St. There are neck-bending views of the ridgetop homes to the left and some great vistas into distant Santiago Canyon beyond the crest. Coast past Newport Blvd. and reach Jamboree Rd. in two miles from Chapman Ave. Another 0.6 mile north on Jamboree Rd. returns bikers to Chapman Ave.

Santiago Creek Trail. From Prospect St., this south side Class I path was open for about 0.6 mile, ending at a turnaround. This might eventually become part of a trail which extends from Irvine Lake to near the Santa Ana Fwy. provided rights-of-way and other issues can be resolved.

Santiago Oaks Park. At Meads Ave./Windes Dr., turn north and take a right at Oak Ln. to remain on rural, two-lane Windes Dr. Ride to Lewis Dr. and turn right. In a short distance is the ranger station and the Santiago Oaks Park entry kiosk. The oak-studded park has interesting flora, water, both hiking and horse trails and limited on-road biking areas. The distance from Santiago Canyon Rd. to the park entry is about 1/2 mile.

CONNECTING TRIPS: 1) Connection with the Santiago Canyon Road route (Trip #27) - the two tours share a common segment on Jamboree Rd. just outside the Irvine Park entrance; 2) connection with the Anaheim Hills tour (Trip #44) - at Katella Ave. and Santiago Blvd., go north on the latter street.

TRIP #27 - SANTIAGO CANYON ROAD

GENERAL LOCATION: Santiago Canyon

LEVEL OF DIFFICULTY: One way - strenuous; up and back - strenuous
Distance - 12.6 miles (one way)
Elevation gain - continuous moderate-to-steep grade to the summit

HIGHLIGHTS: This is an excellent workout trip through a scenic, but highly sun-exposed canyon. It is one of the most popular for serious bikers training against the clock. The tour is l2.6 Class III miles (rides like a Class II) in rolling hills with a near-continuous moderate-to-steep six-mile grade to the summit. On a hot day, this is a strenuous one-way trip. The route has several scenic points, passes near Irvine Lake, and ends near Cook's Corner at a rustic restaurant/bar. Just beyond this terminus is stately Saint Michael's Abbey. This trip also links up with three alternate canyon routes for the more adventurous: Silverado Canyon Rd., Modjeska Canyon Rd., and Live Oak Canyon Rd., all described as separate tours.

TRAILHEAD: From the Orange Fwy. or Costa Mesa Fwy., take the Chapman Ave. turnoff east. The distances to the Jamboree Rd. intersection are 4-1/2 miles and 7-1/2 miles, respectively. Turn left (north), get into the right-hand lane and go 1/3 mile to the Irvine Regional Park entrance. From the Eastern Transportation Corridor, exit at Chapman Ave./Santiago Canyon Rd. and drive west one mile to Jamboree Rd. Turn right and motor 1/3 mile to the park entrance.
Pay the entree fee and enjoy the park after the ride. (See Trip #26 for detailed park information.) A non-paying alternative is to start at the shopping center at the southwest corner of the Chapman Ave./Jamboree Rd. intersection.
Bring a conservative supply of water (two filled water bottles) and munchies. There is water at Irvine Lake Park, although this is a diversion off the main course. The next convenient stop is at Cook's Corner at the trip's end or turnaround point.

TRIP DESCRIPTION: **Trailhead to Irvine Lake Park.** Leave the park and take Jamboree Rd. to Chapman Ave. Turn left onto a four-lane, Class III roadway (with spaced signs asking truck drivers to stay out of the bike lane) and cycle into an open, flat area. Begin a steady moderate climb, then pass over the Eastern Transportation Corridor (State Hwy. 241) at (1.3). Parallel the corridor, then climb to a local summit and observe the toll road's bend to the south.
Coast on a long downgrade which flattens near a viewpoint above the Irvine Lake area. The roadway proceeds modestly uphill again for about 0.4 mile, leveling out just before the Irvine Lake turnoff (3.7). There are rental boats, swimming, shady picnic areas, athletic fields and water at Irvine Lake Park. Better yet, there is a little restaurant/bar here. If you have doubts by now, this might be an fine spot to rest and ponder turning back.
Irvine Lake Park to Silverado Canyon Road. Beyond the turnoff, cycle a moderate uphill and reach the top of the grade where there is a lightly-treed area and the wide Limestone Canyon creek bed to the right. Bike through light rolling (mostly uphill) terrain along the creek in an area with a superb view of Mt. Saddleback (5.5). This is the first 0.5 mile of a sweaty six-mile climb. In another 0.5 mile is the first view into the Santiago Creek watershed and a bridge crossing not far beyond (6.6). In

114

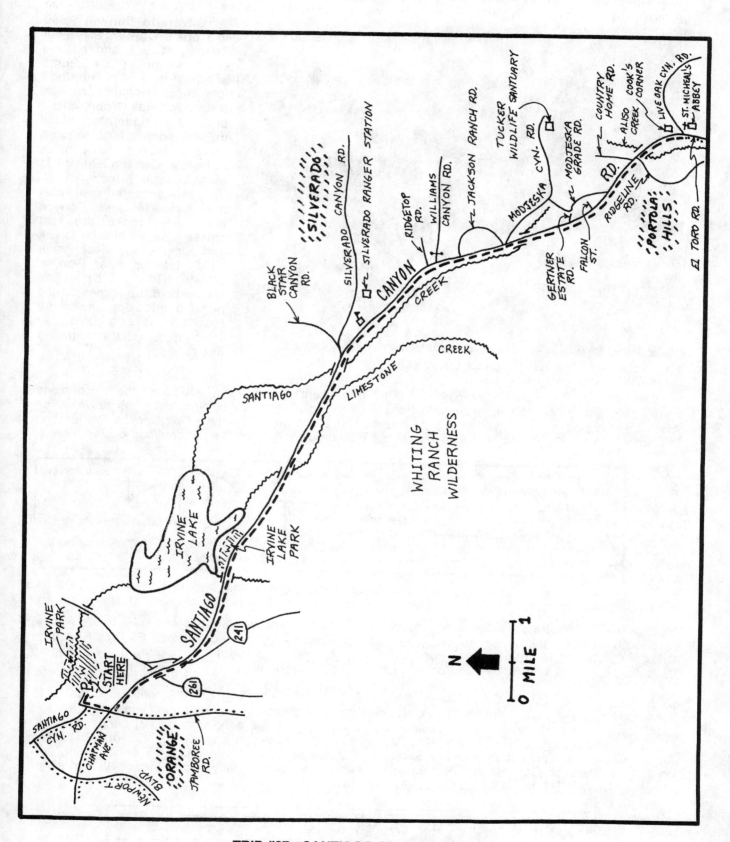

TRIP #27 - SANTIAGO CANYON ROAD

another 0.1 mile is the Silverado Canyon turnoff. The Silverado Forest Station is about 3/4-mile further up that road.

East Santiago Canyon Road

Silverado Canyon Road to Cook's Corner. Stay near Santiago Creek and pass a small school (7.0). Pump another mile-plus upgrade and reach a local crest at Ridgetop Rd. Soon after, pedal the moderated uphill under some high-tension lines (8.3), then pass William's Canyon Rd. (8.7) and Jackson Ranch Rd. N. (8.9) in a scattered residential area. Cross Modjeska Canyon Rd. (9.6), make the last crossing over Santiago Creek and pump a very steep grade which lets up near Gertner Estate Rd. (10.6). (The residents in the homes on the ridge overlooking the climb probably have a field day watching cyclists climbing this segment.)

Now all the hard uphill work pays off! First is a scenic turnout with a view of the surrounding canyonland and a "peek" southward into Portola Hills and Mission Viejo. Next is a long downhill, an Aliso Creek crossing, Ridgeline Rd. (12.0) and the route terminus at the Live Oak Canyon Rd. junction at Cook's Corner (12.6). Stop and take a well deserved break at the rustic restaurant/bar located there.

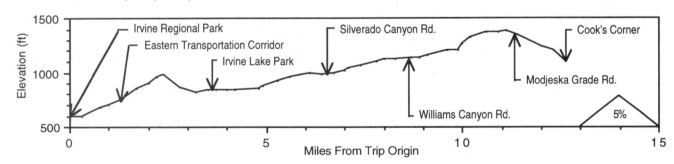

Excursion: St. Michael's Abbey. A neat side trip is to examine the grounds of St. Michael's Abbey, reached by turning east a few hundred feet down the main highway (now named El Toro Rd.) from Cook's Corner. The interesting atmosphere includes little rolling hills, abundant overhanging treecover, the interesting abbey and other buildings on the grounds.

CONNECTING TRIPS: 1) Continuation with the Aliso Creek Trail (Trip #29A) - continue south on El Toro Rd. beyond the trip terminus; 2) connection with the Orange/Irvine Park Loop (Trip #26) - the two tours share a common segment on Jamboree Rd. just outside the park entrance; 3) connection with the Cities and Canyons tour (Trip # 47) - the trips share a common segment on El Toro Rd. below Cook's Corner; 4) connection with the Silverado Canyon ride (Trip #48) - at the 7.6-mile point, turn north onto Silverado Canyon Rd.; 5) connection with the Modjeska Canyon ride (Trip #49) - at either Modjeska Canyon Rd. or Modjeska Grade Rd., turn east.

TRIP #28 - O'NEILL REGIONAL PARK

GENERAL LOCATION: Trabuco Canyon, Rancho Santa Margarita

LEVEL OF DIFFICULTY: Up and back - easy
Distance - 7.4 miles
Elevation gain - moderate grades in Mesa Day Use area

HIGHLIGHTS: The focus of this trip is O'Neill Regional Park with over four miles of bikeway on roads within an oak forest. The trip is a winner for families as it is contained within an enticing natural environment well removed from high traffic streets. The park roadway/bikeway visits the central picnic area and nature center, crosses Trabuco Creek, cruises the elevated Mesa day-use area, visits the Equestrian Camping area, then ends with a countryside ride north, paralleling Live Oak Canyon Rd.

Family Outing Near Oak Grove

TRAILHEAD: From the intersection of El Toro Rd. and Santiago Canyon Rd. at Cook's Corner, turn east onto Live Oak Canyon Rd. and drive about three scenic and hilly miles to the park. From Rancho Santa Margarita, follow Plano Trabuco north to where it turns sharply west and becomes Trabuco Rd. In 1-2/3 mile, on a road now named Trabuco Canyon Rd., is the park entrance.
Only a light water supply is needed. There are scattered sources within the park.

TRIP DESCRIPTION: Minors must accompany adults and a minimum traveling party of two is required -- there are limited inherent dangers such as mountain lions, rattlesnakes, poison oak, and rugged terrain in the park. This is particularly applicable for off-road hiking and biking.
From the park entry area, first cruise the (Oak Grove) day-use picnic area. Pass the gate to the north camping area near the park entrance and the nature center (spring and summer interpretive programs) near the end of the picnic area. There are picnic facilities, turf play area, a softball diamond, playground, water and restrooms in this part of the park.
Leave the picnic area (0.5) and follow the curving road to the right. Cross Trabuco Creek, bike to the intersection with the parking loop (0.9) and follow hard left, pedaling on a short, steep upgrade. Note that there is a hiking trail below which parallels Trabuco Creek. Pedal a more modest incline along the southern park boundary on the Plano Trabuco and pass the Mesa day-use areas. This is prime territory for nature viewers. At the end of the line is a parking/turnaround loop (2.0).
Return across Trabuco Creek to the park office area (4.0) and bear to the right, following the flat roadway past the group camping area and turning right again just beyond. Stay to the right (south) at each junction until reaching a single roadway which veers right (4.55). Cross a feeder creek in 0.1

117

mile, then bear right at the next major junction to reach the Equestrian Camping area (4.9). (We expected to see horses bedded down in sleeping bags!).

Retrace the route back to the park office area (5.8) and turn north just beyond, Pass through the gate and follow that tree-covered road as it passes alongside (but remains fenced from) Live Oak Canyon Rd. Note the abundance of hiking/off-road biking trails to the left all along this section. There are two west-side spurs off the main route for those who want to explore every "nook and cranny" of this beautiful park with a group camping cluster near the second. Near road's end is a series of group camp sites and a turnaround area at the terminus (6.6). Now, simply return to the park entrance (7.4)!

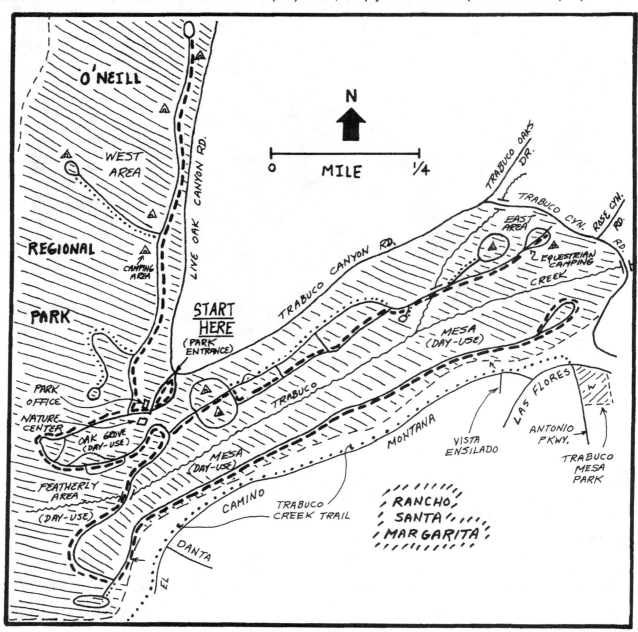

TRIP #28 - O'NEILL REGIONAL PARK

Excursion: Rancho Santa Marguerita. From the Mesa area, there are exits from the park onto Class I Camino Montana. This Trabuco Creek Trail goes 3/4 mile from the Danta exit to Antonio Pkwy's. end.

CONNECTING TRIPS: 1) Connection with the Aliso Creek Trail (Ride #29A) - ride west three miles on Live Oak Canyon Rd. to El Toro Rd.; 2) connection with the Cities and Canyons ride (Trip #47) - exit the park and turn in either direction.

TRIPS #29A & #29B - ALISO CREEK TRAIL

The moderate-level Aliso Creek Trail from Cook's Corner to the terminus in Laguna Niguel (31.8 miles round trip) is broken up into two sections. The general area map for the entire trip is provided below. The ride is entirely Class I. The upper segment (Trip #29A) leaves from the foothills above El Toro, winds its way downhill and southward along Aliso Creek and ends at El Toro Park. The lower segment (Trip #29B) leaves the park and continues the creekside cruise, except for a short Class I on-road stint in the Laguna Woods area. The subsequent creek revisit ends near the Orange County History Museum, is followed by a tour of Laguna Niguel Park/Sulphur Creek Reservoir and ends at Crown Valley Community Park.

There are sections of the trail near El Toro Park and further downstream of Laguna Hills Dr. where the trail may be flooded during winter storms. Plan ahead for route alternates if trips are scheduled under adverse weather conditions.

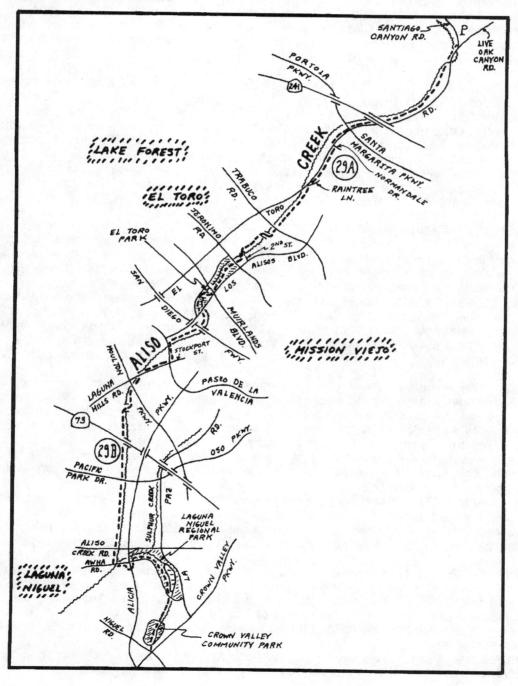

TRIP #29A - ALISO CREEK TRAIL (Northern Segment)

GENERAL LOCATION: El Toro, Lake Forest

LEVEL OF DIFFICULTY: One way - easy; up and back - easy to moderate
Distance - 7.7 miles (one way)
Elevation gain - periodic moderate grades

HIGHLIGHTS: The upper segment starts in the foothills above El Toro, winds its way downhill and southward along Aliso Creek and terminates at El Toro I Park. One of the most pleasant rides in Orange County, this route explores significant stretches of relatively unspoiled bottomland in the middle of high-density residential areas. The upper portion of the trip segment takes cyclists through lightly developed high-desert terrain, while the lower portion winds through the developed cities of El Toro and Lake Forest below, all on Class I bikeway. Inviting, shaded El Toro Park at segment's end is a delightful end point or a fine rest stop for bikers continuing on to the southern trip segment. Portions of this route may be flooded during storms.

TRAILHEAD: From the San Diego Fwy., exit north at El Toro Rd. and continue about eight miles north to the road junction at Oak Canyon Rd. Park in the lot at the junction at Cook's Corner. From the Foothill Transportation Corridor (State Hwy. 241), exit south at Portola Pkwy. and go 1/2 mile to El Toro Rd. Turn left (east) and drive 2-3/4 miles to Cook's Corner. From the Costa Mesa Fwy., exit east at Katella Ave./Villa Park Rd. Follow that roadway, which becomes Santiago Canyon Rd., roughly eight miles to Cook's Corner. This option is presented since the route is scenic.
Bring a filled water bottle. There are few reliable and available water stops directly along the path. The single public water stops that we found are at the baseball diamonds in El Toro Park II and at the tennis courts at the southern end of El Toro I Park.

TRIP DESCRIPTION: **Cactus Country to Raintree Lane.** From Cook's Corner, pedal south just past Ridgeline Rd. (about 1/4 mile) on El Toro Rd. and follow a signed small asphalt path leading diagonally away from the main roadway (on the right hand or west side). (Note that there is also an entry on the east side of the road just south of St. Michael's Abbey.) Observe the Portola Hills ridgeline homes high up to the right while transiting lightly-developed Whiting Ranch Wilderness Park.
Pass the McFadden Ranch House and Interpretive Center and observe the jumble of natural foliage near the trail. Pass the first exit and go under Glenn Ranch Rd. (1.1), staying parallel to and below El Toro Rd. while continuing through high-desert terrain. The path swings toward the west and steepens, passing an area with an abundance of cactus (1.5). Contrast this with the developments on the ridges to the left (east) and the huge monolith that is the Foothill Transportation Corridor in another 0.3 mile.
Just south of the Marguerite Pkwy. (2.0) undercrossing is an alternate entry to the trail. In a short distance, pass alongside an extended eucalyptus grove that is next to El Toro Rd. Cross additional bike entries and exit the eucalyptus-lined portion of the route, remaining next to El Toro Rd. Next is the Santa Margarita exit followed by an undercrossing which dips to near creek level (it floods during rainy periods). The trail leaves the eucalyptus stand and meets the Normandale Dr. undercrossing at (3.3). Exit the creekside trail at the traffic signal, cross over to the east side of El Toro Rd. and bike on the sidewalk/bikeway. (The Class I path does continue on the west side, but there are no convenient street crossings prior to Raintree Ln.)
Raintree Lane to El Toro Park. Bike 0.9 mile further through this higher-density residential area to Raintree Ln. (4.2). At the southeast corner of that intersection, follow the Class I path beyond the trail sign. Just beyond Raintree Ln., Aliso Creek shifts to the southeast side of El Toro Rd. The bikepath transits a pleasant treed, rural setting alongside the creek through a residential community for the next two miles.
In 0.5 mile, the bikeway follows a moderate downhill past Creekside, then spends the next 0.7 mile alongside a mini forest. The trail goes under Trabuco Rd. (5.9), crosses the creek to the west side on a wood walk/bike bridge, and soon follows between the creek and Cherry Ave. alongside stands of fragrant eucalyptus and other trees. Near the end of 2nd St. the path recrosses the creek to the west side on another bikeway/walkway (6.6). In this section the creekbed is concrete and there are residences on both sides.
The path returns to near creek level (this may flood during storms as may the undercrossings at Muirlands Blvd. and Los Aliso Blvd.) and crosses under Jeronimo Rd. It comes up on the opposite side

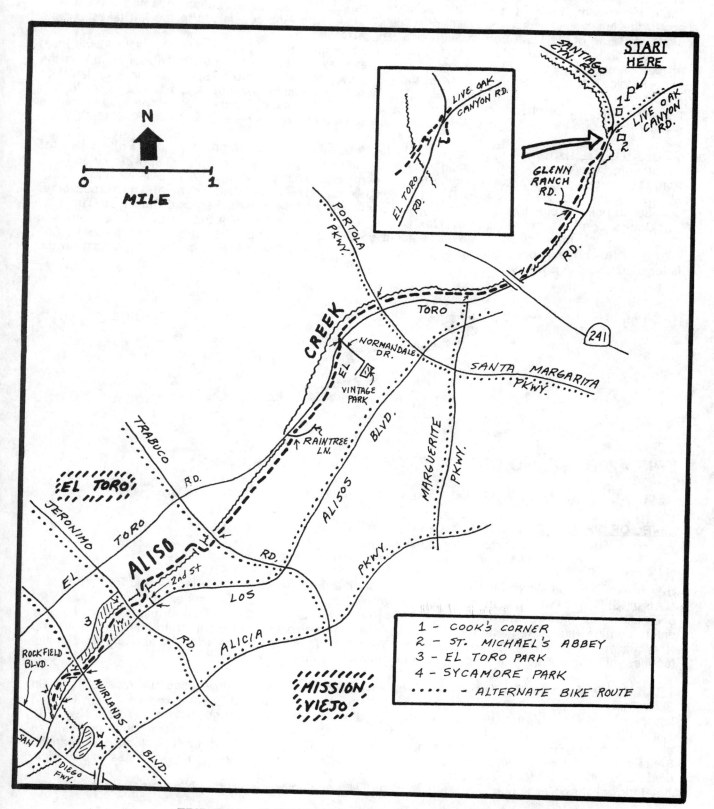

TRIP #29A - ALISO CREEK TRAIL (Northern Segment)

at El Toro II Park with its baseball diamonds and water fountain. (Just up the park pathway to Jeronimo Rd. is a restroom.) Follow the signed route on the periphery of the baseball diamonds and make a wide arc to the left, passing under a railroad trestle (7.0). Another sharper sweep to the left takes cyclists along the edge of the Lake Forest Golf and Practice Center.

Next the trail takes a wide turn to the right (southwest), climbing to and paralleling Los Alisos Blvd. at road level (7.4), then ducks back down near creek level below Muirlands Blvd. It comes up on the opposite side into the most scenic part of the park (7.6), named El Toro I Park. There is abundant tree shade, water near the tennis courts along Larkwood Ln., picnic benches and barbecues, children's play area and a maze of criss-crossing bikeway/walkways. The park's southern edge and trip terminus is just north of Rockfield Blvd. where Aliso Creek turns east and crosses below Los Alisos Blvd. (7.7).

CONNECTING TRIPS: 1) Continuation with the lower Aliso Creek segment (Trip #29B) - bike east underneath Los Alisos Blvd.; 2) continuation with the Santiago Canyon Rd. trip (Trip #27) - ride north from the trip origin on Santiago Canyon Rd.; 3) connection with the Mission Viejo Bikeway (Trip #30) - at Los Alisos Blvd. and Jeronimo Rd., turn north onto Los Alisos Blvd. There are numerous other connection points (refer to Trip #30 map); 4) connection with the O'Neill Regional Park tour (Trip #28) - at Cook's Corner, turn east on Live Oak Canyon Dr.; 5) connection with the Cities and Canyons ride (Trip #47) - the trips have a common segment on El Toro Rd. south of Cook's Corner; 6) connection with the Arroyo Trabuco Loop (Trip #50) - at El Toro Rd. and Santa Margarita Pkwy., go east on the latter roadway to Alicia Pkwy.

TRIP #29B - ALISO CREEK TRAIL (Southern Segment)

GENERAL LOCATION: Lake Forest, Laguna Hills, Laguna Niguel

LEVEL OF DIFFICULTY: Up and back - easy
Distance - 8.2 miles (one way)
Elevation gain - periodic light grades

HIGHLIGHTS: This Class I trip segment is the southern connector for the Aliso Creek Trail. The route starts at El Toro I Park, proceeds 1-1/2 miles along Aliso Creek, plies the trail along surface streets for one-plus miles, then returns to the creek all the way to the Aliso Creek Trail terminus. Next the tour enters Laguna Niguel Regional Park and follows a scenic and interesting trail from this park to the trip terminus at Crown Valley Community Park. The trip highlight is Laguna Niguel Park with its plentiful facilities, offerings of several interesting family mini-tours and a lake to explore.

TRAILHEAD: From the San Diego Fwy., exit north on El Toro Rd. and drive about 1/4 mile to Rockfield Blvd. Turn right and go 0.6 mile to Larkwood Ln. (the street just before Los Alisos Blvd.). Turn left and find parking next to El Toro I Park. From the San Joaquin Hills Transportation Corridor (State Hwy. 73), exit north at El Toro Rd. and head 3-1/4 miles to the San Diego Fwy. undercrossing, then continue as above. From the Foothill Transportation Corridor (State Hwy. 241), exit south at Portola Pkwy./Rancho Santa Margarita Pkwy. and drive 1/2 mile to El Toro Rd. Turn right and go 4-1/2 miles to Rockfield Blvd., turn left and motor 0.6 mile to Larkwood Ln., turning left again.

Bring a light water supply. This is a short trip with strategically-placed public water sources.

TRIP DESCRIPTION: **El Toro I Park to Sheep Hills Park.** Follow the bikepath nearest Los Alisos Blvd. and look for an entry trail into the creekbed. (This may be inaccessible in rainy weather.) Dip down into the concrete bottom and cross the creek over a metal plate. Just beyond, pass under Los Alisos

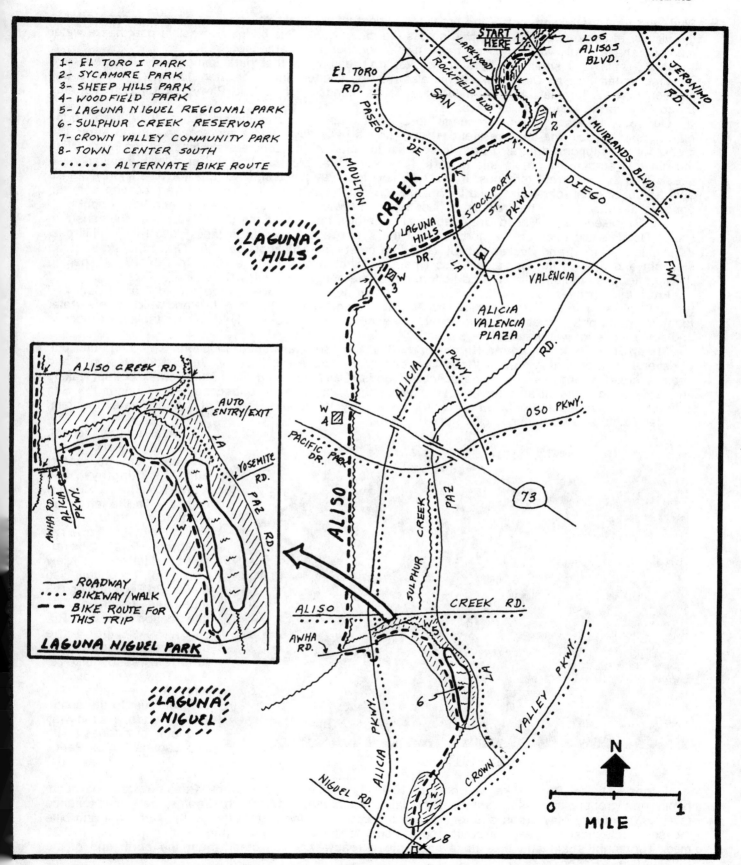

TRIP #29B - ALISO CREEK TRAIL (Southern Segment)

Blvd. and turn east. Climb out of the creekbed almost immediately; the trailway opens up soon after in the vicinity of Sycamore Park, which is across the creek (0.3). This bridge-accessible park has a water fountain, shade trees, walking/biking trails, picnic benches and barbecues.

In 0.2 mile is a small concrete cross-over trail leading to that park immediately followed by a passage under the San Diego Fwy. (This also may be flooded during or after storms.) There is a trail junction here. A turn left and 1/4-mile pedal leads alongside the Alicia Pkwy. turnoff from the San Diego Fwy. to the Laguna Hills Plaza.

Our route heads right and proceeds up a short grade past a commemorative Juan Avila Adobe marker, skirts below the local residences, then heads back down into a more open canyon area. The creek bottom supports natural growth in contrast to some of the concrete stretches to the north. Note the dirt trail across the creek; this is part of the equestrian trailway that will parallel the paved Aliso Creek Trail to it's current terminus. In 0.3 mile is a four-way junction. Two legs travel a short distance and die out at local roadways. Take the middle leg which has a trail marker for bikers coming from the opposite direction (0.7). This trail climbs just below the walls of nearby residences and heads south.

Shortly, bikers reach Paseo De Valencia and the bike trail leaves the creek. Turn left (southeast) on Paseo De Valencia (stay on the north side of the street) and follow the signed Class I trail uphill past Kennington Dr. (1.1) and Beckenham St. (1.3) to a crest near Stockport St. (1.5). Cross the street at the stoplight and ride on the westside Class I path on what is now Laguna Hills Dr. Coast a steepening downgrade, pass Indian Hills Ln. and bottom out at the bridge over Aliso Creek in 0.6 mile.

From the northeast side of the bridge, drop down near creek level on the signed Class I path and turn left, passing under Laguna Hills Dr. Almost immediately is Sheep Hills Park which offers water fountain, porta-potty, scattered tree cover, baseball diamond, soccer field, picnic tables, barbecues and several interior walkway/bikeways.

Sheep Hills Park to Laguna Niguel Park. Skirt the park, pass under Moulton Pkwy. and enter one of several segments of Aliso and Wood Canyons Wilderness Park. Cross to the creek's west side and begin a broad sweep, skirting some school grounds. Continue along the natural creek bottom, taking time to look into the hillside residences which pepper the route's landscape. Pedal under the San Joaquin Hills Transportation Corridor (3.0), pass cozy Woodfield Park to the right (water fountain, baseball fields) and go under Pacific Park Dr. (3.8).

Sulphur Creek Reservoir

Pass another school, Foxborough Park (many facilities, but no water) and the lengthy Aliso Niguel High School campus. To the left is the mammoth, hard-to-miss Hollyfield Federal Building. Pass pocket-sized, waterless Hillview Park (4.8), go under Aliso Creek Rd. in another 0.3 mile and reach a "T"-intersection at Awma Rd. (5.3). As per the directional signs here, turn left (east), bike to Alicia Pkwy. and cross the street at the walker/biker stoplight just to the south. Return north a short way and look for a Class I path into Laguna Niguel Park

Laguna Niguel Park. Bike east on park roadway next to Sulphur Creek. Pass covered and open, family and group picnic sites (some of the latter with running water), restrooms, park maintenance facilities, children's play areas and tennis courts before reaching a road fork (5.8). Turn right and bike the semicircle past a volleyball court, more picnic facilities, restrooms and another junction in 0.25 mile. Turn right again and bike up a short steep roadway which crests near the north end of the Sulphur Creek Reservoir (6.2).

Bring a fishing pole; this reservoir is an inviting spot for a short biking diversion. There are numerous great fishing spots spread along the edge of the reservoir, with numerous waterfowl sharing the territory. The road passes the Laguna Niguel Lake concession and boat rental (6.7) and runs near the tree-lined southern end of the reservoir in 0.3 mile. That area is reached by crossing a small bridge over the outlet creek.

Laguna Niguel Park to Crown Community Park. The bike route reaches a parking lot cul-de-sac; just beyond is a small trail heading south. That trail parallels the outlet creek, passes a small water treatment plant (7.3), then enters a wide-open canyon. There is a direct view of hillside residences and the first glances at Crown Valley Pkwy. At (7.9), the trail passes between the Crown Valley Community Park and a gymnasium/pool. There is a small footbridge over to the park, a putting green, and restrooms.

Continue along the path across a road access to the park's parking lot. There are small picnic/barbecue spots here. The bikeway passes through a shaded corridor along the creek and ends soon near Niguel Rd. and Crown Valley Pkwy. (8.2).

CONNECTING TRIPS: 1) Continuation with the upper Aliso Creek Trail segment (Trip #29A) - from the trip origin, bike north along Los Alisos Blvd.; 2) connection with the Laguna Niguel Bikeway (Trip #11) - at the trip's end at Niguel Rd., proceed in either direction on Crown Valley Pkwy.; 3) connection with the Mission Viejo Bikeway (Trip #30) - at Paseo De Valencia and Stockport St., continue southeast on the former roadway. There are numerous other connection points (refer to Trip #30 map); 4) connection with the Aliso Viejo Figure "8" (Trip #46) - at Aliso Creek Rd. or Pacific Park Dr., exit the creek path.

TRIP #30 - MISSION VIEJO BIKEWAY

GENERAL LOCATION: Mission Viejo, El Toro, Laguna Hills

LEVEL OF DIFFICULTY: Loop - moderate to strenuous
Distance - 15.6 miles
Elevation gain - frequent moderate grades; periodic moderate-to-steep
grades

HIGHLIGHTS: A loop trip that tours a part of the Mission Viejo Bikeway System, this route is primarily a mixed Class I/II adventure that hits several of the local highlights. The trip is hilly with moderate mileage, providing a wide variety of natural and man-made scenery.

The tour leaves the Village Center and passes near the Marguerite Recreation Center, Lake Mission Viejo, Mission Viejo Youth Center, cruises through Wilderness Glen Park, and picks up a segment of the Aliso Creek Trail that goes through El Toro I and II Parks. The northern and middle portions of the route are in established residential environs, while the most southern portion is in the more recently developed hillside areas.

TRAILHEAD: From the San Diego Fwy., exit east at La Paz Rd. and continue about 1-1/4 miles to Marguerite Pkwy. Cross that street, turn right, and find parking under a tree in the Village Center parking area. From the San Joaquin Hills Transportation Corridor (State Hwy. 73), exit east on La Paz Rd. and drive one mile to Marguerite Pkwy., then continue as described above. From the Foothill Transportation Corridor (State Hwy. 241), exit west at Oso Pkwy. and go 3-1/4 miles to Marguerite Pkwy. Turn right (north) and motor two miles to Village Center. If you prefer to start at a park, the best on-route options are El Toro I or II Parks.

Bring a filled water bottle for hot days and refill at the public water sources at El Toro I or II Parks or Sycamore Park, all located near the trip mid-point. No other on-route public sources were found.

125

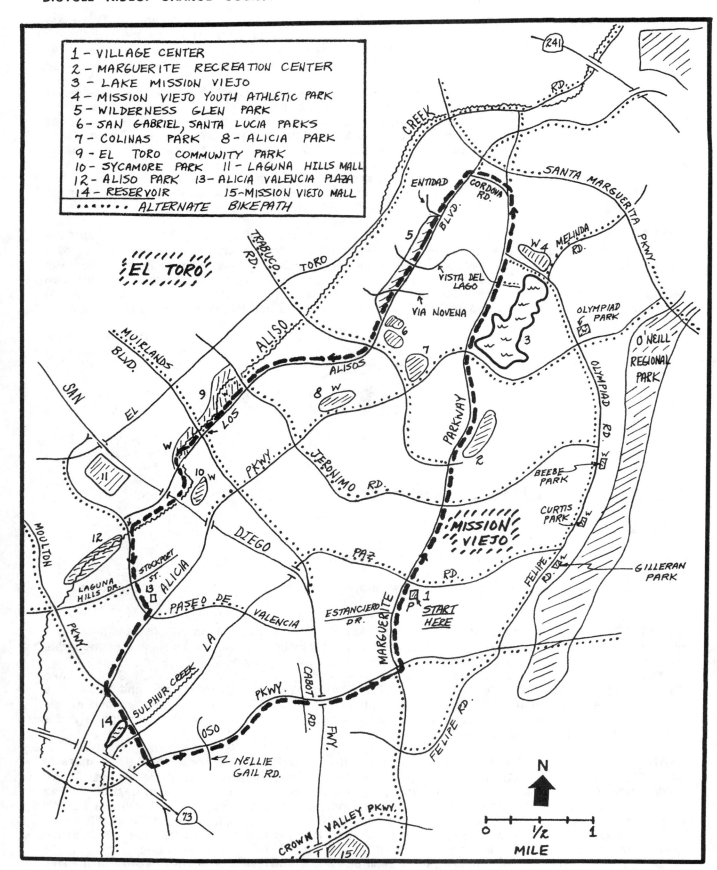

1 – VILLAGE CENTER
2 – MARGUERITE RECREATION CENTER
3 – LAKE MISSION VIEJO
4 – MISSION VIEJO YOUTH ATHLETIC PARK
5 – WILDERNESS GLEN PARK
6 – SAN GABRIEL, SANTA LUCIA PARKS
7 – COLINAS PARK 8 – ALICIA PARK
9 – EL TORO COMMUNITY PARK
10 – SYCAMORE PARK 11 – LAGUNA HILLS MALL
12 – ALISO PARK 13 – ALICIA VALENCIA PLAZA
14 – RESERVOIR   15 – MISSION VIEJO MALL
········· ALTERNATE BIKEPATH

TRIP #30 - MISSION VIEJO BIKEWAY

TRIP DESCRIPTION: **Village Center to Marguerite Recreation Center.** Exit the Village Center and bike north on Class II Marguerite Pkwy. The surrounding area is residential with some tree cover and a developed hillside above the roadway to the left (west). Much of the northern segment of the trip is on hillside-surrounded roadways. Pass Via Florecer (0.3) and head into a steady, light upgrade past Jeronimo Rd. (0.7) to a crest near Trabuco Rd. (1.1). Just across the intersection is a shopping center to the west and the Marguerite Recreation Center to the east. The center has accommodations for a wide variety of sports activities, including an Olympic-size aquatic center.

Lake Mission Viejo. In 0.5 mile the path is alongside the Casta Del Sol Golf Course. There is a view of the hills to the west from this point into what we labeled "Condo Canyon" (1.6). The bike route begins another steady upgrade and reaches Alicia Pkwy. in 0.6 mile and the crest 0.1 mile further. There is a magnificent view into the local mountains from this area. Bike to Vista Del Lago, turn right (east), and ride 0.2 mile past the Market On the Lake shopping center to a great overlook of Lake Mission Viejo.

Cordova Road. Return to Marguerite Pkwy. (3.1) and continue the hilly route 0.3 mile further to Olympiad Rd. Check out the over-the-shoulder Mission Viejo views in the next mile before reaching the Cordova Rd./Mustang Run trip summit. Turn left and cycle 0.3 mile further to Los Alisos Blvd. (4.6). The Portola Plaza shopping center is just to the north.

Wilderness Glen Park. Turn left again and start south and downhill on a Class I path. Bike through this residential area with a high hillside and homes to the left (east). Pass a school and recreation field and reach Entidad at (5.1). There is a maze of trails below this street along English Creek, which allow bikers and walkers to pass under Entidad. This style of "through route" is the same at Vista Del Lago and Via Novena.

Cruise on the Class I sidewalk/bikeway along the north edge of Wilderness Glen Park (5.4). There are trees and a forested creek bed with some canyon-like areas for the next mile, as well as some off-road bicycle paths scattered through the park. Cycle downhill past Vista Del Lago to Via Noveno (5.8); stop and look back at the line of condos that look like a castle on a hill. In 0.4 mile, head steeply downhill and pass a particularly well-forested section of the park. The roadway levels and passes Via Santa Lucia across the street. In a short distance the park ends and soon the path meets Trabuco Rd. (6.2). There is a small shopping center and some eateries at this intersection.

Lake Mission Viejo

El Toro Park. Cross the intersection and bike through a residential area passing Vallejo (6.5), Madero (7.4) and then Jeronimo Rd. in another 0.35 mile. There is a shopping center at this intersection. Shift over to the sidewalk and, in 0.25 mile, join the Class I trail coming up from El Toro II Park. Pedal another 0.25 mile and follow the bikepath under Muirlands Blvd. near creek level (see the discussion on flood warnings from Trip #29A). Come back up on the opposite side into the northern edge of popular and scenic part of El Toro I Park (8.3). There is a water fountain near the tennis courts, reached via a wooden bridge over Aliso Creek.

El Toro Park to The Aliso Creek Trail Exit. The reference route follows the bikepath nearest Los Alisos Blvd. where there is an entry trail into the creekbed. (This may be inaccessible in rainy weather.) Dip down into the concrete bottom and cross the creek over a metal plate. Just beyond, pass under Los Alisos Blvd. and turn east. Climb out of the creekbed almost immediately; the trailway opens up soon after in the vicinity of Sycamore Park, which is across the creek in 0.3 mile. This bridge-accessible park has a water fountain, shade trees, walking/biking trails, picnic benches and barbecues. (Note that no public water sources were identified between here and the trip's end.)

In another 0.2 mile is a small concrete cross-over trail leading to that park immediately followed by a passage under the San Diego Fwy. (This also may be flooded during or after storms.) The trail has now entered Laguna Hills. There is a trail junction here. A turn left and 1/4-mile pedal leads alongside the Alicia Pkwy. turnoff from the San Diego Fwy. to the Laguna Hills Plaza.

Our route heads right and proceeds up a short grade past a commemorative Juan Avila Adobe marker, skirts below the local residences, then heads back down into a more open canyon area. The creek bottom supports natural growth in contrast to some of the concrete stretches to the north. Note the dirt trail across the creek; this is part of the equestrian trailway that will parallel the paved Aliso Creek Trail to it's current terminus. In 0.3 mile is a four-way junction. Two legs travel a short distance and die out at local roadways. Take the middle route which has a trail marker for bikers coming from the opposite direction. This trail climbs just below the walls of nearby residences and heads south.

Shortly, bikers reach Paseo De Valencia and the bike trail leaves the creek (9.5). Turn left (south), staying on the east side of the street, and follow the signed Class I trail uphill past Kennington Dr. and Beckenham St. to a crest near Stockport St. (10.2). Leave the Aliso Creek Trail and coast 0.3 mile downhill to Alicia Pkwy. using either the Class II roadway or the Class I sidewalk, now on the street's west side; there is a shopping plaza at this intersection.

The Southern Section. Turn right (southeast) on Alicia Pkwy. and take the Class I path down into the drainage of an alternate Aliso Creek branch. Follow this wide trail downhill in the broad canyon area 0.7 mile to Moulton Pkwy. Cross at the intersection and follow that street southeast. This Class II roadway heads uphill through a relatively new section of Mission Viejo. In another 0.6 mile is La Paz Rd., the trip minimum elevation point, and just beyond is Oso Pkwy. (12.0).

Turn left (west) on Oso Pkwy. and either use the Class II roadway or join up with the Class I trail on the north side of the highway. Pass under the homes in the low hills in an area with limited tree cover near the path itself. Cross Nellie Gail Rd. and proceed through a small canyon. Pump uphill to a crest near Bridlewood Dr. (13.3); at this point Oso Pkwy. heads downhill with the Class I bikeway parallel to and above the roadway. In 0.2 mile, cross Cabot Rd. and return to Mission Viejo.

The "Home Stretch." Transition to Class II roadway and cross a bridge over Oso Creek and the San Diego Fwy. In 0.3 mile cut through the center of the Mission Viejo Golf Course, then head downhill past Montanoso Dr. (14.3). Proceed uphill to a crest at Marguerite Pkwy. (14.7), turn left (north) and bike past the Mission Viejo Fire Station. There is a fine view of Mt. Saddleback from this area (16.0). Begin a moderate upgrade which passes Estanciero Dr. (15.3) and reach a crest near the trip origin at La Paz Rd. and Village Center (15.6).

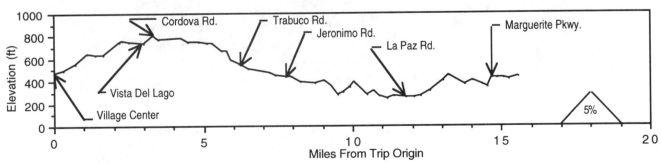

CONNECTING TRIPS: 1) Connection with Aliso Creek Trail (Trip #29) - multiple connections by riding west from Los Alisos Blvd. (for example, Cordova Rd., Trabuco Rd., or Jeronimo Rd.) or by turning south onto La Paz at the Moulton Pkwy. intersection; 2) connection with Laguna Niguel Bikeway (Trip #11) - from the Oso Pkwy. intersection, continue I-l/2 miles south on Marguerite Pkwy. to Crown Valley Pkwy. and turn right (west); 3) connection with the Oso Viejo ride (Trip #42) - bike east on La Paz Rd. at Marguerite Pkwy.; 4) connection with the Cities and Canyons ride (Trip #47) - at Marguerite Pkwy.

and Cordova Rd., continue north on the former street to Santa Margarita Pkwy; 5) connection with the Arroyo Trabuco Loop (Trip #50) - on Alicia Pkwy., turn east at either Oso Pkwy., La Paz Rd., Jeronimo Rd. or Alicia Pkwy. and bike to Felipe Rd./Olympiad Rd.

TRIP #31 - LAGUNA HILLS LOOP

GENERAL LOCATION: Laguna Hills, Irvine, Laguna Beach

LEVEL OF DIFFICULTY: Round trip - moderate to strenuous
Distance - 14.3 miles
Elevation gain - continuous steep grade on lower El Toro Rd. and moderate-to-steep grades on Laguna Canyon Rd.

HIGHLIGHTS: Relatively short, but with a wallop, this is a mixed canyon and flatland adventure. The initial climb from Hummingbird Park is a short, but steep, canyon-like workout to a super-scenic crest, followed by a refreshing coast to Moulton Pkwy. That roadway is predominantly flat and Class II or III, but has heavy traffic and a short Class X stint. It is only for cyclists who are "traffic hardened." The loop transitions westward via Barranca Pkwy. on a Class II stretch through a modern commercial area. The finale is a rustic tour of upper Laguna Canyon and a return to the park via lower El Toro Rd.

TRAILHEAD: From the San Joaquin Hills Transportation Corridor (State Hwy. 73), exit south at Laguna Rd. (State Hwy. 133) and drive 3/4 mile to El Toro Rd. Turn northeast, go 1-1/2 miles to Aliso Creek Rd., turn (west) and proceed 0.1 mile to Hummingbird Ln. A right here leads to the park. From the San Diego Fwy., exit south at Laguna Canyon Rd. and drive 5-1/2 miles to El Toro Rd. Continue as described above. The park has a water fountain, tree cover, and a children's playground on the westside segment and both trees and a walking/biking path on the east side.

Bring a filled water bottle, or two on hot days. The single public source is at the trip origin. However, there are commercial water sources at the many shopping plazas along the route.

TRIP DESCRIPTION:

Over the Top. Backtrack to Class II El Toro Rd. and turn right. Cycle a workout upgrade in the lower tree-lined residential area past Calle Corta (0.3) and Canyon Wren Ln. (0.8), reaching the crest in 0.1 mile. From the top is a panorama that includes El Toro, Irvine, Mt. Saddleback and an over-the-shoulder view of the undeveloped lower El Toro Rd. area. Glide past the shopping complexes on either side of the road at Calle Sonora (1.2) and continue coasting another 0.4 mile to a cluster of shopping centers at Moulton Pkwy.

Northbound. Turn north onto this busy Class III thoroughfare and make a short climb to a crest at Gate #12, then cruise by Moulton Plaza to Santa Maria Ave. (2.3). Navigate a 0.3-mile Class X stretch between this street and Ridge Route Dr, then enjoy the transition to a Class II bikeway that extends all the way to Laguna Canyon Rd. (An alternative after the turn onto Moulton Pkwy. is to bike the entire one-mile stretch one the westside sidewalk.). Cross over little Veeh Lake and pass Lake Forest Dr., where the road changes name to Irvine Center Dr. (3.1).

In this less-developed section, pass over San Diego Creek and meet Bake Pkwy. at (4.0). In 0.2 mile is Hubble/Lion Country, where a left turn leads to the Irvine Meadows Amphitheater and Wild Rivers Waterpark. Pedal over the San Diego Fwy. (4.8) and bike past Pacifica, an entry to the Irvine Spectrum Center shopping area in 0.3 mile. Continue on the flat past Alton Pkwy. and reach Barranca Pkwy. at (5.7).

Westbound Connector. Turn left and cycle though a series of modern commercial sites on Class II roadway, passing over the Laguna Fwy. at (6.0). The commercial development thins as the parkway heads west and meets Laguna Canyon Rd. (6.6).

Laguna Canyon Entry. Turn left onto Class II bikeway, which becomes Class X at Pasteur. Bicycle over the San Diego Fwy. and cruise through agricultural environs. Laguna Canyon Rd. fuses with the

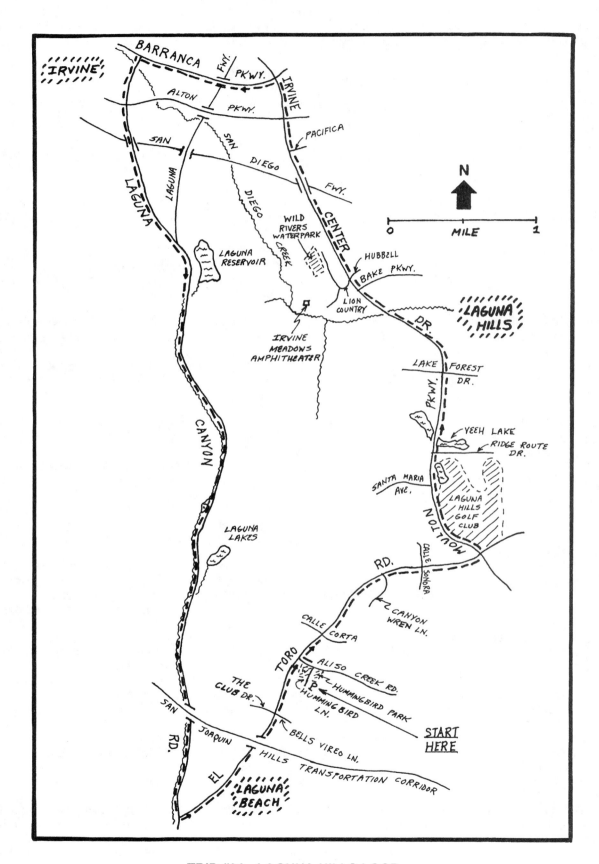

TRIP #31 - LAGUNA HILLS LOOP

Laguna Fwy. outlet traffic in an area surrounded by open fields (8.1). In 0.1 mile, the bikepath starts heading into the canyon opening; the Laguna Reservoir is high on the hillside to the left. There are rolling hills and a small creek along the roadway as the route proceeds into the canyon proper. The roadway becomes a signed Class III at (8.4).

The Canyon Tour. Follow a moderate upgrade (9.0) and reach the top of the grade in an area with a few small shade trees (9.3). In another 0.4 mile, pass a small hamlet to the left (east); to the right are small tree stands and overgrowth. In about 1.3 miles of light rolling hills and nearly treeless roadway, cross over the outlet creek from North Laguna Lake (11.0). This creek has paralleled the road through much of the canyon.

Bike over the rolling hills within the canyon and head up a grade with a "Laguna Beach City Limit" sign near the summit (11.4). In 0.3 mile, pass under State Hwy. 73., then observe the interesting rock formations just beyond and to the right. In a short distance is El Toro Rd. (12.5).

The Return Segment. Turn northeast onto this Class II road which is sandwiched between undeveloped Aliso/Woods Canyon Regional Park (right) and the Laguna Coast Wilderness Park (left). Pass under Hwy. 73 again (13.5), enter the first housing developments, then continue climbing 0.2 mile past Bells Vireo Ln./The Club Dr. Groups of plush residences appear high on the hillside to the left. In another 0.4 mile of spirited uphill is Aliso Creek Rd. and a return to Hummingbird Park (14.3).

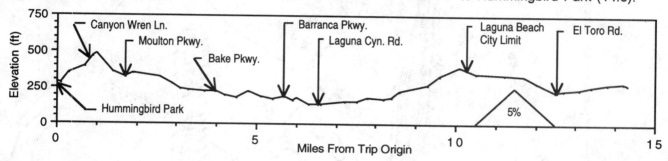

CONNECTING TRIPS: 1) Connection with the Laguna Canyon Rd. tour (Trip #9) - the trips share a common segment of northern Laguna Canyon Rd.; 2) connection with the San Diego Creek trip - at Barranca Pkwy. and Laguna Canyon Rd., take the former road east to Jeffrey Rd.; 3) connection with the Aliso Viejo Figure "8" (Trip #46) - At El Toro Rd. and Aliso Creek Rd., go east on the latter street to Glenwood Dr.; 4) spur trips - at the trip origin, take hilly, Class II Aliso Creek Rd. eastbound. Another neat option is to take Class II Moulton Pkwy. southeast at the El Toro Rd. intersection.

TRIP #32 - LAKE FOREST TOUR

GENERAL LOCATION: Lake Forest

LEVEL OF DIFFICULTY: Loop - easy
                          Distance - 5.3 miles
                          Elevation gain - periodic light grades

HIGHLIGHTS: The Lake Forest loop trip is entirely on Class I/II bikeways within this very pleasant community. The trip includes a tour along residential streets as well as a romp through Serrano Creek Community Park. The street route includes a passby of a lovely man-made lake community along Toledo Wy. The park ride meanders through a major loop with several minor spurs and provides a very pleasant tree-sheltered environment. The park cruise might serve as a good family bike trip, while only more experienced riders should use the Class II roadways.

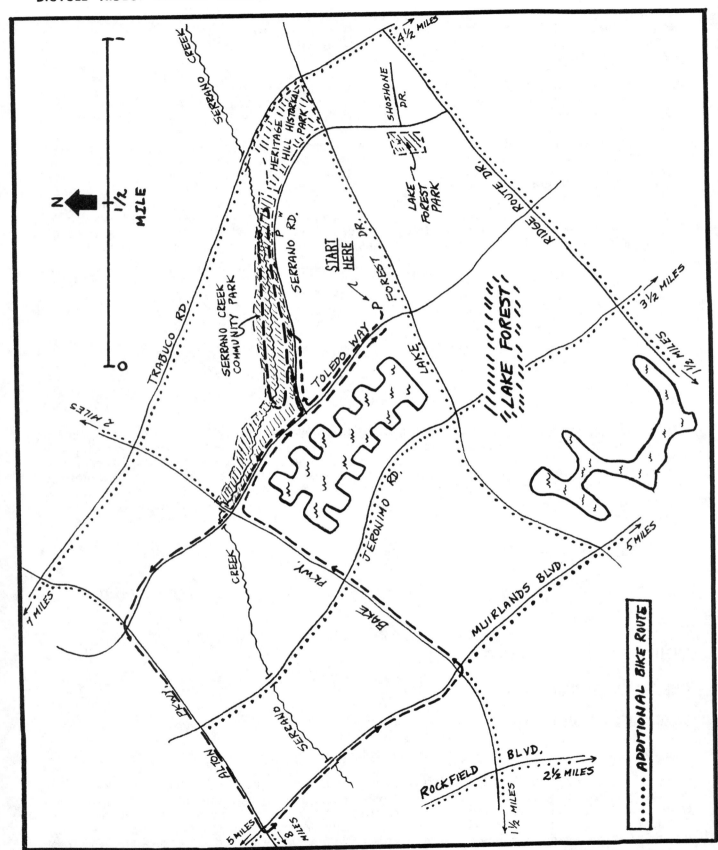

TRIP #32 - LAKE FOREST TOUR

TRAILHEAD: From the San Diego Fwy., exit north on Lake Forest Dr. and travel about two miles to Toledo Wy. Turn left (northwest) and find parking within the local residential area. Check local parking signs and carefully avoid parking on any private streets, specifically those along Toledo Wy. An option for low-use park days is to park alongside Serrano Creek Park.

Bring a moderate supply of water. The trip is short, but the only on-route public water source we found was at Serrano Creek Park.

TRIP DESCRIPTION: Serrano Creek Community Park. From the parking area, proceed in the direction away from Lake Forest Dr. (northwest) on a Class II bikepath. Turn right at Serrano Rd. (0.3) and cycle along the north sidewalk to a downramp that leads to the Class I trail within Serrano Creek Community Park. Bike along the park's trail through lush, tree-shaded surroundings to the picnic/playground area at the east end of the park (0.8). There is a water fountain here plus some unique kid's props such as a small "tire mountain" and a tree house.

The trail goes through a tight turn, crosses the creek and continues to parallel the creek. There are several small trail spurs off this section of path and a horse trail as well. There are also a few short "ups and downs" on the route to give it some variety. The path reaches the west end of the loop, recrosses the creek and returns to the park starting point (1.1). Turn around and head back across the creek, but turn left at the next junction and cycle 0.2 mile to the trail exit near Serrano Dr. and Lake Vista Dr.

The Industrial Loop and Toledo Way. Turn right on Serrano Rd. and return to Toledo Wy., admiring the view of the residences surrounding the man-made lake. Turn right (northwest) on Toledo Wy. and proceed on the Class II bikeway across Bake Pkwy. (1.7). This begins a 2.9-mile loop through a modern, light industrial/high-tech area on a Class II bikeway. Bicycle 0.5 mile to Alton Pkwy., turn left and pedal 0.6 mile to a bridge over a railroad. There is a fine view into the foothills to the southwest from this point (and a long-distance view of the Wild Rivers area).

Cruise 0.2 mile to Muirlands Blvd. and turn left. Next, ride another 0.8 mile to Bake Pkwy. and follow that roadway another 0.8 mile to complete the industrial loop (4.6). On the way is another panoramic vista from the bridge over the railroad tracks. Turn right at Toledo Wy. and continue 0.7 mile, admiring the waterfront Lake Forest community and return to the starting point (5.3). Note there are entries to the lake area at two points off of Toledo Wy., one near Lost River Ct. on the lake's east side and the other near Quiet Oak Dr. on the west side.

Optional Tours. There are a multitude of lengthy Class II roadways which pass through the Lake Forest area. A few of the longer routes are noted on the tour map. Exceptional examples are the Muirlands Blvd./Barranca Pkwy., Alton Pkwy. and Trabuco Rd./Irvine Blvd. bikeways.

CONNECTING TRIPS: 1) Connection with Aliso Creek Trail (Trip #29A) - take Bake Pkwy. northeast to Trabuco Rd. Turn right and proceed about 2-1/2 miles across Lake Forest Dr., Ridge Route and El Toro Rd. to the Aliso Creek Trail. Turn left to head northeast toward Santiago Canyon and right to head southwest toward El Toro.

THE "BIG GUYS"

Santa Ana River near Ocean Outlet

TRIP #33 - WESTERN ORANGE COUNTY LOOP

<u>GENERAL LOCATION</u>: Strand Bike Trail - San Gabriel River - Coyote Creek - Fullerton - El Cajon Trail - Santa Ana River

<u>LEVEL OF DIFFICULTY</u>:   Loop - strenuous
                             Distance - 63.5 miles
                             Elevation gain - periodic moderate grades in Fullerton
                                        and El Cajon Trail areas

<u>HIGHLIGHTS</u>: This grand "looper" provides a testy mileage workout combined with a wide variety of bikeways and scenery. Well over half of the trip is on Class I bike trails. The tour begins at Huntington Beach State Park near the Santa Ana River outlet, proceeds along the coastal strand bikepath, then follows the San Gabriel River and Coyote Creek inland. The route meanders through Buena Park and Fullerton, joins up with the El Cajon Trail in Yorba Linda, and follows a 21-mile runout down the Santa Ana River to the trip origin. The scenery along the coastline, the lower San Gabriel River, the El Cajon Trail, and selected Santa Ana River segments is exceptional. There are numerous top-of-the-line parks on or near this tour, including El Dorado Regional Park, Craig Park, Yorba Regional Park, Centennial Regional Park, and both Huntington Beach and Bolsa Chica Beach State Parks.
    A reduced mileage trip option using Heil Ave. is also provided. This 25-mile alternative visits both Huntington Beach and Bolsa Chica Beach State Parks, Centennial Regional Park and adds Mile Square Park to the itinerary.

<u>TRAILHEAD</u>: From the San Diego Fwy., exit south at Brookhurst St. Continue about five miles to the road's end, turn right, and drive 3/4 mile to Magnolia St. and turn left into the Huntington Beach State Park entrance. There is also free parking off of the inland residential streets.
    From Pacific Coast Hwy. (PCH) southbound, continue four miles past the Huntington Beach Pier and turn right at Magnolia St. For northbound traffic, drive 1-1/4 mile beyond the Santa Ana River and turn left at Magnolia St.
    Bring a couple of filled water bottles in order to minimize water stops. There are scattered water sources at the parks on the route. Bikers may have to buck the on-shore late afternoon winds on the last leg of the Santa Ana River segment. If this is of concern, select an alternate starting point.

<u>TRIP DESCRIPTION</u>: **Huntington Beach State Park to the San Gabriel River.** The Trip #33 description discusses only new or potentially confusing portions of the ride. Refer to the individual trip writeups as identified below for details. The tour starts at Huntington Beach State Park and continues northwest on the coastal strand trail to the northern end of Sunset Beach (see Trip #4, Middle and Northern Segment Maps). Follow the Seal Beach/Sunset Beach Tour (Trip #1) through Seal Beach to the San Gabriel River (10.0).
    San Gabriel River and Coyote Creek. Stay right at the junction and follow the Coyote Creek Trail (Trip #20), exiting at La Palma Ave. (19.0).
    The Inland Jigsaw (Buena Park to Fullerton). Turn right and bike 3.2 miles west on La Palma Ave. on mixed Class II and Class X path. At Western Ave., directly under the Knott's Berry Farm parachute and "free-fall" rides, turn left (north) and ride 1.9 miles on Class III bikeway. Pass under the Artesia and Santa Ana Fwys., turn right at Artesia Blvd., and left in 0.5 mile at Dale St. (25.2).
    From here to Chapman Ave., we found no single route with continuous bike route signs or unsigned roadway with continuous wide bike shoulder. One option is: Bike 1/4 mile to Malvern Ave. and turn right. After one mile of biking on narrow-shouldered Class X roadway, the street transitions to Class III beyond Gilbert St. Cycle past Bastanchury Rd. and, in another 0.4 mile (two miles from Dale St.), turn right onto Basque Ave. (27.3) and then left at Chapman Ave. The second option is: Cycle 1/8 mile on Dale Ave. and turn right at Artesia Blvd. Follow that lightly-used Class X road alongside the Fullerton Municipal Airport and turn left (north) at Gilbert St. Bike 0.3 mile on another Class X street to Malvern Ave. and continue as described above.
    This is the beginning of a 4-1/2 mile Fullerton residential tour. Follow Chapman Ave. 3/4 mile until it reaches Woods Ave., turn right and bike to Wilshire Ave., then turn left. Follow Wilshire Ave. 2.3 miles to Acacia Ave. Turn right and then left again at Commonwealth Ave. until this roadway takes a long 90-degree curve northward and meets Nutwood Ave. (31.5).
    Calfornia State University, Fullerton to Yorba Linda. Cross Nutwood Ave. on the west side of the intersection. At the "can't miss" CSUF sign, turn right and bike on Class I trail through the campus to

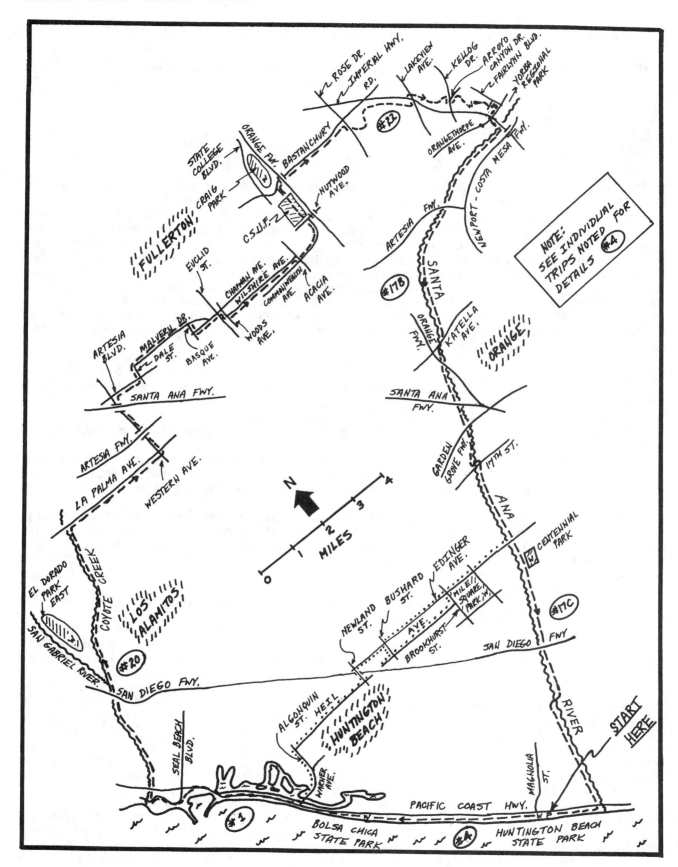

TRIP #33 - WESTERN ORANGE COUTY LOOP

Associated Rd. at the north end. Follow this Class II road 0.3 mile to Bastanchury Rd. and turn right, pedaling uphill on the Class III street under the Orange Fwy. The route peaks in 0.3 mile and the ride flattens for the 2.0 miles to Rose Dr. (35.0).

Santa Ana River Near Ocean Outlet

El Cajon Trail. Turn right on Rose Dr. and in 0.2 mile cross the street to the east side at the Class I path entrance. Follow the El Cajon Trail (Trip #22) for 5.6 miles to the intersection of Fairlynn Blvd. and Esperanza Rd. Turn right (this departs from the Trip #22 route) and bike 0.3 mile to Imperial Hwy. Turn left and continue 0.7 mile to the bridge across the Santa Ana River (41.8).

Santa Ana River. Follow the Class I Santa Ana River Trail (Trips #17B and #17C) 21.4 miles to the ocean, then take a short cruise on the beach bikeway to the trip origin. The total trip mileage is 63.5.

Excursion: Shortcut Loop. Note that the loop can be altered by using the Heil Ave. segment in Huntington Beach. The Heil Ave./Santa Ana River coastal loop is a nice 25-mile ride in itself. The route uses Class II Warner Ave. and Algonquin St. to get to the Class II main thoroughfare on Heil Ave. Near the San Diego Fwy., a short Class X ride on Bushard St. leads to Class II Edinger Ave., which serves as the throughway to the Santa Ana River. At Edinger Ave. and Brookhurst St., this shortcut route passes Mile Square Park, one of the premier parks in Orange County (see Trip #5).

CONNECTING TRIPS: 1) Connection with the Carbon Canyon Workout (Trip #23) - at Rose Dr. and Bastanchury Rd., bike north on Rose Dr.; 2) connection with the Fullerton Tour/Craig Park ride (Trip #24) - at Malvern Ave. and Bastanchury Rd., turn north onto the latter road. Also see individual trip writeups for the myriad of other connectors.

TRIP #34 - EASTERN ORANGE COUNTY LOOP (The "Granddaddy")

GENERAL LOCATION: Santiago Canyon - El Toro - Laguna Niguel - Laguna Beach - Newport Beach - Santa Ana River - Villa Park

LEVEL OF DIFFICULTY: Loop - very strenuous
Distance - 76.9 miles
Elevation gain - periodic moderate grades; frequent long and steep grades in Santiago Canyon area

HIGHLIGHTS: The granddaddy of Orange County trips, this super 77-mile journey covers the southeastern half of the county and has the Santa Ana River as a common boundary with Trip #33 The variety in biking territory is mind boggling! The itinerary includes the rolling hills of Santiago Canyon, the mountains-to-sea ride down the Aliso Creek corridor, a 15-mile grand tour of the southern Orange County coastline, a pedal up the Santa Ana River, and a short return segment through the cities of Orange and Villa Park. Most of the trip is on Class I or Class II routes.

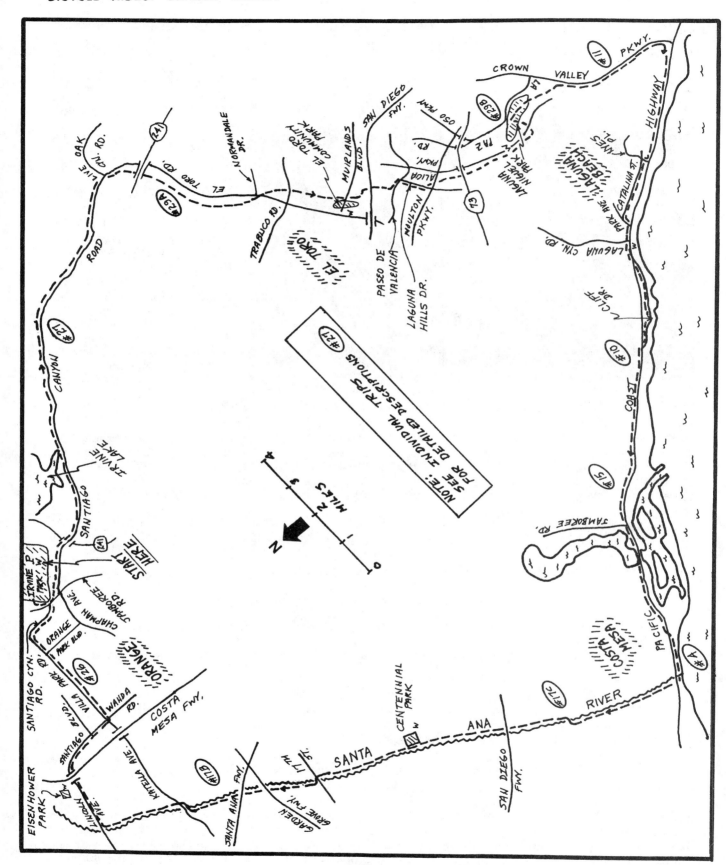

TRIP #34 - EASTERN ORANGE LOOP

With a modest Santa Ana River/Santa Ana Canyon Rd. extension, this trip can be turned into a "Century" tour.

TRAILHEAD: From the Orange Fwy. or Costa Mesa Fwy., take the Chapman Ave. turnoff east. The distances to the Jamboree Rd. intersection are 4-1/2 miles and 7-1/2 miles, respectively. Turn left (north), get into the right-hand lane and go 1/3 mile to the signed Irvine Regional Park entrance at Irvine Park Rd. From the Eastern Transportation Corridor (State Hwy. 241), exit at Chapman Ave./Santiago Canyon Rd. and drive west one mile to Jamboree Rd. Turn right and motor 1/3 mile to the park entrance.

Pay the entree fee and enjoy the park after the ride. (See the detailed map provided in Trip #26 for park facilities.) An alternative is to start at Santiago Hills Park off of Trail's End Ln. and Chapman Ave. The park has water, restrooms, walkway/bikeways, scattered tree cover, sheltered picnic/barbecue facilities and children's playground.

Bring a couple of filled water bottles in order to minimize water stops. There are scattered water sources along the route as noted in the individual trip writeups. The hilly and exposed 12.2-mile Santiago Canyon segment is essentially waterless.

TRIP DESCRIPTION: **Santiago Canyon and Aliso Creek Corridor.** The Trip #33 description discusses only new or potentially confusing portions of the ride. Refer to the individual trip writeups as identified below for details. Bike back to Santiago Canyon Rd., turn left and follow the Santiago Canyon Rd. tour (Trip #27) (12.0). From the road's end at Cook's Corner, pedal about l/4 mile south on El Toro Rd. and pick up the origin of the Aliso Creek Trail (Trip #29). Follow that route to Crown Valley Community Park in Laguna Niguel (27.6).

Laguna Niguel Bikeway. Follow the southern segment of the Laguna Niguel Bikeway (Trip #11) from the Crown Valley Community Park to the trip's end at Pacific Coast Highway (PCH) (30.8).

Cook's Corner

Coastal Segment. Turn right at PCH and bike 2.3 miles on Class X roadway through rolling coastal hills to Aliso Beach County Park. From this point, bike the Laguna Beach Tour (Trip #10) in reverse to Seaward Rd. in Newport Beach (42.2). Bike PCH to Tustin Ave. or follow one of the paths shown for the Newport Beach/Corona Del Mar Tour (Trip #15). The former option is more direct, but is on some narrow and heavily-trafficked roads (47.2).

Bike one mile further on PCH to Balboa Blvd./Superior Ave. and turn left. Turn right at 46th St. and pedal 0.2 mile to Seashore Dr. Follow the Sunset Beach to Newport Beach Strand (Trip #4) back to the Santa Ana River (49.4). On the north side of the river, look for a path that drops below road level, makes a tight turn to the north and goes under PCH. Note that there is a faster pace option to stay on PCH in this stretch on good biking road. For the PCH alternative, stay on PCH to Orange St., turn left at the signal and bike to Seashore Dr., then cycle to the north side of the Santa Ana River.

Santa Ana River. Follow the Santa Ana River Rides #17C and #17B in the northerly direction in that order. Exit the river east at Lincoln Ave. (67.8).

The Return Segment. Follow Class X Lincoln Ave. 1.5 miles on a steady workout upgrade to Tustin Ave.; Eisenhower Park is just north of the intersection. Cruise under the Orange Fwy., turn right onto Class II Santiago Blvd. and follow that road 2.0 miles. Continue straight ahead on Wanda Rd. at the point where Santiago Blvd. veers sharply eastward; in 0.3 mile turn left at Katella Ave./Villa Park Rd. (71.6). Follow the eastbound segment of the Orange/Irvine Park Loop (Trip #26) to the trip origin at Irvine Park (76.9).

"Century Trip." A modest trip extension can easily turn this into a hundred-miler. A recommended option is to continue north on the Santa Ana River to Green River Road (Trips #17A and #17B). For variety on the return leg of this extension, continue south on Santa Ana Canyon Rd. beyond Weir Canyon Rd. and return to Lincoln Ave. via that roadway (Trip #25). Follow **The Return Segment** described above beyond this point.

<u>**CONNECTING TRIPS**</u>: Certainly you are kidding! See the individual trip writeups.

TRIP #35 - ORANGE COUNTY CENTURY

<u>**GENERAL LOCATION**</u>: Santiago Canyon - Laguna Niguel - Laguna Beach - Huntington Beach - Coyote Creek - Fullerton - Villa Park

<u>**LEVEL OF DIFFICULTY**</u>: Loop - very strenuous
Distance - 105.3 miles
Elevation gain - frequent, long and steep grades in Santiago Canyon; frequent moderate-to-steep grades in Laguna Beach area

<u>**HIGHLIGHTS:**</u> Yes Martha, you can build a "century" trip by riding the periphery of the Eastern and Western County Loops (Trips #34 and #33, respectively). This early morning-to-afternoon adventure provides a bike tour of the best that Orange County has to offer: Santiago Canyon, the Aliso Creek Corridor, nearly 20 miles of scenic coastline, the San Gabriel River and Coyote Creek, and the El Cajon Trail. Go for it!! However, if this is your first "century," bring some phone change.

<u>**TRAILHEAD**</u>: Start at Irvine Park (see Trip #34) in order to complete most of the toughest trip segments in the first 40 miles. The 4.7-mile return segment from Villa Park Rd./Santiago Canyon Rd. to Irvine Park is also a hilly workout. If your persuasion is to end the trip on an easier, more laid-back note, start it at Eisenhower Park near Lincoln Ave. and Tustin Ave. (see Trip #25).

<u>**TRIP DESCRIPTION**</u>: The route starts from Irvine Park and follows the Eastern Orange County Loop for the 49.4 miles to the Santa Ana River. Cross the river and bike along the coast, following the Western Orange County Loop. Bike the latter loop 46.8 miles to the Santa Ana River exit at Lincoln Ave. From this intersection, follow **The Return Segment** described in Trip #34 an additional 9.1 miles back to Irvine Park.

<u>**CONNECTING TRIPS**</u>: See Trips #33 and #34. Also refer to the maps for those trips.

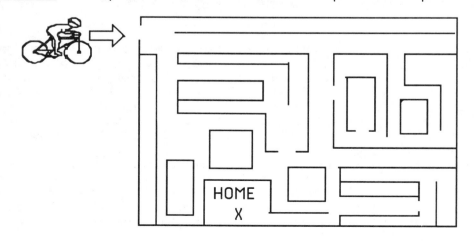

NEW TRIPS

Jeronimo Greenbelt Park in Mission Viejo

TRIP #36 - TURTLE ROCK ROAD

GENERAL LOCATION: Irvine

LEVEL OF DIFFICULTY: Loop - moderate
Distance - 4.3 miles
Elevation gain - two moderate grades

HIGHLIGHTS: This low-mileage loop on Class II roadway surveys the upscale Turtle Rock neighborhood with its classy residences and grand landscaping. After leaving well-stocked Turtle Rock Community Park, cyclists follow a short climb to Ridgeline Dr., coast past Campus Dr., then pump a 1.5-mile moderate upgrade before coasting back to the park. There is also a fun Class I spur trip which originates near the park, wanders through the well-maintained neighborhood, crosses Turtle Rock Rd. near Campus Dr. and ends in the eastern grounds of William R. Mason Regional Park.

TRAILHEAD: From the San Diego Fwy., exit south at Culver Dr., drive 1-1/2 miles to Campus Dr. and turn left. In 1/4 mile, go right at Turtle Rock Dr. and motor two miles to Sunnyhill, then turn right to reach the Turtle Rock Community Park entry. From the San Joaquin Hills Transportation Corridor (State Hwy. 73), exit northbound at Bonita Canyon Dr. Drive two miles to Campus Dr., turn right and continue as described above.

Bring a light water supply for this short trip. There is water at the trip origin and at the water fountain near the Campus Dr. intersection. Turtle Rock Community Park is a large, well-stocked base of operations. It has a visitor center, nature center, water, restrooms, abundant tree cover, walkway/bikeways throughout, picnic areas and shelters, tennis courts, athletic fields and hiking trails.

TRIP DESCRIPTION: **Turtle Rock Community Park to Campus Drive.** Exit the park on Sunnyhill and turn right on Class II Turtle Rock Rd. The surrounding well-manicured grounds and stately residences are typical of those found throughout the tour. Pedal past Silkwood (0.4) and start a mild climb just beyond. In 0.2 mile on the right is one of the few undeveloped local hillsides (the frontal San Joaquin Hills).

Reach a crest near Highland View, then pass Ridgeline Dr., a scenic Class II ride in itself (0.8). Enjoy the quickie view of Irvine below and the estates high on the ridge to the left and coast past Canyon Park (grassy knolls, limited shade, children's playground). Pass Hillsborough with some more barren hillsides to the right (1.3), then continue downhill to West Concordia, which is one entry to Concordia University (1.8). The road opens to a four-lane nearby and cyclists reach the trip low point at Campus Dr. in 0.2 mile.

The Uphill Return. Cycle uphill on Class II roadway past Paseo Segovia, beyond which Turtle Rock Rd. skinnies back down to two lanes. At Amalfi is a short flat, then bikers continue the climb through a heavily tree-lined section to Emporia Ave. (2.8). Near Briarcrest is an open grassy area between residences, one of many open spaces planned into this purely residential community. At Sierra Boca (3.4) is the western edge of Chaparral Park, which provides trees, grassy knolls, children's play area and picnic benches. Just beyond is the crest and cyclists are treated to a mild downgrade, passing Sierra Lisa Rd. at (3.7) and returning to Sunnyhill. A short ride to the park entrance completes the loop (4.3).

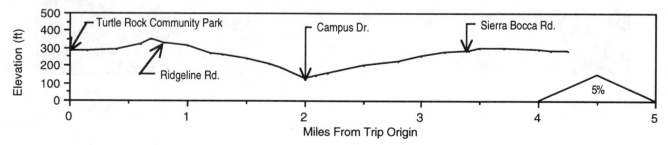

Excursion: Spur Trip. There is a fine Class I bikepath that starts across Turtle Rock Rd. at Sunnyhill and snakes its way between the classy local residences, letting out just across the street at Campus Dr. (1.4 miles). By taking the tunnel under Turtle Rock Rd., bikers can connect with the northern path section which meanders 0.5 mile further into the eastern grounds of William R. Mason Regional Park.

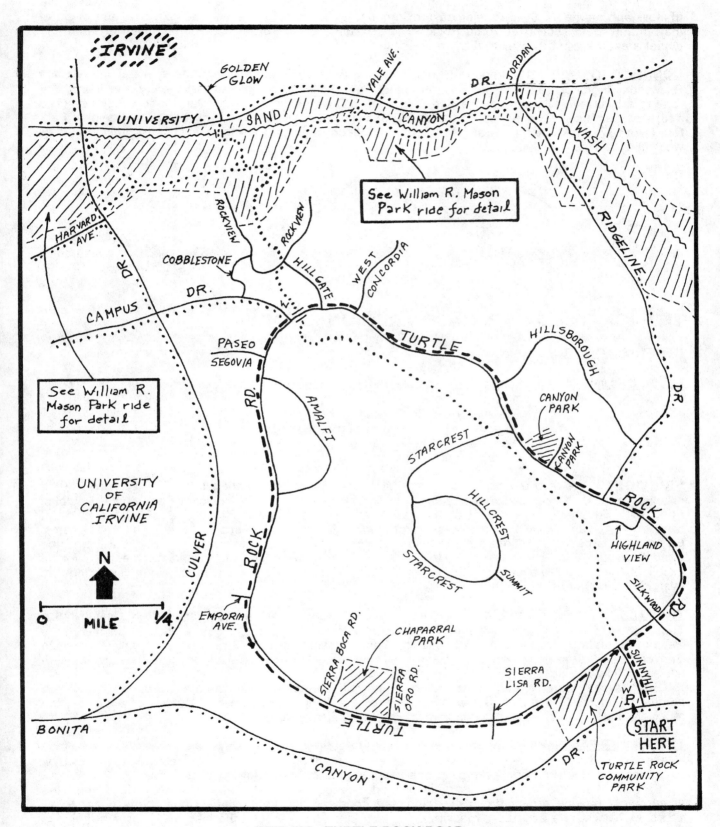

TRIP #36 - TURTLE ROCK ROAD

The path reaches "The Triangle Junction" with park benches and an information kiosk within the triangle and merges with the major eastern grounds trail. There is a water fountain near the origin of the northern path section at Turtle Rock Rd. The return ride to Turtle Rock Community Park from the tunnel area is a climb similar to that on the eastern half of the Turtle Rock Rd. loop.

CONNECTING TRIPS: 1) Connection with the Irvine Bikeway (Trip #8) - take the spur trail into William R. Mason Regional Park to "The Triangle Junction," bike east to the Yale Ave. entry and follow that road to a bikeway/walkway over the San Diego Fwy.; 2) connection with the San Diego Creek ride (Trip #18) - at Campus Dr., bike west to the creek; 3) connection with the William R. Mason Regional Park tour (Trip #37) - take the spur trail into William R. Mason Regional Park to its end, turning either east or west at "The Triangle Junction."

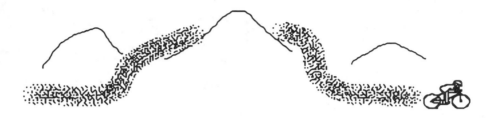

TRIP #37 - WILLIAM R. MASON REGIONAL PARK

GENERAL LOCATION: Irvine

LEVEL OF DIFFICULTY: Loop - easy (sample western grounds peripheral tour)
Distance - 1.9 miles
Elevation gain - essentially flat
Up and back - easy (eastern grounds tour)
Distance - 2.4 miles
Elevation gain - essentially flat

HIGHLIGHTS: We've biked quite a few, but William R. Mason Regional Park has got to be one of the premier parks for family bike rides, along with others such as O'Neill Regional Park, Irvine Regional Park, Mile Square Park and El Dorado Park (eastern Los Angeles County). Besides the miles of excellent bikeways/walkways, the western grounds have a lake, treecover, well-located restrooms, picnic and barbecue facilities, athletic fields, playgrounds, picnic shelters, an amphitheater and the Sand Canyon Wash. The eastern grounds are relatively undeveloped other than the clearings for an excellent Class I bikeway which has numerous access points. (There are precautionary warnings on this side for both poison oak and wildlife.)

TRAILHEAD: From the San Diego Fwy., exit south at Culver Dr. and proceed one mile to University Dr. Turn right and go 0.2 mile to the main entrance (across from San Joaquin) which is on the park's western grounds. From the San Joaquin Hills Transportation Corridor (State Hwy. 73), take the Bonita Canyon Dr. off-ramp north and drive 1-3/4 miles (the street becomes Culver Dr.) to University Dr. Turn left and follow the directions above from this junction.
    Bring a light water supply for a tour of either/both the western and eastern grounds. There are numerous public sources on the western side of the park. There are no sources of water on the relatively undeveloped eastern grounds, however tour mileage is short.

TRIP DESCRIPTION: **Western Grounds.** Pay the fee at the gate (weekdays are far less expensive than weekends) and find parking. There are an unlimited number of ways to connect walkway/bikeways, streets and parking area and we provide the peripheral route below only as an example.
    From the parking area nearest Culver Blvd., head north and make a semi-circle around the easternmost parking group, cross the main park roadway and keep making right turns (ignoring all accesses back to the main park roadway). This will take bikers around the lake and across a drainage channel. At the first exit bikeway to Harvard Ave., turn left, then continue the pattern of right turns, making a semi circle around the southern end of the lake on the outermost path.

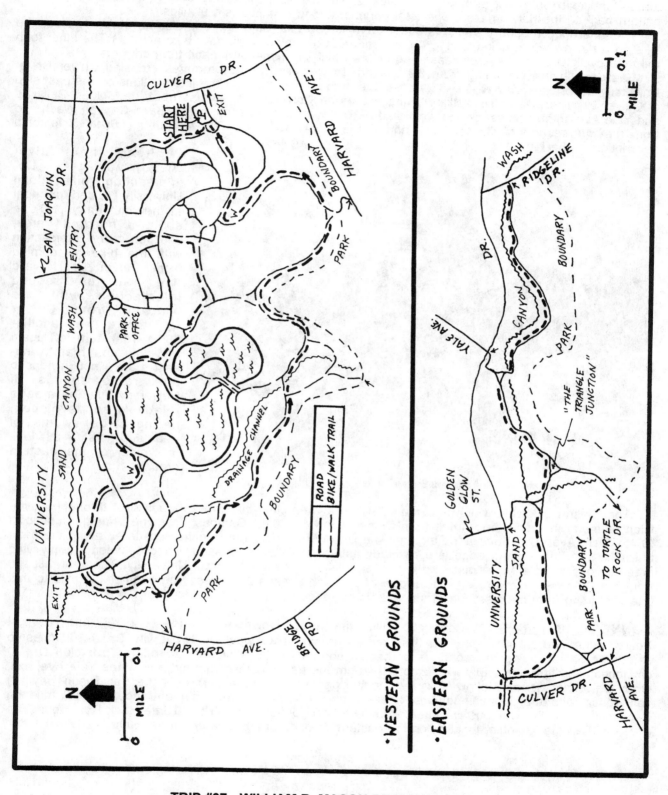

- **WESTERN GROUNDS**
- **EASTERN GROUNDS**

TRIP #37 - WILLIAM R. MASON REGIONAL PARK

Ignore the right turn along the drainage channel's origin, then continue the right turns, bypassing the second exit route to Harvard Ave. Recross the main park roadway and continue the right-hand pattern back to the parking area. The total peripheral loop distance is 1.9 miles.

The inner loop around the lake is about 0.7 mile. On this route, there is also an option to cross the lake on a narrow walker/biker bridge. (If the bridge is occupied, walk your bike across.) The inner loop will treat cyclists with a bevy of geese and ducks which permanently inhabit the park.

Eastern Grounds. Going from the eastern to western grounds requires crossing Culver Dr. at University Dr. or Harvard Ave. In either case, the path entries are near the intersections on the east side of Culver Dr. There are also walking/biking entries on University Dr. across from the Golden Glow St. and Yale Ave. intersections, on the west side of Ridgeline Dr. just south of the Sand Canyon Wash and from the intersection of Campus Dr. and Turtle Rock Rd. (See Trip #36 under **Spur Trip** for a description of the latter.)

Western Grounds: Bridge Over Lake

From the Culver Dr./University Dr. intersection, bike along University Dr. and turn right at the path entry (0.0). In about a hundred yards, veer left at the intersection with the bikeway coming from Culver Dr./Harvard Ave. At the second intersection with the bikeway from Culver Dr./Harvard Ave. (another 200 yards), turn left again and join the main west-east route. Though near to the traffic sounds of University Dr., the area is relatively undeveloped, having large swaths of trees and brush -- this look is typical of the eastern grounds.

The Class I bikeway, which is centered within a wide clear-cut swath, heads east through wildlife-filled environs, meeting the entries from Golden Glow St. (0.4), Campus Dr. ("The Triangle Junction") (0.45), Yale Ave. (0.65) and ends at Ridgeline Dr. (1.05). There are benches scattered along the path, but no water. The eastern edge is particularly natural, with the path sandwiched between the low-lying greenery of Sand Canyon Wash and the steep hillsides below Concordia University. The total mileage from the Culver Dr./Harvard entry to Ridgeline Dr. and back is 2.1 miles. Add another 0.3 mile to that total if starting from the westside grounds main entrance.

CONNECTING TRIPS: 1) Connection with the Upper Newport Bay ride (Trip #6) and Newport Beach/Irvine Tour (Trip #7) - from the main entrance, bike west on University Dr. 1-1/2 miles to Jamboree Rd. For Trip #6, continue across Jamboree Rd. to a street now named Eastbluff Dr.; 2) connection with the Irvine Bikeway (Trip #8) - from the park's eastern ground, follow the Yale Ave. exit, cross University Dr. and follow Yale Ave. to the pedestrian/bicycle path over the San Diego Fwy.; 3) connection with the San Diego Creek tour (Trip #18) - from the main entrance, go 1/2 mile on University Dr. to the Campus Dr. intersection/entry; 4) connection with the Turtle Rock Road tour (Trip #36) - bike to the "triangle"-junction on the eastern grounds of the park and turn south.

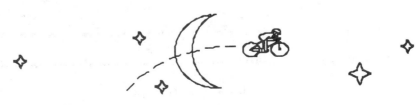

TRIP #38 - SIGNAL PEAK AND PELICAN HILL

<u>**GENERAL LOCATION**</u>: Orange County/Newport Coast

<u>**LEVEL OF DIFFICULTY**</u>: Loop - strenuous
Distance - 8.1 miles
Elevation gain - steep-to-sheer grade on Ridge Park Rd.;
moderate-to-steep grade on Newport Coast Dr.

<u>**HIGHLIGHTS**</u>: This is a ride for serious "hillies." The steep-to-sheer climb on Ridge Park Rd. is early in the ride, but it is a "doozie," with an average 8-plus percent incline. The return up Newport Coast Dr., though more moderate, will also keep your blood moving. The payoff for the hard work are fabulous views of the Pacific Ocean, Catalina Island, Newport Bay and the City of Irvine scattered over the Signal Peak and Pelican Hill areas. Both sections are on wide-shouldered Class X roadways, while Newport Coast Dr. is Class II.

<u>**TRAILHEAD**</u>: From the San Joaquin Hills Transportation Corridor (State Hwy. 73), take the Newport Coast off-ramp southbound and go about one mile to San Joaquin Hills Rd. Turn right and drive 1/4 mile to Newport Ridge Dr. E., then turn right to reach Newport Ridge Community Park. From Pacific Coast Hwy. (PCH), turn north at Newport Coast Dr. and motor 2-1/2 miles to San Joaquin Hills Rd. Turn left and continue as described above.
　　Bring at least a quart of water as there are no public water sources once you leave Newport Ridge Community Park. That park has limited shade, water, restrooms, grass, athletic fields and children's playground.

<u>**TRIP DESCRIPTION**</u>: **Signal Peak.** Leave the park and bike east to Newport Coast Rd. (0.3), turn right and pedal another 0.2 mile to Ridge Park Rd. Almost immediately, begin a steep upgrade that becomes sheer for the remaining 0.8-mile of the pumpathon to the crest. Established residences give way to newer developments as the road passes Tesoro (0.8) and Campobello (1.1).
　　In another 0.3 mile, turn right onto Vista Ridge Rd., enjoying a moderating upgrade and a joyful crest at (1.5). In the early portion of the downgrade on the south flank below Signal Peak, the Pacific Ocean and Catalina views appear. Near Ocean Heights Dr. (2.2) are similar vistas plus drop-dead gorgeous looks into Newport Bay and the City of Irvine. Continue gliding past Altezza Dr. (2.5) and reach road's end at Newport Coast Dr. in 0.3 mile.
　　Pelican Hill. Turn left and bike south to Pelican Hill N. (3.5), passing patchy hillside residences along the way. Turn right and climb to Pelican Crest in 0.2 mile, taking in the ocean views that open just beyond. As the road curves to the south beyond the first Pelican Hills Cr. junction (4.2), scope out the hillside estates, particularly the palatial digs on the ridge to the west. There are more Pacific Ocean vistas in this area. (While taking them in, the road name has changed to Pelican Hill Rd. S.)
　　While circumnavigating Pelican Hill on the south side, the Pelican Hill Golf Club comes into view below. Further downhill is the entry to the pleasing-to-the-eye club itself (5.1). In another mostly-downhill 0.5 mile is Newport Coast Dr.
　　The Return. This is the low point of the tour, which can only mean one thing! Time to cycle in earnest on a 1.5-mile moderate-to-steep climb which crests just south of Vista Ridge Rd. (6.9). A mix of flats and downhill lead back to San Joaquin Hills Rd. and a return to Newport Ridge Regional Park (8.1).

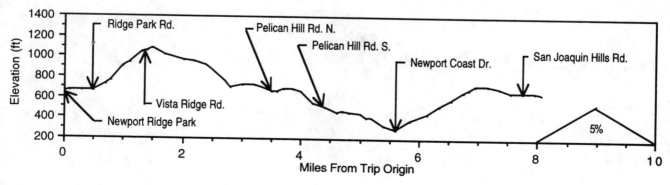

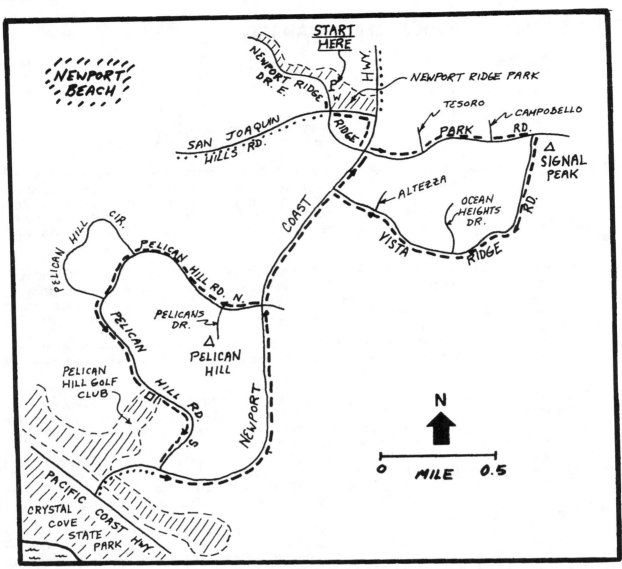

TRIP #38 - SIGNAL PEAK AND PELICAN HILL

Excursion: Continuation Option. Bikers seeking additional mileage and elevation change can coast south beyond Pelican Hill Dr. S. to PCH and return. This adds about 120 feet of elevation gain and an up-and-back mileage of 0.7 mile.

CONNECTING TRIPS: Connection with the Laguna Beach Tour (Trip #10) - take the **Continuation Option** described above to PCH.

148

TRIP #39 - WESTSIDE LAGUNA NIGUEL

GENERAL LOCATION: Laguna Niguel

LEVEL OF DIFFICULTY: Loop - strenuous
Distance - 8.4 miles
Elevation gain - two steep grades; moderate elsewhere

HIGHLIGHTS: This 100% Class II ride plies the westside hillsides of Laguna Niguel, primarily on Highlands Ave. and Pacific Island Dr. The upgrades on those two roadways are short, but very steep. There are grand local and distant vistas near the Highlands Ave. summit and almost all the way up and down Pacific Island Dr. Another primo vista point is just below Niguel Hill on Talavera Dr. at Seaview Park. The return segment on Crown Valley Pkwy. is a pleasant warmdown before completing the loop at the South Coast Regional Civic Center.

Seaview Park Looking East

TRAILHEAD: From the San Joaquin Hills Transportation Corridor, exit south at Aliso Creek Rd. and motor 2-1/4 miles to Alicia Pkwy. Turn right and go 2-1/4 miles, passing Niguel Rd. In another 1/3 mile turn right into the South Coast Regional Civic Center. Park as directed by the signs. From the San Diego Fwy., exit south at Crown Valley Pkwy. and drive 3-3/4 miles to Alicia Pkwy. Turn right, then left at the Civic Center in 0.1 mile.

Bring a filled water bottle, as there are no on-route public sources on the loop. If you plan to roam the side streets off Highlands Ave. or Pacific Island Dr., it might be wise to bring a detailed street map in addition to the tour map provided here.

TRIP DESCRIPTION: **Highlands Ave.** Exit the Civic Center and turn left on Class II Alicia Pkwy., cycling by Ivy Glenn Dr./Pacific Island Dr. in about 0.1 mile. Pass a small shopping center just beyond, then cross Niguel Rd. (0.4) and pedal under the rows of trees. In 1.4 miles of easygoing biking in a nicely-landscaped residential neighborhood, reach Highlands Ave. and turn left.

Immediately start a steep 0.8-mile climb with over-the-shoulder vistas that improve with each pedal. (Consider a diversion to Ridgeview Park for a grand look at the Aliso Creek Drainage and Wood's Canyon.) Near the Niguel Rd. summit, an impressive Laguna Niguel panorama opens to the left (east). A modest downhill leads past Tamarron (2.5) and goes to Pacific Island Dr. in another 0.5 mile.

Pacific Island Dr. Turn right and start an equally steep 1.1-mile climb below the hillside homes to the right. Pass Club House Dr. (3.4) and take in the ever-improving sweeping vista to the left. At Belle Maison (3.7), the view is nothing short of tremendous! Pump another 0.3 mile to a crest and turn right at Talavera Dr. A short, mild pedal leads to Seaview Park, a grassy overlook with benches which follows the curving road just below the Niguel Hill summit. While going from one end of the park to the other, the panorama shifts from northward to the Sheep Hills to westward into the Aliso Creek drainage and the ocean.

Return to Pacific Island Dr. (4.6) and prepare for a swift coast on grades ranging from 7-10%. Glide between the hills on the downgrade in an area with relatively undeveloped hillsides, save for the scattered ridgetop homes on both sides. Pass Ocean Wy. (5.1) and reach a road segment where there

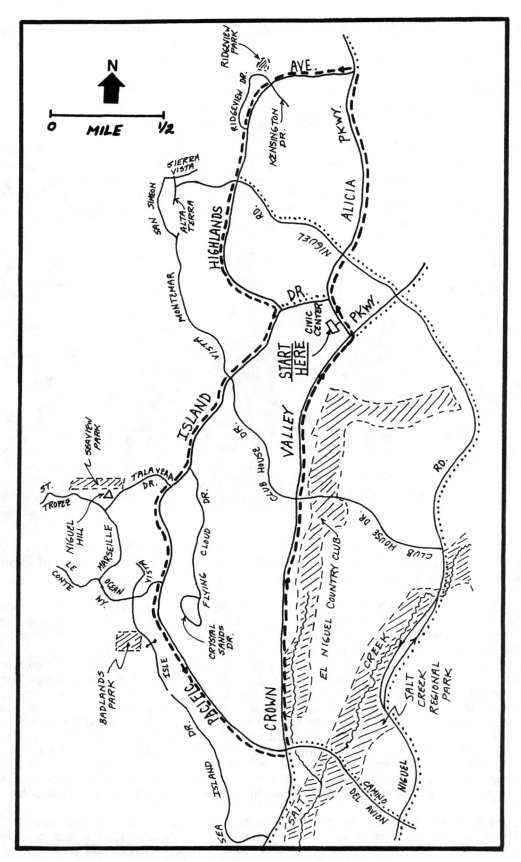

TRIP #39 - WESTSIDE LAGUNA NIGUEL

are hillside-framed views into Dana Point. Continue downhill through this lightly-developed terrain, then pass a cluster of residences near Highcrest Rd., just before reaching Crown Valley Pkwy. (6.2).

   The Return Segment. Turn left (north) and bike a mild uphill in a well-manicured neighborhood with an abundance of trees. Pass West Nine Dr. in another 0.9 mile, then reach a crest 0.7 mile further near Paseo Del Niguel (7.8). Coast pass Hillhurst. Dr. before reaching Alicia Pkwy. at (8.3). Turn left and cycle 0.1 mile to the Civic Center.

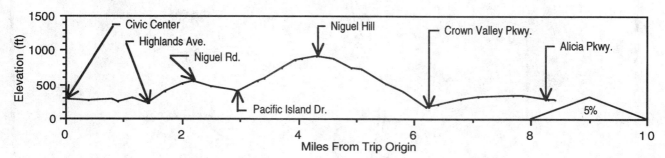

Ride Extensions: There are several scenic diversions off the described route; examples are the Flying Cloud Dr., Isle Vista and Vista Miramar areas in the hills. Another option. which is more to extend trip mileage, is to add Niguel Rd. to the tour.

CONNECTING TRIPS: 1) Connection with the Laguna Niguel Bikeway (Trip #11) - the two trips share a common segment on Crown Valley Pkwy.; 2) connection with the Aliso Viejo Figure "8" (Trip #46) - at Highlands Ave. and Alicia Pkwy., continue north on the latter street.

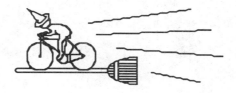

TRIP #40 - HILLSIDE SAN CLEMENTE

GENERAL LOCATION: Capistrano Beach, San Clemente

LEVEL OF DIFFICULTY: **Northern Loop** - moderate
   Distance - 9.7 miles
   Elevation gain - periodic moderate grades; single steep grade
   Southern Loop - strenuous
   Elevation gain - periodic moderate to very-steep grades
   Distance - 15.1 miles

HIGHLIGHTS: This San Clemente adventure plies two different parts of the city (on predominantly Class II roads) that may be connected via Camino Vera Cruz one day. The **Northern Loop** heads inland using Avd. Vaquero and Camino De Las Mares and has a testy workout spur on Camino Vera Cruz. The area east of the freeway is hilly and particularly scenic, with the best views found at the current Camino Vera Cruz' terminus. The return segment beyond Camino De Estrella is a pleasant downhill with a nice coastal stretch along Camino Capistrano.

   The **Southern Loop** starts near the ocean at Ole Hanson Beach Club and heads north on Avd. Pico, the route's main thoroughfare. A steady 3.5-mile moderate climb is followed by a 0.9-mile coast to road's end at a private test facility. Next is a backtrack to Avd. La Pata and a scenic workout to Steed's Park at the San Diego County border. The next delight is a strenuous loop off of Avd. La Pata on Calle Del Cerro and Avd. Vista Montana. On the loop there are varied local hillside vistas and a single area with a long-distance view of Dana Point. The return from Avd. La Pata to the trip origin is a refreshing 3.4-mile downhill.

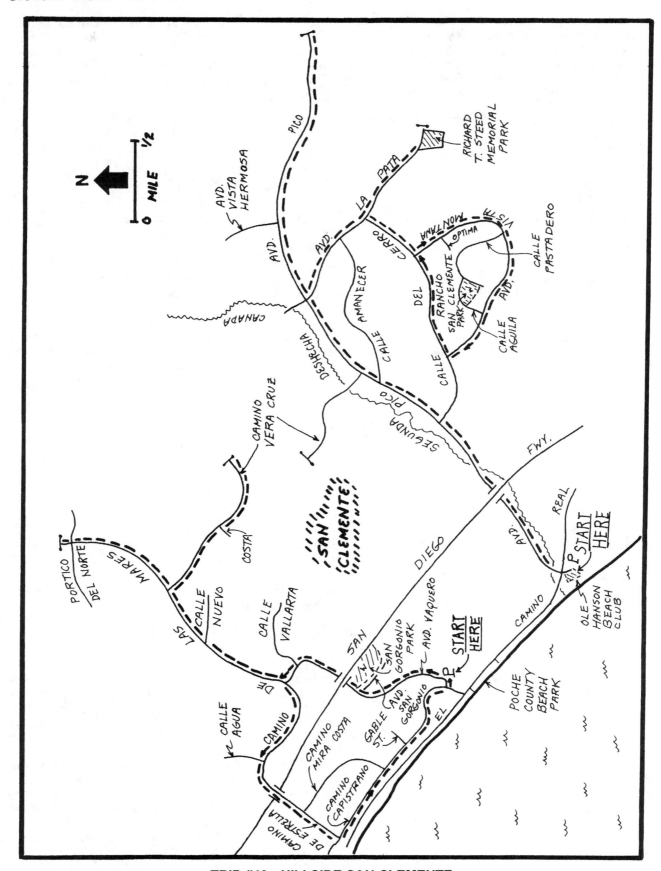

TRIP #40 - HILLSIDE SAN CLEMENTE

TRAILHEAD: **Northern Loop.** From the San Diego Fwy., exit south at Camino De Estrella and drive 1/2 mile to its terminus. Turn left (southeast) on Camino Capistrano and go 1-1/4 miles to Avd. Vaquero. Park in the shopping center on the latter street.

Southern Loop. Follow the "option" directions above, but continue past Avd. Vaquero on Camino Capistrano to El Camino Real. Turn left (southeast) and go one mile to Avd. Pico. Park at Ole Hanson Beach Club, which has limited tree shade, the club and some nearby commercial refreshment stops.

Bring a couple of water bottles if doing both loops. We found no on-route public water sources on either loop. In a pinch, there are scattered commercial water sources on both loops.

TRIP DESCRIPTION: **Northern Loop.** From the shopping center, bike north on Class II Avd. Vaquero through a residential area. Cross the lower portion of the Shorecliffs Golf Course, pass Avd. San Gorgonio (A steep upgrade on this road leads to the like-named park, which has water, numerous facilities and a great view.) and go under the San Diego Fwy. at (0.9). Continue on the long, mild upgrade and follow a sharp road curve left past Calle Vallarta while staring into the hills directly ahead. Cross the middle portion of the golf course just before reaching a "T"-junction at Camino De Los Mares (1.4).

Turn right (northeast) onto that Class II street and bike in residential environs while craning to view the hillside estates above and to the left. Just beyond Calle Nuevo (1.9), there is a Class I path on the east (right) side which transits a grassy, tree-laden area with scattered benches, picnic areas and sheltering pagodas. Pass Camino Vera Cruz (2.4) and cycle to the end of Camino De Los Mares (3.2).

Coast back to Camino Vera Cruz and turn right (southeast). (Skipping this segment turns the trip into an easy 7.6-mile ride.) Start climbing immediately and pass Costa at (4.6); in this area, the grade steepens dramatically. The good news is that the views also improve with each pump of the pedals. At the current road's end (It may be extended eastward to connect with Avd. Vista Hermosa in the near future.) are excellent coastal and City of San Clemente vistas (5.1). Reverse the incoming route and enjoy the refreshing downhill back to Camino De Los Mares (6.1).

Turn left and cruise back to the intersection with Avd. Vaquero (7.1), then continue on the now-Class X roadway. Climb past Calle Agua and a shopping complex in 0.5 mile, reaching a crest near Camino El Molino (7.9). Follow a sharp bend left toward the ocean, where the road becomes Camino De Estrella, then cross over the San Diego Fwy.

Coast 0.5 mile to Camino Capistrano, then turn left. This road parallels El Camino Real, but is on the bluffs above. Glide through residential neighborhood with scattered peeks at the ocean between the bluffside homes. Beyond Gable St., the road veers left and heads more steeply downhill to Avd. Vaquero and the trip start point (9.7).

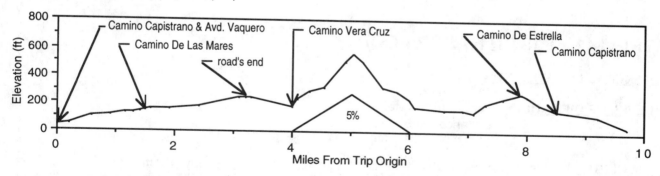

Southern Loop. From Ole Hanson Beach Club, bike inland on Class III Avd. Pico and pass under the San Diego Fwy. (0.7). Follow a short Class X section, then pass San Clemente High School and return to Class II roadway. Continue the modest climb and cross Calle Frontera/Avd. Presidio (1.1), Camino Vera Cruz (2.0), Avd. La Pata (2.5) and Avd. Vista Hermosa (3.0) in an area of rolling hills and numerous new housing developments. In another 0.5 mile is a crest followed by a refreshing coast to the end of Avd. Pico at the Capistrano Test Site entrance (private) (4.4).

Backtrack to Avd. La Pata and turn east onto that Class II street. Pump steeply uphill past several high-tech businesses, enjoying a sweeping vista that improves with elevation. Pass Calle Del Cerro (6.9) and reach a crest in about 0.1 mile. There is a manicured grassy area on the north side worth visiting just to take in the scenic panorama. Next, enjoy a 0.7-mile mild coast to road's end at austere Richard T. Steed Memorial Park (7.7).

Repeat the incoming route to Calle Del Serro (8.5) and turn uphill, climbing 0.5 mile to Avd. Vista Montana. Head left and pump another 0.3 mile to a crest. From here are views to the surrounding electronics-bedecked hilltops and a breathtaking long-distance look into Dana Point and the harbor.

Fly by Calle Pastadero (9.6), then make a decision near Calle Aguila (10.4). Uphill in a couple of hundred yards is San Clemente Park (water, restrooms, picnic areas, pagodas, children's playgrounds and basketball courts). If a rest stop is not in order, continue cruising down to Calle Del Cerro (10.7).

Another decision point! Make a left and coast down to Avd. Pico if "enough is enough!" (This cuts out the loop's most rugged hill climb and reduces total trip length to 12.6 miles.) However, the reference tour goes right and follows a 0.8-mile, sheer uphill through an upscale neighborhood to Avd. Vista Montana and passes over a nearby crest.

From this point, "life is good!" Freewheel downhill to Avd. La Pata, turn left and coast all the way to Avd. Pico, the Southern Loop's main thoroughfare (12.6). Turn left again and repeat the incoming route, returning to Ole Hanson Beach Club at (15.1).

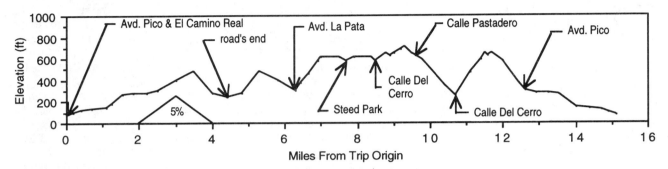

CONNECTING TRIPS: Connection with the Doheny/San Clemente Bike Route (Trip #14) - from the origin of either Northern or Southern Loops, bike to El Camino Real.

TRIP #41 - TUSTIN RANCH LOOP

GENERAL LOCATION: Tustin

LEVEL OF DIFFICULTY: Loop - moderate
Distance - 8.0 miles
Elevation gain - steady moderate grades

HIGHLIGHTS: This is a moderate workout completely on Class II bikeway. Starting from Cedar Grove Park, cyclists climb to Jamboree Rd., then enjoy a three-mile runout. The loop is closed with a flat segment on Alton Pkwy. and finishes with a steady climb on Tustin Ranch Rd. Cyclists can link a 3.9-mile ride to the basic loop using the Class I Peters Canyon Bikeway.

TRAILHEAD: From the Santa Ana Fwy., exit northeast at Jamboree Rd. and drive 2-1/4 miles to Tustin Ranch Rd. Turn left, go 1/4 mile and turn right at Pioneer Wy. In less than 1/4 mile, turn right on Pioneer Rd. and proceed about 100 yards to the Cedar Grove Park entrance. From the Eastern Transportation Corridor (State Hwy. 261), take the Portola Pkwy. turnoff west and motor 1/2 mile to Tustin Ranch Rd. Turn right and go 1/4 mile to Pioneer Wy., then turn left. Proceed as described above.

Bring a light water supply, as there are two strategically-located parks along the route. Cedar Grove Park, at the trip origin, has restrooms, water, limited tree shade, a children's playground and bikeways/walkways. A section of Peters Canyon Bikeway is on the western perimeter, as described in the **Spur Trip Option** below.

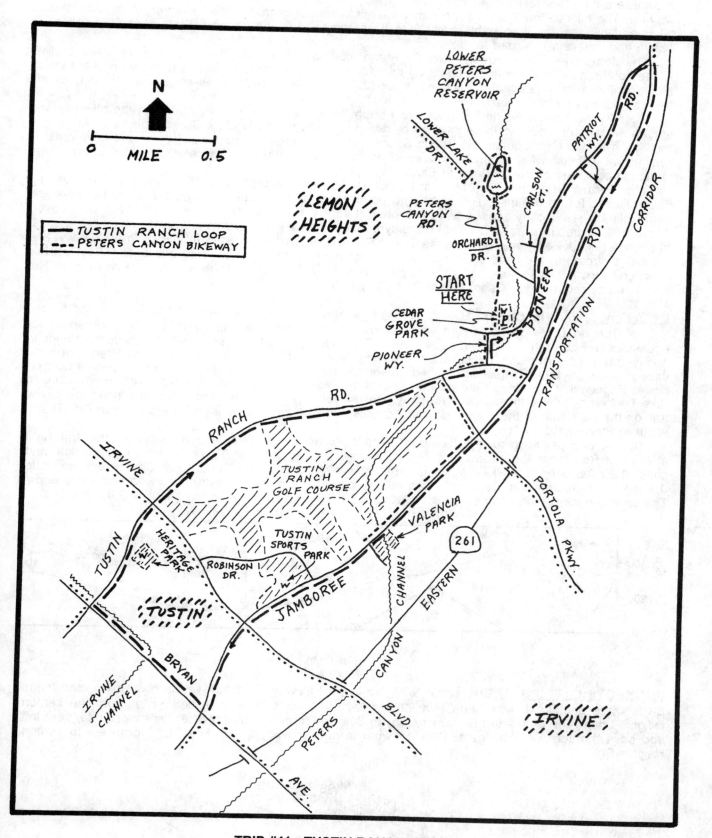

TRIP #41 - TUSTIN RANCH LOOP

TRIP DESCRIPTION: **Pioneer Road.** Leave the park and turn left on Pioneer Rd., beginning a 1.4-mile moderate climb. This residence-lined Class II road passes Carlson Ct. (0.5) and Patriot Wy. (0.9) on the way up. The hills to the left separate the residential community from Peters Canyon, a superb off-road biker and hiker area. Turn right onto Class II Jamboree Rd. and observe State Hwy. 261, which is above and parallels this road to the left.

   The Jamboree Road Downgrade. Enjoy the moderate three-mile downgrade which takes cyclists to the southern edge of the loop. Once on this main thoroughfare, there is a long series of walls which block off the nearby residential sections. Near (2.6), pockets of residences appear on the left, as the freeway pulls away to the east.

   Pass Tustin Ranch Rd. in 0.4 mile and Portola Pkwy. 0.3 mile beyond, taking in the bikeway and separate equestrian path to the right. The cycling path is part of the Peters Canyon Bikeway. At (3.9) is the Tustin Ranch Golf Course; the Tustin Sports Park (numerous athletic fields, water and restrooms) is reached at Robinson Dr. (4.3). Pass Irvine Blvd. and the beginning of The Market Place, a very large shopping complex, before cruising to Bryan Ave. (5.0).

   The Return Segment. Turn right on this Class II street and cross over the Irvine Channel, meeting Tustin Ranch Rd. in 0.6 mile. Turn right onto yet another Class II route, recross the Irvine Channel and begin climbing a steady moderate grade past Heritage Park (water, restrooms, limited tree cover, picnic and barbecue area and children's playground). Cross Irvine Blvd. (6.2) and continue the climb through residential environs, passing the Tustin Ranch Golf Club entry at (6.9). Cross Portola Pkwy. and parallel a stretch of the Peters Canyon Bikeway, continuing the sustained upgrade until (7.7). Reach a crest and turn left at Pioneer Wy. just beyond. A short flat pedal leads to a right turn at Pioneer Rd. and a nearby return to the Cedar Grove Park entry (8.0).

Excursion: **Spur Trip Option.** Bike to the west side of Cedar Grove park and take the wood-fenced Peters Canyon Bikeway northward (staying out of the paralleling dirt path which is reserved for equestrians). Follow the path as it comes along Peters Canyon Rd., passes a small school, then ends in about 200 yards from the Orchard Dr. crossing (about 0.5 mile from Pioneer Rd.). Pedal or walk through a couple hundred feet of crushed gravel and head over for the north side of the Peters Canyon Lower Reservoir. Bike around the paved head of the reservoir to a junction with the dirt Peters Canyon Bike Trail entry, where there is a porta-potty. Unless you have a fat-tire bike, return south via the paved trail on the east side of the reservoir, which outlets near the small school on Peters Canyon Rd. Return south to Pioneer Rd. (1.1).

   To continue on the bikeway's southern section, follow the bikeway and paralleling horse trail right at Pioneer Rd., cross the street and follow Pioneer Wy. 200 yards to Tustin Ranch Rd. Turn right and coast 0.2 mile to Portola Pkwy., then go left. Pass along the Tustin Ranch Golf Course and continue 0.3 mile to Jamboree Rd. Turn right and coast another 0.7 mile to Trevino Dr., where the trail ends. The up-and-back on the southern section totals 2.6 miles and the total bikeway tour is 3.9 miles.

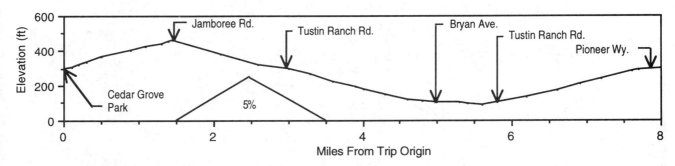

CONNECTING TRIPS: 1) Connection with the Irvine Bikeway (Trip #8) - at Jamboree Rd. and Irvine Blvd., cycle southeast over State Hwy. 261 1-3/4 miles to Yale Ave; 2) connection with the Lemon Heights Loop (Trip #45) - at the Peters Canyon Bikeway terminus on the reservoir's west side, veer left and pass through a locked gate. Bike on what is now (paved) Lower Lake Dr. northwest to Lemon Heights Dr.

TRIP #42 - OSO VIEJO PARK

GENERAL LOCATION: Mission Viejo

LEVEL OF DIFFICULTY: Up and back - moderate
Distance - 4.4 miles
Elevation gain - periodic moderate grades

HIGHLIGHTS: This is actually a tour through a collection of side-by-side parks, of which Oso Viejo Park is the centerpiece. Most of the ride is on Class I trail through lush, treed environs passing through Pavion Park, Jeronimo Greenbelt Park, Oso Viejo Park and World Cup Center Park. Our personal favorite segment is the "high road" through the greenbelt. Besides the pleasant park visits are numerous different looks at Oso Creek and its creekside attractions (e.g., the Butterfly Garden), as well as excellent distant views of Mt. Saddleback.

TRAILHEAD: From the San Diego Fwy., exit east at La Paz Rd. and drive 2-1/2 miles to road's end at Olympiad Rd. Turn left (north) and go one mile to Jeronimo Rd., then turn left again. At the next road on the left (Pavion), turn left and find parking within Pavion Park. The park has water fountains, limited tree cover, athletic fields, children's play area, benches and a few barbecues.
  From the Foothill Transportation Corridor (State Hwy. 241), exit west at Santa Margarita Pkwy., then turn southwest in 1-1/4 miles on Alicia Pkwy. Motor another 1-1/4 miles to Olympiad Rd. and turn right (south), then turn left at Pavion, the first street.

TRIP DESCRIPTION: **Outgoing Route.** Bike along the park periphery on Pavion to Jeronimo Rd. and turn left. In a short distance, take the Class I trail that leads away from the street. It passes along the park 's northern edge and a fenced school playground. Follow an up-and-down path through this lovely treed section below the hillside residences and take in the lush creek drainage below. This is the Jeronimo Greenbelt Park. Pass the path entry from Cascabel (0.7) and follow the roller-coaster trail to a point where crests, then descends steeply to Silleros (1.1).

"High Road" in Jeronimo Greenbelt Park

Bike down to Jeronimo Rd., turn left and parallel that street on a widened walkway which is a also a Class I path. Turn left on Arbolitos in 0.2 mile and follow the signed path through a residential area; here, the creek through the greenbelt merges with Oso Creek and the route officially becomes the "Oso Creek Trail." An option is to continue on Jeronimo Rd. to Oso Creek and follow the signed path down to the creek. Turn left (south) and cross the bridge over the feeder creek to rejoin the Oso Creek Trail. (Due to construction, only the former option was available in the Winter of 2000.)

Follow this classy, wooden-fence-lined trail below the hillside residences above on both left and right. Note the many plantings which are part of a concerted effort to restore this creekside area to its former grandeur. Pass the walk/bike uphill entry to Oso Viejo Park and reach a small bridge over the creek just beyond (1.7). Continue on the creek's east side toward the marked World Cup Center Park entry and follow the signed bikeway/walkway as it swithbacks up to the grassy open fields of the park.

157

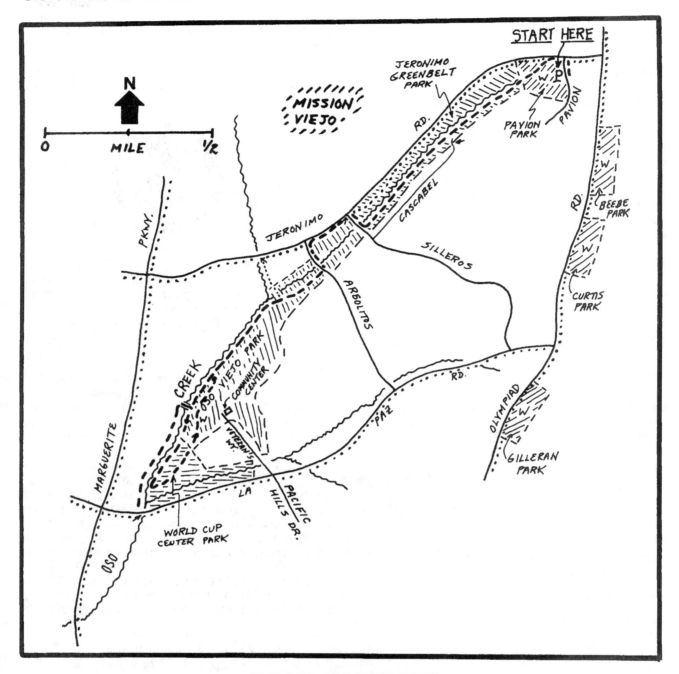

TRIP #42 - OSO VIEJO PARK

Turn back north and cycle through Oso Viejo Park with porta-potties, children's play area, benches barbecue facilities and the Norman P. Murray Community Center (2.0).

There are two options at this juncture to return to the bridge across Oso Creek. One is to retrace the incoming route, while another is to find the Oso Viejo Park walk/bike entry and take that trail back down to Oso Creek. Once there, cross over the bridge and turn left (southwest), cycle past the "Oso Creek Trail Butterfly Garden" and continue to the La Paz Rd. underpass (2.4). This is the nominal trip turnaround point, since the trail is packed dirt and gravel from La Paz Rd. to its end at Marguerite Pkwy.

Return Route. Return along the Oso Creek Trail and Jeronimo Rd. to Silleros. Note that there are several excellent head-on views of Mt. Saddleback when biking in this direction. The best workout is to retrace the incoming route on the "high road." Less-motivated souls can bike on the Class I "low road," which follows a short paved trail along the creek, then returns to the Class I sidewalk trail along

Jeronimo Rd. for the trip's remainder. (Jeronimo Rd. also has a signed Class II bike route as yet another option.) The total trip mileage for all options is about 4.4 miles.

CONNECTING TRIPS: 1) Connection with the Mission Viejo Bikeway (Trip #30) - at trip's end at La Paz Rd., bike west to Marguerite Pkwy.; 2) connection with the Arroyo Trabuco Loop (Trip # 50) - from Pavion Park, bike east on La Paz to Olympiad.

TRIP #43 - YORBA LINDA BITS N' PIECES

GENERAL LOCATION: Yorba Linda

LEVEL OF DIFFICULTY: Loop - very strenuous
Distance - 23.6 miles
Elevation gain - periodic sheer grades

HIGHLIGHTS: Why "Bits and Pieces?" Because we pieced together three different and separated climbs into the hills north of Yorba Linda into a single ride. (It is a "bit" of a quadriceps burner besides!) The full ride is only for serious "hillies" in excellent shape or "advanced poke-alongs" like us who gut it out but always eventually get there. (Besides, we book authors need to stop frequently for elevation readings!) The rewards are an excellent aerobic workout and some serious panoramic views spread throughout the ride.

The tour is a mix of Class I, Class II and Class X, although most of the latter sections are on lightly-traveled roadway. There are options to do a single climb on Fairmont Blvd., two climbs including Hidden Hill Rd. or the full three-climb ride which adds Camino de Bryant. The key decision points for these options are noted in the detailed trip writeup.

TRAILHEAD: From the Riverside Fwy., exit north at Weir Canyon Rd. and drive into Yorba Linda, where the street becomes Yorba Linda Blvd. In 3-1/2 miles from the freeway exit, turn right (north) on Fairmont Blvd., then left on Cordova Ln. in 1/2 mile to reach the Fairmont Knolls Park access. The park has scattered benches under light treecover, grassy knolls and tennis courts. Another option is to park in the small shopping center on the northwest corner of Yorba Linda Blvd. and Fairmont Blvd.

Bring a couple of quarts of water, particularly on hot days. Beyond San Antonio Park, easily-accessible public sources were non-existent on the eastern portion of the tour.

TRIP DESCRIPTION: **Fairmont Road Climb.** Leave the park, head left (northeast) and begin an immediate climb with residences to the right and open hillsides to the left. The Class II roadway disappears, although the horse trails which pervade this general territory continue. There are over-the-shoulder views into Santa Ana Canyon and across to the Anaheim Hills area. The residences increase in both size and grandeur on the way up to the local summit, a general characteristic of the entire tour.

In 1.1 miles near Rim Crest Dr., the upgrade gives way to a flat and subsequent downhill. This brief respite gives way to a steeper 0.9-mile climb to a crest just before reaching San Antonio Rd. (2.3). Coast downhill and enjoy the view of the Santa Ana River flood plain, reaching View Park Dr. and San

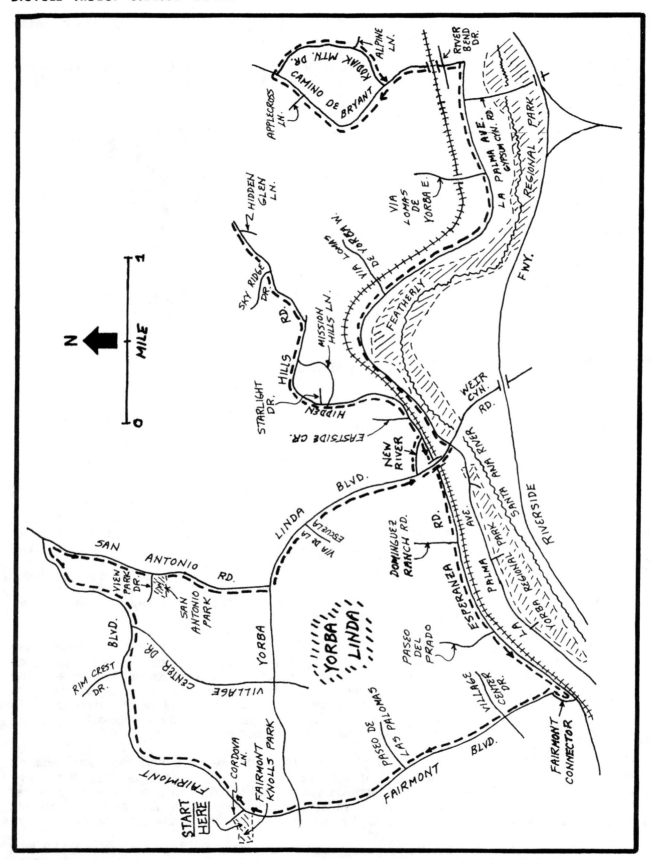

TRIP #43 - YORBA LINDA BITS N' PIECES

Antonio Park at (3.0). The park has water, restrooms, limited shade, recreation fields, equestrian staging area and peripheral trail, modest picnic/barbecue facilities and children's playground.

Continue the downhill to Yorba Linda Blvd. and turn left on that busy Class X (with wide shoulder) road (3.75). A more-moderate downgrade leads past Via de La Escuela (4.2) to New River in another 0.7 mile. Turn left and take that curving street 0.3 mile to Esperanza Rd. -- there is a shopping center across the street. By turning left at this junction, cyclists can return to Fairmont Knolls Park as described in **The Return Leg** below. The single-climb option is a total of 9.2 miles.

Hidden Hills Road Climb. Turn left and take a short easy pedal alongside railroad tracks and above the Santa Ana River flood plain past scattered commercial complexes. Just beyond Eastside Circle (5.4) the road bends left becoming Hidden Hills Rd. The grade steepens, starting the 1.9-mile and toughest climb of the full tour. Grind upward past Starlight Dr. (6.0), then make a hard left in 0.5 mile at a short flat to stay on Hidden Hills Rd. (staying straight leads to a visible deadend).

While sucking air, take in the impressive well-spaced residences to the right and less-developed hillsides to the left. At 7.0 is Sky Ridge Dr. where sweeping southerly views of Santa Ana Canyon and its hillside backdrop open majestically. In another 0.4 sweaty mile is Hidden Glen Ln. and the current road's end. (The road may be extended eastward to connect with Camino de Bryant in the future.) Enjoy the magnificent panoramic vista for a spell, then spin down the road and retrace the incoming route to Esperanza Rd. and New River (9.8). If you opt out of the final climb, continue west on Esperanza Dr. The double-climb option is a total of 13.8 miles.

Camino de Bryant Climb. Turn right on New River and make the short climb to Yorba Linda Blvd. Turn left and pedal 0.3 mile to La Palma Ave., then make another left. An easy 2.1-mile cruise on a Class I bikeway alongside the Santa Ana River flood plain leads to a sharp left turn, where the street name changes to Camino de Bryant. On the La Palma Ave. segment is Via Lomas de Yorba W. (11.2), Via Lomas de Yorba E. and a small shopping complex, and Gypsum Canyon Rd. (12.8). Cyclists must exit the Class I path to follow Camino de Bryant.

Pass Riverbend Dr., then bike under the railroad overpass (13.4) and follow a steepening upgrade. Pump past Kodiak Mountain Dr. in another 0.3 mile and note the large, plush residences scattered alongside the road. There are excellent vistas in this sheer-climb area and opportunities to take "Lookie Lou" breaks. Reach a heaven-sent flat near Applecross Ln. and cycle a short distance to Kodiak Mountain Dr. (14.6). A 0.5-mile steep coast leads past Alpine Ln., an area with a particularly clear look at the Eastern Transportation Corridor across the canyon.

At the intersection with Camino de Bryant (15.5), turn left and coast back to La Palma Ave., then retrace the incoming route to Yorba Linda Blvd. (19.1). Go right, then right again at New River, returning to Esperanza Rd. (19.6).

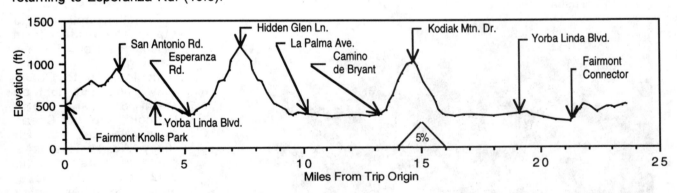

The Return Leg. Pedal under La Palma Ave. and continue west on the Class I bikeway on the street's north side. Pass Dominguez Ranch Rd. (20.1) and Paseo Del Prado (20.6) before reaching Fairmont Connector at (21.2). Turn right and climb to road's end at Fairmont Blvd. in 0.2 mile. Turn left and continue the climb on the Class X road with paralleling horse trails.

Pass by Paseo de Las Palomas at (22.8) and the Class I trail to the right which plies Kingsbriar Park (See Trip #22.) just beyond. Enjoy a short downhill on a suddenly-emerging Class II roadway, then cross Yorba Linda Blvd. at (23.1). A modest uphill leads back to Cordova Ln. and Fairmont Knolls Park (23.6).

CONNECTING TRIPS: 1) Connection with the Santa Ana River Trail (Trip # 17A) - at La Palma Ave. and Yorba Linda Blvd., go west on the former street and enter Yorba Regional Park, then bike toward the river; 2) connection with the El Cajon Trail (Trip #22) - the trips share a common segment on Esperanza Rd. east of Fairmont Connector; 3) connection with the Santa Ana Canyon Road ride (Trip

#25) - bike south across the Santa Ana River on either Yorba Linda Blvd. (becomes Weir Canyon Rd.) or Gypsum Canyon Rd.

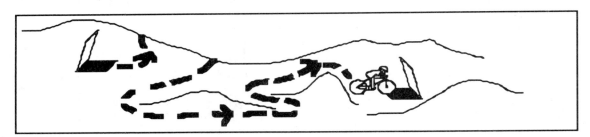

TRIP #44 - ANAHEIM HILLS

GENERAL LOCATION: Anaheim Hills, Orange

LEVEL OF DIFFICULTY: Loop - strenuous
Distance - 14.2 miles
Elevation gain - periodic steep-to-sheer grades

HIGHLIGHTS: This roller-coaster ride in the Peralta Hills is essentially a tour of the plush Anaheim Hills residential area. The tour is primarily on Class X roadway and has several well-spaced hearty climbs, reserving it for well-experienced in-traffic cyclists in good condition. The payoffs are the healthy workout itself, the grand scenic panoramas scattered through the trip and the pleasant residential surroundings. Traffic is relatively light during non-rush-hour weekday periods and weekends.

TRAILHEAD: From the Costa Mesa Fwy. southbound, use the Lincoln Ave./Nohl Ranch Rd. exit which lets out at Tustin Blvd. across from Eisenhower Park/The Brickyard. Go south, cross Lincoln Ave. and turn right into the Park and Ride area just beyond. Northbound traffic should use the same exit, which puts traffic onto Santiago Blvd. Go north a few hundred feet and turn left onto Lincoln Ave., then left again onto Tustin Ave. and enter the Park and Ride area.

West Side of Walnut Canyon Reservoir

Another option is to start the ride from Eisenhower Park. There is parking to the west (Lincoln Ave. to Ocean View Ave. and right on Main St.) and north (Lincoln Ave. to Ocean View Ave. and right on Bixby Ave.). This is a pleasant, shaded little park with a small lake, picnic benches, play areas, a mini-barnyard and bikepath to boot! The park sits right next to The Brickyard, a shopping plaza. There is a fine restaurant with a verandah area that looks out over the lake -- a great place to end the trip.

Bring a filled water bottle to see you through the hardest hill climbs. There is easily accessible water at Imperial Park, Oak Park and Canyon Rim Park, which are strategically placed along the route.

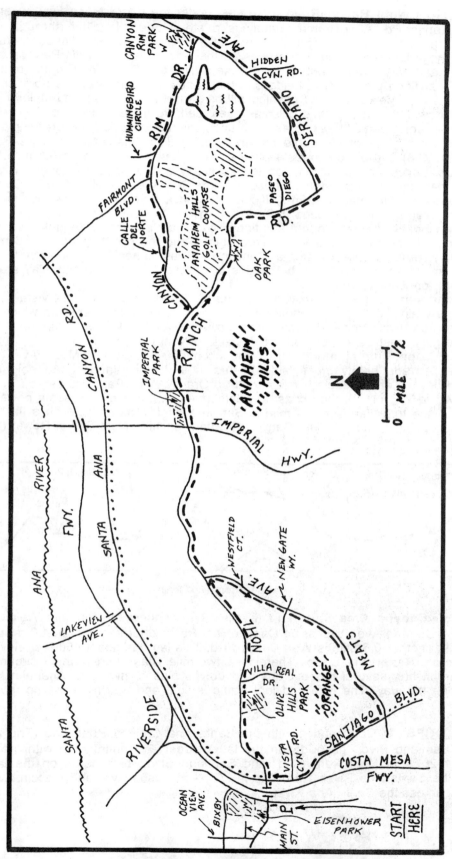

TRIP #44 - ANAHEIM HILLS

TRIP DESCRIPTION: **Nohl Ranch Road.** Bike east under the Costa Mesa Fwy. where Lincoln Ave. becomes Nohl Ranch Rd. Almost immediately is a steep one-mile climb through well-manicured residential environs on Class X roadway with little or no shoulder. These local features are characteristic of those found on most of the ride. On the way up is Olive Hills Park off of Nohl Canyon Rd. (tennis courts and porta potties, but no water), then Villa Real Dr. (0.9). The first of many views into the Santa Ana River flood plain, Yorba Linda and the frontal Chino Hills opens up in this area. A nice coast takes cyclists past Meats Ave. (1.8), which will be part of the trip's second major loop.

An extended downhill with a couple of small rises leads to Imperial Hwy. and Imperial Park (3.0), which has water, a porta-pottie, trees, grassy grounds, recreation fields, children's playground and a scenic northward vista. More of the same terrain takes cyclists past Anaheim Hills Rd. and a small shopping center at (3.8) and a local low elevation point at Canyon Rim Rd. in 0.1 mile.

The Eastside Loop. The eastside loop is essentially a ride on the Anaheim Hills Golf Course periphery. Climb past the western edge of those grounds, the Anaheim Hills Saddle Club and tiny Oak Park (benches and water fountain and magnificent old oaks), then begin a 0.4-mile sheer pumpathon to a much flatter uphill near Paseo Diego (5.2). In 0.2 mile is Serrano Ave.

Turn left and mostly climb through additional well-maintained residential areas, enjoying the views which reopen to the Santa Ana River, Yorba Linda and the hills beyond. In 1.6 miles is Canyon Rim Rd. (7.0) and a turn left, unless a stop at Canyon Rim Park is needed. (The entry to the park, which has a restroom, limited shade, benches, barbecues, sports fields and children's play area, is accessed a little further north on Serrano Ave.)

Now begins the start of a well-deserved downgrade. The scenic northward vistas are frequent on this road. Pass the Walnut Canyon Reservoir and revel in a particularly steep drop which starts near the Hummingbird Cr. area. Pass under the mammoth power towers and power lines near Fremont Blvd., then continue the glide past Calle Del Norte (8.7) back to Nohl Ranch Rd.

The Westside Loop. Turn right and retrace the incoming route back to Meats Ave. (11.3). Turn left and pump a steep grade below the hillside homes in this nicely-landscaped neighborhood. Near Westfield Ct. and beyond are sweeping vistas south to Orange, Villa Park and Lemon Heights. Reach a summit near Newgate Wy. (11.9), then coast to Featherhill Dr., passing near some power towers and a seemingly out-of-place truck farm. In 0.5 mile is Santiago Blvd. (13.0). Cycle on a flat, Class II street passing a small shopping center at Vista Canyon Rd. and reaching Nohl Ranch Rd. at (14.0). Turn left and return to the Park and Ride zone in 0.2 mile.

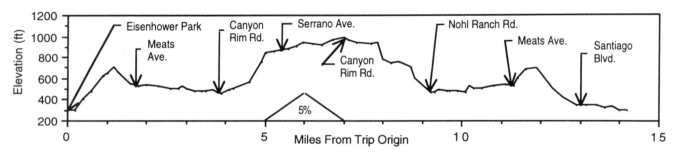

Excursions: **Weir Canyon Area Spur Trip.** Cyclists can connect the trip with Weir Canyon Rd. by staying on Class II Serrano Ave., bypassing Canyon Rim Rd. and turning right in 1.2 miles onto Class II Oak Canyon Dr. In another 0.6 mile is Weir Canyon Rd. This leg has about 450 feet elevation of drop.

Walnut Canyon Reservoir Loop. There is a two-mile Class I trail which circumnavigates the reservoir. The circuit has several modest ups and downs plus a myriad of Anaheim Hills and more distant vistas along the way. The bike and foot traffic is light and the there are no motorized vehicle accesses.

CONNECTING TRIPS: 1) Continuation with the Santa Ana Canyon Road ride (Trip #25) - at Nohl Ranch Rd. and Santiago Blvd., go north on the latter street; 2) continuation with the Orange/Irvine Park tour (Trip # 26) - at Nohl Ranch Rd. and Santiago Blvd., bike south on the latter street; 3) connection with the Santa Ana River Trail (Trip # 17B) - at Tustin Ave. and Lincoln Ave., cycle west on the latter road across the Santa Ana River.

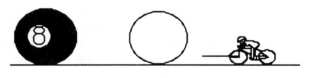

TRIP #45 - LEMON HEIGHTS SIGHTS

GENERAL LOCATION: Lemon Heights

LEVEL OF DIFFICULTY: Loop - moderate to strenuous
Distance - 6.1 miles
Elevation gain - two short, strenuous grades

HIGHLIGHTS: Though short on distance, this route is reserved for veteran bikers who are comfortable sharing narrow roadways with traffic and who like a challenging climb. The reward for doing the winding Class X portion of the tour are the excellent vistas provided on both Skyline Dr. and Foothill Blvd. There is an extended stretch of roadway with views of Tustin and Irvine, Mt. Saddleback and Peters Canyon. A bonus is the myriad of upscale hillside homes that surround the route on its higher elevation segment.

TRAILHEAD: From the Santa Ana Fwy., exit northeast on Red Hill Ave. and drive 1-1/2 miles to Skyline Dr. Park under the trees to the south of the intersection, subject to posted laws. From the Eastern Transportation Corridor (State Hwy. 261), exit northwest on Irvine Blvd., motor 1-1/2 miles to Red Hill Ave. and turn right. In 1/2 mile is Skyline Dr.

Bring a quart of water on hot days. The single easily-accessible source on the route is Bent Tree Park which has a water fountain, walkway/bikeway, tree shade, children's play area and volleyball court.

TRIP DESCRIPTION: **The Workout.** Bike southeast through an upscale, tree-lined rural neighborhood on Class X roadway. In 0.5 mile, the straight-line street follows a curve to the left. The grade changes dramatically in another 0.2 mile just beyond Beverly Glen Dr. and bikers begin a strenuous 0.6-mile winding uphill to a summit near Foothill Blvd. The shoulder is narrow and cyclists will have to work with the limited auto traffic on the climb. (Note that, at Beverly Glen Dr., a turn left is required to remain on Skyline Dr.)

Lemon Height Drive Near Skyline Drive

At Wilding Rd. is a three-way intersection where the reference route goes right on Foothill Blvd./Skyline Dr. (1.2). In a couple of hundred yards, Skyline Dr. splits off to the left and we head right on Foothill Blvd., reaching a crest just beyond. Cruise the next 1.5 miles on a mildly-downhill, sinuous roadway, admiring the hillside estates and the panoramic vista that has Tustin and Irvine laid out below and Mt. Saddleback in the distance. Foothill Blvd. becomes Lemon Heights Dr. just beyond La Questa Dr. (2.0). In the latter portion of this downhill stretch are scenic views into Peters Canyon and its upper reservoir.

At 0.2 mile beyond Sharon Ln. (2.6) is a steep 0.4 mile climb. In this stretch, a left turn at Lower Lake Dr. is required to stay on Lemon Heights Rd. (2.9). A right turn leads to nearby Bent Tree Park. The road ends at a crest where cyclists turn right, rejoining Skyline Dr. and enjoying an expanded road shoulder.

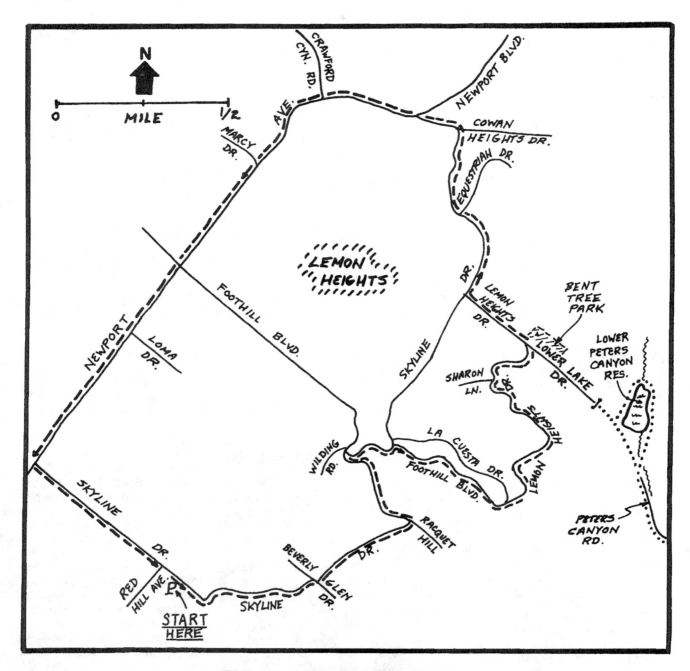

TRIP #45 - LEMON HEIGHTS SIGHTS

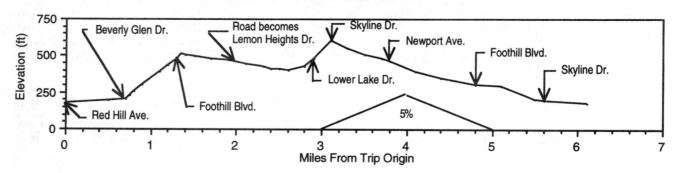

The Downhill Return. Enjoy additional looks at Peters Canyon and coast by additional plush hillside residences before reaching Newport Ave./Newport Blvd. (3.8). Turn left onto this busy Class X street and continue gliding the mild downhill through pleasant (but less opulent) neighborhood. On this straight-line road, a marked Class II section appears near Marcy Dr. (4.4).

Keep coasting past Foothill Blvd. (4.8) and reach Skyline Dr. at (5.6). Turn left, returning to a smaller and tree-lined roadway on the flat. In 0.5 mile after the turn is Red Hill Ave.

CONNECTING TRIPS: Connection with the Tustin Ranch Loop (Trip #41) - at Lower Lake Dr., turn right and coast 0.9 mile to pavement's end. Pass through the locked gate, cross a short section of crushed rock, then bike south on Peters Canyon Rd. to the Class I Peters Canyon Bikeway on the west (right) side of the road.

TRIP #46 - ALISO VIEJO FIGURE "8"

GENERAL LOCATION: Aliso Viejo

LEVEL OF DIFFICULTY: Dual loop - moderate
Distance - 8.2 miles
Elevation gain - steady moderate grade on Pacific Park Dr.

HIGHLIGHTS: This 100% Class II ride wanders through the heart of Aliso Viejo in the form of a double loop. From a low point near the Aliso Creek drainage, cyclists work over to Pacific Park Dr. and tackle a testy, but scenic, upgrade to a panoramic crest. Not long after crossing State. Hwy. 73 on a portion of the long and vista-laden downhill, bikers meet Aliso Creek Rd. and follow it on a broad turn from north to east to return to the trip start point. A fun spur trip on Wood Canyon Rd. is also provided.

TRAILHEAD: From the San Joaquin Hills Transportation Corridor (State Hwy. 73), exit south at La Paz Rd. and drive 1-1/4 miles to Aliso Creek Rd. Turn right and go a couple hundred yards to the Aliso Village shopping center entrance on the south side of the street. From the San Diego Fwy., go west at Oso Pkwy., pass under State Hwy. 73 (the street becomes Pacific Park Dr.) and continue 1/4 mile to La Paz Rd. Proceed left (south) one mile and turn right at Aliso Creek Rd.

An alternate is to start from Laguna Niguel Regional Park. Bike north on the park path leading to the intersection of Aliso Creek Rd. and La Paz Rd., then turn north on the latter street. (Refer to the Trip #29B detail map.)

Bring a light water supply. There are shopping plazas and centers scattered throughout the route; however, we did not find any convenient, on-route public water sources.

TRIP DESCRIPTION: Outwardbound and Upward. Leave the shopping center and bike 0.2 mile to La Paz Rd. Turn left (north) and bike past an interesting collection of commercial centers, residential and modern industrial complexes. Pass Avila Rd. at (0.7) and proceed to Pacific Park Rd. in 0.4 mile.

Turn left, cycle past the large Plaza De La Paz shopping complex and cross Alicia Pkwy. at (1.5). Pass over the Aliso Creek watershed and bike through residential development, reaching Aliso Creek Rd. in 0.5 mile from Alicia Pkwy. Start a steady mild climb past Wood Canyon Dr. (2.75) and take in the over-the-shoulder views of Aliso Creek and the surrounding metropolis. Also notice the line of large residences on the ridge to the left and above. The vista only improves for the next 3/4 mile of steady pumping on the trip's steepest grade. The road swings gradually north and reaches a crest near Chase/Peppertree (3.3).

167

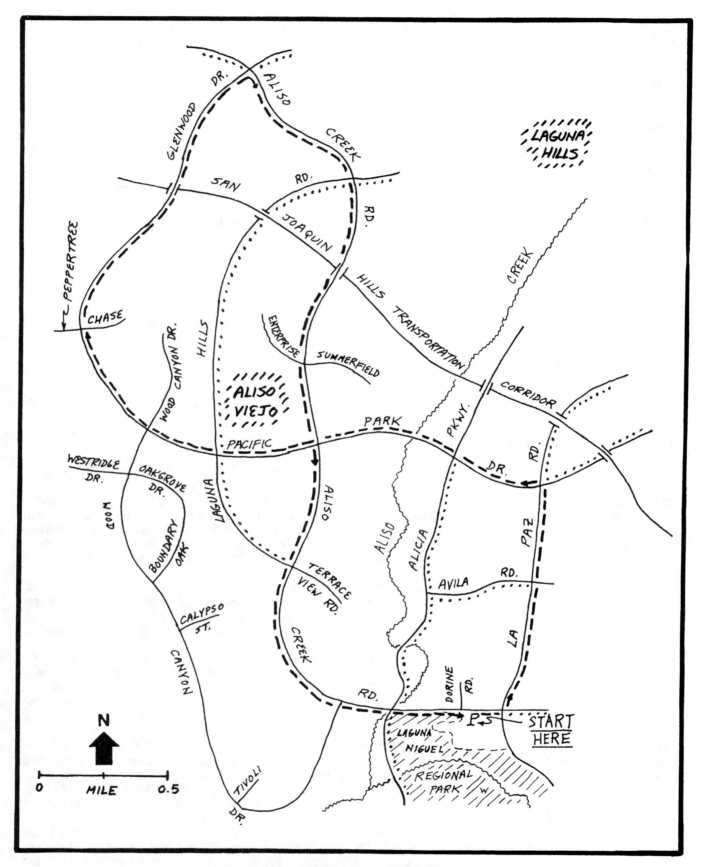

TRIP #46 - ALISO VIEJO FIGURE "8"

Closing the Figure "8." Coast past a large residential complex below and to the right, taking the time to enjoy the panoramic views on the downgrade. Pass over State Hwy. 73 (the road is now named Glenwood Dr.) and seemingly reenter the world of light industrial and commercial enterprises. At (4.6) is Aliso Creek Rd. and a turn right. The remainder of the tour will be on this street.

The downhill steepens and the views to the Aliso Creek drainage and surrounding cities continue. Pass the Laguna Hills Dr. northern segment (5.3) and yet another shopping center, then recross State Hwy. 73 and pedal on flattening terrain past the mammoth Aliso Viejo Town Center. Cross Pacific Park Dr., make a short climb, reaching a crest at Laguna Hills Rd. S./Terrace View Rd. (7.0). Coast over Aliso Creek and reach Alicia Pkwy. at (7.9). In another 0.3 mile is the entry to Aliso Village shopping center.

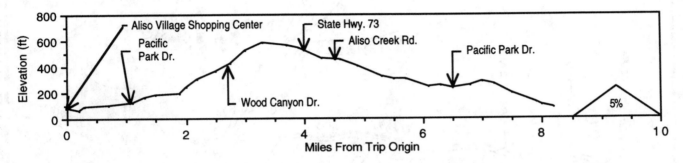

Excursion: Wood Canyon Road Spur Trip. Wood Canyon Rd. is an off-the-beaten track Class X ride below the Sheep Hills and above Wood Canyon. The most interesting segment is the 2.3-mile, predominantly residential stretch south of Pacific Park Dr. Just south there are sweeping views of lower Aliso Viejo and Laguna Niguel. A short climb to Westridge Dr./Oak Grove Dr. gives way to a brief coast to Boundary Oak. There are superb views to the nearby hillside homes, Wood Canyon and the Sheep Hills, the latter two being within the Aliso/Woods Canyon Wilderness area. On the last downhill mile to Aliso Creek Rd. are the most impressive looks into Wood Canyon.

CONNECTING TRIPS: 1) Connection with the Laguna Niguel Bikeway (Trip #11) - at Aliso Creek Rd. and La Paz Rd., take the former street south to Crown Valley Pkwy.; 2) connection with the O'Neill Regional Park tour (Trip #28) - turn into the park entrance on Trabuco Canyon Rd.; 3) connection with the southern segment of the Aliso Creek Trail (Trip #29B) - at Aliso Creek Rd. and Alicia Pkwy., go west on the former road to the Aliso Creek Trail entry; 4) connection with the Laguna Hills Loop (Trip #31) - at Aliso Creek Rd. and Glenwood Dr., bike west on the former road to El Toro Rd.; 5) connection with the Westside Laguna Niguel tour (Trip #39) - at Aliso Creek Rd. and Alicia Pkwy., bike south one mile on the latter street.

TRIP #47 - CITIES AND CANYONS

GENERAL LOCATION: Mission Viejo, Rancho Santa Margarita, Trabuco Canyon, Live Oak Canyon

LEVEL OF DIFFICULTY: Loop - strenuous
    Distance - 13.2 miles
    Elevation gain - periodic moderate grades; steep grade in Live Oak Canyon

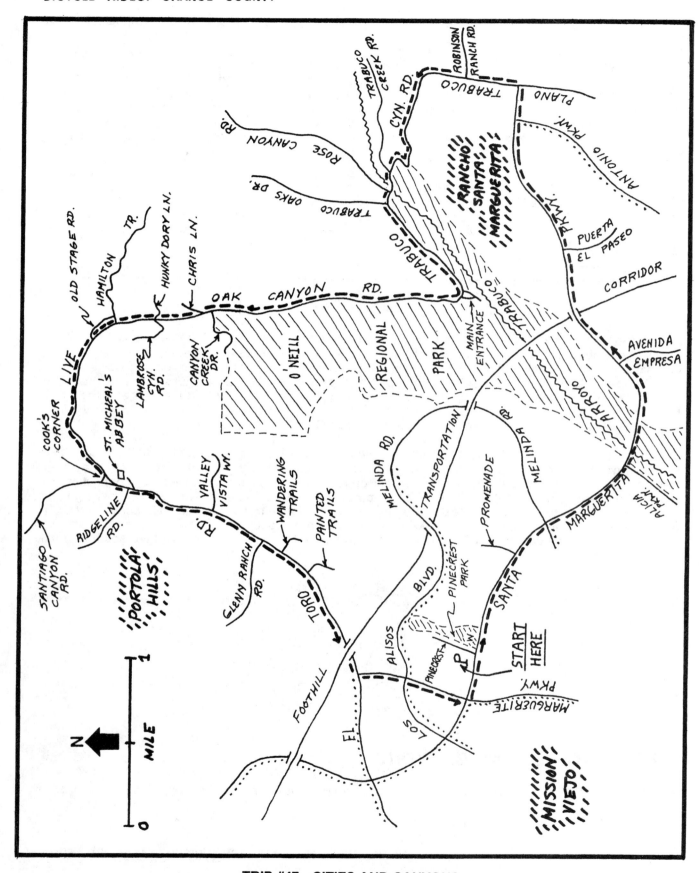

TRIP #47 - CITIES AND CANYONS

<u>HIGHLIGHTS</u>: This is a trip reserved for cyclists with the strong legs and experience riding narrow roads shared with auto traffic. It plies the cities of Mission Viejo and Rancho Santa Margarita, then dives into Trabuco Canyon and climbs steeply out of Live Oak Canyon. The return leg beyond the trip summit at Old Stage Rd. is essentially a four-mile runout back to the start point at Pinecrest Park. The canyons segment is especially scenic with cyclists riding for miles under the oak-dominated tree cover.

<u>TRAILHEAD</u>: From the San Diego Fwy., exit north on El Toro Rd. and proceed five miles to Santa Margarita Pkwy. Turn right (southeast) and drive 1/2 mile to the Pinecrest Park entry at Pinecrest. From the Foothill Transportation Corridor (State Hwy. 241), exit south at Santa Margarita Pkwy. and go 1-1/2 miles to Pinecrest. The grassy park lies within the Oso Creek flood plain just to the east and below Pinecrest. It has water, tree shade, bikeways/walkways, recreation fields, children's play area, but no restrooms.

Though a relatively short ride, bring at least a quart of water to see through the climbs. There are water and restrooms within O'Neill Park which are available to cyclists without an entree fee, but few other convenient public sources.

<u>TRIP DESCRIPTION</u>: **City Ride.** Join Class II Santa Margarita Pkwy. heading eastbound and climb to a crest in a residential zone at Promenade (0.8). A 0.9-mile coast leads past Alicia Pkwy. to a nearby low point and a passage over the Arroyo Trabuco, initiating a three-mile modest climb to San Antonio Pkwy. Proceed by the first of Santa Margarita Pkwy.'s plethora of shopping centers and pass over State Hwy. 241 at (2.8).

Pedal closer to the base of Mt. Saddleback and reach San Antonio Pkwy. at (4.1). Bike across that street and turn left in 0.2 mile at road's end onto Plano Trabuco. A mild 0.6-mile climb through a mix of residential properties and commercial complexes on this northbound stretch leads to a sharp left. At this local crest, the street name changes to Trabuco Canyon Rd. while the road remains Class X.

The Canyon Tour. Begin a winding dive toward Trabuco Creek (below and to the right) while stealing a glance at the dense stand of oaks to the left. Further down the narrow serpentine road, the tree cover begins to surround it. Shortly, the road straightens again and flattens in a more open area which holds Trabuco Creek. Nearby is unpaved Trabuco Creek Rd. (5.7).

After a short climb through a continuous tree canopy, begin a one-mile coast on continued narrow roadway alongside the eastern reaches of O'Neill Park and reach the main entrance at (8.6). (See Trip #28 for the park's features.) On what is now Live Oak Canyon Rd., start the tough four-mile climb out of the canyon, probably working with an impatient driver or two on the way up. Pump up the wiggly route past the western park edge through the sometimes dense and over-hanging tree cover, passing scattered offset-from-the-road residences.

Climb past Canyon Creek Dr. (10.3) and note the thinning tree line just before reaching Hamilton Tr. in 0.9 mile. Cyclists gain the summit in another 0.2 mile at Old Stage Rd., where the road is now sun-exposed. In the distant hillsides ahead, the dense Portola Hills developments can be seen. A 0.9-mile runout through scattered residences and small farms follows, mostly on a more open and exposed roadway. At road's end is El Toro Rd. and Cook's Corner, with its rustic bar/restaurant.

Live Oak Canyon Road Near O'Neill Park

City Return. Turn left and take the Class I Aliso Trail described in Trip #29 or coast down Class II El Toro Rd. Pass Ridgeline Rd. followed by the entry to St. Michael's Abbey, bike a short uphill, then continue coasting below the Portola Hills homes on the ridge to the right. Aliso Creek is below and to the near right.

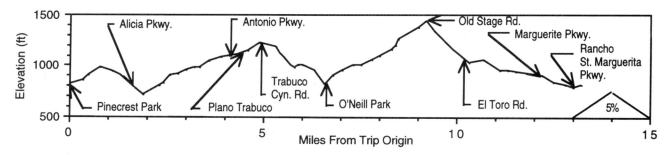

Glide past Valley Vista Wy. (10.7), Glenn Ranch Rd. (11.1), Wandering Trails (11.3) and Painted Trails (11.5) through this open territory before passing under State Hwy. 241 (12.0). Pass a shopping center, then turn left at Class II Marguerite Pkwy. at (12.2), reentering residential environs and continuing downhill. Bike left at Santa Margarita Pkwy. in 0.8 mile near a shopping complex, then coast to the Pinecrest Park entry at (13.2).

Excursions: Rose Canyon Road and Trabuco Oaks Drive Spurs. An interesting spur just north of the Trabuco Creek crossing is Rose Canyon Dr. It climbs modestly uphill alongside Rose Canyon Creek on a narrow roadway, passing through a collection of rustic abodes in a rural setting. Tree cover is plentiful on this mile-plus side road. The accessible upper portion is signed private property.

A second and similar spur is Trabuco Oaks Rd. Once past the Feed, Tackle and General Store and the venerable Trabuco Oaks Steak House (Don't wear a tie to this excellent eatery unless you want to have it "modified."), this slim road climbs for just less than a mile to a gated and locked entry to private grounds. It follows the course of Hickey Canyon Creek through sections of dense, overhanging tree cover.

CONNECTING TRIPS: 1) Connection with the Santiago Canyon Road tour (Trip # 27) - the trips share a common segment on El Toro Rd. below Cook's Corner; 2) connection with the O'Neill Regional Park ride - turn into the park at the main entrance at the junction of Trabuco Canyon Rd./Live Oak Canyon Rd.; 3) connection with the Aliso Creek Trail (Trip #29A) - take the Class I path on the west side of El Toro Rd. at Cook's Corner; 4) connection with the Mission Viejo Bikeway (Trip #30) - at Marguerite Pkwy. and Santa Margarita Pkwy., continue south on the former street; 5) connection with the Arroyo Trabuco Loop (Trip #50) - the tours share a common segment on Santa Margarita Pkwy. between Alicia Pkwy. and Antonio Pkwy.

TRIP #48 - SILVERADO CANYON

GENERAL LOCATION: Silverado Canyon (Cleveland National Forest)

LEVEL OF DIFFICULTY: Up and back - moderate to strenuous
Distance - 11.3 miles
Elevation gain - steady moderate grade beyond Ladd Canyon Rd.

HIGHLIGHTS: This superb canyon ride is for experienced cyclists who are comfortable biking on Class X roadways with little or no shoulder. Note that traffic is light and the speed limit in most stretches is below 25 mph. The tour starts at the Silverado Forest Station and winds its way modestly up an ever-narrowing canyon about four miles to road's end. Residential pockets line the road, squeezed so tight to the canyon walls in the upper stretches that some homes are built directly over Silverado Creek.

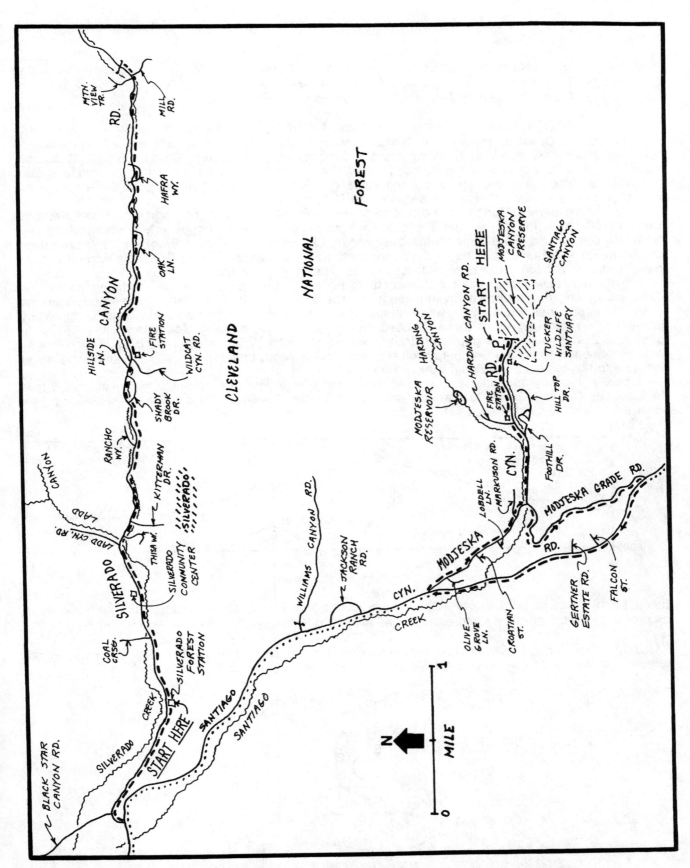

TRIP #48 - SILVERADO CANYON & TRIP #49 - MODJESKA CANYON

Along the way are interesting scenery, scattered overhanging tree cover and both cafes and a country store available for a pleasant rest stop.

TRAILHEAD: From Santiago Canyon Rd., turn north on Silverado Canyon Rd. and go 3/4 mile to the Silverado Forest Station. Bring a light water supply. There is a water fountain at the trip origin and a combination of taverns, cafes and markets along the road.

TRIP DESCRIPTION: Leave the parking area and turn right while noting the Silverado Creek flood plain to the left. Coast by the elegant Calvery Chapel of the Canyons. and take in the nearby scrub-filled hillsides. Make the first of many creek crossings, then pass Ladd Canyon Rd. (1.1) on the beginning of a four-mile upgrade to road's end. The canyon walls begin to narrow and a mixed residential/commercial pocket opens beyond Thisa Wy. (Love that name!) In this area are a restaurant with patio dining, a post office and a second cafe (1.5).

The canyon narrows further and the road follows suit. Take note of the homes built with sections lying directly over the creek and the scattered auto and walking bridges interspersed along the Silverado Canyon Rd. Pass beneath the overhanging tree cover near Shady Brook Dr. (2.7) and reach the Silverado Fire Station just beyond. Then work the pedals past the Shady Brook Country Store and more scattered canyon-squeezed residences in the Hazel Bell Dr. area.

Continue pedaling past scattered pockets of homes in the narrow canyon, reaching Belha Wy. (3.8) and cycling under another overhanging tree stand. Pass through a short undeveloped zone and cross Silverado Creek once again, where it shifts from the north to south side of the road. Drop slightly into a last residential pocket with a "flooded during storm" sign, passing Mountain View Tr. (4.7). In another 0.2 mile is a metal gate with travel beyond restricted to authorized vehicles. There is also parking here for hikers and mountain bikers with Forest Adventure Passes who are planning to go further into the Cleveland National Forest area.

Coast all the way back to the start point (9.7), then bike a relatively flat but winding stretch 0.8 mile to Santiago Canyon Rd. A turnaround and return to the Silverado Forest Station makes cyclists veterans of the full canyon road (11.3).

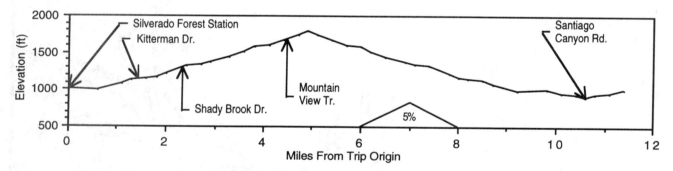

Excursions: Additional Options. Cruise some of the side streets to get a better feel for the canyon area and lifestyle. Particularly interesting areas are off of Kitterman Dr. and near Hazel Bell Dr.

CONNECTING TRIPS: Connection with the Santiago Canyon Rd. tour (Trip #27) - turn in either direction at the Silverado Canyon Rd./Santiago Canyon Rd. intersection.

TRIP #49 - MODJESKA CANYON

GENERAL LOCATION: Modjeska Canyon (Cleveland National Forest)

LEVEL OF DIFFICULTY: Loop - moderate to strenuous; up and back on Modjeska Cyn. Rd. - moderate
Distance - 6.2 miles (loop)
Elevation gain - single steep-to-sheer grade on Modjeska Grade Rd. (loop)

HIGHLIGHTS: This ride starts at Tucker Wildlife Sanctuary parking lot and cruises under the overhanging trees of the rural canyon environs to Modjeska Grade Rd. A steep-to-sheer 0.8 mile climb on that street leads to a couple of excellent vantage points, then rockets down to Santiago Canyon Rd. A short climb and refreshing downhill on that street leads to Santiago Canyon Rd. Next is a short pedal through the treed lower Santiago Canyon Rd. residential area, a return to the Modjeska Grade Rd. intersection and a backtrack to the start point.

The canyon and grade areas are Class X on narrow roadways with limited shoulder. However, because the road is somewhat winding and narrow, autos travel at slow speeds. (The locals are also very courteous.)

TRAILHEAD: From Santiago Rd. exit at Modjeska Canyon Rd. and drive one mile to the Modjeska Grade Rd. junction. Turn left and go another mile to road's end at the Tucker Wildlife Sanctuary parking lot.

Bring a filled water bottle for Modjeska Grade Rd. on hot days. There is a single source of water at the store near Markuson Rd.

TRIP DESCRIPTION: **Outgoing on Modjeska Grade Rd.** Glide back down Modjeska Canyon Rd. on a 1-1/2 to 2-lane mildly winding road. Santiago Creek is to the left and rural residences are scattered within the broad canyon. Pass Harding Canyon Rd. and veer left, then cross Santiago Creek (0.5). Continue through light residential environs and cycle under a light tree canopy before reaching a four-way junction: Modjeska Grade Rd. is left, the Modjeska Canyon Rd. continuation is right and Shadowland Circle is sandwiched in-between (1.1).

Turn left and start an immediate steep climb on a winding road which turns west and reaches Canyon Heights Dr. at (1.4). There is an impressive vista here that includes the Santiago Canyon Rd. area. The road switches sharply southward, the grade steepens and cyclists pass alongside several ridgetop homes. Near Oriole St. and a set of powerline towers is a crest with a commanding view southward to the Portola Hills area (1.9). Soar down the winding roadway another 0.5 mile to its terminus at Santiago Canyon Rd.

Return on Modjeska Canyon Rd. Turn right and bike a modest upgrade to Santiago Canyon Rd.'s highest point, then coast below the ridgeline residences near Falcon St. and Gertner Estate Rd. (3.2). Pass a nursery/plant farm and recross Santiago Creek in another 0.6 mile. The wide flood plain of this creek emanating from Modjeska Canyon is impressive. In another 0.4 mile is Modjeska Canyon Rd. and a turn to the right (4.2).

Start a modest climb through overhanging treecover in a scattered residential area, mostly concentrated to the right. Pass Croatian St. in 0.5 mile and stare ahead and above to the ridgeline estates that you passed on the Modjeska Grade portion of the tour. Enter a short, sun-exposed valley area, pass the Modjeska Country Store and recross Santiago Creek near Markuson Rd. (5.0). In another 0.1 mile is the junction with Modjeska Grade Rd. Turn left and retrace the outgoing route back to Tucker Wildlife Sanctuary parking lot (6.2).

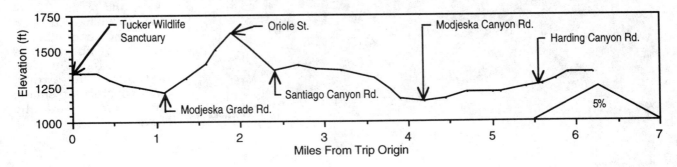

Excursions: Additional Options. Cruise some of the side streets to get a better feel for this peaceful sylvan area. Best bets are in the Hill Top Dr. and Harding Canyon Rd. areas.

CONNECTING TRIPS: Connection with the Santiago Canyon Rd. tour (Trip #27) - turn in either direction at the Modjeska Canyon Rd./Santiago Canyon Rd. or Modjeska Grade Rd./Santiago Canyon Rd. intersections.

TRIP #50 - ARROYO TRABUCO LOOP

GENERAL LOCATION: Mission Viejo, Rancho Santa Margarita, San Juan Capistrano

LEVEL OF DIFFICULTY: Loop - strenuous
Distance - 27.1 miles
Elevation gain - periodic moderate-to-steep grades

HIGHLIGHTS: This predominantly Class II loop takes bikers around the lower reaches of Arroyo Trabuco before it fuses with Oso Creek in Mission Viejo. The route passes over the arroyo in the county area between Mission Viejo and Rancho Santa Margarita and in San Juan Capistrano. Antonio Pkwy. parallels its flood plain above Oso Pkwy. The general tour includes three cities, the relatively undeveloped southern section of Antonio Pkwy., a brief stretch of Ortega Hwy. and a passage over San Juan Creek. There are excellent vista points in both the cities and outland areas. There are no terrifying grades on this tour, but the 1600-plus feet of elevation gain will wear at your legs with time. There is an option to cut the mileage roughly in half using Oso Pkwy. as a connector.

Tijeras Canyon Crossing at Antonio Parkway

TRAILHEAD: From the San Diego Fwy., go east at Oso Pkwy. and drive 1-3/4 miles to Felipe Rd. Turn left and motor one mile to Gilleran Park entrance just north of Tamarind. From the Foothill Transportation Corridor (State Hwy. 241), exit west at Oso Pkwy. and proceed 2-1/4 miles to Felipe Rd. Turn right and continue as described above. The park has water, restrooms, an-awning covered area for shade, and several athletic fields.

Bring a couple of quarts of water for hot days. There was one public park with water and restrooms (Oak Tree Park) directly on-route on the eastern half of the loop. Though commercial centers are plentiful on much of the ride, there were almost no "pit-stops" on Antonio Pkwy. below Oso Pkwy. or on most of the eastern section of Ortega Hwy.

TRIP DESCRIPTION: **Gilleran Park to Antonio Parkway.** From the park exit, turn left and bike 0.2 mile to La Paz Rd., where Class II Felipe Rd. becomes Olympiad Rd. Pass Curtis and Beebe Parks, which are similar in design to Gilleran Park, then climb to a crest at Stonegate, enjoying the excellent panorama north and east (1.9). In another 0.4 mile is Alicia Pkwy. and a turn right (northeast).

Bike to a nearby crest, then cruise downhill on this Class II road, enjoying one of the many views of the Santa Ana Mountains and Mt. Saddleback (the popular name for the combination of side-by-side Santiago and Modjeska Peaks). The terrain flattens at San Benito and cyclists reach Class II Santa Margarita Pkwy. at (3.5). Turn right, pass over the Arroyo Trabuco and continue the climb to San Antonio Pkwy. Proceed by the first of this street's plethora of shopping centers and pass over State Hwy. 241 at (4.6). Cycle closer to the base of Mt. Saddleback and reach San Antonio Pkwy. (5.9), making a right turn.

San Antonio Parkway to Rancho Viejo Road. Surprisingly, this downhill-dominated segment starts with a short climb to the trip's summit. In the 5.6-mile section north of Oso Pkwy., cyclists start through mixed dense residential/commercial development, then glide past mixed patches of development and open space. Pass over State Hwy. 241 again (7.6) and stare down into little Tijeras Canyon on the left.

Avd. Empresa comes up at (8.0), followed by the first peeks at the Tijeras Creek Golf Course and a transit over Tijeras Creek (9.6). In 1.3 miles is Meandering Tr. while Oaktree, the entrance to Oak Tree Park, is 0.3 mile further. This was the single easy-access public park with water on the eastern half of the loop when we passed through. (It also has restrooms, athletic fields and a covered patio area.) Oso Pkwy. follows in another 0.4 mile, best recognized by the sudden appearance of residential pockets and shopping complexes (11.7).

Antonio Pkwy. changes complexion beyond this cross-street, remaining Class II, but passing through even more-lightly developed environs with Arroyo Trabuco paralleling to the right. There is a pocket of development near Crown Valley Pkwy. (12.8), then Arroyo Trabuco pulls away to the west and cyclists enter open spaces on a Class X roadway with wide shoulder. Near (14.3), Antonio Pkwy. follows a ridgeline, where there are open views of a successive line of hills, then the first looks at Ortega Hwy. below. The hillside San Juan Capistrano residences come into sight and bikers pass over San Juan Creek at (15.7). In another 0.5 mile is Ortega Hwy.

Turn right and cruise on this flatter Class X road, passing a nursery and recrossing San Juan Creek (15.7). As the shoulder narrows, cyclists have the option to bike on the wide walkway along the highway. (There are few stoplights and the intersections are lightly-trafficked by cross traffic in this rural zone.) Pass a produce market at Shade Tree Ln./Ave. Siega (17.1), then enter a sparse rural residential area and cross La Novia Ave. at (18.3). In 0.3 mile is Ranch Viejo Rd. at the lowest point of the tour.

Rancho Viejo Road to Gilleran Park. Turn right and climb uphill on a Class I path on the right side of the street, then pass the entry to the Marbella Golf and Country Club at Golf Club Dr. (19.0). The road creeps next to the San Diego Fwy. (as it will stay for the next three miles), passes through the first commercial area in a while and meets Junipero Serra Rd. at (19.9). In 0.6 mile, the Class I path leaves the roadside and passes over Arroyo Trabuco, then cyclists arrive at Via Escolar (21.6). (There is a Class I path that follows Arroyo Trabuco under the San Diego Fwy. to the west side, as described in Trip #12.) This is the San Juan Capistrano/Mission Viejo boundary where there is a transition to Class II bikeway and the street name becomes Marguerite Pkwy.

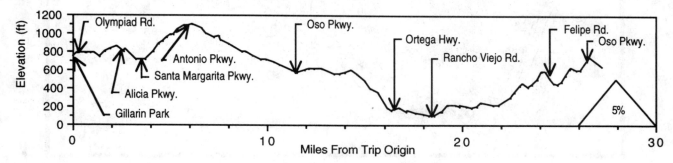

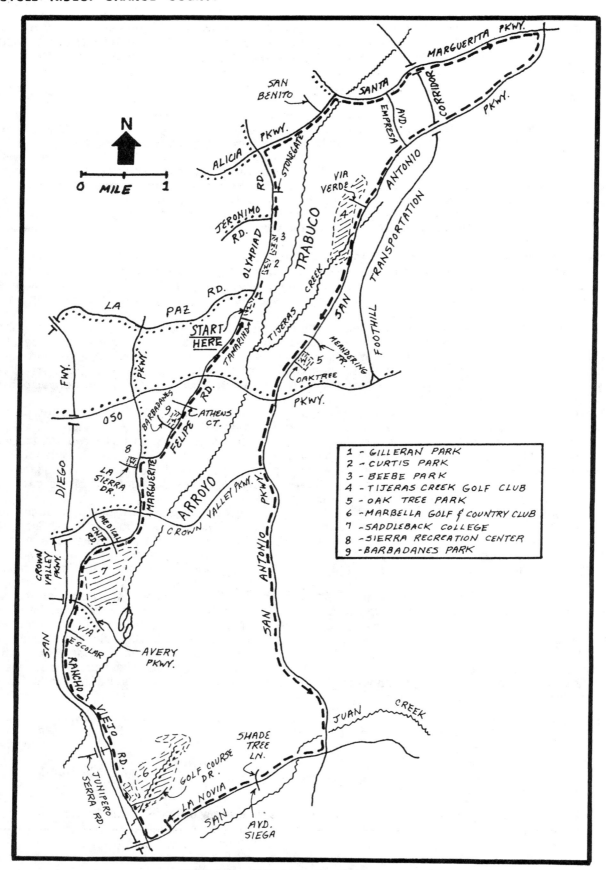

TRIP #50 - ARROYO TRABUCO LOOP

Cross Avery Pkwy., climb past several shopping centers and bike alongside the Saddleback College campus, meeting College Dr./Medical Center Rd. at (23.0). In 0.1 mile is Hillcrest and an exceptional view northward to Mission Viejo. Coast to Crown Valley Pkwy., then begin climbing again to La Sierra Dr. (24.1). A turn left leads to the Sierra Recreation Center, which has public water and restrooms; however, other facilities are for members only. Another crest and pleasant downhill lead to Felipe Rd. where the route heads right.

Pass Barbadanes (left is Barbadanes Park with water, limited shade, grass and children's playground) (25.1) and pump uphill once again to a crest just beyond Athens Ct. in 0.5 mile. Here is another broad vista point. Glide past Oso Pkwy. then start pumping uphill past Tamarind and return to the park entrance at (27.1).

Excursions: **Mini-Tour of the Arroyo Trabuco.** Either northern or southern segments can be ridden separately using Class II Oso Pkwy. as the shortcut connector. The northern and southern loops are 14.6 miles and 12.5 miles, respectively. The southern loop requires a more skilled rider, passing through somewhat desolate surroundings having some Class X sections.

Horno Creek Trail. At the Marbella Golf and Country Club entrance at (19.0), the Class I path along Golf Club Dr. follows the rough contour of Horno Creek. The one-way distance is 1.2 miles. Admittance is a courtesy. Cyclists are expected to respect bicycling rules of good conduct.

Trabuco Creek Trail. There is a Class I trail at the northern end of Antonio Pkwy. Pass the trailside kiosk and bike north and west 1/4 mile, then follow El Camino Montana or enter the O'Neill Regional Park Mesa area at one of the fence entries. (See the Trip #28 Map for detail.) With the former option, the trail continues southwest under State. Hwy 241 on a bike/walk bridge. (Two miles one way.)

CONNECTING TRIPS: 1) Connection with the Laguna Niguel Bikeway (Trip #11) - at College Dr./Medical Center Rd., bike northwest on the latter road to Crown Valley Pkwy.; 2) connection with the Doheny Bikeway (Trip #12) - at Junipero Serra Rd., cycle west under the San Diego Fwy. to Camino Capistrano; 3) connection with the Del Obispo Bikeway (Trip #13) - at Ortega Hwy. and La Novia Ave., turn left (southeast) on the latter street to reach San Juan Creek or follow Ortega Hwy. under the San Diego Fwy. to Camino Capistrano; 4) connection with the Aliso Creek Trail (Trip #29A) - at Santa Margarita Pkwy. and Alicia Pkwy., go west on the former road to El Toro Rd. 5) connection with the Mission Viejo Bikeway (Trip #30) - from Felipe Rd. and Oso Pkwy. bike west on the latter street to Marguerite Pkwy. From Olympiad Rd. and Alicia Pkwy., bike west on the latter street to Marguerite Pkwy.; 6) connection with the Oso Viejo ride (Trip #42) - at Jeronimo Rd. and Olympiad Rd., turn west on the former street; 7) connection with the Cities and Canyons ride (Trip #47) - the tours share a common segment on Santa Margarita Pkwy. between Alicia Pkwy. and San Antonio Pkwy.

TRIP #51 - COTO DE CAZA TOUR

GENERAL LOCATION: Coto De Caza

LEVEL OF DIFFICULTY: Loop - moderate
Distance - 11.2 miles
Elevation gain - long moderate grade on Coto De Caza Dr.

HIGHLIGHTS: **This tour is for Coto De Caza residents or guests only, as Coto De Caza is entirely private.** The route is 100% Class X with wide biking shoulder. The initial five-mile upgrade on Coto De Caza Dr. is tedious, but moderate; in addition, there are a few short climbs on the east side. The vistas include Mt. Saddleback and Coto Valley with it's surrounding hillsides. Slow down and admire the classy residences, equestrian center, as well as the Golf and Racquet Club. Who knows? This tour may convince you take a long look at living in this well-planned enclave.

TRAILHEAD: From the Foothill Transportation Corridor (State Hwy. 241), exit at Oso Pkwy. and continue two miles to its terminus at Coto De Caza Dr. Turn left, pass through the guard gate (a guest or resident pass is required), then turn right at Water Lily Wy. (the first street on the right). From the San Diego Fwy., exit east at Oso Pkwy. and go 6-1/4 miles to road's end. Continue as described above.

The above trailhead starts near the trip's low point. An option (which leaves the hard climbing until the end of the trip) is to start at the Coto Sports and Recreation Park near Coto De Caza Dr. and Vista Del Verde.

Bring a filled water bottle. Though a reasonably short trip, there are no on-road (i.e., direct access) water sources within Coto De Caza. A strategically-located option is to divert to the Coto Sports and Recreation Park near the trip's mid-point.

TRIP DESCRIPTION: **Coto De Caza Dr. and Plano Trabuco.** Return to Coto De Caza Dr. and turn right (north).This segment has the heaviest (but still modest) traffic and the major amount of the trip's climb. Start uphill immediately and take in the stately residences scattered over the Coto Valley floor and more-distant hillsides to the right and in the nearby hillsides to the left. Pass Cantamar (0.2) and take in the head-on view of Mt. Saddleback, which will remain in direct sight for over 1-1/2 miles.

Follow a stair-step upgrade past Hilldale Wy. and the southern edge of the Coto De Caza Golf and Racquet Club (1.1). Pump past Shoal Creek in 0.4 mile, where the hills on the left squeeze toward Coto De Caza Dr. Cross San Miguel (2.0), the single road through the golf course, and reach a false crest at Calle Castile in another 1.3 miles. Enjoy a flat stretch for about 0.3 mile and pass Vista Del Verde, which has directional signs to such places as the CVCC Restaurant (right) and the Coto Sports and Recreation Park (left).

Further climbing leads to Trigo Trail where there is an exceptionally revealing view south highlighting the valley floor and the residence-pocketed hillsides (4.1). In 200-300 yards, Coto De Caza Dr. veers to the left and our reference route swings right on Plano Trabuco. Cycle another 0.6 mile in less-developed and more heavily treed environs and meet Via Pajaro at (4.8).

Via Pajaro and Vista Del Verde. Turn right, make a short climb to the trip's crest and coast past Vinedo Rd. (5.1), tiny Pajaro Park (5.7) and Trigo Trail (5.9). The lots are larger, the homes more stately and there is an abundance of horses in this stretch. Also, the traffic from here to Cantamar is significantly lighter than on the west side (Coto De Caza Dr.).

Pass a general store and the CVCC Restaurant, then turn left onto Vista Del Verde (6.5). Cross Canada Gobernadora, which runs down the center of Coto Valley, and bike on a more winding road with its little ups and downs (but generally downhill). The golf course comes into view again and the route hugs the course before taking a slow turn to the right past Oakmont at (7.4). Continue between the course and the nearby residences, completing the turn near Cherry Hills Dr. Reach San Miguel and a nearby fire station, then coast past the entry to the Club House of the Golf and Racquet Club (8.8).

A mild 0.3-mile upgrade near Atherton Dr. (9.8) interrupts the refreshing coast from the club house to Cantamar (10.5). There was no outlet by continuing south on Vista Del Verde (in early 2001), so our reference route turns east onto Cantamar, cruises to the second Canada Gobernadora crossing and returns to Coto De Caza Dr. in another 0.2 mile. From here, simply retrace the outgoing route to Water Lily Wy. (11.2).

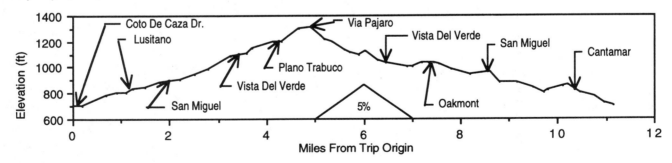

CONNECTING TRIPS: REVISIT 1) Connection with the Mission Viejo Bikeway (Trip # 30) - at the northern gate at Coto De Caza Dr. , continue on what is now La Promesa, turn right on San Antonio Pkwy., left on Santa Margarita Pkwy. go four miles to Marguerite Pkwy. and turn left again; 2) connection with the Cities and Canyon ride (Trip #47) - at Via Pajaro and Plano Trabuco, stay north on the latter street; 3) connection with the Arroyo Trabuco Loop (Trip #50) - at La Promesa and San Antonio Pkwy., go in either direction on the latter road.

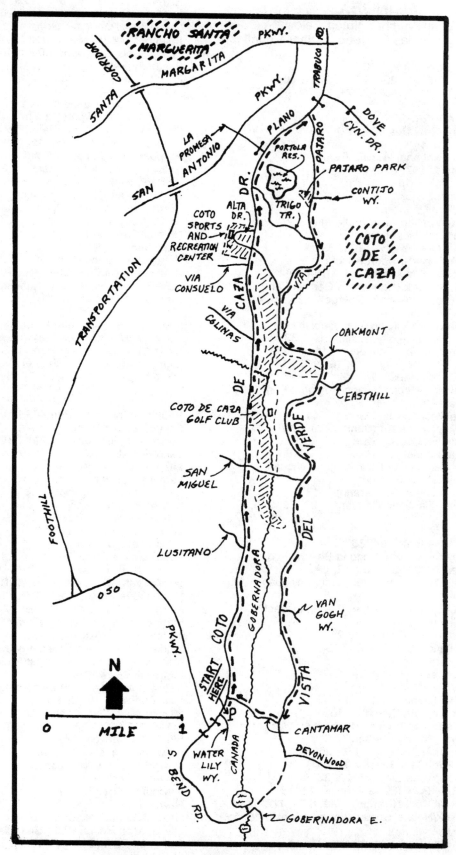

TRIP #51 - COTO DE CAZA

INDEX

(Trip Number Noted Below)
(Bracketed Entries { } Denote Other Counties)

B-D Enterprises Books

Nothing to It!

B-D Enterprises books are available at better bicycle stores, both walk-in and on-line book stores, recreational outlets and from the publisher. For additional information about our books, write us at 122 Mirabeau Ave., San Pedro CA 90732 or e-mail us at <bnyduk@aol.com>.

All cycling books have a master county map(s), master trip matrices, detailed trip maps, elevation contours, a detailed index and numerous photos. Prices noted in the book summaries which follow are suggested retail prices. The cost may vary in individual stores.

BICYCLE RIDES: LOS ANGELES COUNTY

Published 4/89; second printing (revised) - 8/91;
third printing (revised) - 5/95
Completely revised/updated edition 6/00
ISBN 0-9619151-8-8
Library of Congress Cat. Number 99-097150

8-1/2 " X 11" Format; 244 pages; $13.95
71 Trips and 85 Individual On-road Rides

Sample Book Contents by Section:
   • **The Coast** - South Bay Bike Trail, Palos
Verdes Peninsula, L.A. Harbor, Long Beach
Shoreline Park, Santa Monica Mountains, PCH
Coastal Century
   • **River Trails** - Upper Rio Hondo, Lario Trail,
San Gabriel River, "Big Banana", West Fork of
Upper San Gabriel River
   • **Inland** - Whittier Narrows, Arroyo Seco Trail,
Kenneth Newell Bikeway, Griffith Park, Elysian
Park, Mulholland Drive, Sepulveda Bike Basin,
Diamond Bar, San Jose Hills, Bonelli Park
   • **Potpourri** - L.A. Civic Center, Tour de Los
Angeles, Santa Catalina Island
   • **New Trips** - Agoura Hills, Santa Susana
Pass, Hansen Dam, San Dimas Canyon, San
Francisquito & Bouquet Canyons, Old Ridge
Route, California Aqueduct

BICYCLE RIDES: ORANGE COUNTY

Published 9/88; second printing (revised) - 4/90;
third printing (revised) - 8/93; fourth printing
(revised) - 11/96
Completely revised/updated edition 2/01
ISBN 0-9619151-0-2
Library of Congress Control Number 2001130129

8-1/2 " X 11" Format; 183 pages; $12.95
51 Trips and 58 Individual On-road Rides

Sample Book Contents by Section:
   • **The Coast** - Huntington Central Park,
Sunset to Newport Beach Strand, Upper Newport
Bay, Laguna Beach, Laguna Niguel & Del
Obispo Bikeways, Doheny/San Clemente Bike
Route, Newport Beach/Corona Del Mar, San
Clemente to San Diego
   • **River Trails** - Santa Ana River, San Diego
Creek, San Gabriel River, Coyote Creek
   • **Inland** - El Cajon Trail, Carbon Canyon,
Orange/Irvine Park, Santiago Canyon Road,
O'Neill Park, Aliso Creek Trail, Mission Viejo
   • **The "Big Guys"** - Western & Eastern County
Loops, Orange County Century
   • **New Trips** - Turtle Rock, Signal Peak &
Pelican Hill, Tustin Ranch, Oso Viejo Park,
Anaheim Hills, Lemon Heights, Aliso Viejo,
Silverado & Modjeska Canyons, Arroyo Trabuco

BICYCLE RIDES: INLAND EMPIRE

Published 4/90; second printing (revised) - 4/94
ISBN 0-9619151-4-5
Library of Congress Cat. Number 89-091606

8-1/2 " X 11" Format; 154 pages; $8.95
30 Trips and 37 Individual On-road Rides

Sample Book Contents by Section:
- **Riverside County**
  - Riverside City: Upper Santa Ana River, Tour de Riverside, Lake Perris, Pigeon Pass
  - Western Interior Valleys: Perris & Temescal Valleys, Badlands & Fault Lines, Temecula Wine Tour, Lake Elsinor
  - Coachella Valley: Upper Whitewater Rvr., Palm Springs, Coachella Bikeway, Indio Hills
- **San Bernardino County**
  - San Bernardino/Redlands Cities: San Antonio & Cajon Canyons, Prado Park, Timoteo & Live Oak Canyons, Sunset Drive, Oak Glen
  - Mountains: Big Bear Lake, Lytle Creek
  - Desert: Joshua Tree National Park, National Trails Highway (Old Route 66)
  - Colorado River: Parker Strip, Needles-Bullhead City Loop
  - California Aqueduct Bikeway

BICYCLE RIDES: SAN DIEGO AND IMPERIAL COUNTIES

Published 6/92; second printing 6/97
ISBN 0-9619151-5-3
Library of Congress Cat. Number 90-093234

8-1/2 " X 11" Format; 218 pages; $11.95
62 On-road Rides

Sample Book Contents by Section:
- **The Coast**
  - Metropolitan San Diego: Mission Bay, Balboa Park, San Diego Bay, Point Loma, La Jolla, Old Town, Scenic Drive, Techolote Canyon, Imperial Beach, San Diego River, Otay Lake, San Diego to San Clemente
  - North County: Rancho Santa Fe, Lake San Marcos, Vista Lagoons Loop, Oceanside
- **Inland**
  - Urban: El Cajon, Santee Lakes, San Pasqual Valley, Escondido to Sea, Fallbrook, Ramona, Mount Helix, Blossom Valley
  - Mountains/Backcountry: Mount Palomar, Julian, Laguna Mountains, Pala Mission, Lake Morena, Bonsall Canyons, Crest-Dehesa. Barona Valley, Bear Ridge Loop
  - Desert: El Centro, Salton Sea, Borrego Springs, Great Overland Stage Route
  - Colorado River: Winterhaven

BICYCLE RIDES: SANTA BARBARA AND VENTURA COUNTIES

Published 9/94; second printing - 7/98
ISBN 0-9619151-6-1
Library of Congress Catalogue Number 94-094025
6 " X 9" Format; 274 pages; $10.95
68 Trips Including 15 Best Mountain Bike Rides

Sample Book Contents by Section:
- **Santa Barbara County**
     - City of Santa Barbara: Santa Barbara City, Hope Ranch, UCSB Campus, Mountain Drive, Goleta, Carpinteria
     - East County: Gibralter Road, Romero Canyon, East & West Camino Cielo, Upper Santa Ynez River, Refugio Pass, Paradise Road, Wine County Tours, Solvang Century, Figueroa Mountain
     - West County: Jalama Beach, Casmalia & Solomon Hills, Los Coches Mountain, Point Sal, Oso Flaco Lake, Cuyama River
- **Ventura County**
     - The Coast: Port Hueneme, Ventura-Ojai, Ventura-Santa Barbara, Coastal Century
     - Inland/Urban; Agoura Hills, Westlake, Thousand Oaks, North Ranch, Simi Valley, Rocky Peak, Potrero Road
     - Mountain/Backcountry: Sycamore Canyon, Ojai-Santa Barbara, Sisar Canyon, Sulphur & Pine Mountains, Lockwood Valley, Mount Pinos

BICYCLE RIDES
Santa Barbara & Ventura Counties

BY DON AND SHARRON BRUNDIGE

MOUNTAIN BIKING L.A. COUNTY (Southern Section)

Published 9/96
ISBN 0-9619151-7-X
Library of Congress Cat. Number 95-094085
6 "X 9" Format; 241 pages; $11.95
66 Trips and 100 Individual Mountain Bike Rides

Sample Book Contents by Section:
- **Santa Monica Mountains (SMM): East** - Franklin Canyon, Dirt Mulholland, Sullivan Canyon, Trippet Ranch/Eagle Rock, Will Rogers/Backbone Trail
- **SMM: Central** - Redrock Canyon/Calabasas Peak, Crags Road/Malibu Creek, Bulldog Loop, Paramount Ranch, Puerco Canyon, Castro Peak, Zuma Ridge, The Edison Road, East Los Robles Trail, Conejo Crest
- **SMM: West** - Sandstone Peak, The Grotto, Sycamore Canyon, Guadalasco Trail, Rancho Sierra Vista/Satwiwa, West Los Robles Trail
- **Mountclef Ridge/Simi Hills** - Mountclef Ridge, Wildwood Park, Lynnmere Trail, Cheeseboro & Palo Camado Canyons
- **Santa Susana Mountains** - Rocky Peak, Limekiln & Aliso Canyons, Mission Peak/Bee Canyon
- **Verdugo Mountains/San Rafael Hills** - Brand & Beaudry Mtwys., Summit Ride, Hosteller/Whiting Mtwys.
- **Puente Hills** - East & West Skyline Trails
- **Potpourri** - Walnut Canyon, Bonelli Park, Palos Verdes Peninsula, Santa Catalina Island

MOUNTAIN BIKING L.A. COUNTY
(Southern Section)

BY DON AND SHARRON BRUNDIGE

SANTA MONICA MOUNTAINS
SANTA SUSANA MOUNTAINS   SIMI HILLS
VERDUGO MOUNTAINS/SAN RAFAEL HILLS   PUENTE HILLS
PALOS VERDES PENINSULA   SANTA CATALINA ISLAND

OUTDOOR RECREATION CHECKLISTS
A Unique Book Concept With the Multi-Activity Outdoorsperson in Mind

Published 11/98
ISBN 0-9619151-9-6
Library of Congress Cat. Number 96-095421

5-1/2 " X 8-1/2" Format; 422 pages; $14.95
Predominantly All Major Outdoor Activities Included

Why pay the price to buy a book for every outdoor activity that you plan to explore? *Outdoor Recreation Checklists* provides exhaustive equipment checklists and extensive gear discussions and tradeoffs for a wide range of activities. This four-season book covers both land and waterborne adventures ranging from camping to remote mountaineering to self-guided or chartered rafting or fishing trips. Just check the book's front cover (shown at upper right) to be convinced. There are over 70 checklist pages and over 160 photographs.

How is anyone qualified to write such a book? Don and Sharron Brundige, with 25 years of outdoor recreation experience and authors of nine Southern California on-road and off-road bicycling books, have collaborated with a group of grizzled veterans in a broad range of outdoor activities to create this wide-ranging work. *Outdoor Recreation Checklists* is unique on the market. Literature searches conducted over the two years of book development prove this convincingly.

Why is the book so useful for all of the activities covered? Just read a few reasons noted on the book's back cover (shown at lower right). Besides, having all these checklists and tradeoff discussions in one book assists you in identifying gear that is useful for more than one activity. This may save you money and/or affect your gear investment strategy.

What's in the book that is useful to bicyclists? There are four sections dedicated to cycling; two are for on-road biking (daytime and multi-day) and the other two for off-road biking. The book has general discussions on trip planning/preparation, safety, respect for the territory and logistics/communication. There is a detailed discussion of the classic "Ten Essentials," that gear needed for survival contingencies. There are general-use sections on first-aid kit needs and on outdoors meal planning, with many mealtime suggestions. Finally, there is a separate section identifying gear which is common to multiple outdoor activities. This matrix-formatted section may assist you in prioritizing the investment of your hard-earned bucks.

OUTDOOR RECREATION CHECKLISTS

BY DON AND SHARRON BRUNDIGE

DRIVE-IN & BOAT-IN CAMPING   HIKING & BACKPACKING
GLACIER/WINTER CLIMBING & ROCK CLIMBING
BICYCLE TOURING & MOUNTAIN BIKING   NORDIC & ALPINE SKIING
SNOWSHOEING   SNOWMOBILING   CANOEING & KAYAKING
SAILING/POWER BOATING   WATER SPORTS   INLAND & SEA FISHING
Plus FIRST AID KIT & MEAL SELECTION INFORMATION

Have you ever started on an outdoor adventure and realized that you had left some vital gear behind? When trying a new outdoor activity, have you wondered what you should bring or questioned the verbal advice or equipment list that a friend gave to you? When selecting outdoor gear, have you asked yourself what are the important tradeoffs and what would best suit you? *Outdoor Recreation Checklists* provides a guide to gear selection for the entry- and intermediate-level outdoorsman over a wide range of outdoor activities. This book deals with the fundamental gear that you will need for those activities. It identifies key gear characteristics to look for when renting or purchasing equipment. Once you are ready to go, the checklists provided for each activity will assist you in executing an orderly process for deciding what to take along. All this in one book!

ISBN 0-9619151-9-6